Political Parties in Africa

This book examines the effects of ethnicity on party politics in Sub-Saharan Africa. Sebastian Elischer analyzes political parties in Ghana, Kenya, and Namibia in detail and provides a preliminary analysis of parties in seven other countries, including Tanzania, Botswana, Senegal, Zambia, Malawi, Burkina Faso, and Benin. Elischer finds that five party types exist: the mono-ethnic, the ethnic alliance, the catch-all, the programmatic, and the personalistic party. He uses these party types to show that the African political landscape is considerably more diverse than conventionally assumed. Whereas ethnic parties dominate in some countries, nonethnic parties have become the norm in others. This study also finds a correlation between a country's ethnic makeup and the salience of political ethnicity: countries with a core ethnic group are prone to form nonethnic parties. In countries lacking a core ethnic group, ethnic parties constitute the norm.

Sebastian Elischer is assistant professor of comparative politics at the Leuphana University Lüneburg and the German Institute of Global and Area Studies Hamburg.

Political Parties in Africa

Ethnicity and Party Formation

SEBASTIAN ELISCHER
Leuphana University Lüneburg and German Institute of Global and Area Studies, Hamburg

CAMBRIDGE UNIVERSITY PRESS
Cambridge, New York, Melbourne, Madrid, Cape Town,
Singapore, São Paulo, Delhi, Mexico City

Cambridge University Press
32 Avenue of the Americas, New York, NY 10013-2473, USA

www.cambridge.org
Information on this title: www.cambridge.org/9781107620445

First published 2013

A catalog record for this publication is available from the British Library.

Library of Congress Cataloging in Publication Data

Elischer, Sebastian, 1979–
Political parties in Africa : ethnicity and party formation / Sebastian Elischer.
p. cm.
Includes bibliographical references and index.
ISBN 978-1-107-03346-7 (hardback) – ISBN 978-1-107-62044-5 (pbk.)
1. Political parties – Africa. 2. Ethnic relations – Political aspects. 3. Africa – Ethnic relations – Political aspects. I. Title.
JQ1879.A795E45 2013
324.2096–dc23 2012051703

ISBN 978-1-107-03346-7 Hardback
ISBN 978-1-107-62044-5 Paperback

To my grandfather

Contents

Tables

Abstract

Scholars of comparative politics have no framework by which African parties can be compared across countries or continents. In part, this omission owes to the dominance of individual case studies among area experts working on Africa. It also results from a distinct Western bias in the comparative politics literature. The present study eradicates this conceptual void. Drawing on the work of Richard Gunther and Larry Diamond (2001 and 2003), it designs a global party typology. The typology distinguishes between five primary party types, which are at the heart of this study: the mono-ethnic party, the multiethnic alliance party, the catch-all ethnic party, the personalistic party, and the programmatic party. Although the first two party types are defined as ethnic party types, the remaining three are regarded as nonethnic parties.

In a second step, this study applies this typology to all politically significant and effective parties in three African countries. The goal is to illustrate the political diversity of African party politics. The empirical analysis of parties shows that the African political landscape is considerably more diverse than conventionally assumed. Although ethnic parties feature in two of three countries, nonethnic parties dominate political party competition. Second, enduring multiparty competition decreases the political salience of ethnicity. These results are verified with the help of a greater number of additional cases from seven African countries.

In a third and final step, this study accounts for the variance of party types across countries. The study finds a correlation between a country's social structure and the party type in place: countries with a core ethnic group and a low ethnic fragmentation index are prone to the formation of nonethnic parties. Countries without a core ethnic group and a high ethnic fragmentation index are prone to the formation of ethnic parties. Given the limitations of small-*n* research, these findings constitute preliminary contributions to the formulation of a theory that can account for the formation of ethnic parties in some and nonethnic parties in other nonindustrialized countries.

Acknowledgments

I have been working on this book for more than seven years. Writing it has been a pleasure due to a large number of people, to whom I owe special thanks. The genesis of this book was my PhD thesis on ethnic parties, which I conducted under the auspices of Matthijs Bogaards at the Jacobs University Bremen. Matthijs' intellectual guidance was preeminent, his academic guardianship professional and encouraging at all times. Not many young scholars can rely on such thorough academic support. It has been a privilege being his doctoral student.

I thank David Throup from the Centre for Strategic and International Studies in Washington, DC. His detailed knowledge of African affairs and his enthusiasm proved an inspiration without which I would not have embarked on this adventure. I would like to extend my thanks to my colleagues at the German Institute of Global and Areas Studies, and in particular my colleagues at the Institute of African Affairs. I owe many insights into the workings of African parties to Matthias Basedau, Gero Erdmann, Alexander Stroh, and Andreas Mehler. Without their work, my own research would have been impossible. I am especially thankful to those colleagues in our profession who supported my decision to publish my findings in the format of a book and who did not hide their support. I further thank Nicholas Cheeseman from Oxford University, Charles Hornsby, and Gabrielle Lynch from Warwick University for their help and insights.

At the institutional level, I extend my thanks to the Jacobs University Bremen for the excellent and internationally unparalleled research conditions it provides. I equally wish to thank IFES, and in particular Abigail Wilson, Elizabeth Reiter, Magnus Ohmann, and Rudi Eibling, for allowing me to work for them in various capacities in Washington, DC, Nigeria, and Sierra Leone. This greatly improved my own understanding of African institutions. I wish to thank the Friedrich Ebert Foundation for a generous stipend and travel funds between 2007 and 2009. I thank Kathrin Meissner, the former country director of the Friedrich Ebert Stiftung in Accra, and Klaus Lötzer, the former country director of the Konrad Adenauer Foundation in Accra, for providing me with office space and numerous contacts while I conducted research in Ghana. In Kenya, I wish to thank the staff at the National Institute of Statistics and the Centre for Multi Party Democracy for providing all the sources I needed at a moment in time when their country was on the verge of disintegration. In Namibia, I thank Johann Müller for his friendship and his detailed knowledge on Namibian history that he shared with me while he was conducting his own research. Many thanks also to Carolyn Halladay for proofreading and commenting on numerous chapters as well as for offering suggestions of how to make the material readable to her, the wider academic community, and her cats. I am particularly grateful for the moral support she provided.

Finally, I thank those who supported me throughout the years and far beyond this book, including David Schiefer, Anna Möllering, Akua Mercy, Timothy Cook, Regina Bernhard, Rutha Abraha, Frank Stadelmaier, Elisabeth Heid, and Rebecca Wilkins. May all of you find what you are looking for. Most of all, I thank Christine Le Jeune for her unconditional love, her wit, and her endless support.

North Germany, April 2013

1

Comparative Politics and Political Parties in Africa

This book is about the nature of African political parties. The first such study in book length since the 1960s, it demystifies several long-standing assumptions about politics in ethnically divided societies. Its main argument is that not all African parties are ethnic parties; instead, a wide variety of political party types shape the African political landscape. Although African parties by and large refrain from programmatic ideas, such ideas do feature in African politics. A detailed assessment of political parties in several countries indicates that, over time, the political salience of ethnicity is decreasing. Multiparty competition in Africa does not lead to a hardening of ethnic relations.

This book contributes to the recent and ongoing debate about African parties. It confirms those who claim that the salience of ethnicity in young democracies in general and in Africa in particular has been exaggerated (see, e.g., Chandra 2005, Lindberg and Morrison 2008, Basedau and Stroh 2012). In addition, this work broadens scholars' conceptual understanding of parties in Africa and elsewhere. Its findings are based on the first empirical application of a new global party typology.

For decades, comparative research on parties suffered one major shortcoming: scholars interested in African parties had no conceptual framework by which to identify and compare parties. The study of African parties by "Africanists" traditionally ran toward individual country studies. Although political scientists have recently begun to conduct comparative analyses, their studies of African parties often remain confined to the study of election results or survey data (see, e.g., Ishiyama 2012). Scholars of other non-European areas have equally failed to construct alternative frameworks beyond the prevailing party types derived from the study of Western European parties. The much longer duration of multiparty competition in Europe and the historical particularities of European party formation make Western party models unsuitable for the study of parties in nonindustrialized societies. The lack of comparative-empirical work on African parties and the dearth of conceptual tools for the study of parties in non-Western areas have caused many scholars to base their interpretation of African politics on shaky assumptions. The alleged ubiquity of ethnic parties is the most prominent example.

HARBINGERS OF EVIL? ETHNIC PARTIES AND DEMOCRACY

Many scholars regarded democratic contest in ethnically segmented societies as a hotbed of instability and conflict. Until recently, the political science community was cautious about the possibility of peaceful and successful democratic transitions, let alone democratic consolidation, in Africa. According to some, ethnic loyalties would inevitably become the basis for intense partisanship, thereby fuelling ethnic divisions and making ethnic conflict more likely (Kaplan 1997, Horowitz 2000, Mann 2005, Bremmer 2006, Rudolph 2006, Lewis 2011; for a summary, see Reynolds 2011).

The most cited study on the effect and ubiquity of ethnic parties in new democracies remains *Ethnic Groups in Conflict* (Horowitz 2000). According to Horowitz, ethnically segmented societies and their respective political parties are in a reciprocal relationship.

In the industrialized world, party competition is characterized by multiple cleavages. Communal boundaries constitute one cleavage line out of many. In the nonindustrialized world, communal boundaries constitute the dominant – if not the only (Lawson 1999: 12, Posner 2005) – cleavage line that structures party politics. The inevitable result is the introduction of ethnically based parties into the political system.

Once in place, ethnic parties aggravate ethnic divisions. They depend exclusively on the support of a particular ethnic group. Due to a lack of other cleavage lines, ethnically based parties are unable to diversify their electoral base. There is no transferability across communal boundaries. The total dependency on communal support puts ethnic parties under great pressure to satisfy group demands. They constantly face the possibility of competition within the group the party claims to represent. The potential of "ethnic outbidding" (Horowitz 2000: 348) by an intra-group competitor makes parties adopt radical positions. Party leaders espouse ethnic demands, thereby bolstering chauvinistic elements. These positions are irreconcilable with the positions of other ethnic parties (Horowitz 2000).

Multiethnic parties or nonethnic parties may emerge, yet they are not sustainable over time. Due to severe competition from ethnic parties and the lack of alternative cleavage lines, multiethnic parties disintegrate into ethnic wings. The lack or the dissolution of multiethnic parties leads to a "bankruptcy of moderation" (Reilly 2001: 3) within the party system. Not only is the formation of ethnic parties inevitable – ethnic parties become ubiquitous.

These dynamics make multiparty elections tense and conflict-ridden. The exclusionary political environment transforms democratic election outcomes into an ethnic census. Among the losers, elections produce a feeling of constant political marginalization. The political environment is thus conducive to ethnic violence. Eventually, the prevalence of ethnic parties and the political dynamics they produce can lead either to the imposition of an autocratic one-party state – often imposed by a governing multiethnic party to avoid the further deterioration of state cohesion – or by a military coup conducted by the army to restore stability and peace (Horowitz 2000, Chandra 2005, Rabushka and Shepsle 2009). In short, ethnic parties foster ethnic conflict and electoral violence and are conducive to autocratic forms of governance. Although more recent works on partisan preference in Africa suggest that ethnicity is only one of several factors driving African politics, most scholars studying African politics take the enduring significance of communal boundaries as a starting point for their analysis (Palmberg 1999, Bekker et al. 2001, Daddieh and Fair 2002, Posner 2005, Ishiyama and Fox 2006, Basedau and Stroh 2012).

Scholars of ethnic parties in a Western context have provided more sophisticated concepts of the conduct of an ethnic party. The pursuit of policies directed against the interests of other communities and the pursuit of policies that challenge the legitimacy of the multinational state is only one strategy at their disposal. Alternatively, ethnic parties might try and change the constitutional principles of the multinational state in a peaceful and democratic manner. Instead of cultural irredentism, they may try to foster political autonomy or increase territorial self-determination and thus attempt to alter the status quo by nonviolent means. Or, they might do what programmatic parties do and appeal to a particular socioeconomic group within their community and beyond. The literature on particularistic parties in Europe clearly shows party politics based on particularistic motivations to be congruent with state stability. Western electoral competition entered by ethnic parties is resolved by "mostly ballots, rarely bullets" (Newman 1996). Democratic contest is neither replaced by ethnic conflict, nor does the existence of particularistic parties lead to the collapse of nonethnic parties (Newman 1996, Ishiyama and Breuning 1998, Birnir 2007, Brancati 2009, Ishiyama 2009). It is regrettable that scholars of new democracies do not study the dynamics of group politics in advanced democracies in greater detail. The vast and growing empirical evidence from Western Europe shows that often, communal interests manifest themselves in a different, more complex way as group demands coexist and interact with other interests. Over the course of the last three decades, European politics have been shaped increasingly by parties with a focus on a particular region or community. A number of labels have been created to capture the nature of these parties, including "niche," "ethnic," "regional," "stateless," or "nationalist." In many countries these particularistic parties[1] have entered government coalitions (Massetti 2009, Hepburn 2009, 2011).

[1] The term "particularistic party" was first used in an African context and has recently been used by scholars working on ethnic party bans (Bogaards et al. 2010). I am using the term in a purely descriptive manner.

Ethnic parties, however, can always and anywhere affect the quality of democracy. The proliferation of ethnic parties is likely to increase the number of parties achieving legislative representation. This development is likely to lead to a high degree of party fragmentation, and formation of governments subsequently becomes a cumbersome process. The emergence of ethnic parties or an increase in the number of ethnic parties further minimizes the number of voters with the potential to switch parties. The identification of voters with particularistic parties is at least to some extent based on kinship; accordingly, voters do not assess the performance of the incumbent party vis-à-vis changes in their personal well-being. The number of "available voters" (Bartolini 1999: 465) – voters willing to reconsider changing their previous electoral choice – declines. Thus ethnic parties minimize elite responsiveness and distort competition and choice. The high polarization and the low degree of voter availability make any assessment of the incumbent government less contingent on governmental performance. Incumbent vulnerability instead becomes dependent on the turnout rates of ethnic communities. Even if elections remain peaceful and ethnic parties do not constitute a threat to state stability, elections still resemble an ethnic census.

Overall, scholars concerned with questions of democratization should rightly care a great deal about the impact of ethnic parties. Although the effect on stability and peace is not clear-cut, ethnic parties negatively affect democratic competition and choice. They minimize elite responsiveness, increase political polarization, and make political change at least partly contingent on turnout rates of individual communities (Bartolini 1999, 2000, Müller and Strom 1999, Meguid 2005, Adams et al. 2006, Brancati 2008).

INTERNATIONAL PARTY ASSISTANCE AND ETHNIC PARTIES

Given the detrimental effects of ethnic parties on politics in nonindustrialized societies, international donors and African governments have dedicated significant efforts to combating the impact of ethnicity at the level of political parties. Both appear to have accepted the Afro-pessimism that accompanied the return of multiparty competition in the early 1990s.

By now, international party assistance constitutes roughly five to seven percent of international democracy support (Burnell and Gerrits 2010). One of the main goals of international party assistance is to counteract the formation of ethnic parties; its leading proponents are German and American party foundations. Guidelines for the dispersal of aid highlight the need for parties to have strong local ties, while at the same time, parties ought to be present in all parts of the country. Aiming for a broad support base is essential: the multiethnic nature of parties serves as an important benchmark for the identification of local recipients by donors. In addition, recipients are expected to formulate and adhere to key principles. Ideally, they have the firm intention to translate these principles into policies once elected into office. Furthermore, African parties ought to reach out to interest groups and invest meaningful time in drafting their policy platforms. Finally, political parties are supposed to follow democratic standards in their internal dealings. The international community clearly promotes an image of political parties that in essence represents the programmatic mass-based parties that shaped party competition in Europe in the 1950s (National Democratic Instittue 2003, Norris 2005, Carothers 2006, Erdmann 2010).

African governments themselves have invested significant efforts to rid their countries of ethnically based party competition. The spread of multiparty competition in the early 1990s has been accompanied by widespread legal bans on ethnic and other particularistic parties. Currently, 39 of 45 Sub-Saharan African countries ban particularistic parties. Of these 39 countries, 32 explicitly ban ethnic parties either in their constitutions or in party laws regulating party competition. Party bans state explicitly the aim of creating political stability. In the immediate post-independence period, only 17 countries had similar regulations in place. Party bans are clearly a response to the assumption that the return of multiparty contest in Africa would harden ethnic cleavages and endanger stability (Bogaards et al. 2010, Moroff 2010, Moroff and Basedau 2010). Thus both Western donors and African governments are keen to create a political playing field in which ethnic parties are absent. They have subscribed to the assumption that unless party competition is manipulated, ethnic parties will prevail. Some thus regard ethnic party bans as an institution for peace (Basedau 2011).

FIGHTING GHOSTS? POLITICAL SCIENCE AND AFRICAN PARTIES

Despite a plethora of literature on the role of ethnic parties and the alleged dominance of ethnic parties in Africa, comparatively little systematic scholarship has been written about African parties. Even less work has been conducted that considers parties in a comparative manner. Contemporary studies of African parties are confined to in-depth analyses of election results in a specific country at one particular point in time. If voting behavior occurs along communal boundaries, scholars of African politics are inclined to use the term "ethnic party." This convention raises a variety of issues that carry serious theoretical implications for scholars and direct consequences for aid practitioners.

First, parties are analyzed with the help of only one indicator: election results or survey data (see, e.g., Ishiyama 2012). This is a gross oversimplification of the dynamics of political contest. An analysis of other aspects of party life such as original party documents, party factions, the composition of a party's leadership – all of which constitute very popular tools in comparative politics literature – are missing (Chandra 2011).

Second, preliminary research implies that more often than not, African parties do not rely on the exclusive support of one group (Erdmann 2007a). Yet despite their frequent multiethnic composition, these parties still follow the logic of ethnic politics – especially if the party in question is restricted to culturally similar groups. This observation raises a serious conceptual issue: when is an African party an ethnic party, and when does it constitute a nonethnic party? More important, what types of nonethnic parties exist? Often, scholars do not even admit to this possibility and ignore alternative party types. Instead, the term "ethnic party" is the only point of reference for the classification of parties. For example, some distinguish between "ethnic parties" and "potentially ethnic parties" (Scarritt 2006, Cheeseman and Ford 2007, Chandra 2011). The term "ethnic party" is thus used promiscuously and holds little discriminatory power.

Third, the lack of suitable party classification schemes for African parties and the lack of comparative empirical research on African parties constitute a serious shortcoming for the donor community. An appropriate assessment of which party types in Africa are conducive to democracy is missing. As a result, donors use Western party models as a starting point for the design of international party assistance. Not only are these models unsuitable for the African political contexts, but they also idealize the nature of Western parties (Carothers 2006, Erdmann 2010).

Finally, and most pertinent for ongoing research, recent findings illustrate that ethnicity affects African politics considerably less than conventionally assumed. Since the return of multiparty democracy to Africa in the early 1990s, scholars have dedicated new and more thorough efforts to analyzing the attitudes and opinions of African voters. Their writings have arrived at a much more nuanced picture of African political life. Although ethnicity clearly matters, the extent to which it shapes political action varies significantly between countries (Cheeseman and Ford 2007, Dowd and Driessen 2008, Basedau et al. 2011, Basedau and Stroh 2012). Survey data have revealed some of the most striking findings on political opinion formation in Africa. Accordingly, African democracies are characterized by large segments of swing voters (Young 2009, Keffer 2010). Elections do not correspond to the logic of ethnic census; African voters instead choose candidates on the basis of past performance in office. African political participation in large parts resembles the dynamics of political participation in established democracies (Norris and Mattes 2003, Lindberg and Morrison 2008, Bratton et al. 2011).

Twenty years after the third wave of democratization reached the African continent, comparative political science still lacks the analytical tools necessary to capture the nature of African parties. Yet such an analysis is more urgent than ever. Although practitioners and local governments allocate numerous resources to counteract the centrifugal effects of ethnic parties, recent political science research indicates that the political salience of ethnicity has long been exaggerated.

FILLING IN THE GAPS

First, this book builds on an already existing party typology to systematically classify African political parties. It puts forward an operationalization of an ethnic party and how an ethnic party can be distinguished from a number of nonethnic party types; it names and defines these nonethnic party types. It classifies parties with the help of conventional indicators from the comparative politics literature. The framework of analysis is not confined to the realm of area studies (Schmitter and Karl 1994, Basedau and Köllner 2007, Ahram 2011). This book creates a new tool for comparative scholars interested in African parties and/or in parties in nonindustrialized societies in general. It facilitates future cross-regional comparisons with parties in other regions. The party typology advanced here is not carved in stone; it is a starting point for comparative analyses of parties in Africa and beyond. Other scholars can add to or amend the typology, based on their knowledge and expertise.

Second, this book applies the new party typology to a number of African countries to examine the African political landscape in a comparative and systematic manner. Although party systems have recently enjoyed a surge in interest (Bogaards 2004, Basedau and Stroh 2012), analyses of individual African parties have not been conducted. The results from the application of the party typology prove that a variety of party types exist. Ethnic parties are part of this diversity, yet ethnic parties certainly do not dominate political competition. In some countries, both ethnic and nonethnic party types have strong programmatic anchors – although programmatically inclined parties constitute exceptions, not the rule. However, the programmatic aspect of African parties certainly deserves attention.

The existence of ethnic parties does not mean that nonethnic parties disintegrate; rather, ethnic and nonethnic parties coexist over long periods of time. Most strikingly, the present volume finds that over time, the political salience of ethnicity decreases. As multiparty competition endures, ethnic parties attempt to increase their outreach. There is no indication that democratic competition in nonindustrialized societies fosters conflict or hardens communal relations.

Third, this book finds a variation of ethnic and nonethnic party types within and across countries. As outlined previously, the dominant voices in political science literature assume that in societies lacking an industrial revolution, ethnic parties emerge. In the absence of class- and/or post-material cleavages, the argument goes, ethnic differences become the main pillar on which political participation rests. Although this argument carries internal logic, it does not constitute an empirically grounded theory. Results from the application of the party typology clearly demonstrate that ethnicity exercises a strong salience in party politics in some countries, yet ethnicity holds little to no impact on parties in other countries. The book examines why in some countries the formation of ethnic parties is more likely than in others. The small number of cases under scrutiny requires future studies to test the robustness of this finding.

THE STRUCTURE OF THE BOOK

Chapter Two reviews the manner in which political parties in different regions around the globe have been examined. It examines the major threads of the comparative politics literature on parties elsewhere. The chapter attests to the dual dilemma described earlier: no comparative framework exists by which African parties can be compared, neither across Africa, nor across continents. In reviewing the major works on African politics since independence, it further outlines the main variables African political life is subjected to. Subsequently, the chapter introduces a global typology of political parties designed by Diamond and Gunther (2001).[2] The Diamond and Gunther typology is amended to grasp the full diversity of the African continent. The operationalization of the typology is conducted on the basis of worldwide research on parties. Five party types are at the heart of this study: the mono-ethnic party, the multiethnic alliance, the multiethnic catch-all party, the programmatic party, and the personalistic party. Although the mono-ethnic party and the multiethnic alliance are regarded as ethnic parties, the others are seen as nonethnic parties.

Chapters Three, Four, and Five are dedicated to the empirical application of the global typology to all relevant (Sartori 2005a) and effective (Laakso and Taagepera 1979) parties in three countries: Kenya, Namibia, and Ghana. Individual chapters analyze parties within the remits of each parliamentary cycle and across the whole observation period ranging from the early 1990s to 2010. Kenya, Ghana, and Namibia have been selected because each country entails party types that correspond to the party types in the typology. Kenya represents the archetypical case of an ethnic party system; all parties remain ethnic parties. Namibia represents a mixed-party system; its incumbent party is a nonethnic, its opposition is first an ethnic and later a nonethnic party. Ghana reparesents a nonethnic party system; both government and opposition are nonethnic. Both Ghanaian parties display programmatic undertones. Taken together, the three chapters illustrate the political diversity of the African continent with previously unknown data.

[2] Depending on the publication (Gunther and Diamond 2003 or Diamond and Gunther 2001), the typology could also be referred to as "Gunther and Diamond typology." For reasons of simplicity, I use the term "Diamond and Gunther typology."

Chapter Six summarizes the results from the three empirical chapters and comes to an overall assessment of the analytical efficacy of the amended party typology. The chapter shows that even though ethnic parties prevail overall, in two of three countries, nonethnic parties dominate. Parties also do not retain the same facets over time, and most try to become more inclusive over the course of successive elections. This is particularly true of opposition parties. This study finds that the salience of ethnicity differs across and within countries. These further qualify the conventional assumption that African parties are per se ethnic parties.

These challenging and new findings call for empirical verification by additional cases. The systematic application of the new party typology is labor- and time-intensive; therefore, verification of the results relies on preliminary evidence from seven African countries: Tanzania, Botswana, Malawi, Senegal, Burkina Faso, Zambia, and Benin. The results from the preliminary cases confirm the findings from the in-depth cases. Ethnic parties neither dominate, nor does the duration of multiparty contest increase the political salience of ethnicity. To facilitate future large-N comparisons of parties, Chapter Six also assess the discriminative power of each of the indicators of the new party typology.

Chapter Seven examines which factors might be responsible for the prevalence of ethnic parties in some and nonethnic parties in other countries. The literature assumes a causal relationship between the lack of an industrial revolution and the formation of ethnicity-based parties. Yet the causes for the formation of a particular party type have not been examined in earnest. A number of variables that might account for the formation in ethnic parties in some and nonethnic parties in other countries must yet be tested. The initial focus is again on the three in-depth cases of Kenya, Namibia, and Ghana. Economic inequalities (both at the local and at the national level), the quality of democracy, the electoral system in place, and the provision of ethnic party bans cannot account entirely for the formation of (non-) ethnic parties.

The ethnic structure of countries – the existence of a core ethnic group and a low ethnic fractionalization index – is a key factor for the formation of nonethnic parties. The lack of an ethnic core group and a high ethnic fractionalization index by contrast fosters the formation of ethnic parties. Evidence from the additional cases largely confirms the hypothesized relationship. Given the preliminary nature of the additional case studies and the limited number of cases available, this book arrives at preliminary findings. Ensuing studies can take these findings as a point of departure, as the book facilitates a theory-driven approach to African politics.

The Conclusion summarizes the main findings of the study. It demonstrates that the political saliency of ethnicity in African political life has been widely exaggerated. It illustrates once more the diversity of African party competition. Ethnic parties do exist but by no means dominate African politics. The chapter links the findings from the empirical part back to the much broader question of democracy in Africa. The debate about the democratization potential of parties – in Africa and elsewhere – is under the heavy normative shadow of the European mass party. The European mass party, however, is an inappropriate analytical yardstick to evaluate the democratization potential of any party. The conclusion deliberately highlights the positive contributions African parties make to democratic consolidation. Furthermore, the chapter outlines some general suggestions of what international aid concerned with international party assistance should consider. In particular, international party assistance should analyze more thoroughly the conditions on the ground and try to foster nationwide parties. To achieve this end, mass-based organizations are not necessary. Although ethnic parties do not necessarily spell doom, the empirical evidence shows that countries with catch-all parties are more stable and thus more susceptive to democratic consolidation. The book concludes with some general remarks about future pathways of comparative political science.

2

A New Framework of Comparison for Political Parties

Political parties are indispensable for democratic rule. Parties bridge the gap between the state and civil society; they aggregate the interest of their respective populations and, in doing so, structure the popular vote; they integrate and mobilize the citizenry; and they are in charge of recruiting the national political leadership. In short, parties are the primary vehicle for political participation. The nature of parties determines the nature of political competition. In societies in which particularistic parties prevail, participation is likely to be characterized by exclusion, which holds potentially detrimental consequences for state stability and peace. For a long time, scholars saw political participation in Africa structured around ethnic loyalties. In the last decade or so, a number of studies have challenged that view. Yet despite this growing interest in African politics following the introduction of multiparty competition in the early 1990s, no party typology for African parties has emerged from the scholarship. As a result of the absence of a suitable party typology, scholars know very little about the nature of African parties and thus little about the nature of political competition. This chapter creates a new framework of analysis of parties and thus provides the conceptual basis for empirically grounded research on parties in nonindustrialized societies. Twenty years after the third wave of democratization, such an endeavor is long overdue.

This chapter begins with a succinct overview of the dominant party models in the Western world and beyond. The purpose of this section is twofold. First, it confirms the rising perception among scholars that the conventional party models are unsuited to the analysis of contemporary African parties – more specifically, that the prevailing models do not fit contemporary parties anywhere in post–third–wave democracies. Second, it introduces the indicators that comparative scholars and area experts have applied to operationalize existing party models. On the basis of this discussion, I discard the dominant party models of comparative research as useful analytical blueprints for the study of African parties. The conventional party models clearly cannot contribute to our understanding of African party politics. However, the discussion reveals several indicators that should be used in research on African parties to ensure a maximum of comparability between African parties and parties elsewhere.

Next the chapter examines an existing party typology, which was designed with the explicit purpose of comparing political parties globally (Diamond and Gunther 2001, Gunther and Diamond 2003).[1] The Diamond and Gunther typology responds to the sense among scholars that existing typologies pursue a narrow regional bias or no longer speak to the empirical reality of the contemporary period. It provides a unique opportunity to conduct party research in nonindustrialized societies.

Subsequently, the chapter operationalizes the typology with the help of ten indicators drawn from the literature on parties worldwide. The amended and newly operationalized Diamond and Gunther typology serves as an analytical framework for the study of African parties. Its analytical validity is tested in subsequent chapters, which provide an in-depth examination of parties in Kenya, Namibia, and Ghana.

ON THE STUDY OF POLITICAL PARTIES

The study of political parties is more than a century old. In different periods, scholars emphasized different aspects of party life with different degrees of sophistication and analytical depth. Most, if not all, party models were hatched to illustrate the formation of Western European parties in a specific historical context. The emergence of the mass party in the mid-twentieth century, for example, was deeply embedded in the rise of the social democratic left. The literature on Western European parties dominates the comparative politics literature, whereas scholars working on political parties in other regions joined the debate much later. The rise of post–third-wave democracies has led to few attempts to conceptualize parties. The few party models that exist suffer from numerous shortcomings: they are either underspecified, or purely descriptive, or they suffer from an equally strong regional bias as the Western European models.

Party Typologies in the Western World

The first scholar to depart from examining parties in a historical manner was Maurice Duverger (1954). Duverger set the pace for decades of political science research on parties. He prioritized party organization over

[1] The typology by Larry Diamond and Richard Gunther is sometimes cited as Diamond and Gunther typology, sometimes as Gunther and Diamond typology. I use the former for no other reason than simplicity.

TABLE 2.1. *Party Types According to Duverger*

Features	Mass Party	Cadre Party
membership	large	restricted
unit of organization	branch	caucus
range of activity	wide range including education of the masses, constant factors in members' lives	narrow range, presence restricted to political events during election period
ideological articulation	strong	weak

Source: Author's compilation based on Duverger (1951).

other aspects of party life to identify the nature of parties. Duverger distinguished between two party types – the cadre party and the mass party. The cadre party remains elitist in composition, organized not only minimally, but also loosely outside its parliamentary caucus. The mass party organizes the masses (in particular, the working class), engages in a much wider variety of political activities, and represents a much broader segment of society. Duverger's indicators included party membership, internal structure, party activities, and the degrees to which parties articulate ideology. See Table 2.1.

Duverger regarded mass parties as more conducive to the requirements of political competition in the era of postwar universal suffrage, and he predicted that all parties had to transform into mass parties if they wanted to survive politically. At the time when Duverger was writing, all mass parties were socialist or social-democratic parties. Although such contemporary scholars as Alan Ware still use Duverger's two models, several of Duverger's findings have been reassessed in the light of new empirical findings (Wollinetz 2002, Ware 2005). The notion that the mass party could ensure electoral triumph was proven wrong, as the loose organization and the nonideological nature of parties in the United States and the electoral successes of conservative parties in Western Europe have demonstrated (Epstein 1980). In addition, the distinction between mass and cadre parties was increasingly called into question by new developments in Western European politics.

In the mid-1960s, Kirchheimer (1966) argued that after the Second World War, mass parties underwent a transformation from mass parties to catch-all parties. The following phenomena are typical of a catch-all party: (a) a drastic reduction of the party's ideology, (b) a strengthening role of the party's leadership and consequently a diminishing role of individual party members, (c) the recruitment of voters as main priority, and (d) political access to as many interest groups as is feasible. The erosion of social boundaries, the diminishing effect of class on voting behavior, the emergence of the welfare state, and the professional stratification of the working population at large caused all major parties to adopt catch-all electoral strategies, according to Kirchheimer (1966). At the heart of these new strategies are election campaigns that no longer aim to mobilize particular social groups with the help of their membership; instead, parties try to woo as many voters as possible. The de-ideologization of political competition has put candidates in the spotlight and has simultaneously made parties more elitist and less member-driven (Kirchheimer 1966, Krouwel 1999, 2003).

Kirchheimer (1966) thus assumed an ever-growing degree of uniformity among all politically relevant parties. Kirchheimer himself never systematically provided an empirical application of the catch-all party, and various scholars have criticized his work for failing to outline what exactly a catch-all party is (Wollinetz 1979, Smith 1989, Katz and Mair 1995). The proliferation of adjectives attached to his model – "the catch-all people's party," "the catch-all mass party," "the conservative catch-all party," "the Christian type of the catch-all people's party" – further raised criticism about whether the catch-all party really represents a viable analytical concept or whether the term merely describes a political phenomenon that intuitively makes sense (Krouwel 1999, 2003). Contemporary scholars have subjected the catch-all party to empirical verifications. The results, however, have been disappointing, as these studies do not contrast the catch-all party with alternative party models but focus exclusively on how catch-all parties can be identified (Arter 1999, Krouwel 1999, Forestiere 2009, Smith 2009).

Scholars noted that catch-all parties have become less and less ideological and member-driven (Katz and Mair 1992, Mair and van Biezen 2001). Accordingly, Katz and Mair (1995, 2009) discarded Duverger's mass party and Kirchheimer's catch-all party as extinct. They argued that from the 1970s onward, the Western European party systems started to undergo yet another transformation: from catch-all parties to cartel parties. Katz and Mair (1995 and 2009) reexamined the development of European parties over the course of the twentieth century and noted several historical developments that shatter the idea that a political party represents a predefined section of society. Corroborating many of Kirchheimer's previous findings, they referred to the erosion of traditional social boundaries, the rise of the welfare state, the development of the mass media, and the fact that almost all parties have at some point been in government. In particular, three factors have fundamentally changed the nature of party politics: first, the end of the Cold War, which weakened the political benefits of appealing to class and culture; second, the reliance of parties on the mass media and its dependence on professional expertise in running election campaigns; and third, the increase in the cost of political defeat caused by the professionalization of politics. As a result, parties now resemble each other not only in terms of their organizational structure, but also in terms of their strategies.

As they ascend to political prominence, cartel parties stifle the emergence of new competitors. Cartel parties employ various means to maintain their leading position, such as the imposition of threshold rules, the provision of state subsidies to parties with a larger share of seats, and the over-proportional use of the state media by the incumbent parties. Thus, in contrast to previous authors, Katz and Mair (1995 and 2009) no longer analyzed solely the relationship between parties and civil society but expanded their focus to the relationship between parties and the state. They argued that parties have moved to the state to receive urgently needed financial resources, which can no longer be collected from party members (Katz and Mair 1995 and 2009). The key differences between the cartel model and previous ones are outlined in Table 2.2.

Katz and Mair (1995) operationalized their types with a wide variety of indicators and provided their party models with more analytical substance than all previous scholars. The cartel party type still attracts its critics. For example, the cartel type often remains vaguely defined. The precise differences between the catch-all and the cartel party remain unclear. What appear to be characteristics of a cartel party system might in fact be the consequences of catch-all parties (Katz and Mair 1995, 2009, Koole 1996, MacIvor 1996, Blyth and Katz 2005, Scarrow 2007, Pelizzo 2007). Just like the mass party, the catch-all and the cartel party are embattled concepts among Western European scholars. The explicit links between European postwar history once more illustrate the strong regional bias of all European party types.

It is surprising that scholars who work with the catch-all and the cartel-party model normally fail to incorporate research techniques by which the ideological strength of parties can be quantified. Indeed, a second strand of Western literature has analyzed political parties in terms of a right-left cleavage (Downs 1957, Lipset and Rokkan 1967, Enlow and Hinich 1990, Lipset 2001a, Sartori 2005b). In these works, political parties that share ideological orientations are grouped as "party families" (Seiler 1980, Mair and Mudde 1998). Spatial theory provides us with a typology that is very familiar to the occasional political observer, as Table 2.3 demonstrates. For some scholars, ideologies thus continue to be at the heart of political parties. The Manifesto Research Group (MRG) has provided a coding scheme by which the policy positions of parties can be measured with the help of content analysis of party manifestos (Budge et al. 1987, 2001, Laver and Budge 1992, Klingemann et al. 1994, Volkens 2007). Scholars working with the scheme have shown that parties continue to be influenced by their ideological orientations.

To summarize, Western party research is divided and textually specific. Throughout the course of the last few decades, scholars working on Western European parties have attached great importance to various aspects of the nature of parties. Some still favor organizational criteria, whereas others have designed alternative indicators. A third group regards a party's ideological orientation as the major identifier. The organizational aspect certainly received the most attention. Although there is general agreement that the

TABLE 2.2. *Party Types According to Katz and Mair*

Characteristics	Elite Party	Mass Party	Catch-All Party	Cartel Party
time	19th century	1880–1960	1945–	1970–
degree of sociopolitical inclusion	restricted suffrage	enfranchisement and mass suffrage	mass suffrage	mass suffrage
principal goals	distribution of privileges	social reformation	social amelioration	politics as profession
basis of party competition	ascribed status	representative capacity	policy effectiveness	managerial skills
nature of party work and campaigning	irrelevant	labor-intensive	both labor-intensive and capital-intensive	capital-intensive
principal source of resources	personal contacts	members' fees and contributions	contributions from a wide variety of sources	state subventions
relations between ordinary members and elite	elite are ordinary members	bottom up	top down	stratarchy; mutual autonomy
character of membership	small and elitist	large and homogeneous	membership open to all	neither rights nor obligations important

Source: Katz and Mair 1995.

TABLE 2.3. *Party Typology Derived from Spatial Theory*

Party Type	Communist	Left Socialist	Social Democratic	Center Agrarian	Religious	Liberal	Conservative
Identification	Depending on policy space alongside left–right axis						
countries with type	Italy, France, Luxembourg		U.S., Canada, Australia, New Zealand, Ireland, U.K., Spain, Italy, France, Germany, Austria, Luxembourg, Belgium, Netherlands		New Zealand, Spain, U.K., France, Austria, Luxembourg, Belgium, the Netherlands	Canada, Australia, U.K., Italy, France, Germany, Austria, Luxembourg, Belgium, Netherlands	U.S., Canada, New Zealand, Ireland, U.K., Spain, France, Austria

Source: Budge et al. (1994).

mass party is no longer relevant to our world, there is conceptual confusion regarding how to identify alternative party types – and how useful these alternative concepts are. The literature on Western parties alone is sufficient to fill whole libraries; however, no agreement has emerged regarding which party type is best suited to analyze contemporary Western European politics. Most party models are anchored in a particular era. The design of all party models has been embedded in the historical trajectory of European societies. All of the previously mentioned scholars understand their work to be directed at party politics in established democracies. Thus by definition, their models lack "traveling capacity" (Sartori 1984). Unfortunately, little to no accumulative research has taken place. Empirical applications of existing types are the exception rather than the rule.

Several indicators that scholars of Western European politics work with – most notably, party-membership figures and the funding of parties by the state – are impossible to identify outside the Western world. The relationship between party members and the party elite can be expected to be even more top-down and the relationship between parties and democratic rules to be even more ambivalent. It is very difficult to examine to what extent or whether at all political contests can be regarded as professionalized. The importance that Western scholars have attached to new forms of political communication – via television or the internet – is unlikely to feature in areas where large parts of the population have no access to these amenities. Yet the analytical values of other indicators remain valid, such as, for example, a party's ideology, its sociopolitical inclusion, and its principal goals.

Party Typologies Outside the Western World

Comparatively little conceptual work has been done on political parties in nonindustrialized societies. Whereas scholars of Western European politics have emphasized the organizational aspect of parties, those who focus on parties elsewhere stress the social composition of parties. Most scholars follow the lead of Horowitz (2000) and regard all parties in nonindustrialized societies as ethnic parties. Horowitz distinguished between ethnic, multiethnic, and nonethnic parties. He suggests only one indicator – voting behavior – to distinguish among them. Both the ethnic and the multiethnic parties can have a multiethnic following yet "a party is multiethnic only if it spans the major groups in conflict" (Horowitz 2000: 299). Unfortunately, Horowitz provided no definition of the nonethnic party. Indeed, the lack of nonethnic parties is the major premise on which he rests his work (see Table 2.4). Horowitz "typology" thus is somewhat disingenuous: by virtue of definition, he excludes the possibility to falsify his own assumptions.

Drawing on these party types, Horowitz (2000) proposed several types of party systems: ethnic, nonethnic, and mixed. A party system comprising both ethnic and nonethnic parties is exceptional, as this circumstance would

TABLE 2.4. *Party Types in Ethnically Segmented Societies According to Horowitz*

	Ethnic Party	Multiethnic Party	Nonethnic Party
electoral support	supported by a particular group or a cluster of groups	supported by a cluster of groups spanning the major groups in conflict	not specified
occurrence	frequent	rare	nonexistent

Source: Horowitz (2000).

presuppose the existence of more than one issue axis. For Horowitz, this never occurs in Africa or Asia, as ultimately nonethnic parties will always be replaced by ethnic ones.

A second approach to the analysis of parties beyond Western paradigms focuses on their linkage function. Kitschelt (2000) identified three types of parties according to the manner in which they reach out to voters: the charismatic, the clientelistic, and the programmatic. The three differ in two indicators: party appeal and infrastructure (i.e., organization). According to Kitschelt (2000), charismatic parties convince followers of the leader's ability to create a better future. Charismatic parties lack organizational infrastructure. Clientelistic parties rely on a sophisticated party machinery and create bonds with their followers through material side payments. Programmatic parties compensate voters with selected incentives and advance universalistic public policy solutions (Kitschelt 2000). See Table 2.5.

At first blush, this typology appears well suited to compare and contrast the dynamics of party politics in various regions. Kitschelt's types are not embedded in a particular historical context. Kitschelt also developed a much broader spectrum of models than Horowitz. A priori, one could reasonably assume that politics in Africa, Asia, and Latin America strongly

TABLE 2.5. *Party Types Derived from Kitschelt*

Party Type	Infrastructure	Appeal
charismatic Party	no investment in party organization or in programmatic unity building	persuasion skills of leader; asymmetry of leader and followers
lientelistic Party	heavy investment in party organization	logic of exchange with asymmetric exchange
programmatic Party	investment in both organization and programmatic unity	reimbursement of rents as a matter of codified party programs

Source: Kitschelt (2000).

favor personalistic and clientelistic parties, whereas in Europe, parties with programmatic tendencies prevail. However, although Kitschelt's typology may provide a promising basis from which to compare party types across the globe, it offers rather little to a comparison of parties within regions, as his framework does not deal with the problem of mixed types (Kitschelt 2000). European parties, for example, suffer from clientelism, albeit perhaps to a lesser extent than parties elsewhere. Third-world parties often are both clientelistic and personalistic. Similarly, Kitschelt's second indicator – investment in infrastructure – is highly problematic for any empirical analysis. In most third-world countries, these data cannot be extracted easily, as party funding is at the discretion of powerful individuals (Pinto-Duschinsky 2002). What is striking is that both Horowitz and Kitschelt focused on key elements of third-world politics – ethnicity and clientelism – yet both reduced their respective analyses of parties to one of the two.

Party Typologies in Eastern Europe, Latin America, and Asia

In addition to these general frameworks, area experts have advanced new approaches to the study of parties in their respective regions of interest. Scholarly analyses of Eastern Europe's emerging parties constitute the better part of this growing literature. A great deal of scholarly work outlines the differences from political parties in Western Europe, yet is still using the Western European models (Evans and Whitefield 1993, Markowski 1997, Zielinski 2002). As in the study of Western parties, organizational features have been central aspects of the study of parties. Scholars frequently identify Kirchheimer's catch-all model as the dominant party type (Kopecky 1995, van Biezen 2005).

Ishiyama (1999) conducted one of the rare systematic attempts to differentiate among different party types in Eastern Europe. Ishiyama went back to the classic literature and designed a typology based on two dimensions: the role of membership and ideological coherence. He derived four different party types (see Table 2.6).

Reliance on membership is denoted as "organizational density," which is the ratio of the number of estimated official party members over the number of voters. To measure ideological coherence, Ishyiama used the

TABLE 2.6. *Party Types Derived from Ishiyama*

	High Reliance on Membership	Low Reliance on Membership
party ideologically coherent	mass party	programmatic party
party ideologically incoherent	clientelistic party	cadre party

Source: Ishiyama (1999).

Huber and Inglehart (1995) database, which is based on expert interviews about the political positioning of parties in forty-two countries. Although Ishiyama's typology broadens the comparative horizon of regional experts – and although his indicators are more sharply defined than those of his peers – the applicability of his framework beyond Eastern Europe is questionable. First, data on membership figures in many new democracies are unreliable. Second, although Huber and Inglehart's database covers a wider variety of countries in Latin America and Eastern Europe, in Africa the database is restricted to South Africa and Nigeria. In both cases, the number of expert opinions is small.[2] Finally, doubts remain about the extent to which his indicators – derived from Duverger (1954) – still speak to the empirical reality anywhere in the world.

The area studies literature on Latin America has focused on party systems and the degree to which they have become institutionalized (Mainwaring and Scully 1995, Stockton 2001, Kuenzi and Lambright 2007, Kitschelt et al. 2010). Van Cott (2005) forms a notable exception. Van Cott's party typology consists of three ethnic party types: the mono-ethnic party, which claims to have the best interests of one particular group at heart; the indigenous-only party, which represents indigenous groups; and the indigenous-based party, which represents indigenous interests but incorporates nonindigenous sympathizers. In contrast to Horowitz, van Cott claimed that mono-ethnic parties are the least frequent party type. This assertion is all the more interesting, as her conceptual framework follows Horowitz. Her distinction between ethnic and multiethnic parties is based on Horowitz: multiethnic parties are "spanning the major ethnic groups and cleavages in society" (van Cott 2005: 18). In line with Horowitz, she used electoral data as an indicator. However, her selection of indicators is much broader. She is the first scholar to include party documents and the official statements of party leaders in any analysis of third-world parties. Unfortunately, van Cott did not explain in detail how to distinguish between the three ethnic party types. Her typology thus remains underspecified and unlikely to produce genuinely comparative analyses.

Surprisingly little systematic research has been conducted on political parties in Asia. Only two descriptive analyses make Asian parties the unit of analysis (Fukui 1985, Sachsenröder and Frings 1998). Both studies use a variety of indicators: party programs, social groups that the party targets as supporters, electoral support, internal party structure, member participation in internal party politics, selection procedures of candidates, and party finances. Because both studies remain at the level of description, all of the indicators are not applied comparatively and thus lack discriminatory power. No party typology has been advanced that is germane to the Asian

[2] In the case of Nigeria, four country experts graded the various aspects of ideological coherence. In the case of South Africa, eleven experts were consulted.

context, nor have Western or global concepts been applied to Asia. As in the case of Latin America, the primary focus of scholars has been on party system institutionalization (Reilly 2007, Croissant 2008).

Party Typologies in Africa

The analysis of African parties deserves special attention. The following section distinguishes between three schools of thought: the post-independence school, which focuses on parties in the immediate post- and pre-independence periods; the revisionist school, whose writings reflected the increasing turn to nondemocratic forms of government from the early 1960s onward; and the democratization school, which focuses on African politics in the post–third-wave era. The most recent writings of the democratization school have challenged the idea that ethnicity is the dominant political variable in African life.

The analyses of political parties in the immediate post- and pre-independence period were embedded in the much broader school of modernization theory. Accordingly, political parties were major instruments in the creation of stable nations. The first comparative small-N studies applied Duverger's distinction between mass and cadre parties. As was the case in Western Europe, the study of political parties in Africa suffered from a normative undercurrent; it regarded the mass party as most conducive to the creation of modern, stable states. In addition to the size of membership, the examination of parties also took party ideology into consideration – not, however, on the basis of truly comparative endeavors but in a descriptive, ad hoc manner. The general agreement was that African political parties followed a decidedly left-wing stance (Hodgkin 1961, Morgenthau 1964, McCain 1975).

The first genuine attempt at constructing a typology relevant to the African context was undertaken in an edited volume by Coleman and Rosberg (1964). The contributors' list reads like a "who's who" of African studies at the time. Coleman and Rosberg distinguished between parties that either follow a "pragmatic-pluralistic pattern" or a "revolutionary-centralizing trend" (1964: 5). The major differences between the two are their occupation with ideology, the degree of popular participation in these parties, and their organizational aspects. See Table 2.7.

Coleman and Rosberg's party models constitute the first and last attempt of area experts to construct an African party typology. Their work demonstrates that many organizational features of African parties must be measured by different indicators than in Western Europe. Instead of membership figures, for example, the authors use popular participation. Party ideology is identified by analyzing the attitude of parties toward pressing political issues rather than with the help of an elaborated coding scheme. All their indicators are applied in a purely descriptive and nonsystematic manner.

TABLE 2.7. *African Parties According to Coleman and Rosberg*

Factor of Differentiation	Pragmatic Pluralist	Revolutionary Centralist
degree of ideology	limited	strong preoccupation
approach toward modernization	moderate and controlled modernization	revolutionary
engagement toward the following goals:		
Neutralism	pragmatic	very positive
African unity	pragmatic functional	political unification
Decolonization and Africanization	pragmatic	immediate
popular participation		
Degree of mobilization	partly	high
Type of individual participation	direct and indirect	direct
organizational aspects		
Degree of centralism	varies	high
Degree of fusion	varies	high
Degree to which party and state are integrated	limited integration	total integration

Source: Coleman and Rosberg 1964.

Unfortunately, Coleman and Rosberg failed to apply their typology. Instead they arrived at the disappointing conclusion that African parties cannot be empirically distinguished (Coleman and Rosberg 1964, Rotberg 1966). At the same time, many contributors had previously published their analyses of parties in individual countries (see, e.g., Sklar 1963, Zollberg 1964, and Lofchie 1965). Their main scholarly preoccupation was to highlight the particularities of their pet country rather than to find a common analytical ground for fruitful comparisons. Five decades after independence, their party types and their indicators offer even less to the study of African parties.

The failure of early scholars to come to terms with the nature of African parties owed to many factors. First, scholarship on the early years of African politics was rife with convoluted research questions: the search for suitable party types was linked to the question of whether democratic rule was possible in Africa and to what extent one could speak of successful nation-building (see, e.g., Apter 1955). Little time was spent on the construction of coherent typologies, let alone their application. Second, African parties were simply too young to be analyzed in a systematic manner. Third – and later scholars often overlook this point – scholars of the early years saw it as their goal to increase, or indeed to create, information about Africa in the most general sense. All of these factors militated for description at the expense of analysis.

The downfall of multiparty democracy and its replacement with various forms of nondemocratic forms of government in several African states prompted political scientists to adopt a revisionist approach. Whereas mass parties had been previously regarded as essential tools in creating united and stable nations, they were now seen as outgrowths of the neopatrimonial state held together by the desire of powerful individuals to gain access to state resources (Austin 1964, Zollberg 1964). African parties were now anything but mass parties; they were described as fragile entities driven by the interests of the powerful few. Because one-party regimes were often accompanied by military or personalistic rule, the focus of research on Africa shifted away from parties to the broader subject of political order (Decalo 1976, Jackson and Rosberg 1982, Young 1982, Cartwright 1983). Simultaneously, a variety of scholars noted the high salience of ethnicity in African politics – which the literature of the early years had regarded as less significant given the formation of nationwide mass parties (Young 1965, Kasfir 1976). Although the major studies of the early years pursued comparative – though purely descriptive – research, the literature of the revisionist school focused on individual countries. Because the revisionist school never examined parties as their own unit of analysis, research on African parties never left its infancy.

The third wave of democratization changed the direction as well as the scope of the scholarly debate. The rapid alternation from authoritarian to democratic forms of government made Africa once again the subject of the classic topics of comparative politics. Just as in the immediate post- and pre-independence periods, the research of the last 20 years has been less concerned with political parties. Instead, the question of which factors – external or internal forces – contributed more to the democratic transition process was key to the seminal works on Africa (Wiseman 1996, Bratton and van de Walle 1997). Others have tried to identify the factors that account for an increase in the quality of democracy over time (Lindberg 2007). Although the tone of the revisionist school was distinctly negative, the recent debate can be divided between those who regard the spread of democratic norms as a genuinely new development and those who argue that African societies remain driven by neopatrimonial structures, whose logic is enduring and stronger than formal state structures (Bayart 1993, Chabal and Daloz 1999). Both fail to provide any in-depth analyses of parties.

Recent writings of the democratization school have dedicated significant efforts in examining the role of ethnicity. Results challenge the alleged ubiquity of ethnicity in African political affairs. First, a number of studies have highlighted that ethnic loyalties are man-made. Politicians use cleavages to their advantage or they alter existing cleavages to increase their chances of being voted into office (Posner 2003, 2005). Second, others have shown that some African party systems are more ethnically dominated than others (Cheeseman and Ford 2007, Dowd and Driessen 2008, Basedau and Stroh 2012). Some have even advanced tentative considerations, which factors account for the diverging degree to which ethnicity effects party systems (e.g., Kasara 2011). Third, the prevalence of dominant party systems indicates that incumbent parties do not follow the logic of ethnic politics. If voting occurred exclusively along ethnic lines, Africa's party systems would be more fragmented and dominant parties would be absent. In addition, voter turnout differs significantly between countries and is contingent on institutional factors. Elections therefore cannot be reduced to ethnic census. Most African presidents hail from minority communities – again, a strong indication that ethnic loyalties matter less than expected (Bogaards 2004, Kuenzi and Lambright 2007, Bratton et al. 2011). Fourth, survey data have revealed some of the most striking findings about African opinion formation. African voters display partisan indifference, not ethnic loyalty, in the run-up to elections. Accordingly, African democracies are characterized by large segments of swing voters. Voters choose candidates on the basis of past performance. Thus African democracies bear great similarity to the liberal democracies in the Western world (Norris and Mattes 2003, Lindberg and Morrison 2008, Young 2009, Keffer 2010, Bratton et al. 2011).

Despite these challenging and pioneering findings, research on individual African parties has remained absent. Neither have new African party typologies been developed, nor have existing typologies been applied. Instead, African parties are exclusively analyzed within the context of election results or survey data. This reduces the analysis of political parties to one indicator. Consciously or unconsciously, these studies draw on the assumption that voting in nonindustrialized societies occurs along ethnic lines (for examples, see Kandeh 2003, Throup and Hornsby 1998, Nugent 1999, 2001, Cowen and Laakso 2002, Morrison 2004, Fridy 2007, Basedau and Stroh 2012). Whenever voting occurs along ethnic lines, the term "ethnic party" is used somewhat indiscriminately.

Although the democratization school does focus on political parties, its analysis of political parties is limited in various ways: First, most (though not all) publications refer to a single case, that is, one country and/or one particular election. Second, political parties are analyzed only in the context of election results, which makes a systematic examination difficult, especially if voting does not occur solely along ethnic lines. The more recent literature on African politics suggests that the salience of ethnicity has long been exaggerated. This finding further begs the question: which other party types exist? Does an ethnic party stay an ethnic party in the long run? What are the dynamics between ethnic and nonethnic parties over time? In recent years, scholarly awareness of this shortcoming has risen, and various authors have called on the research community to dedicate greater efforts to come to terms with the nature of African parties (Erdmann 2004, Basedau et al. 2007, Elischer 2008). Still, although new and more sophisticated data are available on voting preferences, there remains a lack of conceptual groundwork and empirical testing. See Table 2.8.

TABLE 2.8. *African Parties in the Literature*

School of Thought	Early Phase	Revisionist School	Democratization School
historical background	pre-independence	post-independence	post–third wave
unit of analysis	political parties	the African state	democracy the African state
methodology	single case comparative	single case comparative	single case large-N
descriptive/ analytical	descriptive	descriptive	analytical
role of parties	dominant	absent	minor
framework for analyzing parties	mass vs. patron pragmatic pluralist vs. revolutionary centralist	none	none

Source: Author's Compilation

TOWARD A NEW FRAMEWORK OF COMPARISON

The overview of party models across the globe reveals the tribalized nature of political science. All party models inhibit a regional or temporal bias. In numerous instances, it is not even clear to what extent we can talk about genuine typologies, as ideally a typology includes several types and indicators by which their types (in this case: party types) can be distinguished. The existing frameworks more often than not fall drastically short of fulfilling even these basic criteria.

Diamond and Gunther (2001, 2003) were the first scholars to openly address the failure of political science to capture the new diversity of political parties following the third wave of democratization. The two authors constructed a global party typology, which was specifically designed to avoid the temporal and contextual bias that has become characteristic of party research. On the basis of three criteria – *formal party organization*, *programmatic commitments*, and a *party's relationship to democratic norms* – Diamond and Gunther arrived at 15 global party types (see Table 2.9). Unfortunately, Diamond and Gunther failed to operationalize the typology with indicators that hold sufficient discriminatory power. The subsequent sections provide the first attempt in doing so, whereas the following chapters apply the operationalized typology to three African countries.

Diamond and Gunther's (2001, 2003) distinction between pluralistic types and proto-hegemonic types is somewhat incongruous. It introduces a dichotomy between those parties conducive to democratic rule (the

TABLE 2.9. *Diamond and Gunther's Party Typology*

Parties	Pluralistic Type	Proto-hegemonic Type
elite-based	local notable	
	clientelistic	
mass-based		
ideological/socialist	class-mass	leninist
ideological nationalist	pluralist nationalist	ultranationalist
religious	denominational-mass	religious fundamentalism
ethnicity-based	ethnic	
	congress	
electoralist	catch-all	
	programmatic	
	personalistic	
movement	left-libertarian	
	post-industrial extreme right	

Source: Diamond and Gunther 2001, 2003.

pluralistic types) and those whose conduct is detrimental to democratic consolidation (the proto-hegemonic types). Proto-hegemonic types strive to replace the existing pluralist society with one that is suited to their goals. They further try to prevail over opposition groups inside the party by excluding them from leadership positions. In contrast, pluralistic types accept victory in free and fair elections as the only legitimate way of achieving their objectives; internally, they comply with democratic rules.

The separation between these two "meta-types" does not derive from the literature, and the two authors advance no justification why, for example, an ethnic party would be any more democratic in its internal or external behavior than a religious fundamentalist party. The distinction becomes even more difficult to understand if one follows the scholarly literature on Western parties, which, practically from its inception, has stressed the ambivalent relationship between parties and intra-party democracy (Neumann 1955). The more recent literature on the cartel party shows that the relationship between parties and democracy is not as clear-cut as Diamond and Gunther assumed (Katz and Mair 2009).

In my empirical application of Diamond and Gunther typology, I discard the attribution of specific party types to democratic behavior.

Diamond and Gunther's individual party types cannot serve as the starting point for comparing African parties without several other amendments, as the analytical validity of some types can be excluded a priori. Diamond and Gunther argued that the left-libertarian type is "quintessentially post-materialist in their attitudinal orientation and behavior" (2001: 29). As an example, the authors cite the German Green Party. African countries are not sufficiently advanced economically to allow for post-material ideology to emerge as major political cleavage. This is not to say there are no ecological (or similar) movements on African soil, but serious doubts can be raised about their political significance.

For similar reasons, the post-industrial extreme right type can be dropped from an analysis of African parties. The term "post-industrial" presupposes large-scale industrialization to have taken place, which is hardly the case in Africa. In addition, Diamond and Gunther pictured this type of movement as one in which "xenophobic, racist hostility towards migrants is a highly salient line of conflict" (2001: 30). The authors refer to Austria's Freedom Movement and France's National Front as examples for contemporary radical right-wing parties. In ethnically segmented societies, subnational identities take the place of national identities and are better analyzed and captured within the framework of ethnicity-based parties. The same argument applies to Diamond and Gunther's pluralist-nationalistic party and ultranationalist types, as well as to the denominational religious party. As I show later, the concept of ethnicity employed in this study leaves sufficient room to classify all of these parties as ethnic. All of them fall into the category of an "ethnic party."

I also drop the elite-based party types – the local notable and the clientelistic party. At first glance this seems controversial, considering the heavily clientelistic nature of African political life. Diamond and Gunther identified both, the local notable and the clientelistic party, as beset by minimal organizational capacities and as structured around established elites, who provide access to resources. This characterization raises two problems. As the literature on African political structures attests, this elitism is characteristic of all significant African parties. These two types lack discriminative power, as their key characteristic is typical of all African parties.

Two further modifications are necessary. The first concerns Diamond and Gunther's congress party type, which is geared toward a consociationalist type of party: "[...] where the consociational system tries to share power and resources among and assures the mutual security of all groups within a coalitional government formed after the election, a congress party constructs the coalitional guarantees in advance, within the broad tent of its party organization" (Diamond and Gunther 2001: 24). Research on consociational parties in Africa suggests that a congress party type modeled too narrowly on the idea of a consociational party does not appear to be of great analytical use for categorizing African parties (Bogaards 2005, Thiven 2005, Lemarchand 2007). As a result, the congress-type party is broken up here into two types of multiethnic parties, the multiethnic alliance and the multiethnic catch-all party.[3] The two basic differences between them are their

[3] In the following analysis, for reasons of simplicity, these are referred to as (ethnic) alliance parties and (ethnic) catch-all parties.

respective motivations and degrees of internal stability. The alliance type corresponds to the logic of Donald Horowitz's *coalitions of convenience* and *coalitions of commitment*. A *coalition of convenience* is formed with the sole motivation of gaining a parliamentary majority. *Coalitions of commitment* indicate more amicable relations, yet anticipated gains on election day provide the key impetus for communities to unite under the roof of one party. Driven by strategic considerations, the alliance party makes extensive use of "ethnic arithmetic"; it tries to include as many groups as necessary to secure electoral victory. Vote-pooling in the form of shared lists or joint association under a new party is sometimes characteristic of such short-lived coalitions. Internally, the alliance type tends toward instability as it suffers from the same constraints as Horowitz's "multiethnic party":

> The incompatibility of ethnic claims to power; the propensity for demands to be made at the expense of other groups; the taint that is often attached to working in political concert with members of opposing ethnic groups; and the incentives politicians have to organize their clienteles along ethnic lines before someone else does so – these are among the forces that undermine multiethnic parties. (Horowitz 2000: 427)

The ethnic catch-all type's purposes transcend election day. This party type corresponds to Horowitz's logic of *permanent coalitions of ethnic parties*. It aims to form a long-lasting political force in which two conditions are fulfilled: It bridges its country's dominant ethnic cleavages (past or present) by incorporating influential community leaders from both sides of the cleavage into its leadership structure. Furthermore, the ethnic catch-all party is formed long before election day and survives electoral defeats as well as leadership contests without any major changes (splits and mergers) in the groups that make up the party. By staying together as a united political force, it demonstrates that it has overcome the divisive logic of ethnic arithmetic. However, ethnicity does matter inside the party, given its centrality in African social and political life:

> An ethnic/tribal affiliation may be perceived as more protective, more equitable and self-assuring, articulating particular own interests and much more adequately so than the impersonal entity nation-state. In such processes ethnicity is not only conceptualized and instrumentalized as a socially binding force but also as a political idea with an inherent mobilizing dynamism. (Tötemeyer 2004: 1)

Contrary to the ideological tendencies of early modernization theory, this study explicitly refrains from making normative statements about the enduring impact of ethnicity. It does not regard the political manifestation of ethnicity as good or bad; it merely takes notice of its significance.[4] The present study posits that one's affiliation with a particular community can

[4] For a discussion on the positive as well as the negative role ethnicity can play, see Berman et al. 2004.

shape one's actions, as in the way suggested by Tötemeyer. Therefore, even in an ethnic catch-all party, community affiliations can come to the fore when the party approaches key political events such as the election of the party's presidential candidate. However, within the catch-all party, ethnicity no longer leads to exclusion from the leadership or from the party as a whole. The catch-all party is therefore not an "ethnic party" as conventionally understood in the literature. Given the diverse social fabric of African societies, Africa's lack of an industrial revolution, and the continent's limited ability to design social welfare policies, the catch-all party is the closest an African party gets to the model of the catch-all party found in Europe and the United States.

The distinction between two multiethnic types corresponds better to recent empirical findings, which indicate that most African parties are multiethnic in composition. The few individual case studies covering African parties show that most African parties can be assumed to be multiethnic (Erdmann 2007). A multiethnic following can but does not per se constitute a national party. The distinction between the alliance and the catch-all party allows for a distinction between those multiethnic parties, which constitute nationwide political forces and those whose outreach is confined to a number of communities or regions. The following three empirical chapters demonstrate that this distinction is essential for a thorough and systematic analysis of African parties.

The second alteration concerns Diamond and Gunther's own catch-all type and is directly related to the creation of two ethnic party types. According to Diamond and Gunther, the catch-all party's goal is to "maximize electoral support through broad aggregation of interests;" its social base consists of "de facto core social groups supplemented by shifting constituencies" (2001: 11). As in African politics, this type can be assumed to be very similar to the multiethnic catch-all party. Furthermore, both its electoral strategy – "broad and eclectic issue appeals and candidate image" – and its organizational structure – "organization primarily around election campaigns, otherwise weak party organization" (2001: 11) – are characteristics of African parties in general. As a result, my catch-all party is collapsed with Diamond and Gunther's catch-all type.

The necessary conceptual changes leave us with a variety of nonethnic parties, including the ethnic catch-all, the personalistic, the programmatic, the Leninist, the class-mass, and the religious fundamentalist. Ethnic parties include the mono-ethnic and the multiethnic alliance.

THE OPERATIONALIZATION OF THE AMENDED DIAMOND AND GUNTHER TYPOLOGY

My main goal is to provide an analytical framework for African parties while ensuring the comparability of African parties to parties elsewhere.

Accordingly, I choose indicators from the mainstream literature on political parties. In addition, I select indicators in terms of their applicability to the particular context in which African politics unfolds. Descending Sartori's ladder of abstraction from a high to a medium level avoids the pronounced Western European bias in party research (Sartori 1970, Collier and Mahon 1993, Erdmann 2007a). The operationalization is the first attempt at devising a party typology that allows for intra-area and a cross-area comparisons. Future research might add new properties to or eliminate properties according to the particularities of the respective region of interest.

Diamond and Gunther (2001) advanced four criteria – party goals, electoral strategy, organizational structure, and social base – by which their party types could be distinguished. I supplement their criteria with indicators, detailed next.

Party Goals

Motive of party formation. What were the historical conditions causing the party's formation? Knowing the societal characteristics that provided a fertile breeding ground for a party is essential for understanding its goals. If a party forms to represent the interests of specific communities, it is either an ethnic alliance party or a mono-ethnic party. Parties that attempt to foster national unity or those with a neutral or catch-all aim indicate multiethnic catch-all parties. In the African context, neutral/catch-all purposes include promoting democracy, fighting corruption, and vaguely claiming to aspire to create a vibrant economy. Parties founded to keep an individual in power hint at a personalistic party. We can expect this type in regimes that have undergone a transition from military dictatorship to multiparty democracy. If at its founding, a party pays reference to programmatic ideas, this indicates a programmatic party.

Rhetoric. A party's rhetoric reveals a lot about its goals; this is particularly true for election-free periods when strategic constraints on vote- and office-seeking are relaxed. Do parties espouse ethnic claims? Is their rhetoric reduced to hailing a leader, or do they clothe their appeals in programmatic ideas? Although what constitutes programmatic ideas has been well established in the context of Western politics (Lipset and Rokkan 1967, Budge et al. 1994, Klingemann et al. 2006), there is currently no agreement among scholars on what could be seen as a genuine programmatic statement by an African party (Elischer 2008). I apply programmatic statements as understood in a Western context and test their analytical validity in an African context. A party's rhetoric during election-free periods has not been systematically analyzed in the literature, which has favored in-depth analyses of election campaigns and electoral performance. Van Cott's (2005) analysis outlined earlier is the first to consider party rhetoric a possible indicator for party types.

Electoral Strategy

Electoral rhetoric. Rallying support in anticipation of election day is a central activity of parties. During election time, parties' rhetoric might change as all parties seek to maximize their votes. Accordingly, I add an additional indicator for electoral rhetoric. Mono-ethnic and ethnic alliance parties might remain relatively mute during election campaigns because they can rely on their core clientele to turn up in large numbers. However, in cases where several parties claim to represent one or several ethnic groups, ethnic parties may be very visible and identifiable by strong appeals to group interests. Catch-all parties are likely to stress themes of national unity and topics that have a neutral character: the fight against corruption, the importance of economic growth, or improvements of the democratic system. Catch-all issues can also be expected to be part of the electoral rhetoric of ethnic-based parties, yet ethnic appeals will prevail over catch-all issues or catch-all issues will be clothed in ethnic language. The programmatic party will try to put forward its ideas, but at a reticent level to maximize its votes. The personalistic party will focus on its leader and highlight his achievements for the nation at large.

Content of election manifesto. Although in the context of European and American politics, election manifestos are regarded as useful tools for the analysis of parties, they are rarely seen as such in an African context (Elischer 2012). In the rare instances in which political scientists have examined them, this was done in a descriptive manner (Emminghaus 2003, Hunter and Sherbourne 2004). I apply the MRG coding technique, a seminal tool for the study of election manifestos in Europe and beyond (Klingemann et al. 2006, Budge et al. 2001). The MRG coding scheme contains 52 policy categories. Twenty-six are regarded as programmatic: 13 categories count as left-wing and 13 qualify as right-wing categories. Every sentence of a party manifesto is assigned to a category. In case a sentence contains more than one policy statement, each statement in favor of a particular policy is counted. The MRG thus identifies the percentage shares of programmatic sentences in election manifestos. Annex B lists all categories in detail and provides an overview of all manifestos collected and coded.

A high share of programmatic content indicates a programmatic party, whereas a low share can be indicative of any other party type. Whenever I find parties with a high share of programmatic statements, I test whether this is due to an overemphasis on individual policy categories. This situation is given if a party allocates a disproportionately large number of policy statements to one category. If, for example, the programmatic share of the election manifesto of party A is relatively high, this circumstance might not be due to its programmatic inclinations but due to the fact that it stresses one or a smaller number of policy issues the MRG coding scheme regards as programmatic. This test serves as a first precautionary measure against reading too much into the allegedly programmatic aims of a party. A second precautionary measure includes the calculation of the number of "effective" programmatic categories. Here, I use the Laakso and Taagepera (1979) formula for the calculation of the effective number of parties. Where manifestos refer excessively to one or a smaller selection of policy categories, the number of significant programmatic categories should remain at a low level. Annex C provides an overview of all results for this test.

Organizational Structure

Conventional analyses of political parties frequently use changes in membership figures over time as key indicators for the nature of the party (Mair and van Biezen 2001). African parties do not keep sophisticated records of their membership, and if they do, the accuracy of these figures cannot be ascertained. In the absence of reliable membership figures, the organizational structure of parties will have to be measured with a variety of proxies.

Regional and national coverage (RNC). The RNC measures a party's ability to reach out nationally by comparing the number of parliamentary candidates it fields in each region with the number of constituencies in each region. This indicator sheds greater light into the extent to which parties are serious contenders across regions and communities. Programmatic, personalistic, and catch-all parties can score highly on this indicator. The alliance and the mono-ethnic party have medium to low coverage depending on which communities they include. In countries with a Proportional Rrepresentation system based on national lists, this indicator is not applicable. National lists do not tell us about the ability of parties to field candidates in regions or provinces.

Party factions. Internal party factions affect party goals and party behavior. Changes in the nature of party factions have the potential to change the nature of the party (Harmel and Janda 1994, Protsyk and Wilson 2003, Reiter 2004, Sartori 2005b, Köllner et al. 2006, Boucek 2009).

In a mono-ethnic party, factions consist of individuals from one major community. Numerically, small minority groups might also participate in the party, yet they do not play a role in intra-party divisions. The nature of these factions is personal. In an ethnic alliance, factions are modeled around ethnic lines headed by leaders from different communities. They have the potential to tear the party apart, corroborating Horowitz's assumed logic of ethnic politics. Factions might defect, subsequently form new parties, or merge with opposing ones. This danger of defection is particularly poignant if factional leaders represent communities that are located at the opposite end of a dominant ethnic cleavage line. Factions around powerful individuals with a nationwide following indicate ethnic catch-all parties. They share this feature with the mono-ethnic party. In a programmatic party, factions are structured around different conceptions of the party's ideological content.

In a personalistic party, factions are absent because party life is structured around its uncontested leader. Factions do, however, occur once the leader leaves the political scene.

Party apparatus. Which internal groupings dominate the party? The literature on African politics at times tentatively refers to the influence of traditional leaders in political affairs (Kilson 1966). If a party shows preference to the elders of a particular community – or several particular communities – this is indicative of an ethnic or alliance party. Given the low institutionalization of African parties, such groupings as a women's wing or a youth wing can be expected in any kind of party, at least on paper. In nonethnic parties, these groupings will have a prevailing influence. If the party has created an additional wing made up of individuals close to the party leader, this indicates a personalistic party.

Social Base

Leadership composition. Leadership composition refers to the top positions in a political party, including the chairperson, the vice-chairperson (or vice-chairpeople), the secretary-general, and the national treasurer. Van Cott (2005) and Chandra (2004) both use the origins of leaders for their analyses; I follow their lead. When positions are named otherwise, the empirical data are adjusted accordingly. Drawing on Horowitz's distinction between ethnic and nonethnic parties, the leadership of the alliance type fails to incorporate leaders from the opposing sides of an ethnic cleavage lines. The ethnic catch-all party, by contrast, manages to do so. Making a straightforward distinction between alliance and mono-ethnic parties is not easy, as parties whose complete leadership is mono-ethnic are unlikely phenomena. I regard a leadership setup where one large community dominates and all other members are from numerically small communities as mono-ethnic. Leadership setups with more than one major group is visible characterize an ethnic alliance. Leadership setups bridging the dominant ethnic cleavage lines characterize an ethnic catch-all party. To qualify as programmatic or personalistic, the party equally needs to bridge the country's cleavage lines. Both the programmatic and the personalistic types are defined as nonethnic parties.

Cabinet appointments. The heavily neopatrimonial nature of African politics provides a strong political imperative for any group to be included at the major level of governance. Cabinets including all major communities whose numerical strength in the cabinet roughly reflects their numerical strength in society are representative of ethnic catch-all, programmatic, and personalistic parties. Cabinets failing to overcome the country's dominant cleavage lines and cabinets in which one community or several major communities are clearly underrepresented indicate alliance parties. Cabinets including only one major group indicate that a mono-ethnic party is in power. By virtue of its definition, this indicator can only be applied to governing parties.

The interpretation of data also requires some flexibility, as even the most integrative (i.e., nonethnic) party might find it difficult to find a proportionate share of cabinet members from each community.

Party nationalization score (PNS) and party divergence score (PDS). Election results are often used as a major analytical yardstick for the classification of African parties. I use two aggregate measurements to identify the spread of a party's electoral support.

The PNS provides a useful means of comparing different parties' electoral support nationwide both within and across countries (Jones and Mainwaring 2008). Thus far, they have not been used in the context of African politics. The PNS is measured by calculating the Gini coefficient of a party's electoral support and subtracting the coefficient from 1. The closer the PNS is to 1, the more the party's support can be seen as national. The closer it is to 0, the less its support is nationwide. Skeptical voices will counter that the unit of analysis for calculating the PNS is a country's region and that, therefore, results are contingent on the spread of communities across regions. To mitigate this problem, the calculation of PNS is supplemented by a descriptive analysis of voting behavior that takes the ethnic make-up of countries and their regions into consideration. In addition, and where data were available, the PNS is calculated with the help of Afrobarometer data. Annex F contains all results for this indicator.

The PDS calculates the percentage share of votes that a region or province contributes to the overall share of a party's performance. This figure is subsequently compared with the percentage share of the region's population in terms of the total population.[5] The following example illustrates how the indicator works in practice: party A received 55 percent of its overall vote share from Region Z. However, only 20 percent of the population lives in Region Z. Accordingly, there is a high discrepancy between these two figures: the electoral contribution of Region Z to party A is 35 percent higher than it would be if the vote spread corresponded to the population spread. The PDS is calculated by adding up the discrepancies for each region. Compared with the PNS, the PDS outlines the performance of parties across regions, which allows us to identify respective strongholds.

Very high, high, and medium PNSs indicate programmatic, personalistic, and ethnic catch-all parties. Medium and low scores indicate ethnic alliances. As the calculation of the PNS uses regional units as its base, PNSs are heavily influenced by the spread of population groups at the subnational level (i.e., the numerical spread of communities across regions or provinces). Therefore, an alliance party might display a medium or high score. PNSs exhibiting low to very low values designate mono-ethnic parties. However, if the mono-ethnic party comprises a numerically large group settling in several regions, the PNS might fall into the medium to low category. PNSs,

[5] The PDS is based on Rose and Urwin's (1974) index of cumulative regional inequality.

TABLE 2.10. *Overview of Key Characteristics and Indicators*

Goals	Electoral Strategy	Organizational Structure	Social Base
motive of formation/party history	electoral rhetoric	national coverage	leadership composition
rhetoric (between elections)	content of election manifesto	party factions	cabinet appointments
		party apparatus	PNS and PDS supplemented by Afrobarometer data

Source: Author's compilation.

therefore, need to be interpreted vis-à-vis a detailed analysis of the ethnic composition of each country.

The PDS classifies parties as follows: (very) low to medium values signal programmatic, personalistic, and catch-all parties. Medium to high values suggest alliance parties. Those falling into the low to very low category indicate mono-ethnic parties. Again, any analysis ought to take the size and the spread of communities into consideration. Annex D summarizes all results for this indicator.

Table 2.10 summarizes the operationalization of the amended Diamond and Gunther (2001) typology.

The major difference between the mono- and the multiethnic alliance party is their composition: the alliance party includes several numerically strong groups, whereas the mono-ethnic party includes one major group and potentially several smaller groups. Both are driven by the same goal: namely, to garner as many votes as possible from the specific group or groups whose interests the party wishes to represent. The differences between the alliance and the ethnic catch-all party have already been elaborated. This leaves only the programmatic party and the personalistic party. The framework employed assumes both the programmatic party and the personalistic party to be nonethnic, an assumption implicit in the outline of the various indicators, yet one that has not been explained further.[6] With regard to the programmatic party, one should note that its only difference from the catch-all party is its programmatic content. This does not exclude the possibility that a mono-ethnic party or an ethnic alliance party is grounded in programmatic ideas.[7] However, the present framework is based on the assumption

[6] For the most obvious example, see *party leadership composition*.

[7] An example would be the Kenyan KPU in the 1960s (Geertzel 1970).

that the programmatic orientation of such a party is derived from its ethnic base. In other words, it supports programmatic ideas because they are conducive to the well-being of its comparatively narrow membership. Thus mono-ethnic and multiethnic alliance parties with programmatic content are regarded as ethnic. To be classified as programmatic, a party is required to have a nationwide following. The same is true of the personalistic party. Personalism is a ubiquitous factor in African politics. A party structured around a strong leader and reduced to particular groups would be the covert version of an ethnic party, as personalism can be expected to feature highly in both mono-ethnic and ethnic alliances. Although the difference between the programmatic party and the catch-all party hinges on the presence of programmatic ideas on a measurable scale, the difference between the catch-all party and the personalistic party is that the latter derives its purpose from its leader in charge, whereas the former provides a national platform for ideas devoid of programmatic ideas.

AGGREGATION

The party types are ideal types in the Weberian sense (Weber 1978). The empirical part will display a variety of parties exhibiting characteristics of more than one party type. This point raises the problem of aggregating the results for individual indicators. One solution could be weighting, that is, giving some indicators a higher status than others. In the absence of previous systematic comparisons of African parties, any such decision would be difficult to justify. The lack of conceptual work on African party types and the lack of global comparisons calls for a framework that is as broad as possible. Favoring one or several indicators over others inevitably would lead to conceptual reductionism.

Therefore, I examine disaggregated results and discuss whether the outcome for individual indicators point to any ideal type. This acknowledges the complexities of social organizations. A comparative small-N research design allows for an in-depth understanding of the cases under scrutiny and enables an accurate classification. The classification is thus framed within a historically informed examination. I chose two different observation periods. The first covers individual parliamentary cycles, each starting with the campaign period for the parliamentary elections and finishing when the campaign period for the next elections begins. In African countries where democratization occurred in the early 1990s, this generally provides three to four observation periods per party. The second observation period covers the whole period under scrutiny starting with the permission of multiparty competition and ending with the present day situation. The second timeline reveals trends that have occurred over a longer period of time. A party might follow the behavioral pattern of a (non)ethnic party over the course of various short observation periods. At a particular moment the party might change strategy; however, such a development only becomes visible incrementally and might initially be displayed in only a small number of indicators. Assessing the same party over a longer period will make long-term trends visible and indicate future tendencies in a more convincing manner.

Table 2.11 outlines the ideal types. At times, indicators contain various criteria: the electoral rhetoric of an alliance party, for example, is characterized by catch-all as well as by ethnic rhetoric. Mentioning catch-all as the first characteristic is indicative both of the higher frequency of catch-all slogans than ethnic rhetoric. The table omits the class-mass, the Leninist, or the religious fundamentalist parties. These party types do not feature in the empirical part of this study. An overview over their operationalization is provided in Annex A.

TOWARD EMPIRICAL RESEARCH

The application of the typology requires a definition of ethnicity. There is no shortage in the political science literature on different conceptions of the term. In the area of African politics, authors have long been divided into those who favor a primordial view of ethnicity (Lemarchand 1972) and those who perceive ethnicity as fluid and interchangeable (Berman et al. 2004, Chandra 2005, 2006). This book applies the latter and uses a constructivist notion of the ethnicity, as previously employed by Kasfir (1976):

> [E]thnicity contains objective characteristics associated with common ancestry, such as language, territory, cultural practices and the like. These are perceived by both insiders and outsiders as important indicators of identity, so that they can become the bases for mobilizing social solidarity and which in certain situations result in political activity. (Kasfir 1976: 77)

Kasfir's concept of ethnicity applies to different political scenarios: ethnic identities may play a significant role – for example, during an election campaign – but they also may cease to matter at all. Recent quantitative studies undertaken by Afrobarometer also encourage a situational approach toward ethnicity (Bannon et al. 2004, Cheeseman and Ford 2007). A constructivist notion of the term is also necessary for practical reasons: without the possibility of a change in the degree to which ethnicity impacts party politics, one is unable to anticipate the possibility of finding nonethnic party types.

Of equal importance is the definition of what constitutes a political party. The most widely used concept is Sartori's definition of a party as "any political group identified by an official label that presents at elections and is capable of placing through elections candidates for public office" (Sartori 2005a: 56). African parties are weakly institutionalized. The weak degree

TABLE 2.11. *Operationalization of the Amended Diamond and Gunther Party Typology*

	Party Indicator and Characteristics									
	Party Goals		Electoral Strategy		Organizational Structure			Social Base		
Party Type	Motive of Formation	Rhetoric	Electoral Rhetoric	Content of Election Manifesto	National Coverage	Party Factions	Party Apparatus	Leadership Composition	Cabinet Composition	PNS, PDS
mono-ethnic	promotion of group interest	geared toward group interest	ethnic; catch-all	low	low	structured around individuals	important role of traditional leaders of a specific group	drawn from one major ethnic group	drawn from one major ethnic group	low/very low PNS high/very high PDS
ethnic alliance	promotion of diverse group interests	hostile toward groups outside the alliance	catch-all; ethnic	low	low to medium or medium to high	structured around ethnic groups	important role of traditional leaders of specific groups	failing to bridge country's dominant cleavage lines	failing to bridge country's dominant cleavage lines	low to medium/high PNS medium to high/ low PDS
ethnic catch-all	catch-all; promotion of national unity	catch-all and promoting national unity	catch-all	low	high	structured around individuals	important role of youth or women's wing or any wing that does not correspond to ethnic groups	bridging country's dominant cleavage lines	bridging country's dominant cleavage lines	medium to high/very high PNS medium to low or very low PDS
programmatic	promotion of ideas	motivated by ideas	moderate promotion of ideas coupled with catch-all phrases	high	high	structured around individuals	existence of programmatic wings	bridging country's dominant cleavage lines	bridging country's dominant cleavage lines	medium to high/very high PNS medium to low/very low PDS
personalistic	promotion of leader	drawing on leader's achievement	drawing extensively on leader's achievements	low	high	none	wings structured around support of leader	bridging country's dominant cleavage lines	bridging country dominant cleavage lines	

PDS, party divergence score; PNS, party nationalization score.

of institutional cohesion among African parties (Salih 2003, Basedau and Stroh 2008) calls for a minimal definition of what a party is.

African parties have dramatically proliferated during the third wave of democratization. Most of these parties hardly stand a chance of sending their candidates to parliament or have a realistic prospect of meaningfully influencing politics. Creating criteria is therefore necessary to enable us to limit our analysis to what can be termed "relevant" parties. This study uses the relevance criteria outlined by Sartori (2005a). Only parties that have blackmail or coalition potential will be considered. Sartori's criteria have been proven to be of great analytical value for the study of African parties (Bogaards 2004). These criteria will be supplemented by Laakso and Taagepera's (1979) index on effective number of parties.

In the subsequent chapters, I apply the Diamond and Gunther (2001) typology to parties in three African countries: Kenya, Namibia, and Ghana. Each country represents a different political dynamic. Frequently used criteria of case selection – the most different and the most similar research design – require in-depth knowledge about the values on the dependent and the independent variable. Little to nothing is known about African party types, and even less work has been done on the factors that might lead to the formation of a particular party type. The lack of data on both dependent and independent variable frequently characterizes research on non-Western societies but is rarely expounded openly as a research problem in itself (Bennett and Elman 2006, Simons and Zanker 2012). Recent works on case selection offer alternative selection criteria. The strategy chosen here approximates the diverse case method to illustrate the diversity of African party politics (Gerring 2004, Gerring 2007, Seawright and Gerring 2008). I use cases in which ethnicity can be expected to yield significant influence on parties and cases in which ethnicity can be expected to have little to none. As my investigation is first and foremost exploratory, I do not claim that my small sample is representative of parties in Sub-Saharan Africa, let alone representative of parties in nonindustrialized societies.

In Kenya, ethnicity is known to exercise particularly high salience (Widner 1994, Throup and Hornsby 1998, Horowitz 2000, Anderson 2005, Banch et al. 2010). Since the return of multiparty democracy, a high number of effective and relevant parties have formed. As the following chapter demonstrates, throughout the last two decades, ethnic parties (mono-ethnic parties and multiethnic alliances) have remained ubiquitous. Every attempt to form nonethnic parties has failed. Kenya thus corresponds to the conventional view of African party politics.

The political dynamics in Namibia challenge much of what has been written about party competition in ethnically diverse societies. Namibia is a mixed-party system. The governing South West African People's Organization (SWAPO) is a catch-all party. It enjoys support from all major communities. The long-term official opposition, the Democratic Turnhalle

Alliance (the DTA), is a multiethnic alliance. After several electoral cycles, the role of the main opposition was taken over by the Congress of Democrats (CoD), a catch-all party. Namibia thus demonstrates that in Africa, nonethnic parties exist and endure. The presence of an ethnic opposition party does not lead to the "bankruptcy of moderation" (Reilly 2001: 3). Instead, regular multiparty competition leads to the decline of the salience of ethnic divisions.

The classification of the Ghanaian National Patriotic Front (NPP), and the National Democratic Congress (NDC), illustrates the diverse nature of African parties even more vividly. The NPP started out as a multi-ethnic alliance, which transformed into, first, a programmatic party and later a catch-all party. As in Namibia, the salience of ethnicity has decreased over time. The NDC started out as a personalistic party and has transformed into a catch-all party. Although the NPP has clearly visible pro-market ideological sympathies, the NDC over time has built up a social democratic profile.

In addition to the 10 indicators of the party typology, the next three chapters outline which policies incumbent parties have passed. This fulfills two purposes. First, it shows whether incumbent parties initiated bills affecting inter-ethnic relations. Second, it illustrates the relationship between particular party types and public policies put in place. Due to reason of space, the analysis focuses on those bills, which received most attention by the media and/or the opposition.

COMPARATIVE POLITICS AND THE DIAMOND AND GUNTHER TYPOLOGY

This chapter provided a concise overview of the conventional party models, which scholars designed to analyze the political parties in their regions of interest. The prevailing models are deeply embedded in the social and political history of Western Europe. The most commonly known party types such as the mass party, the catch-all party, and the cartel-party are explicitly linked to social and economic developments that unfolded between the mid and the late twentieth century. The embeddedness of these types into the historical evolution of Western European society makes them ill-fitted for an application in nonindustrial societies.

Scholars working on parties outside Europe failed to arrive at alternative typologies that made any lasting impact on the literature. Although the clientelistic and ethnic party types have become popular analytical tools, both types have never been operationalized thoroughly, let alone undergone empirical testing. Typologically driven works in areas outside Europe either applied to ill-suited Western concepts or used area-specific frameworks. These frameworks lacked clearly defined indicators and as such remained vague and underspecified. The literature on African parties reveals a particularly bleak picture. No systematic research on parties has taken place since the return of multiparty democracy in the early 1990s. If African parties are analyzed, it occurs exclusively within the context of individual case studies and with the help of election results. In case voting occurs along ethnic lines – which appears to no longer hold in numerous cases – scholars label parties as ethnic. No alternative party types have been developed for Africa. Contemporary research on Africa has yet to conceptualize political parties.

The third wave of democratization and the proliferation of parties in regions where previously democratic contests had never taken place over longer periods exacerbated the perception that the conventional frameworks are ill-equipped to capture the political diversity of our time. Two scholars, Larry Diamond and Richard Gunther (2001, 2003), improved the dire state of research on non-Western parties. Diamond and Gunther put forward 15 party types, yet did not provide a set of indicators by which their typology can be applied.

The operationalization of the amended Diamond and Gunther typology has been at the heart of this chapter. Drawing on the extensive literature on parties worldwide, the chapter put forward 10 indicators by which the individual party types can be distinguished. All of the party types constitute ideal types. Five party types are at the heart of this study – the mono-ethnic party, the multiethnic alliance, the multiethnic catch-all party, the programmatic party, and the personalistic party. The next three chapters apply the typology to three African countries. Kenya, Namibia, and Ghana has been chosen because the political dynamics in all three countries differ. In Kenya ethnic parties prevail, in Namibia ethnic and nonethnic parties co-exist, and in Ghana nonethnic parties are ubiquitous. These three countries, therefore, illustrate the political diversity of the African continent.

3

Kenya

The Ubiquity of Ethnic Parties

Kenya is as the first country to which the amended Diamond and Gunther (2001 and 2003) party typology is applied. Kenyan parties are representative of the typology's ethnic party types. All parties under scrutiny are classified as mono-ethnic or multiethnic alliances. The dynamics of political party competition in Kenya are thus in line with the assumption that multiparty competition in new democracies leads to ethnic conflict and violence. Those who have a pessimistic outlook on the chances of democratic transitions in Africa frequently refer to the political dynamics of Kenyan party politics.[1] However, over time, Kenyan parties try to become nonethnic parties. Although they fail to become national parties, they are undergoing a transformation from mono-ethnic parties to multiethnic alliances.

This chapter starts by setting the historical background against which multiparty politics manifested itself from the early 1990s onward. Particular emphasis is given to the identification of dominant ethnic cleavage lines, as they are important points of reference for my distinction between ethnic and nonethnic parties. Subsequently, this chapter applies the new party typology to three observation periods, each covering one parliamentary cycle. The first observation period covers a slightly longer period starting with the formation of various opposition parties in late 1991. This is necessary to include the circumstances surrounding the processes of party formation. The observation period finishes once campaigning of parties for the 1997 elections starts in earnest. At this point, the second observation period commences, covering the period between November 1997 and November 2002, when the third and final observation begins. Data following the onset of the fourth observation are discussed tentatively to determine whether previous political trends can be expected to match future ones. Tables 3.1 and 3.2 outline the ethnic composition of Kenya nationwide and across regions.

[1] Horowitz (2000) dedicated substantial efforts in outlining the political situation in Kenya. Much of his theory on group conflict in Africa and beyond focuses on Kenya.

TABLE 3.1. *Ethnic Composition of Kenya Nationwide*

Ethnic Community	Percentage of Population
Kikuyu	20.8%
Luhya	14.4%
Luo	12.4%
Kalenjin	11.5%
Kisii	6.2%
Meru	5.1%
Mijikenda	4.7%
Maasai	1.8%

Source: Kenya Population Census 1989, Volume I. Communities that account for less than 1 percent are not listed.

TABLE 3.2. *Ethnic Composition of Kenya's Provinces*

Province	Ethnic Composition
Nairobi	Kikuyu: 32.4%
	Luo: 18.5%
	Luhya; 16.5%
	Kamba: 13.5%
Coast	Mijikenda: 54.4%
	Taita: 10.2%
	Kamba: 6.9%
	Luo: 4.5%
North Eastern	Ogaden: 36%
	Degodia: 25.2%
	Gurreh: 18.5%
	Hawiyah: 6.7%
Eastern	Kamba: 53.9%
	Meru: 27.4%
	Embu: 6.1%
Central	Kikuyu: 93.8%
Rift Valley	Kalenjin: 46.4%
	Kikuyu: 19.3%
	Luhya: 9%
	Turkana: 5.2%
Western	Luhya: 86.2%
	Teso: 5.7%
	Luo: 2.6%
Nyanza	Luo: 57.9%
	Kisii: 32.4%

Source: Kenya Population Census 1989, Volume I. Communities that account for less than 1 percent are not listed.

TABLE 3.3. *Overview of Kenyan Cases and Observations*

Observation Period	Significant and Effective Party
Period 1 (1991–1997)	KANU
	FORD-A
	FORD-K
	DP
Period 2 (1997–2002)	KANU
	FORD-K
	DP
	NDP
	SDP
Period 3 (2002–2007)	NARC
	KANU
Period 4 (2007–2012)	ODM
	PNU[2]

Source: Author's compilation.

Throughout the three observation periods, Kenya's party system has produced a comparatively large number of politically effective (Laakso and Taagepera 1979) and relevant (Sartori 2005a) parties. In the first observation period, the Kenyan African National Union (KANU), the Forum for the Restoration of Democracy–Kenya (FORD-K), the Forum for the Restoration of Democracy–Asili (FORD-A), and the Democratic Party (DP) fulfill both criteria. In the second observation period, five parties are both significant and effective: KANU, the DP, FORD-K, the National Democratic Party (NDP), and the Social Democratic Party (SDP). The merger of the opposition in anticipation of the 2002 elections means that only two parties are the foci of my analysis in the third observation period, the National Alliance Rainbow Coalition (NARC) and KANU. With the exception of KANU, no party managed to remain effective and significant (Laakso and Taagepera 1979, Sartori 2005a) throughout all observation periods. Consequently, the analysis of Kenyan parties is reduced to 11 observations for 7 parties: 3 observations for KANU, 2 for FORD-K, 2 for DP, and 1 each for FORD-A, NDP, SDP, and NARC. Table 3.3 outlines all cases and observations in detail.

[2] The PNU and ODM are not included in my overall results as the fourth observation period has not yet come to an end. However, both are analyzed and classified with the help of the data available at the time of writing.

ONE-PARTY RULE AND THE RISE OF ETHNIC CLEAVAGE LINES

For most of the time between its independence in 1963 and the return to multiparty democracy in 1991, Kenya was a one-party state. Multiparty elections occurred only in the run-up to independence after the defeat of the Mau-Mau uprising and the subsequent legalization of African political activity. Two political parties emerged: The KANU and the Kenyan African Democratic Union (KADU).

KANU was largely a revival of the Kenyan African Union (KAU) of the immediate post–World War II era. Before the Declaration of the Emergency in 1952, KAU had been dominated by the Kikuyu Central Association. Consequently, KANU was heavily influenced by a numerically strong Kikuyu wing led by Jomo Kenyatta, the former President of KAU who was detained by the British administration between 1952 and 1961.[3] During Kenyatta's detention, KANU was led by two Luo – Oginga Odinga, who largely derived his support from the Luo Heartland, Central Nyanza in Nyanza Province, and Tom Mboya, who derived his support from the Trade Unions and the Luo Diaspora in Nairobi. Many saw in KANU the urban side of Kenyan nationalism, whereas its opposition, KADU, represented its rural counterpart. Led by Ronald Ngala (Coastal), Masinde Muliro (Luhya), and Daniel arap Moi (Kalenjin), KADU was largely driven by Kenya's smaller communities. The populations of KADU's core groups had been less penetrated by European colonialism and were less politicized than the Kikuyu, who undoubtedly suffered the most from land alienation and forced labor on European farms (Throup 1987, Wandiba 1996, Ajulu 2002).

Although both parties postulated the immediate release of Jomo Kenyatta, KANU and KADU differed significantly over Kenya's post-independence constitutional order. KADU was advocating a robust federal set-up – "majimboism" – as it feared political domination by the numerically strong Luo and Kikuyu groups. Accordingly, the parties' different stances on majimboism were not based on ideological convictions but on their ethnic compositions. It equally reflected the different socioeconomic positions these groups were assigned to (Geertzel 1970, Anderson 2005). The fact that both parties failed to field candidates in the strongholds of their respective opponent in the pre-independence election of 1960 underlines the ethnic nature of early Kenyan party competition (Bennett and Rosberg 1961). After KADU lost the elections, KANU cajoled KADU leaders into disbanding the party and joining the government. This heralded the beginning of the de facto one-party state under the presidency of Jomo Kenyatta.

Historians and political scientists have dedicated significant efforts in examining KANU in various ways since its formation in March 1961.

[3] A more in-depth analysis of immediate pre- and post-independence Kenyan politics is provided in Chapter Seven.

A reoccurring theme in the literature is the extent to which the Kenyan one-party state was (un)able to integrate the country's ethnic communities. Constitutionally proscribed one-party rule derived its intellectual legitimacy from the notion that political competition in ethnically diverse and nonindustrialized nations would foster ethnic fragmentation; in contrast, reducing political activity to one political entity was seen as conducive to national integration and development (Geertzel 1970, Berg-Schlosser 1984, Schatzberg 1987, Widner 1992, Throup and Hornsby 1998, Omolo 2002). Looking at the party leadership composition of KANU and at cabinet appointments throughout the decades (Ahluwalia 1996), the Kenyan one-party state was inclusive of all communities in the limited sense that it permitted all major communities access to state resources. Cabinet appointments, of course, are of limited explanatory power if taken on their own. As the subsequent section shows, cabinet inclusion notwithstanding, Kenya became haunted by deep ethnic divisions.

An initial dominant ethnic cleavage line developed during Kenyatta's reign between the Kikuyu and the Luo. Their joint formation of KANU was less due to common rather than a lack of opposing interests. Inside the party, Mboya was regarded as the political heir of Kenyatta, a vision that never materialized because the former fell victim to a politically motivated assassination in July 1969. Although the real motives behind the murder have never been established, it was largely perceived to be driven by Kenyatta himself to avoid a political confrontation between his Kikuyu elite and the national populist Luo politician Mboya (Goldsworthy 1982). At the point of Mboya's assassination, Oginga Odinga – the other great Luo personality inside KANU – had attracted the wrath of the whole KANU establishment when he and a sizeable group of 33 members of parliament (MPs) broke away from the government benches on personal as well as ideological grounds and formed the Kenya People's Union (KPU) in 1966. This was a radical and dangerous move against Kenyatta's inner circle given Odinga's status as Kenya's vice-president at the time. Although it would be wrong to consider the KPU a mere expression of Luo protest – Odinga's deputy Kagga was a Kikuyu, and only 10 of the 33 parliamentary defectors were Luo – the results of the so-called 1966 "little general election" left the KPU with mere Luo support. Following unrest surrounding Kenyatta's visit to Nyanza Province in 1969 – after the killing of Mboya – most KPU leaders were detained and their party banned indefinitely (Geertzel 1970).

Odinga's detention and Mboya's assassination caused a sense of betrayal among the Luo. In the run-up to independence, KANU's Luo wing had boycotted the first African-led government until Kenyatta and his Kikuyu entourage were released from prison. They had withheld their own political aspirations and thus facilitated Kenyatta's ascendancy to power. Merely six years after independence, their leaders were either imprisoned or had fallen victim to what appeared to be politically motivated murder (Throup and

Hornsby 1998, Ajulu 2002). The feeling of political marginalization was intensified by the murder of former Foreign Minister Robert Ouko (Luo), one of the most influential and last remaining national Luo politician in early 1990. The murder aroused suspicion that the Moi government had been involved in it, a claim that has never been verified (Kanyinga 2003, Morrison 2007). For many Luo, the Ouko murder was the ultimate proof that the Luo could not trust their fellow Kenyan communities.[4]

A second ethnic rift developed between the Kikuyu and the Kalenjin community over the issue of presidential succession in the late 1970s. The conflict over access to the State House was embedded in the traditional conflict between Kikuyu and Kalenjin over the distribution of land that had shaped pre-independence politics. With Kenyatta's health deteriorating, parliamentarians from the Kikuyu, Embu, and Meru communities assembled under the roof of the Gikuyu, Embua, and Meru (GEMA) welfare association with the aim of changing the Kenyan constitution, which foresaw the vice-president to succeed the president in case of the latter's death. The campaign was targeted at the sitting vice-president, Daniel arap Moi, and mainly aimed to avoid a future Kalenjin presidency. Eventually, Moi successfully fought off GEMA's onslaught and managed to succeed Kenyatta. As in the case of the KPU, it would be too simplistic to regard Moi's fight for the presidency through the lenses of Kikuyu-Kalenjin antagonism only. At the individual level, Moi could rely on the collaboration of Kikuyu politicians. In particular, Charles Njongo's (Kenya's Attorney General) and Mwai Kibaki's (one of Kenyatta's aspiring cabinet ministers) political support proved seminal in securing Moi the Kenyan Presidency (Good 1968, Tamarkin 1979). However, the formation of GEMA and Moi's victory greatly fostered mutual suspicion between the Kalenjin and the Kikuyu, as well as between the Kikuyu and the rest of the nation.[5] Following a failed coup d'état against his government in the early 1980s, Moi radically altered the composition of key cabinet and civil service positions and replaced incumbents with a disproportionate share of Kalenjin. The country further witnessed a shift in resource allocation to those communities, which had initially made up the precolonial KADU alliance. In addition, Moi proved skillful in dividing the Kikuyu by successfully playing leading figures of the community against each other (Ajulu 2002, Widner 1992). At the constitutional level, Kenya was transformed to a de jure one-party state. Table 3.4 summarizes the main cleavage lines in Kenyan politics.

In the months following the legalization of party competition in December 1991, these divisions became the main stepping stones of the newly

[4] Interview with Ralph Michael Peters, political expert of the EU Election Observation Mission to the Republic of Kenya 2007, January 10, 2008, Nairobi.

[5] It deserves notice that GEMA members had to swear an oath promising to never accept a non-Kikuyu president.

TABLE 3.4. *Summary of Historical Cleavage Lines in Kenyan Politics*

Cleavage	Issue	Political Manifestation	Leading Figures
small communities versus large communities: Kalenjin, Masai, Turkana, Samburu versus Luo, Kikuyu	fear of domination by larger communities Federalism/ Majimboism	KADU versus KANU	KADU: Daniel Arap Moi (Kalenjin) Martin Shikuku (Luhya) Robert Ngala (Coastal Communities) Masinde Muliro (Luhya) KANU: Jomo Kenyatta (Kikuyu) Oginga Odinga (Luo) Tom Mboya (Luo)
Luo versus Kikuyu	presidency and political power	Mboya versus Kenyatta KPU versus KANU	Mboya versus Kikuyu elite Odinga and Kenyatta
Kikuyu versus Kalenjin	succession of Kenyatta	Moi wing of KANU versus GEMA	Moi/Kibaki versus GEMA leaders

Source: Author's compilation.

formed democratic opposition that came together under the roof of the FORD. Led by veteran politician Oginga Odinga (Luo), its leadership was able to assemble personalities from all of Kenya's main groups and thus initially represented a formidable challenge to KANU.[6] Most of its leading personalities had been at the forefront of the struggle for independence, and many had been high-ranking KANU figures. Yet its national composition in conjunction with its high density of strong-willed politicians soon became its greatest burden. Less than four weeks after its formation, factions formed around Odinga Oginga (Luo) and Kenneth Matiba (Kikuyu), who both simultaneously announced their intention of becoming Kenya's next president on the FORD ticket. In the following months, both camps could not (and probably did not want to) agree on a procedure for selecting the party's presidential candidate, which ultimately led to the split into FORD-Kenya (FORD-K) headed by Odinga and FORD-Asili (FORD-A) headed by Matiba (Throup and Hornsby 1998). The initial FORD-K leadership

[6] *Daily Nation*, December 12, 1991.

formed in May 1992 and was largely driven by Luhya and Luo politicians, yet also included Paul Muite, an aspiring and popular Kikuyu politician.[7] Right from its inception, FORD-A was overshadowed by the mighty presence of its chairman and presidential candidate Kenneth Matiba, one of the icons of Kenya's democratization movement. Its leadership further included Martin Shikuku, a well-established Luhya politician, and George Nthenge from the Kamba community (Throup and Hornsby 1998). Although the split into FORD-K and FORD-A represented the Kikuyu-Luo ethnic divide in terms of their respective presidential candidates, the impact of ethnicity on both parties was less poignant than at later stages. At rallies, both called for an end of KANU rule and an end to human rights abuses committed by the Moi regime. Their respective constitutions considered the restoration of human rights and civil rights of paramount importance.[8]

In January 1992, the DP formed alongside FORD-A and FORD-K. It was launched by a variety of KANU politicians, including Mwai Kibaki (Kikuyu), John Keen (Masai), and Eliud Mwamunga (Somali).[9] Its goals were congruent to the ones of the FORD parties; however, the DP's constitution emphasized the need for a free market economy to a greater extent.[10] Its more explicit pro–free market stance did not go unnoticed by the Kenyan media, which regarded the DP as KANU reformers whose efforts to democratize KANU from within had failed.[11] Right from its inception, the party was heavily dependent on and structured around its chairman Kibaki and his wealthy Kikuyu entourage, many of whom had been leading members of the GEMA welfare association in the 1970s. Overall, no opposition party managed to bridge the dominant cleavage lines between the Luo and the Kikuyu and the Kikuyu and the Kalenjin in the run-up to the founding election. On the governing benches, KANU managed to do so in terms of its leadership structure,[12] although its cabinets displayed a disproportionately large share of ministers from the Kalenjin and other communities.

Kenya entered the 1992 election campaign with parties whose relationship with ethnicity was ambivalent. On the one hand, the communities that had been marginalized by Moi's economic policies and his cabinet appointments left KANU in large numbers and did so under the leadership of the most prominent politicians these communities had produced. The disintegration of the original FORD and the personal proximity of GEMA to the

[7] *Daily Nation*, May 22, 1992.

[8] For Ford-K, see Constitution of the Forum for the Restoration of Democracy-Kenya. For FORD-A, see *Daily Nation*, December 15 and 16, 1992.

[9] *Daily Nation*, January 8, 1992.

[10] *Daily Nation*, January 8, 1992.

[11] *Daily Nation*, January 13, 1992.

[12] KANU's chairman was Ndolo Ayah (Luo), its vice-chairman was Njoroge Mungai (Kikuyu), and its secretary general was Joseph Kamotho (Kikuyu). Its president was Daniel arap Moi (Kalenjin).

DP displayed the traditional ethnic undercurrents of Kenyan party politics. On the other hand, the opposition was united in their call for democratic change. KANU still presided over a nationwide following in terms of its infrastructure and its leadership composition. Although the Kenyan media speculated about how individual parties would feature in specific regions, the effect of ethnicity was furtive rather than overt.

OBSERVATION PERIOD 1

Between 1992 and 1997, the KANU government introduced, debated, and passed a number of bills. Table 3.5 contains a selection of those bills that received greater attention in public.[13] The 1991 Parliamentary Constituencies Review Bill worsened relations between those communities organized in KANU and those organized in other parties, as the bill created more constituencies in districts with communities organized inside KANU (Peters 1998). Other bills had no effect on ethnic relations. None of the bills passed into law displayed programmatic orientations.

FORD-Kenya: The Enduring Logic of Ethnic Politics

As outlined previously, FORD-K's initial purpose and major goal at the time was the restoration of democracy. Its election campaign resembled an anti-KANU campaign in general and anti-Moi campaign in particular.[14] Table 3.6 displays the percentage shares of programmatic sentences of all Kenyan parties across all four observation periods. Calculating the average percentage share of programmatic content across countries and time, I arrive at an average value of 40 percent, which serves as my benchmark figure to distinguish between programmatic and nonprogrammatic manifestos. A summary of all coding categories is provided in Annex B. A summary of all results is provided in Annex E and in Chapter Six.

For current purposes, I focus only on FORD-K. FORD-K's share of 40 percent matches the cut-off point between those manifestos regarded as nonprogrammatic and those classified as programmatic. Its programmatic content is not due to an overemphasis on one particular policy category, as its amount of effective number of programmatic shares (8.6) corresponds to the total average across time and space (8.7). Therefore, the FORD-K manifesto is a borderline case, which cannot be classified easily. The Manifesto Research Group (MRG) coding scheme reveals which policy issues FORD-K stressed most. In terms of programmatic content, it emphasized category 506 (Education Expansion: positive, 7.2 percentage points of the overall

[13] A full list of all bills passed by the National Assembly is with the author.

[14] *Daily Nation*, November 28, 1992.

TABLE 3.5. *Selection of Bills Passed by the National Assembly Between 1991 and 1997*

Name of Bill	Comment	Impact on Ethnic Relations
1991 Finance Bill	led to changes on import and industry duties	no
1991 Income Tax Bill	removed discrepancies between married and single women	no
1991 Preferential Trade Area Bill		No
1991 Parliamentary Constituencies Review Bill	increased the number of parliamentarians from 188 to 210	yes. The new boundaries benefited the Kalenjin and other groups organized inside KANU.
1992 District and Provinces Act	divided the country into 46 districts	no
1992 Prevention of Corruption Bill	allowed the state to repossess goods or land that had been in the illegitimate possession of a politician found to be corrupt. The bill was delayed considerably.	no
1994 National Assembly Remuneration Bill	foresaw increases for National Assembly members	no
1995 Arbitration Bill	established alternative methods for solving disputes by which people knowledgeable in the matter at hand sit and resolve the issue without going to court	no
1995 Central Bank of Kenya	bestowed on the Central Bank of Kenya the power to issue and revoke licenses	no

Source: Compiled by the author with the help of the Kenyan Hansard.

programmatic content) and category 505 (Welfare State Expansion: positive, 6 percentage points). The party further stressed category 202 (Democracy: positive, 4.8 percentage points), which is in line with its original cause of formation. The subsequent observation periods show that its support for democratic procedures – which the MRG coding scheme regards as

TABLE 3.6. *Percentage Shares of Programmatic Content of Kenyan Party Manifestos*

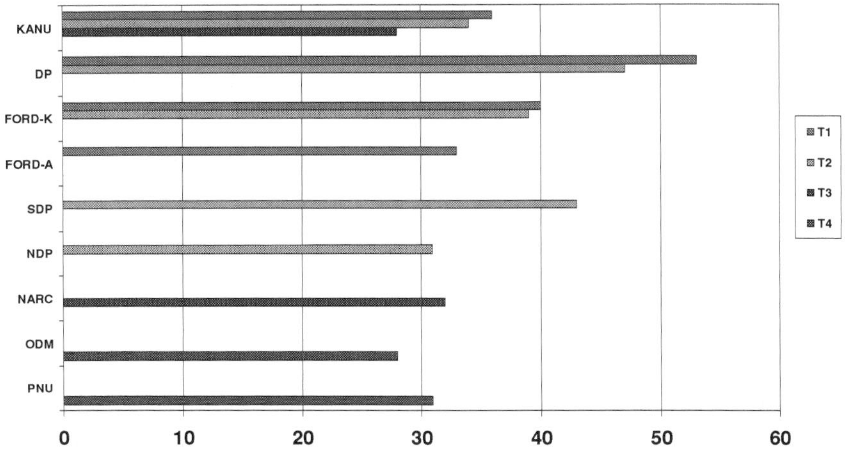

KANU
DP
FORD-K
FORD-A
SDP
NDP
NARC
ODM
PNU
T1
T2
T3
T4
0 10 20 30 40 50 60

Source: Author's compilation.

a programmatic category – declines. This is the main factor in accounting for FORD-K's 1997 programmatic content to be below my 40 percent cut-off point. In retrospect, therefore, the average programmatic content of FORD-K is due to the historical circumstances of the election – the return of multiparty democracy to Kenya – rather than a general characteristic of the party. Accordingly, it is more accurate to regard the party's manifesto as not programmatic.

Entering the first parliamentary cycle as the only party with MPs from every province,[15] FORD-K followed in the footsteps of its predecessor. Increasingly, the Kikuyu/ Meru wing of the party threatened Odinga's leadership and was particularly critical of his informal cooperation with KANU.[16] In September 1993, Paul Muite (Kikuyu) and Gitobu Imanyara (Meru) eventually left FORD-K in protest against Odinga's involvement in the Goldenberg scandal.[17] Muite's constant appeals to fellow Kikuyu leaders to unite under one political umbrella and his accusations that Odinga was running the party like a Luo kingdom[18] illustrate the ethnic connotations that accompanied the party's divisions. The departure of Muite and

[15] Nevertheless, more than two-thirds of FORD-K legislators were from Nyanza province.

[16] *Daily Nation*, July 3, 1993; *Daily Nation*, July 27, 1993; *Daily Nation*, August 26, 1993.

[17] The Goldenberg scandal was Kenya's largest political scandal involving bribery of the country's governing elite. It dominated the headlines for almost a decade. In 1993, evidence emerged that Oginga Odinga had received large sums of money from the government to remain quiet over the government's involvement in it. For details of the Goldenberg scandal, see Wrong 2009.

[18] *Daily Nation*, May 9, 1994.

Odinga's death shortly thereafter in January 1994 paved the way for the party's second vice-chairman, Kijana Wamalwa (Luhya), to take over the chairmanship. In line with these changes, FORD-K's leadership composition in March 1994 displayed paramount Luo and Luhya influence.[19]

Intense factionalism continued between Wamalwa and Raila Odinga,[20] Oginga Odinga's son, who increasingly managed to distinguish himself as the new leader of the Luo community (Badejo 2006). Although Wamalwa won the FORD-K leadership contest unopposed, James Orengo (Luo) and Raila (Luo) vied for the position of the first vice-chairman. Orengo, who could rely on the support of almost all FORD-K Luo MPs, managed to beat Odinga, the candidate of the Luo elders, by three votes.[21] Despite his defeat, the Raila faction maintained its challenge to the Luo-Luhya faction led by Wamalwa and Orengo. In March 1995, FORD-K MPs dropped Raila from the influential parliamentary Public Accounts Committee after the party headquarters was cleansed of employees allied to him.[22] Meanwhile, Raila increasingly advocated a strategic Luo-Kikuyu alliance and challenged Wamalwa more than once to resign over his alleged involvement in the Goldenberg scandal.[23] Behind the scenes of his struggle against Wamalwa, Raila continued to fight for the leadership of the Luo community against Orengo. The party's steady slide into chaos became unstoppable at the end of 1995, when Raila declared himself chairman of FORD-K over the failure of Wamalwa to hold grassroots elections in 1995.[24] Under the auspices of an independent FORD-K arbitrator, FORD-K held party grassroots and (chaotic) national elections in April 1996, which were boycotted by the Raila faction.[25] In January 1997, the Raila faction quit FORD-K and defected to the National Development Party (NDP) after lengthy consultations with traditional Luo leaders (Badejo 2006). Shortly after the dissolution of parliament in late 1997, all Luo FORD-K MPs followed Raila. For Raila, this meant that he had become the uncontested Luo leader; for FORD-K, it meant a decline from an ethnic alliance to a Luhya-based mono-ethnic party. Table 3.7 illustrates the ethnic nature of the party's factions in connection with the causes that led to their departure.

Statements by MPs after the founding election reflect the increasing role of ethnicity after the first multiparty elections. The pro-Kikuyu rhetoric of Muite and other Kikuyu MPs has been touched on. Luo MPs such as Tom Obondo followed this example. They called on Oginga Odinga to lead the Luo to government and leave the opposition to the Kikuyu and Asians, as

[19] *Daily Nation*, March 21, 1994. Data on all leadership positions is with the author.

[20] Raila Odinga will be referred to as Raila; his father will be referred to as Odinga.

[21] *Daily Nation*, March 8, 1994.

[22] *Daily Nation*, November 24, 1995; *Daily Nation*, March 29, 1995.

[23] *Daily Nation*, April 18, 1995.

[24] *Daily Nation*, November 30, 1995.

[25] *Daily Nation*, April 14, 1996.

TABLE 3.7. *Factionalism Inside FORD-K Between 1992 and 1997*

Division	Factions	Issue	Outcome
Luo versus Kikuyu	Oginga Odinga (Luo) versus Paul Muite (Kikuyu)	cooperation with KANU Odinga's leadership	Muite and Imanyara exit party → end of Kikuyu participation in FORD-K
Luo versus Luhya	Raila Odinga (Luo) versus Kijana Wamalwa (Luhya)	party leadership	Raila exits party → end of Luo participation in FORD-K

Source: Author's compilation.

these groups had amassed enough wealth to protect themselves.[26] Oburo Odinga – another son of Oginga – appealed to Luo unity in the face of economic adversity.[27] On various occasions, Luo politicians in other parties were asked to join FORD-K to secure a united Luo front.[28] Taken together, these statements undermined party unity given their contradictory and heavily parochial content. Obondo's crushing comment on Kikuyu wealth, for example, immediately provoked a strong Kikuyu response.[29] Consequently, not too much time was spent on actual policy issues. It would be unfair to ignore that, at times, party legislators took a united stance on the need to increase the national minimum wage[30] or on a decrease in commodity prices.[31] Yet for most of the time, its individual factions were occupied either by appealing to fellow community members to join the party or by degrading others and ousting them from the party.[32] The rapid intensification of ethnicity-based intra-party rivalry – evident in party factions and rhetoric – ultimately led to a redefinition of the party's purpose away from its original motives. Leading party politicians no longer saw the party as a means to fight for democracy and human rights but as vehicle for the political ambitions of their respective communities.

The party's regional and national coverage (RNC) in the 1992 election unveiled important gaps, most notably in the Kalenjin dominated Rift Valley and the Kikuyu dominated Central province. Election results in both regions were equally disappointing. The party's strongholds were clearly Nyanza, home of the Luo, and to some extent Nairobi. Table 3.8 displays FORD-K's

[26] *Daily Nation*, January 4, 1994.
[27] *Daily Nation*, July 25, 1994.
[28] *Daily Nation*, December 28, 1996.
[29] *Daily Nation*, January 4, 1994.
[30] *Daily Nation*, June 7, 1994.
[31] *Daily Nation*, March 19, 1994.
[32] Two years after the founding elections, the Kenyan media almost exclusively focused on tensions inside the party.

TABLE 3.8. *Parties' Electoral Performance and Ability to Field Candidates in 1992*

	Ford-K		FORD-A		DP		KANU		
T1	RNC	PDS	RNC	PDS	RNC	PDS	RNC	PDS	Vote Share of Region[33]
Nairobi	100%	9%	100%	12%	100%	7%	100%	3%	8%
Coast	89%	6%	85%	3%	100%	5%	100%	10%	7%
North Eastern	90%	1%	80%	0%	100%	0%	100%	3%	1%
Eastern	81%	5%	90%	6%	91%	32%	100%	19%	17%
Central	60%	5%	96%	43%	92%	35%	100%	4%	21%
Rift Valley	40%	8%	48%	19%	59%	13%	100%	34%	19%
Western	85%	10%	85%	16%	90%	3%	100%	15%	11%
Nyanza	100%	56%	45%	1%	55%	5%	100%	12%	16%
TOTAL	74%	100%	76%	100%	83%	100%	100%	100%	100%

PDS FORD-K: 83/ average diverging points across time and space: 52
PNS FORD-K: .56/ average PNS across time and space: .67
PDS FORD-A: 62 / average diverging points across time and space: 52
PNS FORD-A: .60/ average PNS across time and space: .67
PDS DP: 58 / average diverging points across time and space: 52
PNS DP: .61/ average PNS across time and space: .67
PDS KANU: 52/ average diverging points across time and space: 52
PNS KANU: .68/ average PNS across time and space: .67

Source: Author's compilation on the basis of data provided by the Electoral Commission of Kenya.

33 The vote share of the region is calculated by dividing the number of total votes cast per region by the number of total votes cast nationwide in the particular election under scrutiny.

RNC, the vote share that each region contributed to its party divergence score (PDS) and its party nationalization score (PNS).

An overview over all PDS and PNS values as well as their respective average values across time and space is provided in Annex D. Comparing these averages with the performance of FORD-K, we note that its PDS falls between the high to very high category. Although this indicates a mono-ethnic party, it is very close to values that are characteristic of an ethnic alliance (ranging between 52 to 81 diverging points). Its PNS falls into the medium to low category, which is indicative of an ethnic alliance. Overall, FORD-K is classified as an ethnic alliance; its manifesto was not programmatic, its party factions ethnic, its intra-party life characterized by defections on the basis of group grievances, and its general rhetoric overshadowed by appeals to communal solidarity. Its leadership never managed to bridge the country's dominant cleavage lines. However, toward the end of the first parliamentary cycle, FORD-K increasingly resembled a mono-ethnic party, as first Kikuyu and later Luo representatives departed from its leadership.

FORD-Asili: The Prisoners of Dr. Kenneth Matiba

Although FORD-A managed to gain the same amount of parliamentary seats as FORD-K, it initially posed a greater threat to KANU and President Moi due to Matiba's impressive performance in the presidential elections.[34] In line with FORD-K, its election campaign was driven by its dedication to democracy and constitutionalism.[35] In addition, it was geared toward Kenya's "common man" and in particular the "common man" among the Kikuyu and Luhya.[36] Kenya's leading newspaper even referred to FORD-A as the "ghetto party."[37] Because the campaign focused on the Luhya and Kikuyu gentry and because of the party's history as a break-away of the original FORD, it campaigned not only against KANU, but also against the rest of the opposition.[38] Campaigning against Kibaki had both an intra-ethnic as well as a class dimension to it; aiming to be the party of the common man required political distance to parts of the economic elite. In this regard, Kibaki served as a useful straw man. In addition, FORD-A – if it wanted to win the presidential elections and a significant amount of seats – required a united Kikuyu voting block. Campaigning against Odinga entertained an inter-ethnic as well as a personal element that resulted from the disintegration of the original FORD. The campaign also had integrative

[34] Some have argued that had it not been for electoral rigging in strategically selected provinces in the presidential elections, Matiba would have been elected president. See Throup and Hornsby 1998.

[35] For an example, see *Daily Nation*, December 5, 1992.

[36] Interview with Eric Shimoli, Editor in Chief, *Daily Nation*, December 24, 2007, Nairobi.

[37] *Daily Nation*, June 5, 1993.

[38] *Daily Nation*, November 23, 1992.

elements to it with regard to Moi's community; Matiba frequently warned against the political isolation of the Kalenjin. On several occasions, he stated that the Kalenjin should not be punished for the exclusionary policies of the Moi period.[39] Overall, however, its electoral rhetoric was more in line with the criteria of an alliance party, as its main goal was the consolidation of the vote of those groups that dominated its leadership. Despite its focus on the "ordinary man," its election manifesto retained a comparatively low programmatic content (33 percent). Its most emphasized categories included category 411 (Technology and Infrastructure: positive, 12 percentage points of the overall content), 202 (Democracy: positive, 9.2 percentage points), and 201 (Freedom and Human Rights: positive, 7.9 percentage points).

Following the 1992 elections, the party proved unable to effectively challenge the Moi regime. In contrast to FORD-K, this was less due to ethnic factionalism, although tensions between the Luhya wing of Shikuku and the Kikuyu wing of Matiba temporarily emerged.[40] However, factions were more of a personalistic than of an ethnic nature, as intra-party life became severely constrained by regular fall-outs between Matiba and the rest. Matiba continuously boycotted parliamentary debates, much to the disadvantage and anger of his party. In October 1994, he single-handedly closed down FORD-A's party headquarters and removed all documents without explaining his actions.[41] His 1996 Shadow Cabinet did not include any sitting FORD-A MP.[42] His consistent failure to hold party elections further damaged the image of FORD-A, as did the fact that Matiba did not attend meetings of the FORD-A National Executive Council. This at times led to his temporary and later permanent suspension from the party.[43] Matiba's erratic behavior also hindered the conduct of leadership elections for most of the time. Contests that did take place were later successfully challenged in court.[44] In response to Matiba's behavior, the "Patriotic Group" formed at the behest of various FORD-A MPs, including Shikuku (Luhya), Nthenge (Kamba), and Nyanja (Kikuyu). It officially defined itself as acting against self-centered individuals and thus tried to contain the impact of their unpredictable party leader.[45]

Party statements appealed to group solidarity of the communities that were represented in FORD-A's leadership. Kikuyu MPs such as Stephen Ndichu expressed their support for the revival of GEMA to keep the Kikuyu united.[46] Robert Mungai (Kikuyu) consistently advised his community

[39] *Daily Nation*, December 22, 1992.

[40] For an example, see *Daily Nation*, July 26, 1993.

[41] *Daily Nation*, October 21, 1994.

[42] *Daily Nation*, May 3, 1996.

[43] See for example *Daily Nation*, June 6, 1997.

[44] *Daily Nation*, March 11, 1996.

[45] *Daily Nation*, June 16, 1996.

[46] *Daily Nation*, October 2, 1993.

to be on guard against a widespread victimization campaign that was underway in all corners of the country.[47] Martin Shikuku issued strong warnings against anyone with the intention "to joke around" with the Luhya community.[48] Thus the purpose of the party increasingly espoused communal-based rhetoric.

FORD-A's electoral performance and its national coverage are in line with these findings. Although it had a huge presence in Eastern, Central, Western, and Coastal province, it performed badly in that regard in Nyanza and the Rift Valley. It had clearly identifiable strongholds, including Central and Western. It further did well in Nairobi, a general stronghold of the opposition. Its PDS as well as its PNS are characteristic of an ethnic alliance. The party is classified as such, as all indicators but party factions match my ideal type of the ethnic alliance.

The Democratic Party: In the Shadows of GEMA

The DP's 1992 election was as anti-KANU as the respective campaigns of the FORD parties, yet its emphasis was slightly more issue-based. Its criticism on KANU concentrated on the way the governing party had (mis)managed the economy and the civil service.[49] The party was forced to dedicate much of its time countering its negative image as a GEMA voting bloc given that many of its high-ranking members and sponsors were standing in high-profile constituencies, including GEMA's former leader Njenga Karume and Dixon Kihika, both key actors in the organization's attempts to stop Moi from claiming the presidency in the late 1970s.[50] Kibaki's team avoided electoral rhetoric targeted at groups that did not participate in the party's leadership composition. Instead, its efforts to unite its major voting bloc were embedded in statements praising Kenyatta. Kibaki's claim that Moi had destroyed the political institutions Kenyatta had successfully created after independence was reiterated at all major DP rallies.[51]

An examination of the DP election manifesto reveals a high number of programmatic content (54 percent). Data do not indicate an overemphasis on any particular policy category; its amount of significant programmatic categories (11) is above the average amount both in a national as well as in a cross-national context (8.7). Therefore, for the first time, this study discovers a party whose election manifesto contains a genuinely high programmatic content. The manifesto shows strong allegiance to several programmatic categories, such as 403 (Market Regulation: positive, 8.6 percentage points of

47 *Daily Nation*, October 21, 1993.
48 *Daily Nation*, May 7, 1993.
49 *Daily Nation*, December 8, 1992.
50 *Daily Nation*, May 29, 1993.
51 *Daily Nation*, November 17, 1992.

the overall content), 401 (Free Enterprise: positive, 6.6 percentage points), 607 (Multiculturalism: positive, 6.9 percentage points), 504 (Welfare State Expansion: positive, 5.9 percentage points), and 506 (Improvement of Education: positive, 4.5 percentage points).

The results from the coding scheme are in line with the party's focus on the Kikuyu vote. Much of the Kikuyu core clientele of the party belongs to the country's trading class. Support for pro–free market statements matches the political preferences of the community the DP represented first and foremost. The DP's high support for the social-market economy that the MRG coding scheme allocates to the political left appears contradictory only to those who approach African parties with an analytical approach that is grounded in Western politics. A political agenda that advocates both free-market forces and market control are, however, perfectly in line with the expediency of a party that aims at reaching out to a comparatively well-situated political community as well as taking into account the economic reality of most ordinary citizens. The high support for cultural diversity might come as a surprise given the DP's parochial setup. This, however, must be compared against the historical context in which the election took place. Ever since the death of Kenyatta, there has been a sense of marginalization among the Kikuyu both politically and economically (Ajulu 2002, Wrong 2009). Under the pretext of fighting for cultural diversity hide long-held political grievances.

In terms of its leadership composition and party factions, the DP maintained its nature as an alliance party. The party's first leadership election conducted by a national congress saw the confirmation of Kibaki and the inclusion of Kamba, Kisii, Masai, and Somali politicians.[52] In response to protests against sidelining of the Meru community, the DP further created additional senior posts that were filled by Meru party functionaries.[53] Between 1992 and 1995, Kibaki's leadership was questioned more than once by several representatives, including those of his own community, which was caused by the self-centered manner in which he led the party.[54] Factionalism was thus initially cross-cutting with regard to the ethnic composition of the group that challenged Kibaki. This changed from mid-1995 onward, when MP Agnes Ndetei (Kamba) announced that she would challenge Kibaki for the leadership of the party at the next available opportunity, a statement supplemented by rallying cries to the Kamba to claim the party's leadership.[55] Her defection back to KANU in early 1996 occurred in protest

[52] *Daily Nation*, July 6, 1993.
[53] *Daily Nation*, July 19, 1993.
[54] For details, see *Daily Nation*, March 28, 1995; *Daily Nation*, May 1, 1995; *Daily Nation*, May 13, 1995.
[55] *Daily Nation*, June 9, 1995.

against Kibaki's failure to convene a new national party congress.[56] It was anticipated by John Keen's (Masai) re-defection to KANU one year earlier. Keen justified his walk-out from the party he had helped found by alluding to Masai elders, who had advised him to rejoin the governing party.[57] The departure of Ndetei and Keen could not be compensated by members of the same communities. At the end of the first observation period, the DP had followed the same example of the FORD-K; its leadership composition was tilting toward that of a mono-ethnic party.

The party's appeal to the Kenyan electorate after the 1992 elections was its allegiance to the principles of good governance, especially with regard to budget spending and the condemnation of corrupt activities.[58] These, however, were often overshadowed by issues related to ethnicity, such as Keen's call for the smaller tribes to unite to increase their political leverage,[59] his ridicule of the Kalenjin's fear of being marginalized,[60] or his tribute of the way the Kikuyu behaved after ethnic clashes in the Rift Valley.[61] Programmatic ideas did feature, yet these were overwritten by praising the groups represented within the party and by attacking those who were not. The original purpose of the party outlined in its statute was still visible as manifested in its pro-market–based rhetoric, yet the longer the party endured, the more it became a political laboratory for various attempts of ethnic hijacking, as exemplified by Ndetei's failed palace coup. Yet compared with other party leaders, Kibaki never overtly advocated Kikuyu unity, and his own rhetoric was devoid of strong ethnic undertones.

Its ability to field candidates nationwide was more enhanced than the rest of the opposition, yet there were still significant gaps, in particular, in the Kalenjin- and Luo-dominated areas. Its electoral strongholds can be identified quickly and are in line with the examination conducted thus far; the DP excelled in Kikuyu- and Kamba-dominated regions. Its PDS is at a medium to high level, and its PNS displays medium to high values, both indicating an ethnic alliance in terms of its electoral performance. Therefore, despite its high programmatic content, all indicators define the DP as yet another example of a multiethnic alliance.

The Kenyan African National Union: Entering the Democratic Age

KANU entered the period of multiparty democracy as a party that had been in government for almost three decades. The legacy of one-party rule

[56] *Daily Nation*, February 5, 1996.
[57] *Daily Nation*, February 3, 1995.
[58] *Daily Nation*, October 6, 1993; *Daily Nation*, June 17, 1994.
[59] *Daily Nation*, September 5, 1994.
[60] *Daily Nation*, July 4, 1994.
[61] *Daily Nation*, November 5, 1993.

provided a variety of advantages. First, it presided over party offices on a nationwide scale, even before the registration process for opposition parties began, enabling it to field candidates in all constituencies. Second, despite a distinct pro-Kalenjin bias under Moi's presidency during the period of de jure one-party rule, KANU had always been able to include representatives of all communities in its internal setup, as well as in terms of cabinet appointments before the 1992 elections. Since its 1988 party elections, the party's leadership positions were filled by Ndolo Ayah (Luo) as party chairman (hierarchically below the position of party president filled by Moi), Njoroge Mungai (Kikuyu) as party vice-chairman, and Joseph Kamotho (Kikuyu) as secretary-general.[62] In terms of party leadership, KANU thus entered the new era of democratic competition as a party that had a national outreach on paper. Out of all the political parties, it certainly represented the most national one at the time, even though this was the legacy effect of the one-party period rather than a product of an explicitly inclusive political approach.

Keen on trying to portray itself as party of national unity and stability – the two catchphrases of its election posters[63] – its campaign rhetoric revealed strong ethnic undertones.

In regions where opposition leaders originated from and where the party was in real danger of losing its decade-grown foothold, the call to rally behind KANU was exceptionally strong and driven by hostility and open threats. In the Luhya-dominated Western region – where political loyalties were particularly contested, given that all parties managed to include Luhya community members in high-ranking positions[64] – KANU cabinet minister Elijah Mwangale (Luhya) warned his community against the possibility of a Kikuyu (i.e., a DP or FORD-A) president.[65] Another minister, Burudi Nabwera, called on Kikuyu traders in Western province to leave the area and to hand over trading spots to the indigenous Luhya community. He stated that "the time has come for the Kikuyu community to leave Western province to the Luhya to run businesses to raise their living standards."[66] Simultaneously in Nyanza province, various KANU candidates called on the Luo community to not vote for the opposition, as this would lead to the political isolation of the Luo.[67] Leading KANU figures further aimed at the political mobilization of the Embu community against the Kikuyu to divide the two groups, which had previously been close allies in the days of GEMA.

[62] Based on various sources of the Kenyan printing press.

[63] *Daily Nation*, December 17 and 21, 1992, pp. 15, 16, and 22.

[64] Historically, the Luhya have never been united under the roof of one party with the exception of the 2002 election. As a result, Western province has traditionally been a hotly contested political ground.

[65] *Daily* Nation, November 24, 1992.

[66] *Daly Nation*, December 2, 1992.

[67] *Daily Nation*, November 2, 1992.

In a variety of speeches, the Kikuyu were portrayed as a group that aspired to isolate others.[68] The anti-Kikuyu element had a dual purpose; it raised the fear of a return of Kikuyu/ GEMA rule and thus increased pressure on communities other than the Kikuyu to rally behind KANU. Accordingly, the failure to support KANU would lead to political isolation either because the Kikuyu would triumph or because KANU would win, and communities that had withdrawn their support would suffer the consequences of abandoning KANU.

These potential consequences were spelled out more explicitly in the years that followed KANU's 1992 electoral triumph, in which the party maintained a divide-and-rule rhetoric. Most frequently, this was pursued by cabinet ministers. Cabinet member Johnstone Makau, for example, warned his Kamba community against forming any kind of alliance with members of GEMA, as this would lead to their exploitation by the GEMA communities.[69] KANU's minister for cooperative development, John Munyi, appealed to his Embu people to vote for KANU if they wanted to receive further government assistance.[70] Attempts to deter people from abandoning KANU were underscored by luring back communities that had voted for the opposition. Dalmas Otieno, one of the few remaining Luo ministers, urged his community to return to KANU to harvest the fruits of independence.[71] After the surprise takeover of the FORD-K leadership by Wamalwa (Luhya), KANU's stance in one of its strongholds was seriously endangered. The party propaganda machinery reacted promptly; Cabinet Minster Masinde (Luhya) and Luhya KANU MPs appealed to their community not to be tricked by FORD-K's Luo membership, who were out to cheat the Luhya community.[72] On various occasions, Moi called on his own group, the Kalenjin, to remain united inside the party and not to fall prey to intra-ethnic divisions (Lynch 2007).[73] This strategy had already started in the run-up to the 1992 election, when Moi's confidants – mainly Kalenjin politician and elders – portrayed the democratic opposition as anti-Kalenjin. In addition, KANU politicians from the Kalenjin and other nomadic communities began to re-advocate "majimboism" by stating that greater regional autonomy would be a suitable instrument by which the Rift Valley and other regions could get rid of Kikiyu settlers (Oyugi 1997). This tendency increased throughout the 1990s. By the mid-1990s, Kenya had come full circle. The same communities that had supported majimboism under the roof of KADU in the 1960s were in charge of KANU. The same communities that had opposed

68 *Daily Nation*, December 21, 1992.
69 *Daily Nation*, June 7, 1993.
70 *Daily Nation*, February 22, 1994.
71 *Daily Nation*, February 21, 1994.
72 *Daily Nation*, February 8, 1994.
73 For one example, see *Daily Nation*, May 3, 1996.

federalism in the immediate postcolonial period inside KANU now formed the opposition. Throughout the observation period, the same rhetorical pattern was evident; KANU's fear of losing key communities – needed to ensure a numerical survival on election day – resulted in warnings of the potential consequences a betrayal of KANU might constitute for these communities. This was followed by a vicious condemnation campaign of groups challenging KANU. Yet the governing party was as eloquent in describing the dangers of certain groups as they were in inviting them back to KANU. On various occasions, KANU leaders reached out to the Luo and the Kikuyu and called on them to return to the party they once had founded.[74] Moi consistently called for national unity and the need to work together for the common good of Kenya. An important leitmotif in his speeches was his rejection of multiparty competition by invoking fears that these will foster ethnic tensions (Throup and Hornsby 1998). Yet by using rhetoric to play communities against each other, KANU contributed to several ethnic clashes, which haunted the country throughout the 1990s. As various human rights agencies noted, high-ranking KANU personalities, such as Moi's right-hand Nicholas Biwott, were directly involved in organizing these clashes (Human Rights Watch 1993).

In its 1992 election manifesto, KANU showed a below-average concern with programmatic issues (36 percent). The programmatic issues it stressed most included categories 403 (Market Regulation: positive, 4.4 percentage points of the overall content), 107 (Internationalism: positive, 4.3 percentage points), 504 (Welfare State Expansion: positive, 3.8 percentage points), and 506 (Education Expansion: positive, 3.2 percentage points). The 1960 KANU party statutes stated that the party aimed at creating a socialist society. In the early 1990s, this intention was long gone. Neither its content nor its electoral rhetoric displayed an exceptionally strong allegiance to socialist values.

The same is true of bills the KANU government passed in the National Assembly, which were free of ideological preferences. The 1991 Parliamentary Constituencies Review Bill, however, further worsened ethnic relations. The bill created 30 new parliamentary constituencies. In effect, the bill allocated a higher number of new constituencies to ethnic groups, who supported the incumbent party. Ethnic gerrymandering thus ensured power maintenance (Peters 1998).

Although KANU was the most united party in the 1992–1997 period, party factions emerged over the question of whether or not increasing intraparty democracy was desirable. The party wing known as "KANU A" was in favor of new party leadership elections. It was led by cabinet minister Simon Nyachae (Kissi) and William ole Ntimama (Masai). "KANU B" represented the hardliners of the party, including Kenyan vice-president Saitoti

[74] For examples, see *Daily Nation*, January 18, 1997; *Daily Nation*, July 22, 1996.

(Masai), KANU's Secretary-General Kamotho (Kikuyu), Cabinet Minister Kipkalia Kones (Kalenjin), and Nicholas Biwott (Kalenjin). At the heart of this division was the position of the vice-presidency, which was connected to the looming question of who would most likely succeed Moi.[75] Individual power considerations thus were the dominant line of division, which in turn were affected by strategic-ethnic considerations of which group would dominate KANU in the post-Moi era. KANU A was in favor of the political reintegration of (parts of) the Kikuyu in the KANU power machinery given their numerical strength, a strategy supported by Moi. The more hawkish group of KANU B feared that increasing Kikuyu participation would ultimately lead to a neglect of the political interests of the smaller communities (Peters 1998). In addition, community representatives of the Luo and the Luhya occasionally complained about being marginalized deliberately by the party's power brokers.[76] Thus ethnic divisions also featured inside KANU, although to a much lesser extent than inside the FORD parties or the DP – again, a legacy effect of several decades as ruling party, which facilitated patronage and a higher degree of party institutionalization.

President Moi sought close relations with traditional leaders, in particular with those on his community. After ongoing ethnic clashes between Kikuyu and Kalenjin in the multiethnic areas of the Rift Valley, Moi presided over meetings between GEMA leaders and representatives of the Kalenjin and other smaller communities[77] (Lynch 2007). In doing so, he invited traditional elements of Kenyan society to play an active role in politics.[78]

The lion's share of his 1993 cabinet went to three communities – the Kamba, the Luhya, and the Kalenjin – whereas the Luo and the Kikuyu got one ministerial position each and can thus be seen as comparatively underrepresented. Five cabinet positions went to representatives of smaller communities.[79] As Table 3.9 illustrates, KANU's first cabinet after independence was an immediate reaction to the ethnicization of Kenyan politics along party lines and demarcates KANU's ethnic bias; numerically the founding communities of KADU prevail, whereas the Luo and the Kikuyu are underrepresented.[80] The underrepresentation of the Kikuyu is all the more striking when the 1992 cabinet is compared with the ethnic

[75] *Daily Nation*, September 21, 1996; *Daily Nation*, November 1, 1996; *Daily Nation*, November 13, 1996; *Daily Nation*, January 16, 1997.

[76] *Daily Nation*, October 14, 1996; *Daily Nation*, November 15, 1996.

[77] The literature frequently refers to these as KAMASATU tribes – Kalenjin, Maasai, Samburu, and Turkana.

[78] *Daily Nation*, September 11, 1995. This was criticized by some segments of the Kenyan media.

[79] *Daily Nation*, January 14, 1993.

[80] George Saitoti has been classified by Ahluwalia as Kikuyu although he frequently described himself as Masai. If this is taken into consideration, the participation rate of the Kikuyu would be 10 percent.

TABLE 3.9. *Ethnic Composition of Kenya's 1979, 1983, and 1992 Cabinets*

Community	Number of Cabinet Ministers Allocated in 1979	Percentage of Cabinet Allocated	Number of Cabinet Ministers Allocated in 1983	Percentage of Cabinet Allocated in 1983	Number of Cabinet Ministers Allocated in 1992	Percentage of Cabinet Allocated in 1992
GEMA	10	37%	5	24%	3	15%
Kikuyu					1	5%
Embu					1	5%
Meru					1	5%
Luo	3	11%	2	10%	1	5%
Kalenjin	4	15%	5	24%	4	15%
Luhya	3	11%	3	14%	3	15%
Kamba	2	7%	2	10%	4	20%
Other (smaller communities)	5	19%	4	18%	5	30%
TOTAL	27	100%	21	100%	20	100%

Source: Author's compilation based on Namibian media sources and Ahluwalia (1996).

composition of previous cabinets. The comparison over time is important, as taken on its own, the 1992 cabinet still displays integrative elements of the one-party age.

The bias in favor of the KAMATUSA communities also corresponds to the party's electoral strongholds in the Rift Valley, North Eastern, Coastal, and Western provinces. The PDS is characteristic of an alliance party, whereas its PNS falls into the medium to high category and is thus indicative of a catch-all party.

The discussion of individual indicators demonstrates that KANU is more difficult to classify than other parties, as it contains several elements indicative of a catch-all and alliance party. Its rhetoric is clearly ethnic, and so is its cabinet composition, whereas its factions and its national coverage are indicative of a catch-all party. Out of all Kenyan parties, it was beyond doubt the most national one. However, the data supporting its catch-all nature are limited in terms of its sustainability over time. Indicators derived from KANU's electoral performance date back to 1992, a period in which the party could thrive on its infrastructural heritage of one-party rule. Its last leadership election dates back to 1988 and was again reminiscent of very different political circumstances. In addition, several voices have stressed that the 1992 and 1997 elections were in some areas rigged in favor of KANU, which manipulates data in favor of a higher PNS and PDS (Peters 1998, Throup and Hornsby 1998). Moreover, in a variety of constituencies, KANU candidates were elected unopposed. As this occurred mainly in KANU strongholds in the Rift Valley, the PNS and PDS are further biased in favor of higher values; if elections had taken place, KANU would have taken them in a landslide, which would have led to a less equal spread of its vote nationwide. Most importantly, KANU incorporated politicians, which were involved in organizing ethnic clashes. It would thus be incorrect to classify KANU as a catch-all party, although it is a borderline case. Drawing on Horowitz's (2000) three logics of ethnic coalitions, KANU clearly represented an ethnic *coalition of commitment*, in contrast to the opposition, which displayed characteristic of *coalitions of convenience*. My analysis of subsequent observation periods confirms the classification of KANU as an ethnic party.

OBSERVATION PERIOD 2

Throughout the early years of the era of multiparty competition, parties became increasingly embroiled in the dynamics of ethnic politics. This process reached its peak at the beginning of the second parliamentary cycle, which saw an increase in the number of significant parties, now including the DP, FORD-K, the NDP (the former Luo wing of FORD-K), the SDP (the former Kamba wing of the DP), and KANU. Statistically, the number of effective parties increased from four to five. Toward the end of the second period, a change in political strategy occurred. Constant disintegration gave way to reintegration, which in turn was followed by renewed disintegration.

A selection of bills passed by the Kenyan National Assembly is outlined in Table 3.10. None of them altered or fostered the relationships between Kenya's major ethnic communities.

FORD-Kenya: From Alliance to Mono-Ethnic Party

Following the departure of FORD-K's Luo wing and the increasing number of political parties catching the spotlight of the Kenyan media, FORD-K was less able to attract attention. Observers of the 1997 campaign noted less excitement about the second elections, as the disintegration of the opposition had made another KANU triumph almost inevitable (Peters 1998, Rutten et al. 2001). As in 1992, the party stressed its anticorruption credentials and promised constitutional reforms without specifying them in detail.[81] Its 1997 election manifesto was less programmatic than the previous version due to a decline in statements that were supportive of democracy and human rights. All other programmatic categories changed only marginally.

FORD-K's ability to field candidates decreased by roughly one-third, as Table 3.11 outlines. Particularly affected by this decline was Nyanza and Central province, a direct consequence of the exit of the Luo community

[81] *Daily Nation*, November 17, 1997; *Daily Nation*, December 18, 1997.

TABLE 3.10. *Selection of Bills Passed by the National Assembly Between 1997 and 2002*

Name of Bill	Comment	Impact on Ethnic Relations
1998 Licensing Bill	refined the legal framework of the licensing regime in Kenya	no
1998 Local Authorities Transfer Fund Bill	aimed at transferring funds to local authorities to promote growth	no
1999 Finance Bill	introduced a new taxation measure to provide the government with new funds to fight poverty	no
1999 Constitution of Kenya (Amendment) Bill	provided for the establishment of a Parliamentary Service Commission	no
2000 Supplementary Appropriation Bill	introduced a new system of protecting crops	no
2000 Petroleum Bill	provided a legal framework that covered all petroleum product activities	no
2001 Bill to Amend Section 22 of the Constitution	provided the president the right to appoint a number of permanent secretaries as he may determine	no
2002 Industrial Property Bill	allowed the government to purchase drug-analyzing machines	no

Source: Compiled by the author with the help of the Kenyan Hansard.

from the party. Its electoral stronghold shifted accordingly to Western province while it underperformed in all other regions.

Its medium to high PDS shows FORD-K to be an alliance party, although the party nearly meets the requirements of a mono-ethnic alliance (82). Its PNS is one of the lowest identified in this book. The proximity of the PDS to numerical values characteristic of a mono-ethnic party in conjunction with its very low PNS points toward a mono-ethnic party rather than an ethnic alliance.

The nature of the party factions confirms this, as they were exclusively driven by Luhya politicians. After the disappointing performance at the ballot box, FORD-K chairman Wamalwa was challenged by several younger Luhya FORD-K MPs such as George Kapten and Mikhisah Kitui.[82] Although the party contained a variety of high-ranking non-Luhya functionaries after its party congress in early 1997 – James Orengo (Luo) as vice-chairman and Gitobu Imanyara (Kukuyu) as secretary-general – these

[82] *Daily Nation*, November 2, 1998.

TABLE 3.11. *Parties' Electoral Performance and Ability to Field Candidates in 1997*

	FORD-K		NDP		DP		SDP		KANU		Regional
T2	RNC	PDS	RNC	PDS	RNC	PDS	RNC	PDS	RNC	PDS	Vote Share
Nairobi	87%	2%	100%	11%	100%	9%	89%	9%	100%	3%	**6%**
Coast	66%	3%	81%	7%	81%	5%	62%	6%	100%	10%	**7%**
North Eastern	36%	1%	73%	0%	63%	0%	36%	0%	100%	3%	**2%**
Eastern	25%	7%	47%	4%	83%	20%	67%	51%	100%	19%	**18%**
Central	10%	0%	24%	4%	90%	38%	55%	23%	100%	4%	**17%**
Rift Valley	42%	20%	29%	5%	52%	25%	25%	3%	100%	34%	**22%**
Western	95%	52%	22%	3%	38%	0%	25%	2%	100%	15%	**12%**
Nyanza	29%	15%	94%	66%	34%	3%	63%	6%	100%	12%	**16%**
TOTAL	50%	100%	52%	100%	64%	100%	49%	100%	100%	100%	100%

PDS FORD-K: 80/ average diverging points across time and space: 52
PNS FORD-K: .45/ average PNS across time and space: .67
PDS NDP: 110/ average diverging points across time and space: 52
PNS: .48/ average PNS across time and space: .67
PDS DP: 58/ average diverging points across time and space: 52
PNS DP: .57/ average PNS across time and space: .67
PDS SDP: 84/ average diverging points across time and space: 52
PNS SDP: .42/ average PNS across time and space: .67
PDS KANU: 40/ average diverging points across time and space: 52
PNS KANU: .76/ average PNS across time and space: .67

Source: Author's compilation on the basis of election data provided by the Kenyan Electoral Commission.

were no longer powerful players given their minority status within the leadership rank. Both at times openly admitted that FORD-K had become a Luhya-only party.[83] Given the generational division within the party and its loss of status as the official opposition party, FORD-K's role diminished. Shortly after the elections, James Orengo proposed a motion of no confidence in the Moi government and failed to rally the party behind him.[84] This episode illustrates FORD-K's inability to act as a coherent political unit. Otherwise, the party failed to make any lasting impact on the national scale. During the second observation period, FORD-K shows all the signs of a mono-ethnic party.

The National Development Party: FORD-K's Former Luo Wing

Raila's departure from FORD-K precipitated the departure of all sitting Luo FORD-K MPs shortly after parliament was dissolved.[85] The NDP's party constitution does not outline the main goals of the party. It contains very vague references to the need of a dynamic democratic society and constitutionalism (NDP 1997). The actual purpose of the party was to provide a platform for political bargaining in the interest of the Luo community.[86] At the beginning of the NDP's election campaign, Raila called on the Luo community to understand that even though his party represented first and foremost Luos, he would have to appeal to all Kenyans.[87] His campaign was clearly focused on Nyanza province, where the NDP appealed to regional unity among the Luo and the Kissi.[88] At no moment in time was the regional and ethnic focus of the party concealed. At times, Kenyan commentators compared the NDP with Oginga Odinga's KPU of the 1960s and thought of Raila's party as equally left-leaning. Comparatively low programmatic content in the NDP's election manifesto (31 percent) proves otherwise. Among its programmatic content, the party emphasized category 506 (Education Expansion: positive, 4.4 percentage points of the overall content) and category 504 (Welfare State Expansion: positive, 5.1 percentage points); although both are designated left-wing categories, there is nothing outstanding about these statements or about their degree in an African context.

The party's ability to contest the election was limited to regions where its leading personalities originated from (Nyanza) and areas that were

83 *Daily Nation*, August 20, 1997.

84 *Daily Nation*, October 14, 1998.

85 *Daily Nation*, November 12, 1997; *Daily Nation*, November 13, 1997. The sole exception was James Orengo, who initially also announced that he would leave FORD-K.

86 For an in-depth analysis on the factors that led to the formation of the NDP, see Badejo 2006.

87 *Daily Nation*, December 17, 1997.

88 *Daily Nation*, December 18, 1997.

logistically easy to cover (Nairobi). By contrast, the party hardly featured in Central province and the Rift Valley. This corresponds to its electoral performance. Out of all parties in this study, it was the most regional-based one, deriving two-thirds of its electoral strength from one province alone. Its diverging scores are the highest recorded, whereas its PNS is the second lowest identified.

There has been no public notification of the leadership setup of the NDP, and neither is it known if the party ever held a congress. A variety of its leadership figures were not Luo. Professor Geoffrey ole Maloiy (Masai), Raila's deputy, quit the party during the period under scrutiny. Like many others, he regarded the NDP's cooperation in parliament with KANU following the 1997 election as betrayal of the democratic opposition.[89] The exact motives – whether or not these resignations also had an ethnic dimension – cannot be ascertained. However, just as the KPU did, the NDP ended up as a Luo party. Although the very notion of parliamentary cooperation between KANU and the NDP was historically bizarre given Raila's long-term imprisonment during the era of one-party rule, the rhetoric of the NDP by which it sought to justify this confirms the party's mono-ethnic nature. On various occasions, Raila stressed the benefits cooperation with KANU would bring to the Luo.[90] A variety of Luo NDP MPs publicly warned the Kikuyu against using their numerical strength in seeking the presidency, arguing that the Luo should instead give other communities the opportunity to ascend to power.[91] At times, Raila and the NDP demanded that Kenyans forgive Moi for his past wrongdoings to facilitate peaceful coexistence.[92] In August 2001, Raila and a variety of other NDP leaders were promoted to the cabinet, while simultaneously KANU merged with the NDP.

Founded with the clear intention of giving the Luo a louder voice in Kenyan politics and with a strong organizational, rhetorical, and electoral bias in favor of Nyanza province, the NDP is the proto-type of a mono-ethnic party. Its temporary nature corresponds to the logic of "ethnic arithmetic." Ensuring the political unity of the Luo community, Raila managed to promote himself as guarantor of the Luo voting bloc, which made him and his party attractive to those in need of increasing their vote share (in this case, KANU). In doing so, he managed to position himself in a promising (i.e., multiethnic) environment to try and claim the presidency later. The speed by which Raila and the NDP rushed into the Moi succession was remarkable. Shortly after the merger, NDP legislators demanded a motion of no confidence in Vice-President Saitoti (Kikuyu/Masai), citing his involvement in several corruption scandals. Interestingly, the motion was defeated with

[89] *Daily Nation*, June 19, 1998.
[90] *Daily Nation*, May 11, 1998.
[91] *Daily Nation*, March 15, 1999.
[92] *Daily Nation*, July 6, 1998.

the help of opposition Kikuyu MPs and in particular MPs from Kibaki's DP. Saitoti's Kikuyu supporters argued that a successful motion of no confidence would have prepared the ground for a Raila presidency, which had to be avoided at all costs (Kanyinga 2003). This example of voting behavior along ethnic lines – which was later to be repeated in the context of NARC – nicely illustrates the high salience of ethnic considerations in Kenyan party politics.

The Democratic Party: The Beneficiaries of FORD-A's Collapse

Mwai Kibaki's party focused its election campaign on two overriding motives: the economic failures of the Moi government and the need to embark on improvements in a variety of sectors, such as infrastructure, education, and health care.[93] As such, the campaign was devoid of ideology. It was also more anti-Moi than previously (Jonyo 2003); the party thus reacted to the strong anti-Kikuyu rhetoric of KANU during the first parliamentary cycle. The disintegration of FORD-A and Matiba's decision not to contest the 1997 elections also provided an opportunity to win over previous FORD-A supporters, and public condemnations of Moi provided a welcome opportunity to do so.

Its election manifesto again contained a large share of programmatic statements (47 percent).

Statements in favor of category 202 (Democracy: positive) increased from 3.4 percent of the overall content to 8.6 percent, possibly again a response to the anti-Kikuyu stance of the government. Among the programmatic categories, the party's share of statements in favor of category 401 (Free Enterprise: positive) declined drastically from 6.6 percentage points to 1.3 percentage points, which is the main cause for its overall programmatic content decline. Again, the DP manifesto was genuinely programmatic; the number of effective programmatic categories was higher (10.8) than the cross-national average (8.7).

Its organizational ability to cover constituencies declined even though the DP managed to remain the most effective national opposition party in this regard. Its stronghold remained Central province and the Kikuyu diaspora in the Rift Valley, where it could increase its share of the vote. This was largely a result of the decline of FORD-A and the exit of Kikuyu politician Matiba from the national political scene. The party failed to cover large areas of the Rift Valley as well as large parts of Western and Nyanza. Subsequently, it performed very poorly in Kalenjin-, Luo-, and Luhya-dominated regions. Indicators derived from its electoral output show a medium to high party diverging score and a low to medium PNS. Its electoral performance can be

[93] *Daily Nation*, December 17, 1997; *Daily Nation*, December 16, 1997; *Daily Nation*, December 18, 1997.

attributed to mono- as well as multiethnic alliances. Given the size and the spread of the Kikuyu community, the former type is more appropriate.

This is also in line with our findings for the DP's leadership composition. With Charity Ngilu and John Keen and their respective communities gone for good, Kibaki's leadership was never contested in earnest. There is no documented party congress of the DP during the second parliamentary cycle. The party's rhetoric continued to focus on policies devoid of ideology, such as infrastructure improvements,[94] the fight against corruption,[95] and economic growth.[96] At times, there were speculations that Kibaki was working with high-ranking Kikuyu politicians, such as Paul Muite, former GEMA leader Njenga Karume, and former KANU Attorney General Charles Njongo, on a plan to ensure Kikuyu unity in the upcoming elections.[97] These speculations seem plausible and further underline the enduring mono-ethnic character of the DP with regard to its political strategy. Through large-scale financiers of the party like Karume[98] and other previously high-ranking GEMA members, the party ensured direct coordination with Kikuyu traditional elders.[99] More so than in the first parliamentary cycle, the DP was firmly in the hands of the Kikuyu.

For the study of African politics in general and of African parties in particular, it is important to note that a party that fulfills all criteria of an ethnic party does not necessarily have to be devoid of ideology. The DP represents one of the rare instances in which ethnicity-based political claims are compatible with a high share of programmatic content. Ethnicity and programmatic anchors do not always have to be at the opposing ends of the political debate, as political scientists frequently assume. One should further note that the case of the DP confirms my initial assumption that a programmatic party needs to bridge the country's ethnic cleavage lines to be qualified as such. If one was to classify the DP as programmatic on the basis of its manifesto content, one would inevitably run into trouble justifying this on the basis of the party's goals, its organizational structure, and its social base.

The Social Democratic Party: Toward Kamba Unity

Little is known about the SDP in advance of Charity Ngilu's decision to quit the DP and to contest the 1997 elections on the ticket of the SDP. Initially the party attracted the leadership of a variety of intellectuals, such

94 *Daily Nation*, October 5, 1998.
95 *Daily Nation*, January 4, 1999.
96 *Daily Nation*, April 6, 1998.
97 *Daily Nation*, September 14, 1998.
98 Karume is known to be one of Kenya's first African multimillionaires.
99 *Daily Nation*, January 14, 2006.

as Professor Anyang Nyong'o (Luo), one of Kenya's leading political scientists, and Johnstone Makau (Kamba). Before the SDP entered the national political scene, it had discernible social-democratic underpinnings, although its regional stronghold has always been among the Kamba (Throup and Hornsby 1992). One Kenyan journalist referred to it as a "textbook party, which would have done well in Europe."[100] An analysis of the party's election manifesto confirms this. Much of its high programmatic content (43 percent) focuses on core issues that define social democracy, including support for category 403 (Market Regulation: positive, 5.8 percentage points of the overall manifesto content), category 504 (Welfare State Expansion: positive, 12.5 percentage points), and category 504 (Education Expansion: positive, 4.8 percentage points).

The sudden success of the party at the 1997 polls is largely due to its presidential candidate, Ngilu, who established herself as a strong advocate of the interest of the Kamba community. In several of her campaign speeches, she stressed that "the community will not take anything short of the Presidency – the time has come for us to have our cake."[101] Simultaneously, she represented a new and refreshing element in Kenyan politics; she neither belonged to the political establishment, nor did she have any links to traditional leaders. She was the first female Kenyan politician to attract the national limelight, a strong grassroots campaigner and a fervent advocate of democratic change. When she left the DP, she took almost the whole party infrastructure in the Kamba-dominated areas of Eastern province with her, which subsequently became the powerhouse of the party (Grignon 2001). Ngilu consistently condemned the failure of other opposition leaders to form a united front against KANU.[102] Other than in the manifesto, programmatic statements did not feature in her electoral rhetoric in a way that would be noticeable.

The ability of the SDP to contest the election was reduced significantly; overall, the party contested fewer than half of all seats nationwide. Even in Eastern and Central province, it was unable to cover more than two thirds of all seats. It derived half of its overall votes from Eastern, the home province of the Kamba, and one-fifth of its overall votes from Central, which houses a significant segment of the Kamba population. Indicators derived from its electoral performance are in line with the values assigned to our mono-ethnic party type.

Soon after the elections – in which the SDP finished as fifth strongest party and thus the weakest significant party under scrutiny – intense rivalry developed between Ngilu and the elected leadership of the SDP, in particular, Professor Nyong'o (Luo). Both simultaneously claimed to be the official

[100] Interview with Eric Shimoli, Editor in Chief, *Daily Nation*, December 24, 2007, Nairobi.
[101] *Daily Nation*, July 21, 1999.
[102] *East African Standard*, December 16, 1997.

spokesperson of the party, with the party's National Executive Committee backing Nyong'o.[103] Both equally aimed at becoming the party's 2002 presidential candidate. Much of the division between Nyong'o and Ngilu was centered on diverging interpretations of the party's constitution. Although this is not in any way different to the divisions that led to the disintegration of the original FORD or later FORD-K, ethnic connotations were absent, and much of the struggle between the two camps was personality-driven. In July 2001, Ngilu defected from the SDP and formed her own party, the National Party of Kenya (NPK), which had the support of the SDP parliamentary group.[104] Subsequently, the NPK became the advocate of the same ideas that the SDP put forward after 1997, the urgent need to form a nationwide coalition against KANU.[105]

The essence of the SDP is difficult to capture. Its original purpose – advancing social-democratic principles – indicates a programmatic nature, yet these were not the factors that led to its temporary success. Its party factions were driven by strong antagonisms of individual party leaders. Although its presidential candidate appealed strongly to her own community, both she and the rest of the party equally represented a different type of Kenyan politician. The party appealed to those who were genuinely concerned about democratic freedoms and those who had no direct access to conventional power brokers. The SDP illustrates the difficulties social scientists may face when trying to capture the essence of what constitutes a political party: candidates, factions, history, or rhetoric? In the case of the SDP, all of these factors point in different directions and, further, in different directions at different moments in time. Yet the party never managed to bridge the country's dominant ethnic cleavage lines. This means it cannot be classified as programmatic, despite its high programmatic content. Its leadership was multiethnic, yet its performance and large parts of its campaign rhetoric were typical of a mono-ethnic party. Its focus on the Kamba vote was the pivotal reason why it managed to ascend to parliament. Therefore, elements characteristic of a mono-ethnic party prevail.

The Kenyan African National Union

The governing party's 1997 election campaign was less derogative of multiparty competition than the previous one. Instead of decrying the dangers of political competition and the chaos it might produce, KANU portrayed itself as the guardian of stability and peace.[106] In doing so, KANU could distance itself from the opposition that it portrayed as ethnic (and hence sinister);

[103] *Daily Nation*, July 8, 2000.
[104] *Daily Nation*, June 26, 2001.
[104] *Daily Nation*, July 8, 2000.
[106] *Daily Nation*, December 13, 1997.

in particular, the DP and the Kikuyu community became the victims of this strategy.[107] The KANU election manifesto resembled the 1992 election manifesto in many ways. It neither differed in terms of programmatic content share nor in terms of the issues the party emphasized. The bills passed by the KANU majority in the National Assembly did not indicate any ideological convictions.

The support it received on election day highlights the party's persisting integrative elements. Its PNS value is at the upper bottom of our medium to high category, displaying a more equal spread of the KANU vote than in 1992. The increase is the result of Moi's attempts to increase KANU's vote share among the Kikuyu, which he achieved by lifting the profile of medium-ranking Kikuyu figures within the party. Although the vote share that Central province constitutes of the KANU overall vote remained the same, the absolute number of KANU votes in the region increased, which influences its PNS value. At the same time, however, its diverging party score falls into the medium to low category and thus indicates an alliance party. The party continued to have a clearly identifiable stronghold, the Kalenjin-dominated Rift Valley.

After the election, KANU's parliamentary dominance was constantly under threat, given its narrow majority of only four seats over the combined seats of the opposition. Although KANU profited from the ethnic fragmentation of the opposition at the presidential elections, its majority hold over parliament was reliant on party discipline. Parliamentary unity was difficult to maintain, and on a variety of occasions, KANU failed to pass bills through parliament.[108] Finance Minister Nyachae's outspoken criticism over ongoing corruption and the blank state of the economy weakened the party's ability to stay united.[109] Only with the help of various opposition MPs did KANU survive a vote of no confidence organized by James Orengo (FORD-K).[110] The vote was inspired by Moi's failure to appoint a sitting vice-president for more than 15 months after the 1997 elections, which further deepened tensions in the party over the looming question of who would eventually succeed the self-appointed "professor of politics."

KANU's post-1997 cabinet resembled its predecessor in many ways, yet was even less representative of Kenya's ethnic make-up.[111] As Table 3.12 outlines, Kikuyu and Luo participation declined further, whereas the lion's share of cabinet positions went again to the Kalenjin, the Luhya, and the pastoral communities.

[107] *Daily Nation*, December 16, 1997.
[108] For examples, see *Daily Nation*, April 13, 1998, and *Daily Nation*, April 20, 1998.
[109] *Daily Nation*, April 8, 1998.
[110] *Daily Nation*, October 16, 1998.
[111] *Daily Nation*, January 10, 1998.

TABLE 3.12. *Ethnic Composition of Kenya's 1998 Cabinet*

Community	Number of Cabinet Ministers Allocated	Percentage of Cabinet Allocated
GEMA:	5	22%
Kikuyu	1	4%
Embu	3	13%
Meru	1	4%
Luo	1	4%
Kalenjin	4	17%
Luhya	4	17%
Kamba	3	14%
Other (smaller communities)	6	26%
TOTAL	23	100%

Source: Author's compilation based on Kenyan media sources.

Inside the party, the faction known under the label of KANU A initially appeared to have gained the upper hand, as many cabinet members associated with "KANU B" received low-profile cabinet positions. Parliamentary cooperation with Raila's NDP resulted in a change of the cabinet setup – the Luo community returned to the cabinet holding a variety of cabinet positions[112] – and further led to a merger of the two parties in August 2001. In bringing the Luo back into KANU, Moi managed not only to secure parliamentary superiority but further could keep KANU's options open regarding which community would ascend to the presidency.

The merger with the NDP required new party elections. In March 2002, KANU elected its new leadership for the first time since 1988 and thus for the first time since the return of multiparty competition. In a carefully staged competition, "New KANU" elected Moi as the new chairman and Kalonzo Musyoka (Kamba), Uhuru Kenyatta (Kikuyu), Musalia Mudavadi (Luhya), and Katana Ngala (Coastal) as vice-chairmen. Raila Odinga (Luo) was elected general secretary, and Yisuf Haji (Somali) was elected national treasurer.[113] With the sole exception of the original FORD, this was the first time that a party managed to bridge all of Kenya's dominant ethnic cleavage lines in the post-1991 political environment. In contrast to FORD, it managed to do so by bringing young politicians into party leadership positions. Uhuru Kenyatta, for example, had only held party positions in Central province. The inclusion of Raila and Kenyatta had symbolic character; as the respective sons of the country's founding fathers, KANU appeared to have come full circle and was ready to embark on a future that was likely to

[112] Raila was appointed energy minister and Adhu Awiti was appointed minister in charge of planning and economic development. See Kanyinga 2003.

[113] *Daily Nation*, March 19, 2002.

be as successful as its past. At the time of its congress, the governing party was seen as the expected winner of the upcoming election.

However, the logic of ethnic politics proved too strong for KANU to withstand. Almost immediately after the congress, it became engulfed in the same quandaries that had haunted the original FORD a decade earlier. In July 2002, Moi unilaterally declared Uhuru Kenyatta as his preferred 2002 presidential candidate.[114] Much speculation has gone into what might have been Moi's motivation behind "Project Uhuru." Some regard it as the culmination of Moi's long-term strategy to rebuild KANU's power base in Central province (Peters 1998, Kagwanja 2006), whereas others point to the personal proximity between the Kenyatta and the Moi family despite all divisions between them at the political level. Moi's appointment of Musalia Mudavadi (Luhya) as vice-president at the constitutionally latest possible moment before the 2002 election gives credence to those who saw Kenyatta's candidature as part of a larger plot by which Moi tried to combine the votes of the Kalenjin, the Luhya, and the Kikuyu to secure ongoing KANU dominance.[115] Given the ethnic nature of Kenyan party politics, it does not come as a surprise that large factions of "New KANU" were unhappy about Moi's move and the potential implications of a second Kenyatta presidency. The anger this caused among KANU heavyweights led to the formation of the Rainbow Alliance, a rebel group within KANU under the leadership of Raila. It included former vice-president George Saitoti (Kikuyu/ Masai), former KANU Secretary General Joseph Kamotho (Kikuyu), New KANU's Vice-Chairmen Katana Ngala (Coastal), and Kalonzo Musyoka (Kamba).[116] The Rainbow Alliance openly campaigned against the Moi/Kenyatta slate. Two days before Kenyatta was officially elected as KANU's presidential candidate on October 14, 2002, the Rainbow Alliance formed the Liberal Democratic Party and defected to the opposition.[117]

The analysis of KANU in the second parliamentary cycle provides valuable insight into the dynamics of "ethnic arithmetic" typical of an alliance party. To survive politically, KANU was desperate for the inclusion of communities it had hitherto neglected. Yet by incorporating community representatives from opposing ends of ethnic cleavage lines, it immediately fell prey to the logic of ethnic politics. Although it managed to temporarily bridge Kenya's dominant ethnic divisions, this was tactically motivated and short-lived. One ought to note that the ability of a governing party to build lasting alliances with the help of patronage was not sufficiently strong to overcome the centrifugal tendencies of ethnicity, as is often assumed in the

114 *Daily Nation*, July 14, 2002.

115 *Daily Nation*, November 13, 2002.

116 *Daily Nation*, August 7, 2002. Musalia Mudavadi was originally also part of this group, yet later withdrew his support and backed Kenyatta.

117 *Daily Nation*, October 16, 2002.

exhaustive literature on clientelism (Lemarchand 1972). This should be kept in mind when shifting our analysis to the next parliamentary cycle and the analysis of the National Rainbow Coalition Alliance (NARC).

OBSERVATION PERIOD 3

In the run-up to the 2002 election, the opposition reacted to the formation of "New KANU" and formed the National Alliance for Change (NAC), which later merged with Raila's Liberal Democratic Party into the NARC. Although chronologically the formation of NARC falls into the second observation period, it is discussed in the context of the third parliamentary cycle for reasons of comprehension. This observation period is complex, as political parties underwent reoccurring processes of formation, disintegration, and reformation. It was at times not clear which parties were in government and in opposition, as both were in a constant state of flux. As a result, the discussion of this section proceeds differently; it starts by focusing on the new governing party NARC and in particular on the factors that led to its formation and subsequent disintegration. From this, the analysis shifts to the opposition, whose standing was heavily influenced by NARC's failure to stay united. Significant parties in this period include NARC and KANU.

As in the previous periods, a number of bills that were debated in parliament gained widespread attention. These are listed in Table 3.13. The Kibaki government passed more bills than any previous Kenyan government. None of the bills altered the relationships between Kenya's ethnic communities.

The National Alliance Rainbow Coalition

After the merger between KANU and the NDP, pressure mounted on the opposition to react to keep the option of democratic change alive. In particular, Charity Ngilu was keen on forming an alliance with Kibaki and Wamalwa and managed to convince both to agree to the formation of the National Alliance Kenya (NAK). The construction of this alliance was anticipated by extensive consultation with traditional elders of those groups the DP, FORD-K, and the NPK represented (Badejo 2006, Kadima and Owuor 2006). The joint front against KANU found widespread support around the country, and 14 smaller opposition parties joined the NAK, which was officially constituted as a new party in August 2002. On September 18, 2002, an internal nomination panel that had been set up to vet candidates standing for high posts announced Kibaki as presidential nominee, Wamalwa as his running mate, and Ngilu for the future post of prime minister. The position of the prime minister was created as part of a constitutional amendment package NAK promised to implement. Simultaneously, infighting inside KANU reached its peak after Moi's official support for Kenyatta as KANU presidential candidate. Inside the Rainbow Alliance, Raila aimed for maximum

TABLE 3.13. *Selection of Bills Passed by the National Assembly Between 2002 and 2007*

Name of Bill	Comment	Impact on Ethnic Relations
2003 The Constitution of Kenya (Amendment) Bill	gave more power to the Kenya Anti-Corruption Authority (KACA)	no. But the bill led to many arguments regarding the efficiency of the KACA.
2003 Pensions Bill		no
2004 HIV and AIDS Prevention and Control Bill		no
2003 Anti-Rape Bill		no
2005 Political Parties Bill	helped fund political parties	no
2005 The International Crimes Bill		no
2006 National Famine and Drought Management Bill		no
2007 Person with Disabilities Bill		no
2007 Information and Communication Bill	helped foster e-commerce and e-government	no

Source: Compiled by the author on the basis of information provided by the Kenyan Hansard.

ethnic representation and proved skillful in replacing those high-ranking Rainbow members who withdrew from the group due to Moi's pressure with members from the same community. When, for example, Musalia Mudavadi backtracked to the Moi camp, another Luhya, Moddy Awori, was elevated as the main Luhya figure inside the Rainbow (Badejo 2006).

Thus both NAK and the Rainbow Alliance learned the lessons of Kenya's short history of multiparty competition; only by uniting as many groups as possible could KANU be challenged in earnest. The period of fragmentation thus was succeeded by a period of fusion. This process reached its peak when the Rainbow leaders and MPs loyal to them unveiled their defection to the Liberal Democratic Party on October 14, 2002, parallel to the KANU congress that opted for Kenyatta as KANU presidential candidate. On this occasion, the LDP invited the leadership of the NAK to Uhuru Park, where the LDP held its first public rally. No formal agreement existed between the two at the time, and an electoral contest between three major forces, KANU, NAK, and the LDP, appeared the likeliest option. At the end of the rally, to the great surprise of everyone, Raila asked the crowd if they thought

Kibaki was good enough as the presidential candidate, in Kiswahili, "Kibaki Tosha?" The crowd's overwhelming approval and Raila's unforeseen question created a fait accompli, which ended all speculation regarding whether or not there would be an electoral super-alliance against KANU and who the opposition's challenger would be.

Raila's encouragement for Kibaki was largely born out of strategic considerations. First, it seemed unlikely that the LDP – should it contest the election on its own – could agree on a candidate. After all, it was personal disappointment with Moi's selection of his successor that had drawn them together (Mutua 2008). Leaving the candidacy to Kibaki would postpone these problems, as all presidential aspirants of the LDP were younger than him. Second, the LDP was unlikely to win the election on its own. Kenya's recent electoral history strongly suggested that a divided opposition would once again provide KANU with a chance to win. KANU's alleged rigging of the 1992 and 1997 elections was an additional motivation behind the formation of a super-alliance; only by beating the Moi political machinery by a high margin could the effect of rigging be counterbalanced.[118] Most importantly, a Kibaki candidacy would split up the Kikuyu voting bloc and cost Kenyatta dearly; by contrast, combining Kibaki's Kikuyu vote share in connection with Raila's Luo, Wamalwa's Luhya, and Ngilu's Kamba votes might be sufficient to fight off KANU (Jonyo 2003, Kadima and Owuor 2003, Badejo 2006).

These considerations led to the merger of the NAK and the LDP into the NARC, which was officially formed on October 22, 2002. In its Memorandum of Understanding (MoU), the leaders of NAK and the LDP set down the terms of cooperation and its purpose. Raila was now promised the position of prime minister, and both sides agreed on a 50/50 power-sharing formula with regard to cabinet ministers. The first article of the memorandum states explicitly that NARC was established "for the purpose of winning the next general election."[119] Affiliation to NARC was only possible through cooperate membership; only parties, not individuals, could join the party. These arrangements underline the strategic considerations that were at the heart of NARC, the formation of a powerful majority by beating KANU at ethnic arithmetic. The only policy issue to which all of its power brokers were committed was constitutional reform.

In contrast to previous opposition campaigns, NARC campaigned nationwide and managed to challenge KANU in all constituencies. In its election campaign, ethnicity featured, albeit at a toned-down level. The various leaders of NARC, and in particular, Kibaki, Raila, Ngilu, Musyoka, and Wamalwa, appealed to their communities to turn out in large numbers and

[118] See EU 2002.

[119] A copy of the MoU is attached in Badejo 2006.

to support NARC.[120] The crucial difference to previous elections was that negative rhetoric attacking other communities remained largely absent. This novelty was due to the fact that the two contending parties were headed by a Kikuyu candidate. Clearly NARC was the more national party of the two despite its lack of a strong Kalenjin element in its leadership. Nevertheless, at the time of going to the polls, it did bridge the division between the Kikuyu and the Luo.

Its campaign highlighted constitutional reform, the need to fight corruption, and the need to implement greater transparency in the country's decision-making process.[121] Kibaki at times tried to give the campaign a slightly ideological spin, calling for tax reduction and the privatization of state-run enterprises on a large scale.[122] The overarching theme of the campaign nevertheless was the notion of a united front against KANU and the need for democratic transition to become a reality.

The NARC election manifesto was fairly low in terms of programmatic content (32 percent). It strongly favored category 506 (Education Expansion: positive, 5.6 percentage points of the overall content), category 201 (Freedom and Human Rights, 3.8 percentage points), and category 606 (Social Harmony: positive). Bills passed by the NARC government also were not ideological in nature. What proved to be the most contested items on the NARC policy agenda was the strengthening of the anticorruption agency and the establishment of a new constitutional committee. Both would soon haunt the new government.

As outlined in Table 3.14, NARC's electoral support corresponded in almost all regions to the vote share that each region represented of the overall vote. Only in the Kalenjin-dominated Rift Valley did NARC underperform slightly.

In terms of its PNS, NARC achieved the highest value identified in Kenya. The PNS calculated on the basis of Afrobarometer 2003 data confirms this. Simultaneously, its PDS was the lowest found in Kenya and one of the lowest found in this study. Its electoral performance shows the catch-all nature of the party at the time of going to the polls. NARC's spectacular electoral triumph was hailed by many as a new beginning in the democratic history of Kenya. This was reflected in its new cabinet setup, as outlined in Table 3.15. Kibaki's 2003 cabinet included all communities and corresponded more accurately to the ethnic makeup of the country than all previous ones.

Immediately after NARC's electoral victory, Kenyan politics lapsed back into its modus operandi. Shortly after President Kibaki had appointed his cabinet, many in Raila's LDP felt shortchanged. The NARC cabinet did

[120] For an in-depth analysis of the 2002 campaign, see the edited volume by Maupeu et al. 2005.

[121] *Standard*, November 19, 2002.

[122] *Standard*, December 3, 2002.

TABLE 3.14. *Parties' Electoral Performance in 2002*

Province	NARC 2002	KANU 2002	Average Vote Share of Regions
Nairobi	9%	4%	7%
Coast	5%	7%	6%
North Eastern	0%	5%	1%
Eastern	18%	16%	18%
Central	18%	14%	17%
Rift Valley	20%	40%	24%
Western	15%	9%	12%
Nyanza	15%	5%	15%
TOTAL	100%	100%	100%

PDS NARC: 24/ average diverging points across time and space: 52
PNS NARC: .84 / average PNS across time and space: .67
PNS NARC based on Afrobarometer data collected in 2003: .93/ average PNS across time and space: .72
PNS NARC based on Afrobarometer data collected in 2005: .69/ average PNS across time and space: .72
PDS KANU: 42/ average diverging points across time and space: 52
PNS KANU: .73/ average PNS across time and space: .67
PNS KANU based on Afrobarometer data collected in 2003: .66/ average PNS across time and space: .72
PNS KANU based on Afrobarometer data collected in 2005: .52/ average PNS across time and space: .72

Source: Author's compilation on the basis of election data provided by the Kenyan Electoral Commission.

not achieve an equal share of the cabinet between NAK and the LDP.[123] Raila's supporters complained that the ministry of public works allocated to him was too small in scope.[124] In March 2003, Raila surprisingly failed to become the chairman of the Parliamentary Committee for Constitutional Reform because Kikuyu NARC MPs decided to opt for Paul Muite (Kikuyu), who had become an MP on the party ticket of a smaller opposition party. Muite also found the support of Kikuyu KANU MPs. This not only shows that ethnic loyalties proved stronger entities than parties, but also further indicates strong antipathy of the notion of a Luo prime minister on the side of the Kikuyu.[125] Kibaki's Kikuyu appointments further raised fears of a return of Kenyatta's hawkish Kikuyu elite, represented by Njenga Karume, John

[123] *Standard*, January 4, 2003, and *Standard*, January 29, 2003. Out of the 125 NARC MPs, 59 were allied to the LDP and 56 to the NAK.

[124] *Standard*, January 29, 2003.

[125] *Daily Nation*, March 20, 2003. See also Mutua 2008. Raila was expected to take over the commission on constitutional reform because he was promised the position of prime minister that the commission was expected to create.

TABLE 3.15. *Ethnic Composition of Kenya's 2003 Cabinet*

Community	Number of Cabinet Ministers Allocated	Percentage of Cabinet Ministers Allocated
GEMA	8	31%
Luo	4	15%
Kalenjin	3	12%
Luhya	4	15%
Kamba	2	8%
Other (smaller communities)	5	19%
TOTAL	26	100%

Source: Author's compilation based on Kenyan media sources.

Michuki, and Kiraitu Murungi,[126] who became members of the cabinet. All three had unlimited access to Kibaki, whereas others like Raila and Ngilu soon complained about marginalization by the president's cabinet. In addition to the old GEMA group, Kibaki's inner-circle further included a variety of Kikuyu businessmen who had previously supported his DP, such as Nat Kang'ethe (the chairman of Saatchi & Saatchi in Kenya), Joe Wanjui (a former industrialist, now the chancellor of the University of Nairobi and former close ally of Michuki in the days of Kenyatta), and Peter Kanyago (the former director of the Kenyan Tea Development Authority).[127] Taken together, they represented the kind of Kikuyu establishment many politicians – including Moi and Raila – had always seen as threatening.

The longer NARC was in power, the more apprehensive became the relationship between the Luo (and the non-Kikuyu) side of the NARC alliance and its Kikuyu counterpart. In particular, Raila and Kurungi, Kibaki's minister for justice and constitutional affairs, clashed on issues affecting constitutional reform.[128] Ironically, constitutional reform – the decade-old question of *majimboism* – became the major obstacle to the survival of NARC, even though constitutional reform had been the only genuine policy issue that had brought NARC together. Although Raila and his supporters called for the immediate creation of a prime minister with executive powers and a federal state structure, the conservative forces around Kibaki effectively tried to slow down the process (for details, see Mutua 2008). Tensions reached a peak in January 2004, when Kurungi proposed that the official representation of the government delegation at the national constitutional conference ("Bomas Conference") should not include Wamalwa, Raila, Ngilu, or indeed

[126] Karume was the chairman of the Gikuyu, Embu, and Merus welfare association in the 1970s, which aimed at ensuring the continuation of a Kikuyu presidency after Kenyatta's death, while Michuki was his assistant secretary-general.

[127] *Standard*, April 4, 2004.

[128] *Standard*, April 6, 2003, and *Standard*, November 28, 2004.

any other leading figure of NARC. The delegation list he put forward did not include any Luo or Kamba politicians.[129] Simultaneously, other ministers such as Ngilu or Anyang' Nyong'o also faced a wall of Kikuyu leaders opposed to any of their ideas or initiatives inside the cabinet.[130] In June 2004, Kibaki appointed several opposition leaders into governmental positions, which he justified on the grounds of the potential benefits of political inclusion. His unwillingness to consult all other NARC members over this decision further exacerbated tensions inside the governing alliance.[131]

These various theatres of conflict not only affected the day-to-day work of the government but soon were reverberated inside the NARC. Kibaki and his allies started various attempts to take total control of NARC by building up parallel party structures.[132] Consequently, the leading players inside NARC consistently rejected the idea of merging the NARC's member parties, which Kibaki advocated. Less than two years after its formation, the LDP and FORD-K boycotted the NARC party congress. At the NARC congress, several Kikuyu ministers dominated the political agenda. In addition, the congress was attended by several Kikuyu opposition leaders, most notably Paul Muite.[133] The NARC congress decided to engage in a major recruitment drive and thus in forming a party on its own. PNS values calculated on the basis of Afrobarometer data that were collected in 2005 indicate the increasing loss of trust the Kenyan electorate as a whole had in NARC. Although in 2003 its PNS was .93 shortly after the elections, over two years later, it had declined to a value of .69, which is below the cross-country average value of .71.

NARC finally collapsed after Kibaki announced a constitutional referendum scheduled for November 21, 2005. Even though throughout 2003 and 2004 the National Constitutional Conference had called for the establishment of a strong Prime Minister, the constitutional draft put to the people of Kenya by the Kibaki government ("Wako draft") still contained a strong presidency.[134] Growing tensions between FORD-K and the LDP further contributed to the party's breakdown. After Wamalwa's death in September 2003, Kibaki had appointed Moodi Awori, another Luhya, as his new vice-president. This provoked tension between FORD-K and the LDP, as

[129] *Standard*, January 31, 2004.

[130] *Standard*, November 28, 2004. Professor Nyong'o was returned to parliament and his SDP became a member of NARC. The same was true of Ngilu's NPK.

[131] *Daily Nation*, July 2, 2004.

[132] *Standard*, October 31, 2004.

[133] *Standard*, December 5, 2004. At the same time, various NARC member parties held their own national congresses. Their line-ups confirmed the results of these parties as mostly mono-ethnic. The LDP never held a national congress after its take-over by the KANU rebels.

[134] For a very detailed analysis of the different constitutional drafts negotiated at various national conferences, see Mutua 2008: 185–204.

TABLE 3.16. *Constitutional Proposals Compared*

Section/Issue	Draft Constitution (Bomas draft)	Proposed Constitution (Wako Draft)
executive	president as Head of State but largely ceremonial. prime Minister with executive powers.	president as chief executive president appoints and dismisses Prime Minister impeachment of President by 75% of MPs
devolution	creates quasi-federal system. establishes strong regional governments.	districts are basic units of devolution. district assembly elected.

Source: Mutua 2008: 184–204.

Awori was a leading LDP figure.[135] With FORD-K MP Musikari Kombo emerging as the new FORD-K leader, an intense political fight developed between the two parties over the Luhya vote and political domination over Western province.[136] On various occasions, Kombo denounced Awori and LDP Luhya Minister Mudavadi as traitors of the Luhya. Other prominent FORD-K MPs such as Soita Shitanda and Bonny Khalwale explicitly warned LDP leaders not to enter Western province, as it was "owned" by FORD-K.[137]

During the months leading up to and following the constitutional referendum, Kenya's political parties transformed into a state of fluidity, which made Kenyan party politics increasingly unpredictable. For the purpose of the referendum, the LDP faction of NARC teamed up with parts of KANU and formed the NO camp, together with Ngilu's NPK (formerly SDP), campaigning under the banner of an orange. The DP, FORD-K, FORD-P, and the many smaller parties that had originally made up the NAK came together in the YES camp, campaigning under the banner of a banana. Table 3.16 summarizes the different stances between the supporters of the draft constitution as supported by ODM-Kenya ("Bomas draft") and the constitutional amendment package put forward by the government ("Wako draft").

The outcome was the humiliation of the president and his YES camp. Although the results say less about political affiliations than election results – referenda provide an opportunity to raise one's opinion on a single policy issue and are thus less indicative of political affiliations of ethnic communities – it nevertheless showed the weakened position of Kibaki, whose campaign was unable to gain a majority outside the Kikuyu-dominated areas.

135 *Daily Nation*, December 7 2003.

136 *Daily Nation*, October 19, 2003.

137 *The East African Standard*, December 21, 2004. Party recruitment drives in Western province frequently caused violence between LDP and FORD-K supporters.

TABLE 3.17. *Political Changes Immediately After the 2005 Referendum*

Pre 2005 Referendum	Post 2005 Referendum
government alliance: NARC member parties: FORD-K, DP, NPK (formerly SDP) and 11 smaller parties	government alliance: NARC-K member parties: FORD-K, FORD-P DP, KANU[138] plus smaller parties

Source: Compiled from various media reports.

In an unprecedented step, Kibaki sacked his entire cabinet and called for a government of national unity, appointing prominent members of KANU and FORD-P to government, now known under the label of NARC-Kenya. In return, the LDP refused to return to the cabinet table, and once more Raila Odinga became the leader of the country's opposition, now known under the label of the Orange Democratic Movement–Kenya (ODM-K). Table 3.17 summarizes the process of reformation on the government benches.

In this study, NARC proves to be the second example – after KANU's merger with the NDP into New KANU – of a governing party that failed to bridge the cleavage line between the Kikuyu and the Luo. Again, unlimited access to state patronage was not a sufficient condition to overcome the centrifugal tendencies of ethnicity.

NARC's successor, NARC-K, officially opened as a party on May 24, 2006, under the leadership of the minister for immigration, Gideon Konchela (Masai).[139] Due to a lack of money and an acute shortage of registered party members, NARC-K was never able to engage in membership recruitment drives or grassroots elections.[140] At no point in time did the party manage to build additional organizational structures. It never issued party statutes. At its inception, the party opted to confer membership to all MPs that showed loyalty to Kibaki.[141] Although the party could quickly agree on Kibaki as its presidential candidate for many months, it proved unable to agree on a leadership setup. A variety of high-ranking party MPs engaged in endless debates regarding which personality would be best suited to become the party's leader. In the end, Raphael Tuju (Luo) emerged as the new chairman. His communal background should not be overstated or misinterpreted. Although a confidante of Kibaki, Tuju never managed to establish himself as political representative of the Luo community. As a former development consultant, he had entered the cabinet as a novice politician. Attempts to establish himself as a Luo leader in opposition to Raila proved futile, and his decision to stick with Kibaki proved his electoral downfall in the 2007

[138] The status of KANU is not clear. See debate about opposition parties that follows.
[139] *Standard*, May 24, 2006.
[140] *Standard*, May 26, 2007 and *Standard*, July 7, 2007.
[141] *Standard*, January 7, 2007.

elections. Tuju's failure to rally Luo support behind him was the principal reason why his leadership of NARC-K was heavily contested by other party heavyweights such as Musalia Mudavadi (Luhya) or Arap Kirwa (Kalenjin) from the very day Tuju was appointed as Narc-K chairman.[142] What further undermined the party were allegations that the Kikuyu leadership of the party had attempted to rig the failed grassroots elections in their favor. Kibaki's re-appointment of David Mwiraria (Kikuyu), his former minister of finance, into the cabinet after Mwiraria had been forced to resign over his involvement in various corruption scandals further contributed to the image of NARC-K as a party driven by cut-throat Kikuyu interests.[143]

With NARC-K unable to move forward in any meaningful way and the 2007 elections around the corner, Kibaki decided to form a new political vehicle to secure his reelection in late September 2007.[144] Just like its predecessor NARC-K, the newly founded Party of National Unity (PNU) lacked Luo participation yet did include a variety of representatives from the Luhya, the Kalenjin,[145] and the Coastal groups, as well as of the Masai and many smaller communities. Also in line with NARC-K, it never conducted any party elections or membership drives but instead remained an entity designed to rally support around Kibaki.

Although it is not possible to speak of one governing party in Kenya during the third period, one can identify various alliances structured around the Luo-Kikuyu divide, which eventually pitched Kibaki against Odinga in the December 2007 elections. At the moment of its foundation, NARC was a catch-all party in terms of its electoral performance and rhetoric. In terms of its declared goal, its factions, and, most importantly, its inability to bridge Kenya's dominant ethnic cleavage lines over the long run, it was an ethnic alliance and therefore is classified as such.

KANU, THE ORANGE DEMOCRATIC MOVEMENT–KENYA, AND THE ORANGE DEMOCRATIC MOVEMENT

In terms of its electoral rhetoric, KANU mirrored the 2002 NARC campaign. It supported the formation of an all-inclusive government, declared war on corruption, and called for far-reaching health reforms.[146] Similarly, the Kenyatta campaign called for a renewal of Kenyan politics, which it associated with a young president. Accordingly, at his rallies Kenyatta called on older Kenyan politicians not to stand in the way of generational renewal, which was more than a subtle hint at Kibaki's mature age.[147] Many

[142] *Standard*, May 4, 2007. While campaigning in Nyanza province, Tuju's entourage frequently encountered violence by the local population.

[143] *Standard*, July 7, 2007, and *Standard*, July 27, 2007.

[144] *Standard*, September 27, 2007.

[145] Kibaki's reelection campaign was backed by Daniel arap Moi.

[146] *Standard*, November 19, 2002.

[147] *Standard*, December 2, 2002.

leading KANU leaders followed his lead, including Musalia Mudavadi (Luhya), Kenyatta's running mate.[148] As already outlined, ethnicity featured considerably less as both parties were putting forward a Kikuyu presidential candidate to the electorate. Ethnically inclined statements – to the extent that they featured at all – were employed to reassure communities that KANU's presidential candidate would work toward the benefit of the community. Mudavadi (Luhya), for example, informed the Luhya that "when Uhuru Kenyatta takes over the leadership of this country Kenya, he will form the next government with mutembe (Luhya community) children."[149] The same occurred among the Kalenjin, where William Ruto served as spokesperson for the Kenyatta campaign (Jonyo 2003). KANU attempted to sell a Kikuyu presidency to core KANU communities, and in particular, the Kalenjin revealed the instrumental nature of ethnicity in Kenyan party politics. The ethnic spin of NARC's as well as KANU's campaign had strong elements of inclusion, in great contrast to the rhetoric of KANU in the 1990s.

KANU's 2002 election manifesto displayed a further decline in the party's programmatic content (28 percent). Among the programmatic categories, it emphasized category 506 (Education Expansion: positive, seven percentage points of the overall content), whereas the remaining programmatic categories dwell at very low levels.

The party's electoral output displayed a medium to low PDS and a high to medium PNS, which means that KANU maintained its catch-all character with regard to its electoral indicators (see Table 3.12). It is interesting to note, however, that in 2002 the party's ability to gain votes on a national scale was lower than in 1997. In retrospect, this underlines Moi's ability to reach out to groups outside the core KANU clientele in 1997 and confirms the devastating impact of the break-away of the LDP on the party's electoral fortunes.

KANU's electoral defeat proved too much for the party to withstand, which confirms our previous classification of ethnic alliance in periods 1 and 2; party coherence – to the extent that it was present between the core groups that made up the party – was facilitated by access to state resources. Shortly after the 2002 elections, former Vice-President Mudavadi (Luhya) ditched the party, thus further undermining the party's support base in Western province.[150] Just as with NARC, the opposition became deeply divided along ethnic lines. In the months following its defeat, tensions increased between Uhuru Kenyatta's Kikuyu camp and the Kalenjin faction led by Moi's previous right-hand man, Nicholas Biwott. At the party elections in February 2005, KANU managed once more to include representatives of all major communities, with Kenyatta taking over Moi's position as chairman; Chris Okemo (Luhya), Noah Ngala (Coastal), Dalmas Otieno (Luo), and

[148] *Standard*, December 7, 2002.

[149] *Standard*, December 19, 2002.

[150] *BBC Monitoring Africa*, November 22, 2003.

Henry Kosgey (Kalenjin) serving as Kenyatta's vice-chairmen; and Nicholas Biwott claiming the position of secretary-general after being defeated by Kenyatta for the party leadership.[151] Immediately afterward, Biwott started to launch an alternative party in the Rift Valley.[152] KANU's PNS based on 2003 and 2005 Afrobarometer data confirms the decline of political support among Kenya's key communities. Both the 2003 and 2005 PNS values are below the cross-country average. The decline from .66 to .52 shows the increasing lack of support among those Kikuyu who voted for Kenyatta in the 2002 elections.

Given the very visible disintegration of NARC, public interest in KANU began to fade in the nationwide media. Its political stance never followed a clearly articulated agenda. KANU formally joined the government after Kibaki appointed former GEMA leader Njenga Karume to his cabinet in late June 2004. Karume had long been a major sponsor of Kibaki's DP in the 1990s yet had temporarily shifted his support to Kenyatta as he saw Kikuyu interests best represented by the son of his former mentor. Given Karume's old allegiance to Kibaki, however, this act was not representative of KANU as a party, which remained in opposition. For the purpose of the constitutional referendum, the Kenyatta wing of KANU teamed up with the NO campaign, whereas the Biwott wing appeared to take a somewhat neutral stance (Lynch 2006). Following Kibaki's humiliating defeat and the dismissal of his cabinet, the opposition changed in terms of format and composition.

Former government ministers and leading NARC figures, most notably Raila Odinga (Luo), Najib Balala (Coastal), Kalonzo Musyoka (Kamba), and Anyang Nyong'o (Luo), teamed up with (KANU) opposition figures Musalia Mudavadi (Luhya) and William Ruto (Kalenjin) to form the Orange Democratic Movement–Kenya (ODM-K). Initially, Uhuru Kenyatta and KANU were part of this alliance, and Kenyatta was at times seen as a potential future presidential ODM-K candidate. After the referendum, it was unclear whether KANU was supporting the government or whether it constituted part of the opposition. As the 2008 elections drew closer, Kenyatta decided to shift his loyalty to Kibaki's Party of National Unity. Yet until the run-up to the 2008 elections, Kenyatta was a member of the so-called "Pentagon," consisting of the eight leading figures of ODM-K, which apart from him included Raila (Luo), Musyoka (Kamba), Mudavadi (Luhya), Balala (Coastal), Kenyatta (Kikuyu), Ruto (Kalenjin), ole Ntimama (Masai), and Anyang' Nyong'o (Luo). On August 24, 2006, ODM-K was

[151] *Daily Nation*, February 2, 2005.

[152] *The East African Standard*, January 22, 2006. Ruto was at times advocated as a presidential contender by KANU Rift Valley MPs. For a deeper analysis on the political reorientation of the Kalenjin after Moi's departure from power, see Lynch 2006 and 2008.

TABLE 3.18. *Composition of Opposition After 2005 Referendum*

Pre 2005 Referendum	Post 2005 Referendum
opposition: KANU, FORD-P[153]	opposition: ODM-K member parties: LDP, KANU

Source: Author's compilation.

constituted as a new party and served as de facto new opposition following the disintegration of NARC.

Table 3.18 summarizes the new composition of the opposition, which grew in numbers after the failed 2005 constitutional referendum.[154]

To fully understand the impact of ethnicity on opposition and government, it is noteworthy to look at the disintegration of NARC at the level of individual parliamentarians. Of the 122 MPs elected on the NARC ticket, 54 MPs remained loyal to the government. Of these, 40 were from the Kikuyu, the Embu, or the Meru (GEMA) communities. With the sole exception of one legislator (Maoka Ntonyiri, KANU[155]), all Kikuyu MPs threw their support behind Kibaki. By comparison, 52 MPs took an antigovernment stance after the referendum. With the exception of one legislator, all Luo MPs decided to back ODM-K. A smaller group of MPs decided to take a neutral stance. All of these were largely unknown politicians who left their options open to exchange their parliamentary support on an ad hoc basis. See Table 3.19.

This illustrates the ethnic nature of party wings inside NARC and KANU/ODM-K; ethnicity proved to be a more reliable base for political loyalty than political parties. Even though government and opposition managed to overcome their previous disintegration into mono-ethnic entities, both failed to bridge the division between the Luo and the Kikuyu.

In terms of its rhetoric, ODM-K called on Kibaki to stop favoring his own tribesmen in public appointments. On looking back at his time in the Kibaki cabinet, Raila stated that "only one community was being favored with high-profile jobs while others were being hounded out of office."[156] A distinct rhetorical element that accused the Kikuyu of favoritism was thus

[153] FORD-P was in opposition until late June 2004, when Kibaki nominated FORD-P presidential candidate Simon Nyachae to the cabinet.

[154] *Standard*, April 6, 2007; *Standard*, August 26, 2008; *Standard*, August 27, 2008. ODM-K agreed on a leadership setup, which in essence was similar to the one represented by its founding members with the exception of Kikuyu participation. After the departure of Kenyatta, ODM-K lacked a foothold among the Kikuyu. The same is true of its Council of Elders that was set up in April 2007.

[155] *Daily Nation*, December 11, 2005.

[156] *Standard*, October 9, 2006.

TABLE 3.19. *Situation Inside the NARC Parliamentary Group*

progovernment MPs in total: 54	GEMA: 40
	Coastal: 5
	Luhya: 4
	Kalenjin: 2
	Masai 1
	Luo: 1
	Other 1
antigovernment MPs in total: 52	Luo: 23
	Luhya: 12
	Kamba: 9
	Coastal: 4
	GEMA: 1
	Kalenjin: 1
	Masai: 1
	Other: 1
undecided MPs in total: 16	Luhya: 11
	Other: 2
	GEMA: 2
	Kamba: 1

Source: *Daily Nation*, December 11, 2005.

visible from ODM-K's inception.[157] Simultaneously, the party tried to position itself as one that cherishes the people's will – after all, it had emerged as a movement that had managed to deal a blow to Kibaki's *other-than-promised* constitutional draft. Raila further tried to portray himself in ideological clouds, making frequent use of Marxist quotes decrying the working conditions of Kenyan manual laborers.[158] At times he referred to ODM-K as a center-left movement, which other ODM-K leaders never subscribed to.[159] ODM's 2007 election manifesto displays low programmatic content (28 percent), which illustrates that one should not over-interpret Raila's left-wing bias when looking at the party as a whole.[160] Taken together, ODM-K tried to foster an image of itself as a party of good governance and national unity. This fact notwithstanding, its rhetoric contained aversions to the Kikuyu.

After the split of NARC into the PNU and ODM-K, ODM-K again underwent a period of internal turmoil in the months leading up to the party

157 See also *Standard*, May 7, 2007.

158 *Standard*, April 20, 2007.

159 *Standard*, March 18, 2007.

160 Data from the 2007 ODM manifesto (i.e., from the party that constituted the larger part of ODM-K) do not fall into the fourth observation period but have been used to verify the party's incorporation of programmatic ideas.

congress that was to decide on its presidential candidate. Since the formation of the LDP, tensions had been visible between Raila and Musyoka. During the LDP's grassroots elections in May 2006, local candidates were aligning with either of the two, and many Raila allies such as Najib Balala (Coastal) failed to secure local leadership positions.[161] For the best part of ODM-K's existence, Musyoka was heralded as the alliance's most suited presidential aspirant. On June 16, 2007, the party's Council of Elders issued a statement declaring Musyoka the candidate with the best chance of beating Kibaki. It further advocated for the selection of its presidential candidate by the method of consensus rather than by electing him or her by delegates.[162] This proved an unacceptable condition to an ever-increasing amount of high-ranking party officials the closer that the party moved to take its decision. Ultimately, the personal rivalry between Raila and Musyoka led to the break-up of ODM-K. Much of this rivalry dates back to the late 1980s, when Musyoka had been an aspiring KANU politician (and in the 1990s, Kenya's youngest ever foreign minister) while Raila had been imprisoned for being involved in illegal political activities.[163] Therefore, personal ambitions rather than ethnic antagonism tore ODM-K apart. On August 14, 2007, the Raila camp broke away and formed the Orange Democratic Movement (ODM), taking most of ODM-K's leading officials with him.[164]

Both KANU and ODM-K (before the split into ODM and ODM-K) are classified as ethnic-alliance parties. KANU once more displays a national setup at the early stages in period 3. However, it soon fell apart into a Kikuyu and Kalenjin wing before it departed into political oblivion. ODM-K initially also included leading politicians from all communities, yet Uhuru's departure meant that a national leadership setup was unsustainable.

KENYA AFTER THE 2007 ELECTIONS

Kenya's 2007 presidential and parliamentary elections resulted in one of the largest turnouts in history. Its aftermath led to ethnic clashes on an unprecedented scale, leaving thousands of Kenyan citizens dead and hundreds of thousands displaced. The scale and the impact of the 2007 clashes constituted a novelty and carried very strong ethnic undertones (Human Rights Watch 2003, 2008, Elischer 2008).

At the beginning of the fourth observation period, Kenya found itself in the same political setup as after the 2002 elections: an ethnically balanced government presiding over a vast parliamentary majority that aims at tackling constitutional reform and in particular tackling the issues of the

[161] *Standard*, May 29, 2006.
[162] *Daily Nation*, June 17, 2007.
[163] *Standard*, March 18, 2007.
[164] *Daily Nation*, August 14, 2007.

TABLE 3.20. *Ethnic Composition of Kenya's 2008 Cabinet*

Community	Number of Cabinet Ministers Allocated	Percentage of Cabinet Allocated
GEMA:	8	20%
Luo	6	15%
Kalenjin	5	12%
Luhya	8	20%
Kamba	3	7%
other (smaller communities)	11	26%
TOTAL	41	100%

Source: Author's compilation based on Kenyan media sources.

all-domineering office of the president and majimboism (Anderson 2005, Kindiki and Ambani 2005, Lynch 2006). Table 3.20 outlines the cabinet composition of the Kenyan government after the formation of the externally induced grand coalition (Brown 2009). As in 2002, it is representative of the Kenyan state yet heavily over-bloated in terms of the number of ministerial appointments.

Thus far, the devastating loss of human life in early 2008 did not result in a new era of party politics. Reviewing the dynamics of Kenyan party politics, it seems unlikely that the current political setup is sustainable. The events of early 2008 not only confirm the high salience of ethnicity, but also further validate Horowitz's (2000) expectations about politics in countries in which the formation of nonethnic parties is unsuccessful. Accordingly, electoral performance turns into an ethnic census, which in turn causes ethnic violence. Table 3.21 outlines the election results of the vote share of each province for each party.

Nearly two-thirds of ODM-K's electoral support comes from Eastern province, the home province of the Kamba. Both electoral indicators prove it to be a mono-ethnic party. The ODM derived two-thirds of its electoral base from the Rift Valley and Nyanza province, which is indicative of its Luo and Kalenjin support. It underperformed dramatically in Central and Eastern. Its PNS is slightly above average, and so is its PDS. This is indicative of a catch-all party, yet the circumstances of its formation, its lack of Kikuyu participation, and its rhetoric are more indicative of a multiethnic alliance. The PNU managed to gain strong support among the Kikuyu in Central province yet remains virtually absent in Nyanza. Party composition and election results show that the division between Kikuyu and Kalenjin has been bridged, whereas the division between Kikuyu and the Luo has not. As a result, both ODM and PNU must be seen as ethnic alliances.

At the time of writing, Kenya is approaching the 2013 elections. Although formally its grand coalition remained intact, deep divisions characterize its various ethnic pillars ever since its formation (Hornsby 2012). The legal

TABLE 3.21. *Parties' Electoral Performance in 2007*

Province	PNU (%)	ODM (%)	ODM-K (%)	Average Vote Share of Regions (%)
Nairobi	8	8	5	6
Coast	4	7	8	6
North Eastern	1	2	2	2
Eastern	18	2	62	17
Central	38	1	0	18
Rift Valley	22	36	16	25
Western	9	14	4	10
Nyanza	0	30	3	16
TOTAL	100	100	100	100

PDS ODM-K: 86 / average diverging points across time and space: 52
PNS ODM-K: .49 / average PNS across time and space: .67
PDS ODM: 62 / average diverging points across time and space: 52
PNS ODM: .70 / average PNS across time and space: .67
PDS PNU: 46 / average diverging points across time and space: 52
PNS PNU: .66 / average PNS across time and space: .67

Source: Author's compilation based on official election results provided by the Kenyan Electoral Commission.

position of Raila Odinga as prime minister was never clarified. Both Raila and Kibaki did their best to compromise the other by leaking information about corruption affairs of their respective political foes. Inside the ODM, Raila was regularly at loggerheads with the Kalenjin camp of Ruto. This was particularly visible during the 2010 constitutional referendum campaign and in the referendum results, as Ruto managed once more to rally the Kalenjin to vote as an ethnic bloc against the constitution. Inside the PNU, tension erupted between Kenyatta and Musyoka over the Kibaki succession. The investigations of the International Criminal Court into the role of Kenyatta and Ruto during the ethnic clashes of 2008 greatly complicated the nomination procedures. Thus, although the coalition stuck together and produced a new constitution, it failed in ending the ethnic feuds, which have haunted Kenya since independence (Economist Intelligence Unit Reports 2009, 2010, 2011, 2012; Africa Yearbook 2009, 2010, 2011, 2012; Hornsby 2012).

POLITICAL PARTIES IN AFRICA: FINDINGS FROM KENYA

The analysis of Kenyan party politics has shown all significant parties in Kenya to be ethnic in nature. This applies both to government and opposition. On several occasions, parties managed to become nationwide forces, all of which were unsustainable and born out of ethnic-strategic considerations.

What is striking about the Kenyan case is that party fragmentation occurs regularly and affects both government and opposition. Access to unlimited state patronage – the privilege of any governing party – has proven deficient in countering the centrifugal tendencies of ethnicity.

Given the ubiquity of ethnic parties, I classify the Kenyan party system as ethnic. This notwithstanding, programmatic ideas do feature in Kenyan politics. Kenyan party manifestos (of the DP and SDP) at times display a high programmatic content. This proves the compatibility of ethnicity with programmatic ideas. It further confirms the conceptualization of a programmatic party as national in composition; neither the SDP nor the DP could be envisioned as any of the nonethnic types given the disaggregated results for each indicator. Yet these two parties provide initial evidence that programmatic ideas do occur in African politics, even though they are overshadowed by other social phenomena. The disintegration of FORD into FORD-A and FORD-K, for example, incorporated strong personal elements and cannot simply be reduced to ethnic politics. The same is true of the disintegration of ODM-Kenya into ODM and ODM-K.

It would be wrong to deny that Kenyan politicians had an intention to include groups that are on the opposite end of ethnic cleavage lines and a willingness to change things for the better. The formation of FORD, New KANU, and NARC demonstrates that political leaders are (at least temporarily) willing to cooperate with as many groups as possible. Yet ever since the return of democracy, all attempts to form nonethnic parties have failed. Despite good intentions, parties eventually became structured around the country's dominant ethnic cleavage lines. For individual politicians, ethnicity has remained the building block of their respective careers; both Kibaki and Raila had to spend significant time and effort to position themselves as their respective communities' uncontested leader before they could qualify as serious contenders for the presidency on a multiethnic ticket. After his break-away from Raila, Kalonzo Musyoka has been similarly successful among the Kamba and it does not come as surprise that he is regarded as a potential Kibaki successor of a Kamba-Kikuyu alliance in 2012. The same applies to William Ruto with regard to the Kalenjin.

The distinction between ethnic alliances and catch-all parties has shown particular analytical use in the Kenyan context. To be in a position to theoretically differentiate between multiethnic parties that bridge dominant cleavage lines and those that fail to do so makes the identification of ethnic parties possible. Table 3.22 displays a summary of all results for all parties examined.

It is noteworthy to reflect on the differences between party politics in Kenya as it played out in the 1990s and how it manifested itself in the decade thereafter. Although the first two observation periods were characterized by an increasing ethnicization of political parties, from the second half of the second observation period onward, Kenyan politics was marked

TABLE 3.22. *Summary of Disaggregated Results for all Political Parties in Kenya*

	Party Scoring Sheet										
	Party Goals		Electoral Strategy		Organizational Structure			Social Base			
Party: FORD-K Observation Period	Motive of Formation	Rhetoric	Electoral Rhetoric	Content of Election Manifesto	National Coverage	Party Factions	Party Apparatus	Leadership Composition	Cabinet Composition	PDS and PNS	Classification
T1	pro-democracy; provide platform for FORD breakaway:	catch-all first then ethnic	catch-all	low	low to medium	ethnic	not visible	failing to bridge cleavages	n/a	high to very high; medium to low	ethnic alliance
T2	pro-democracy; provide platform for FORD breakaway:	empty	catch-all	low	low	based on individuals from one group	not visible	drawn from one group	n/a	medium to high; low to very low	mono-ethnic
Across Time	increasingly mono-ethnic	empty	catch-all	low	low	based on individuals from one group	not visible	drawn from one group	n/a	high to very high; low to very low	mono-ethnic
Party: Ford-A Observation Period											
T1	pro-democratic provide platform for FORD breakaway:	catch-all; ethnic	ethnic	low	medium	personalistic	not visible	failing to bridge cleavages	n/a	medium to high; medium to low	ethnic alliance
Party: NDP Observation Period											
T2	FORD-K Luo break-away	ethnic	ethnic	low	low	none	strong links with Luo elders	unknown	n/a	very high; very low	mono-ethnic
Party: SDP Observation Period											
T2	promotion of ideas	ethnic; pro-grammatic	ethnic	high/ due to policy overstretch	medium to low	based on individuals	n/a	failing to bridge cleavages	n/a	high to very high; low to very low	**mono-ethnic**

(continued)

TABLE 3.22 (*continued*)

	Party Scoring Sheet										
	Party Goals		Electoral Strategy		Organizational Structure			Social Base			
Party: DP Observation Period	Motive of Formation	Rhetoric	Electoral Rhetoric	Content of Election Manifesto	National Coverage	Party Factions	Party Apparatus	Leadership Composition	Cabinet Composition	PDS and PNS	Classification
T1	pro-democracy; promotion of ideas	catch-all and program-matic	catch-all and program-matic	high	medium to high	ethnic	important role of Kikuyu leaders	failing to bridge cleavages	n/a	medium to high; medium to low	**ethnic alliance**
T2	pro-democracy; promotion of ideas	catch-all	catch-all	high	medium to high	none	important role of Kikuyu leaders	drawn from one major group	n/a	medium to high; medium to low	**mono-ethnic**
Across Time	pro-democracy; promotion of ideas	catch-all	catch-all	high	medium	none	important role of Kikuyu leaders	drawn from one major group	n/a	medium to high; medium to low	**mono-ethnic**
Party: KANU Observation Period											
T1	catch-all with socialist aims	ethnic	catch-all; ethnic	low	high	based on individuals	important role of Kalenjin elders and elders of smaller groups	bridging cleavages	failing to bridge cleavages	medium; medium to high	**ethnic alliance**
T2	catch-all though initially socialist	ethnic	catch-all; ethnic	low	high	ethnic	not visible	failing to bridge cleavages in the long-run	failing to bridge cleavages	medium to low; medium to high	**ethnic alliance**
T3	catch-all	catch-all	catch-all	low	high	ethnic	not visible	failing to bridge cleavages	n/a	medium to low; medium to high	**ethnic alliance**
Across Time	catch-all	ethnic	catch-all; ethnic	low	high	ethnic	important role of elders	failing to bridge cleavages in the long-run despite "integrative moments"	failing to bridge cleavages	medium to low; medium to high	**ethnic alliance**
Party: NARC Observation Period											
T3	claim power and constitutional change	catch-all	promoting unity; catch-all	Low	high	ethnic	not visible; no grassroots	bridging cleavages in the short term	bridging cleavages in the short	low to very low; high to very high	**ethnic alliance**

Source: Author's compilation.

by attempts to create catch-all parties. Although all of these attempts failed, Kenyan leaders reacted to their previous inability to challenge KANU. Following the spectacular victory of NARC, reaching out to as many groups as possible now appears to be the rule of the day; mono-ethnic parties have given way to much broader ethnic alliances. This shows that even though ethnicity exercises great salience in Kenya's party system, the system itself is not static. Changes in political strategies do occur, although they fall short of bridging dominant cleavage lines. The turn toward more inclusive multiethnic alliances has led to reoccurring processes of party merger, disintegration, and renewed merger. Acknowledging the changing dynamics of Kenya's party system over time makes the transformation of the system from an ethnic one into a nonethnic one possible. With the exception of ODM-K, mono-ethnic parties have now ceased to matter. In the medium to long run, this might cause Kenyan politicians to recognize the benefits of reaching out across the Kikuyu-Kalenjin and the Kikuyu-Luo divide in a sustainable manner. This might happen for purely ulterior (i.e., strategic) motives and yet might lead to the formation of nonethnic parties.

Overall, I find ethnic parties to be the dominant party type in Kenya. My first empirical case clearly confirmed some of the worries political scientists have raised about the feasibility of multiparty competition in ethnically segmented societies. The return of party politics to Kenya has contributed to a further strengthening of ethnic division between communities that have historically been at opposing ends of cleavage lines. Democratic competition under Moi did not vitiate the tensions between the Kikuyu and the Kalenjin but rather fostered them. The same is true of the relationship between the Luo and the Kikuyu under the presidency of Kibaki. Ethnic clashes have haunted Kenya before or after every election since 1992, with the sole exception of 2002, when parties pursued a more inclusive approach than previously and both presidential contenders originated from the same community. Kenya's political history since 1991 thus points to a mutually reinforcing relationship between ethnic parties, their methods of electoral mobilization, and electoral violence. The next two chapters apply my party typology to Namibia and Ghana. They illustrate that in contrast to Kenya, political party competition in Africa is not exclusively structured along ethnic lines.

4

Namibia

The Dominance of Nonethnic Parties

In Kenya, ethnicity is a major obstacle for the formation of stable political parties. All parties could be identified as ethnic parties. Kenya is representative of countries in which ethnic parties prevail. The Kenya case further confirmed that ethnic divisions can lead to the formation of ethnic parties. Ethnic parties in turn can have detrimental effects on state stability.

The case of Namibia demonstrates that nonethnic parties exist and endure in Africa. This chapter provides apt evidence that Namibia's dominant party, the South West African People's Organization (SWAPO), is the prototype of a catch-all party. For long, the Democratic Turnhalle Alliance (DTA) was the official parliamentary opposition party (1989–2005). The DTA is the prototype of a multiethnic alliance. The evolving dynamics of party competition in Namibia are particularly intriguing. The coexistence of an ethnic opposition does not cause the disintegration of the nonethnic party in government, as predicted by Horowitz (2000). Following the 2005 elections, the Congress of Democrats (CoD) managed to become the new official parliamentary position. The CoD is another example of a catch-all party. A mixed-party system thus transformed into a nonethnic party system. In Namibia, enduring party competition does not foster ethnic antagonism but leads to the rise of nonethnic parties.

Namibia has been a multiparty democracy since its independence in March 1989. As Namibian parties antecede the independent Namibian state, the first part of this chapter is devoted to the historical background against which democratic contest unfolded. Subsequently, four observation periods are covered. The only party that is both effective and significant is the governing SWAPO. The official opposition is only statistically effective. Both the CoD and the DTA lack coalition or blackmail potential. However, a more comprehensive perspective of the Namibian party system requires an analysis of both the governing as well as the strongest opposition party. See Table 4.1.

TABLE 4.1. *Overview of Namibian Cases and Observations*

Observation Period	Significant and/or Effective Party
Period 1 (1989–1994)	SWAPO DTA
Period 2 (1994–1999)	SWAPO DTA
Period 3 (1999–2004)	SWAPO DTA
Period 4 (2004–2009)	SWAPO CoD

Source: Author's compilation.

APARTHEID, ETHNIC CLEAVAGE LINES, AND POLITICAL PARTIES

At independence in March 1989, Namibia's main political parties had been long in existence. SWAPO had its origins in the Ovambo People's Congress (OPC). The OPC was founded by Namibian migrant workers in Cape Town in 1958. After it was renamed Ovambo's People's Organization (OPO), it opened an office in Windhoek (Pütz et al. 1990: 119–126). Although its name indicates an ethnic agenda, its original purpose was to protest the harsh conditions of the South African contract labor system, which – given the mechanism of the system and the geographical location of the Ovambo community – affected mainly workers from Ovamboland. Right from its inception, the OPO represented a nationalist challenge to the continuation of apartheid rule (Lindeke et al. 1992, Cliffe 1994). Sam Nujoma (Ovambo), one of the founding members of the OPO, the OPC, and SWAPO, described the major stimulus behind the formation of OPO as follows:

> (...) we the youth, set out to break the system of ethnic segregation, even by intermarriages, and by the close alliance we from the North had formed with the Herero's Chiefs' Council, and with the Damaras and Namas United Front. (Nujoma 2001: 46)

Accordingly, the OPO constitution called for the creation of a democratic government, the territorial unity of what the apartheid state referred to as Ovamboland, Hereroland, Damaraland, and Namaland. Its ultimate goal was independence from South Africa (Nujoma 2001). Its constitution implied the future SWAPO slogan of "One Namibia, One Nation." The OPO was renamed SWAPO and managed to establish itself as Namibia's major nationalist movement.[1] In 1976, the party was designated the status

[1] For many years, SWAPO had to compete with the South West African National Union (SWANU) to become Namibia's leading nationalist movement. For an analysis of what led to the disintegration of SWANU, see Herneit-Sievers (1984) and Leys and Saul (1995).

of the sole and the authentic representative of the Namibian people by the United Nations. Little is known about SWAPO activism in its early years (Ansprenger 1984). Its leadership line-up of 1969 indicates its all-inclusive nature. Sam Nujoma (Ovambo) managed to establish himself as uncontested leader and party president. Its chairman and founding member was Herero and several of its administrative secretaries Damara (Geingob 2004). In 1976, an internal crisis hit the SWAPO leadership in its Zambian exile. A massive exodus of Namibians from their country in 1974 – facilitated by the fall of the Portuguese Empire and the opening of the Angolan-Namibian border – led to a rapid increase of military recruits at the party's main base in Lusaka. Most recruits were members of the SWAPO Youth League, which had been very successful in rallying resistance against the apartheid regime. The Youth League demanded greater influence in running the affairs of the movement, accused the former OPO leadership of negligence in questions of party ideology, and severely criticized the abuse of party finances for personal gain. The growing dissent – mainly directed against Nujoma – was put down with the help of the Zambian army. Over one thousand SWAPO fighters were detained, and an unknown number were killed. Similar incidents occurred in the 1980s, when approximately two thousand SWAPO members were accused of spy activities in Angola (Leys and Saul 1976, Hunter 2008). These episodes highlight the ambiguous relationship between SWAPO and basic democratic principles.

Namibia was ruled along ethnic lines by the Southern African administration, and contact between the different communities was very limited. Ethnic cleavages are difficult to decipher. Studies on cultural relations indicate prejudices and precolonial tensions between the Ovambo and Herero (Tötemeyer 2004). Ever since its formation, SWAPO was able to not only bridge the division between the Herero and the Ovambo, but also further managed to integrate Namibia's smaller communities, such as the Damara and the Caprivians, into the liberation movement (Lindeke et al. 1992). The deepest line of division in Namibian politics ran between the country's white and black population. During its armed resistance, the desirability of white membership was debated, which in the end became an option (Harneit-Sievers 1984). SWAPO's most prominent white member was Anton Lubowski, a German-Namibian human rights lawyer. Luboswki was shot dead in broad daylight in September 1989 under circumstances that remain unknown (Lush 1993).

The historical roots of SWAPO's former long-term main opposition, the DTA, also predate Namibian independence. It formed in reaction to the increasing importance of SWAPO at the international level. The party emerged out of the dust of the failed Turnhalle conference of 1975. The South African apartheid regime had organized the Turnhalle conference to form a political force loyal to Pretoria. To counterbalance SWAPO, it assembled all traditional authorities and tried to unite them under the roof of one political party (Cooper 2001). The conference failed as a result of diverging

TABLE 4.2. *Ethnic Composition of Namibia Nationwide*

Ethnic/Language Community	Percentage of Population
Oshivambo	51%
Nama/Damara	13%
Rukavango	10%
Otjiherero	8%
Caprivi	5%
San	2%
German	1%

Source: Republic of Namibia. 1991 Population and Housing Census.

views between the South African National Party and the deputy leader of its Namibian wing, Dirk Mudge. The Mudge camp opposed many apartheid laws in the education sector. His opposition to "petty apartheid" bade well with many traditional African leaders. When the South African delegation refused to compromise, numerous delegates staged a walk-out. Two years later, they founded the DTA. In the absence of an alternative stooge, South Africa became the party's sponsor.

SWAPO rejected any political association based on traditional and ethnic leadership and had boycotted the Turnhalle conference. Thus, early on, two diametrically opposed conceptions of the future Namibian state emerged. SWAPO called for "One Namibia, One Nation." The DTA maintained the ethnic identities of its founding member parties. Its internal hierarchy was based on the numerical support of ethnic constituents.[2] At its inception, the DTA included the following mono-ethnic parties and interest associations: The Herero Council, the Republican Party (led by Dirk Mudge representing white Namibians) the Kavango Alliance, the Damara United Front, the Caprivian Alliance, the Interessengemeinschaft deutscher Südwester (led by Erik Staby representing the interests of German farmers), National Unity Democratic Organization (NUDO, a Herero party closely allied with the Herero Council), the Rehoboth Bastervereinigung, the Nama DTP, the Bushman Alliance, and the Labor Party (Lister 1981, Voizey 1994). The Ovambo community was represented through the National Democratic Party (NDP). However, the NDP's leader, Reverend Kalungula, and his supporters left the DTA in the early 1980s. Although SWAPO incorporated members of all ethnic groups, the DTA failed to do so for most of the time before independence.

Table 4.2 displays the ethnic composition of Namibia nationwide, and Table 4.3 illustrates the ethnic composition of Namibia's provinces. The census asked respondents to state their first language, which does not always

[2] Interview with Hans Erik Staby, former DTA member of the National Assembly, Windhoek, July 8, 2008.

TABLE 4.3. *Ethnic Composition of Namibia's Provinces*

Region	Ethnic Composition
Caprivi	Caprivi: 70%
	Rukavango: 24%
	San: 4%
Erongo	Nama/ Damara: 33%
	Oshiwambo: 24%
	Otjiherero: 18%
Hardap	Nama/ Damara: 49%
	Afrikaans: 43%[3]
	Oshiwambo: 5%
Karas	Afrikaans: 41%
	Nama/ Damara: 38%
	Oshiwambo: 15%
Kavango	Okavango: 90%
Khomas	Afrikaans: 30%
	Oshiwambo: 27%
	Nama/ Damara: 21%
Kunene	Otjiherero: 44%
	Nama/ Damara: 34%
	Oshiwambo: 14%
Ohangwena	Oshiwambo 99%
Omaheke	Otjiherero: 43%
	Nama/ Damara :24%
	San: 12%
Omusati	Oshiwambo: 99%
Oshana	Oshiwambo: 98%
Oshikoto	Oshiwambo: 88%
Otjozondjupa	Otjiherero: 30%
	Nama/Damara: 25%
	Oshiwambo: 18

Source: Republic of Namibia. 1991 Population and Housing Census.

correspond to people's ethnic identity. The Nama and the Damara languages are merged into one language group.

OBSERVATION PERIOD 1

Namibia's major political players entered the period of multiparty democracy in an environment of mutual mistrust. The killing of SWAPO attorney

[3] The inclusion of Afrikaans speakers makes it difficult to make any inferences about the background of the respondents. However, the data provided are the only data available on the ethnic setup of Namibia's provinces.

TABLE 4.4. *Bills Passed by the National Assembly Between 1989 and 1994*

Name of Bill	Comment	Impact on Ethnic Relations
1990 Bank of Namibia Act	established a Central Bank for the Republic of Namibia	no
1990 Defence of Amendment Act	established the Namibia Defence Force	no
1990 Foreign Investments Act	made provisions for the promotion of foreign investments in Namibia	no
1991 National Fishing Corporation of Namibia Act	made legal provision for the exploitation of the fish and other resources	no
1992 University of Namibia Act	established the University of Namibia	no
1992 Regional Councils Act	established regional councils	no
1993 Income Tax Amendment	established a new income tax structure	no
1994 Walvis Bay and Off-Shore Islands Act	provided for the transfer of control of Walvis Bay from South Africa to Namibia	no
1994 Social Security Act	established a pension scheme	no

Source: Author's compilation based on Economic Intelligence Unit, expert interviews, and the Namibian media. All data are with the author.

Anton Lubowski had generated the fear of retaliation attacks. SWAPO's failed invasion of the country on April 1, 1989, greatly complicated the transition and temporarily put South Africa's cooperative stance at risk. Nevertheless, peace prevailed and generally peaceful elections took place in November 1989.

Between 1989 and 1994, the National Assembly passed numerous laws. Table 4.4 provides an overview of those bills that received wider attention. Policy making was exclusively driven by the intention of creating viable state institutions for the new state. None of the acts passed affected ethnic relations. None of the acts tabled by the SWAPO government had any effect on ethnic relations.

The Democratic Turnhalle Alliance and the Democratic Age

Of the two major political forces, the DTA was financially better equipped to deal with the challenges of political contest. It presided over extensive funds, given its generous donors from apartheid South Africa. It had already gained some experience in running election campaigns. It also had gathered experience as party in government at the regional level and consequently was well

TABLE 4.5. *Programmatic Content of Election Manifestos in Kenya and Namibia*

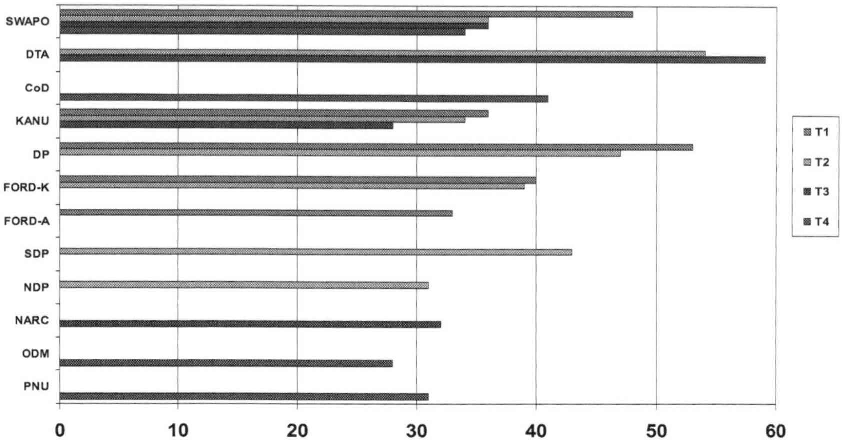

SWAPO
DTA
CoD
KANU
DP
FORD-K
FORD-A
SDP
NDP
NARC
ODM
PNU
0 10 20 30 40 50 60
T1
T2
T3
T4

Source: Author's compilation.

entrenched in local power structures. Its well-established party structures mobilized a sophisticated political machinery underscored by propaganda materials and generous handouts. Its rhetoric projected the image of a party with in-depth regional knowledge. The DTA drew on its close proximity to local chiefs, in particular in the Herero-dominated areas. It dealt with its morally questionable heritage by claiming a Namibian nationalist symbol as its own and by depicting its history as a political force fighting for Namibia independence by peaceful means. Simultaneously, it denigrated SWAPO as a terrorist group. Anti-SWAPO and anti-Nujoma slogans characterized the DTA election campaign. Nujoma was often portrayed as an uneducated terrorist who had organized the assassination of Lubowski. The DTA further paid extensive reference to the "detainee issue," which was resurfacing in the domestic debate in particular in the Southern regions (Lush 1993, Cliffe 1994). The party further appealed to one of its core clientele, Namibia's whites, by stressing that whites were Namibians and that the new Namibian state had to adhere to universal human rights.[4] Table 4.5 compares the programmatic content of Namibian election manifestos with the results from Kenya.

Through this study, the 40 percent line serves as cut-off point to distinguish between manifestos with a potentially programmatic content and those that can outright be rejected as not programmatic. The programmatic content of the DTA's 1989 manifesto constitutes 52.2 percent of its overall content. However, 18 percentage points of its programmatic content is

[4] *Namibian*, November 15, 1989.

composed of two categories: Category 201(Human Rights: positive) and category 202 (Democracy: positive). The DTA was keen on portraying itself as democratic force, and its manifesto is not indicative of a programmatic party.

The electoral indicators of both parties are difficult to assess in comparison with subsequent elections. The PNS is calculated on the basis of regions created by the apartheid state. Shortly after the elections, new regions were created. This complicated within-country comparisons across time. The demarcation lines in place during the 1989 elections inflate the DTA's PNS. The DTA's poor performance among the Ovambo is not adequately reflected because Ovamboland only constitutes one region but more than one-third of the national electorate. As a result, the PNS of the DTA falls into the high to very high and its PDS into the medium to high category. Although this would make the DTA an ethnic-alliance party, a closer analysis of its electoral performance does not warrant such a conclusion.

The Herero- and Caprivi-dominated regions of Caprivi, Kaokoland, and Hereroland were the party's clearly identifiable strongholds. The party drastically underperformed in Ovamboland, where in some areas it received no votes at all. In several areas, the results were rigged in favor of the DTA. In Kavango, the local chiefs forced newly registered voters to vote for the DTA. In Gobabis, many white farmers threatened their African field workers with dismissal in case they voted for SWAPO. Similar incidents occurred in Windhoek (Cliffe 1994). Finally, white interest groups flew South African citizens, who were eligible to vote, into the country (Tötemeyer et al. 1996). Electoral performance of parties in 1989 is shown in Table 4.6.

Shortly before the 1989 election, the DTA's central committee elected a new leadership. Kuaimo Riruako (Herero) was made party president, Dirk Mudge (white) served as party chairman, and Rudolph Kamburona (Herero) was elected secretary-general. The following were elected vice-chairmen: Gabriel Kautuima (Ovambo), Katuutire Kaura (Herero), Max Haraseb (Damara), Daniel Luipert (Nama), and Ben Africa (Baster).[5] In September 1992, Kautuima resigned from his post. Seven prominent Ovambo functionaries followed his example. They explained their resignation by their community's aversion to the party and its goals.[6]

The organizational structure was typical of an ethnic alliance. Its ethnic member parties remained in existence. Party factions were structured around these mono-ethnic entities. The relationship between the Herero and white Namibians was particularly tense. DTA chairman Riruako resigned in March 1990 after the DTA leadership decided to stay organized as an umbrella organization. Riruako opposed the decision – even though he formally was in charge of the very same entity, he opposed. For a long time,

[5] *Namibian*, September, 4, 1989.

[6] *Namibian*, September 18, 1992.

TABLE 4.6. *Parties' Electoral Performance in 1989*

T1	SWAPO PDS	DTA PDS	Vote Share of Region
Bethanie	0.12%[7]	0.69%	0.35%
Caprivi	2.69%	7.2%	3.87%
Damaraland	1.08%	1.35%	2.24%
Gobabis	0.64%	6.1%	2.66%
Grotfontein	0.02%	4.6%	3.01%
Hereroland	0.61%	5.16%	2.40%
Kaokoland	0.34%	4.27%	1.88%
Karasburg	0.62%	5.26%	2.76%
Karibib	0.58%	1.04%	0.97%
Kavango	8%	12.96%	9.02%
Keetmanshoop	1.42%	4.83%	2.83%
Lüderitz	2%	1.12%	1.66%
Maltahöhe	0.22%	0.36%	0.38%
Mariental	0.78%	4%	2.07%
Okahandja	0.96%	2.23%	1.52%
Omaruru	0.33%	1.54%	0.85%
Otjiwarongo	1.04%	2.72%	1.81%
Outjo	0.31%	1.6%	1.01%
Ovamboland	58.37%	5.61%	36.46%
Rehoboth	0.78%	4.04%	2.55%
Swakopmund	3.65%	3.1%	3.54%
Tsumeh	1.88%	2.1%	2.04%
Windhoek	11.43%	18.13%	14.27

PDS DTA: 65 / average diverging points across time and space: 52
PNS DTA: .81 / average PNS across time and space: .67
PDS SWAPO: 47 / average diverging points across time and space: 52
PNS SWAPO: .74/ average PNS across time and space: .67

Source: Author's compilation on the basis of Lodge 1999.

Riruako had been at loggerheads with Mudge. Mudge had remained the dominant personality inside the DTA. He remained its informal leader and main financer.[8] Riruako further accused the DTA of marginalizing Herero interest, as his NUDO party had not been allocated sufficient seats on the DTA parliamentary list.[9] Mishake Muyongo (Caprivi) took Riruako's place as DTA chairman.

7 Due to the small size of regions, results are reported to two decimal places.

8 Interview with Hans Erik Staby, former DTA member of the National Assembly, July 8, 2008, Windhoek. Interview with Gerhard Tötemeyer, former SWAPO deputy minister and member of the National Assembly, July 10, 2008, Windhoek.

9 *Namibian*, March 15, 1990; *Namibian*, December 6, 1991.

Tensions between whites and Hereros also destabilized intra-party relations in the run-up to the local elections. In numerous locations, local functionaries could not agree on the party lists for the municipal elections. Although NUDO members were pushing for Herero candidates, members of the Republican Party rallied support for white candidates.[10] In December 1991, Fanuel Kozonguizi (Herero), a DTA frontbencher, resigned. He claimed that he had been marginalized by the DTA leadership.[11] In January 1994, Riruako announced the withdrawal of NUDO from the DTA. Two days later, he had to backtrack on his earlier announcement, as his defection did not find sufficient support inside NUDO.[12] Many petty disagreements between individual communities over policy issues further worsened intra-party relations.[13]

The increasing deterioration of the party was accompanied by the inability to formulate a coherent political agenda. Failing to anticipate SWAPO's moderate stance on the land question and national reconciliation, the DTA became a victim of its own anti-SWAPO propaganda.[14] It denounced Namibia's democratic order as a façade and accused SWAPO of the hidden implementation of a one-party state. It was desperate to show that Namibian democracy was not working. On one occasion, the party issued a memorandum to American Vice-President Dan Quayle stating that the creation of a one-party state was imminent.[15] The DTA parliamentary caucus tabled several motions of no confidence in the government, most of which failed to make the parliamentary agenda.[16] Its various anti-SWAPO campaigns lacked credibility. Mudge, for example, congratulated SWAPO on its moderate policies and stated publicly that Namibian democracy was in good shape.[17]

The DTA thus internalized the rhetoric of the apartheid state and portrayed SWAPO as an undemocratic terrorist group.[18] The ethnic nature of the DTA was also visible in some of its public statements. When a variety of ancient kingdoms were reinstalled by local traditional authorities, the various ethnic wings of the party welcomed this step. In stark contrast, SWAPO leaders condemned these local initiatives.[19]

[10] *Namibian*, November 9, 1992.
[11] *Namibian*, December 3, 1991.
[12] *Namibian*, January 5, 1994; *Namibian*, January 7, 1994; *Namibian*, January 14, 1994.
[13] Interview with Hans Erik Staby, former DTA member of the National Assembly, July 8, 2008, Windhoek.
[14] *Namibian*, July 23, 1993.
[15] *Namibian*, September 13, 1991.
[16] *Namibian*, February 28, 1991; *Namibian*, May 22, 1992.
[17] *Namibian*, February 5, 1991.
[18] *Namibian*, July 1, 1994.
[19] *Namibian*, October 4, 1993.

The DTA is classified as an alliance party. For most of the time it lacked Ovambo membership and failed to have any electoral support among the largest group of the country. It had clearly identifiable electoral strongholds. The ethnic compartmentalization of the party setup caused the rise of ethnic factions. In terms of its rhetoric, it focused on SWAPO's alleged failures to create a democratic state, but it was keen on satisfying the demands of local communities. It sought close cooperation with traditional leaders.

The South West African People's Organization

After several decades in exile, the SWAPO leadership returned to Namibia shortly before the elections to Namibia's National Assembly. Their successive return reached its emotional peak with the arrival of Sam Nujoma. On September 30, 1989, Nujoma gave his first speech in Windhoek in 30 years. His central theme was the need to reconcile Namibians, independently of their heritage and their political past.[20] The imperative to build a united post-apartheid nation, a political order based on racial equality, and adherence to constitutionalism became SWAPO's main electoral sound bites (Cliffe 1994). The party distanced itself from any previous socialist aspirations; instead, it advocated a moderate role for the state in managing the economy.[21] Despite its pro-Soviet leanings in the past, the SWAPO campaign never embarked on economic rhetoric that was radical in any way. Among the 41 newly elected SWAPO MPs, merely 3 were committed to a socialist agenda. Among the party leadership, a socialist economic agenda was never a serious option.[22] In contrast to its main political opponent, SWAPO rejected appeals to ethnic identity. Instead, it emphasized its decade-long rejection of ethnicity-based political activism. Throughout the 1989 election campaign, SWAPO articulated pan-Namibian nationalism and made extensive reference to its merits in the struggle for Namibia's independence (Lush 1993).

Although 48 percent of SWAPO's manifesto content consists of programmatic statements, this was due to an overemphasis on a few selected categories. Eighteen percentage points consist of two categories: category 201 (Freedom and Human Rights: positive) and category 202 (Democracy: positive). The SWAPO manifesto mirrors the content of the DTA manifesto. The high programmatic content of both manifestos is the result of the historical circumstances in which the elections were conducted. The programmatic categories SWAPO highlighted were category 506 (Education Expansion: positive, 6.8 percentage point of the overall manifesto content), category 504 (Welfare State Expansion: positive, 5.2 percentage points),

[20] *Namibian*, October 9, 1989.

[21] *Namibian*, November 7, 1989.

[22] Interview with Gerhard Tötemeyer, former SWAPO deputy minister and member of the National Assembly, July 10, 2008, Windhoek.

TABLE 4.7. *Ethnic Composition of Namibia's 1989 Cabinet*

Community	Number of Cabinet Ministers Allocated	Percentage of Cabinet Ministers Allocated
Ovambo	10	47%
White	3	13%
Damara	2	10%
Kavango	2	10%
Herero	1	5%
Nama	1	5%
Caprivian	1	5%
Colored	1	5%
TOTAL	21	100%

Source: Author's compilation based on Namibian media sources.

category 606 (Social Harmony: positive, 2.8 percentage points), and category 106 (Peace: positive, 2.6 percentage points). Although the preponderance of the former two categories is typical of any African party, the latter two can again be explained by contextual factors: the desire to build a stable post-apartheid state and to normalize diplomatic relations with Namibia's neighbors.

The same factors that rigged the electoral indicators in favor of the DTA had the reverse effect on the indicators measuring SWAPO's national support. This notwithstanding, SWAPO's PNS displays a medium to high and its PDS a medium to low value. Both indicate a catch-all party.

The national composition of SWAPO's leadership in exile was translated into an all-inclusive cabinet. See Table 4.7.

The high degree of white participation demonstrated goodwill to those who had serious doubts about Nujoma's reconciliation campaign. The inclusion of white Namibians also had pragmatic reasons: the upcoming challenges of nation-building required the new Namibian power holders to rely on experienced administrators.[23] The vast majority of the acts the SWAPO government tabled in parliament were technocratic in nature.

Inside the party leadership, all major communities were included. At SWAPO's extraordinary congress in 1991, Nujoma was reelected as party president, and David Merero (Herero) was confirmed as party chairman. Hendrik Witbooi (Nama) maintained his position as vice-president. In a highly contested election for the position of the secretary-general, Moses Garoeb (Damara), defeated veteran SWAPO leader Toivo ya Toivo

[23] Interview with Hans Erik Staby, former DTA member of the National Assembly, July 8, 2008, Windhoek. Interview with Gerhard Tötemeyer, former SWAPO deputy minister and member of the National Assembly, July 10, 2008, Windhoek.

(Ovambo) by a very small margin. The numerical superiority of Ovambo speakers was not the decisive criterion in determining the composition of the SWAPO leadership.[24] Neither ethnic nor racial heritage determined the outcome of leadership contests throughout the 1990s.[25]

Little is known about party factions during the immediate post-independence period.[26] There has always been a latent rift between the party leadership in exile and the leadership that fought apartheid inside Namibia. SWAPO leaders who had remained inside the country felt that their efforts had not been honored sufficiently. Nevertheless, the division into SWAPO exiles and the former "home front" never translated into the formation of factions.[27]

Disagreements over policies or procedural issues never provided enough substance for the formation of lasting alliances.[28] One example was the appointment of Stanley Webster as deputy minister of agriculture, water, and rural development. Webster was not a member of the National Assembly, and his appointment was unconstitutional. The debate temporarily divided the cabinet but did not cause a long-term division.[29]

Between elections, SWAPO promoted itself as the party of all Namibians[30] and remained averse to the idea of reinstating ancient African kingdoms.[31] Cabinet ministers consistently stressed their desire to eradicate land inequality and the vast economic discrepancies that existed between whites and blacks as well as between the relatively well-developed South and the war-torn North.[32] Much of the government's activities focused on reforming administrative structures and making them accessible to the wider populace. The government further decided to freeze state pensions for whites to increase pensions for all other communities.[33] It also implemented a policy of affirmative actions that gave preference to Africans in filling civil service positions.

24 *New Era*, December 12, 1991.

25 Interview with Hartmut Ruppel, former attorney-general and member of the SWAPO Politbüro, July 21, 2008, Windhoek. Interview with Gerhard Tötemeyer, former SWAPO deputy minister and member of the National Assembly, July 10, 2008, Windhoek.

26 This is partly due to the lack of contested issues at the time and partly due to SWAPO's heritage as liberation movement. During those years, it had been an imperative to keep information regarding its leadership secret.

27 Confidential interview with a former member of the SWAPO Politbüro.

28 Interview with Professor Andre du Pisani, University of Namibia, July 21, 2008, Windhoek.

29 *Namibian*, February 10, 1994.

30 *New Era*, December 12, 1991; *Namibian*, June 17, 1992.

31 *Namibian*, March 19, 1993.

32 *Namibian*, March 19, 1993.

33 *Namibian*, April 12, 1990. At the time of coming to power, the entitlements of Namibia's various groups were as follows: Whites: R382, Coloreds: R192; Basters: R138; Ovambo Caprivians and Kavangos: R75; Tswanas: R85; Namas: R65; Hereros: R65.

SWAPO promoted pan-Namibian nationhood and refrained from programmatic rhetoric or policies. Its electoral stronghold was Ovambo province, but it clearly was not an Ovambo party. Party factions did not emerge. Overall, SWAPO closely resembled the ideal type of the catch-all party.

OBSERVATION PERIOD 2

Between 1994 and 1999, the Namibian National Assembly passed 10 bills, which received greater attention in the media and which were discussed in public by the political class (see Table 4.8).[34]

The 1996 Affirmative Action Bill, the 1998 Human Resources Development Bill, and the 1999 Communal Land Reform Bill caused great antagonism among the white population. White DTA politicians were very vocal in their criticism against these laws. Relations between the African communities were not affected by any of the acts.

The Democratic Turnhalle Alliance Falls Apart

Five years after Namibian independence, apartheid had come to an end in South Africa. The interests of previous South African donors had shifted from containing SWAPO abroad to maintaining a political presence at home. SWAPO's pragmatic stance on the land issue weakened the DTA's mobilization potential (Tötemeyer et al. 1996). During its 1994 campaign, the DTA severely criticized governmental nepotism and insinuated that public appointments had been made in favor of the President's own community.[35] It called on voters to avoid a two-third SWAPO majority.[36] At the local level, the party depicted itself as the champion of the respective ethnic group and stressed the gains it had achieved for that community in the pre-independence period. Although it campaigned on a national scale, its campaign rhetoric and its modus operandi revealed the existence of the various mono-ethnic member parties.[37]

[34] Data have been extracted from Economic Intelligence Reports since 1989 and expert interviews. All data are with the author.

[35] *Namibian*, July 13, 1994. Preference was given to those Namibians who had received administrative training abroad. As most citizens who went into exile were Ovambo, this bias does therefore does not appear to be deliberate. Interview with Gerhard Tötemeyer, former SWAPO deputy minister and member of the National Assembly, July 10, 2008, Windhoek.

[36] *Namibian*, October 19, 1994.

[37] Interview with Justine Hunter, executive director of Namibia Institute for Democracy, July 30, 2008, Windhoek. Interview with Gerhard Tötemeyer, former SWAPO deputy minister and member of the National Assembly, July 10, 2008, Windhoek.

TABLE 4.8. *Bills Passed by the National Assembly Between 1994 and 1999*

Name of Bill	Comment	Impact on Ethnic Relations
1995 Married Persons Equality Bill	gave women equal financial, property, and guardianship rights after marriage	no. The bill led to a heated debate between male and female MPs.
1995 Transport Bill	new road usage taxes meant to take into account the weight of vehicles and adjust for inflation	no
1996 Affirmative Action Bill	gave preference to black and colored Namibians over white Namibians	the bill caused antagonism among Namibia's whites.
1997 Securities Bill	important for regulating firms in the securities market	no
1997 The Company Bill		no
1997 Insurance and Pensions Amendment Bill		no
1997 Investment Promotion Bill		no
1998 Human Resources Development Bill	aimed to promote the indigenization of all posts currently held by expatriates in the public and private sectors	the bill caused antagonism among Namibia's whites.
1999 Communal Land Reform Bill	provided for the establishment of regional land boards and defined the powers of chiefs and traditional leaders over communal areas	the bill caused antagonism among Namibia's whites.
1999 The Industrial Relations Bill		no

Source: Author's compilation based on Economic Intelligence Unit, expert interviews, and the Namibian media. All data are with the author.

The DTA election manifesto displayed a surprisingly high degree of programmatic content (54 percent, see Table 4.5). As previously, this is due to an overemphasis on a few policy categories. Category 605 (Law and Order: positive) and category 506 (Education Expansion: positive) account for 36 percentage points of the DTA's programmatic content. The number of the manifesto's significant categories (6.3) is below the cross-country average (8.8). Therefore, its programmatic content is again the result of an overemphasis on a small selection of individual categories.

At the polls, the DTA could not avoid a two-thirds majority for SWAPO. Analysts have blamed the failure of the DTA to do so on its inability to mobilize its core voters (Tötemeyer et al. 1996). The party continued to perform very poorly in the Ovambo-dominated North, where its vote share was less than one percent. It did well in Caprivi (the home region of its presidential candidate), in the Herero-populated areas, and in regions with a sizable white farming population.

In terms of its electoral output, the DTA is classified as an ethnic alliance. Its PDS almost doubles the cross-country average. Its PNS can be categorized as low to medium.

The party leadership underwent several changes following the 1994 electoral defeat. Mishake Muyongo (Caprivi) was reelected party president. Piet Junius (white) took over the position as party chairman after Dirk Mudge's departure form politics. Katuuire Kaura (Herero) and Rudolf Kamburona (Herero) became vice-president and vice-chairman, respectively. Ben Africa (Baster) took over as secretary-general.[38] Soon, the new line-up suffered from infighting. The departure of Mudge meant that the party lacked a de facto leader. Numerous personnel changes followed. In July 1996, Africa and Junius switched positions; Johan de Waal (white) replaced Kamburona.[39] One year later, the position of secretary-general changed from Junius, who returned to his former role as chairman, to Mike Venaani (Herero).[40] At the heart of any decision regarding its leadership setup was the wider question of providing access to power to a particular ethnic group.[41] The recurring reordering of the ethnic pecking order proved detrimental to the cohesion of the DTA.

Following a failed attempt of Caprivian rebels to secede from Namibia, DTA President Mishake Muyongo (Caprivian) was expelled from the party because of his involvement in the secession campaign. Katuuire Kaura (Herero) was elected party president, and Philemon Moongo (Ovambo) was elected as his deputy.[42] Even though the party's leadership now incorporated an Ovambo, it is doubtful to what extent Moongo's promotion was a genuine attempt to increase the DTA's social base. Moongo had joined SWAPO in the 1960s, where he served in the People's Liberation Army. During SWAPO's 1976 crisis, he belonged to those who were openly critical of the SWAPO leadership, and in particular of Nujoma. In the late 1970s,

[38] *Namibian*, May 2, 1995.
[39] *Namibian*, July 22, 1996.
[40] *Namibian*, September 29, 1997.
[41] Interview with Hans Erik Staby, former DTA member of the National Assembly, July 8, 2008, Windhoek.
[42] *Namibian*, September 7, 1998.

he had become a founding member of SWAPO-D, a party of SWAPO dissidents. SWAPO-D failed to have a lasting impact on the political scene (Hopwood 2007). Thus Moongo was a disappointed SWAPO renegade for whom the DTA provided a new political base rather than a DTA heavyweight with the potential to reach out to a group the DTA had failed to include. To classify the party leadership composition as catch-all would be misleading, as this was not achieved on a long-term basis. As we see later, it was not long before the DTA was to implode.

In the day-to-day political struggle, the party continued to present itself as the party of good governance. Party Vice-President Katuuire Kaura repeatedly stated that SWAPO was turning parliament into a rubberstamp and Namibia into a dictatorship.[43] After Nujoma declared his intention to seek a third presidential term – a move many regarded an incompatible with the constitution – the DTA protested strongly.[44] Nujoma's purchase of a luxurious presidential jet featured highly on the DTA's list of examples of governmental corruption. Other affairs such as the loss of several million Namibian dollars through the Katutura Single Quarters project were also taken up by the opposition.[45] The party's proximity to traditional authorities was visible throughout the period. After SWAPO proposed (and later passed) a bill banning traditional elders from serving as national politicians, the DTA opposed that bill.[46] SWAPO's decision to build a Nydro electric scheme at Epupa became a point of contention; the DTA argued that the government would have to consult the Council of Traditional Himba Leaders, as they were the true representatives of the people in the region.[47] The party's African conservatism toward the emancipation of women was visible during the parliamentary debate on rape and the domestic violence bill. In parliament, DTA MP Kuaima Riruako (Herero) called on women to stop raping men and stated that he had become the victim of female rapists on several occasions.[48] The DTA heavily opposed the 1996 Affirmative Action Bill, the 1998 Human Resources Development Bill, and the 1999 Communal Land Reform Bill, which posed a severe threat to the economic interests of one of its core groups – the white community. The party clearly failed to comprehend the political environment of the post-independence period.

Its proximity to traditional leaders, its ethnic divisions, its failure to attract any support in the Ovambo regions, and the lack of any meaningful programmatic undercurrents make the DTA an alliance party.

43 *Namibian*, February 22, 1995.

44 *Namibian*, August 5, 1998.

45 *Namibian*, June 26, 1995.

46 *Namibian*, June 8, 1995. One should note that this decision had negative consequences for a variety of SWAPO leaders, who were forced to resign from traditional leadership positions. They nevertheless voted in favor of the bill.

47 *Namibian*, February 13, 1997.

48 *Namibian*, June 15, 1999.

SWAPO Extending the SWAPO Kingdom

SWAPO's 1994 electoral campaign was a low-profile affair. No one doubted the party's victory. On the campaign trail, it stressed that it had facilitated access to wealth and power to all Namibians. "Namibianization" became the main theme of the campaign. SWAPO reiterated the DTA's role during the apartheid period. The DTA presidential challenger Mishake Muyongo – a high-ranking SWAPO functionary in the 1960s – became a particularly popular target. On various occasions, SWAPO accused him of having served the former South African government. The party blamed him of building up ethnic tensions in the Caprivi regions between the Subia and the Mafwe communities.[49] In general, SWAPO drew on the notion of "us against them" and insinuated that its opponents would find themselves on the losing side of history.[50]

SWAPO's 1994 election manifesto displayed a lower programmatic content than the previous one (36 percent). The decline was due to its diminished support for category 201 (Freedom and Human Right: positive, a decline from 9.5 percentage points to 2.4 percentage points) and category 202 (Democracy: positive, a decline from 8.4 percentage points to 3.8 percentage points). Other programmatic categories changed only marginally.

None of the bills put forward by SWAPO had any ideological intent. Most bills were technocratic in nature and inspired little to no debate. Exceptions to this rule were bills designed to end disparities in gender relations, which indicate the strong influence of SWAPO women inside the party.[51] Various bills were designed to create a greater degree of racial equality in the public service. These bills contributed to the alienation of Namibia's whites from SWAPO.[52]

In terms of its electoral performance, SWAPO remained a national force. Its PDS remained low, whereas its PNS rose slightly. The party's stronghold remained the Ovambo regions in the North, yet it could count on nationwide support. Outside former Ovamboland (Ohangwena, Omusati, Oshana, and Oshikoto), SWAPO matched the performance of the DTA. Outside the Ovambo regions, SWAPO gained a total of 115,154 votes and the DTA a total of 94,743 votes.[53]

[49] *Namibian*, November 7, 1994.

[50] Interview with Justine Hunter, executive director of the Namibia Institute for Democracy, July 30, 2008, Windhoek.

[51] Even inside SWAPO, many functionaries were opposed to these bills. Interview with Justine Hunter, executive director of the Namibia Institute for Democracy, July 30, 2008, Windhoek.

[52] Interview with Hartmut Ruppel, former attorney-general and member of the SWAPO Politbüro, July 21, 2008, Windhoek. Interview with Gerhard Tötemeyer, former SWAPO deputy minister and member of the National Assembly, July 10, 2008, Windhoek.

[53] Based on official parliamentary election results as reported by Lodge 1999.

TABLE 4.9. *Parties' Electoral Performance in 1994*

T2	SWAPO PDS	DTA PDS	Vote Share of Region
Caprivi	3%	12%	5%
Erongo	5%	8%	6%
Hardap	3%	10%	4%
Karas	4%	9%	5%
Kavango	6%	4%	5%
Khomas	9%	20%	12%
Kunene	2%	7%	4%
Ohangwena	16%	0%	12%
Omaheke	2%	10%	4%
Omusati	20%	0%	15%
Oshana	14%	2%	11%
Oshikoto	12%	2%	10%
Otjozondjupa	4%	16%	7%

PDS DTA: 90/ average diverging points across time and space: 50
PNS DTA: .60/ average PNS across time and space: .67
PDS SWAPO: 30/ average diverging points across time and space: 50
PNS SWAPO: .77/ average PNS across time and space: .67

Source: Author's compilation.

The new cabinet reflected the all-inclusive character of the government. See Table 4.10. Compared with the previous cabinet, no major changes occurred.

Inside the party, tensions became more visible, although again party factions did not emerge. Following its electoral triumph, the party expelled a

TABLE 4.10. *Ethnic Composition of Namibia's 1994 Cabinet*

Community	Number of Cabinet Ministers Allocated	Percentage of Cabinet Ministers Allocated
Ovambo	12	52%
White	3	13%
Damara	2	9%
Kavango	2	9%
Herero	1	4%
Nama	1	4%
Caprivian	2	9%
Colored	0	0%
TOTAL	23	100%

Source: Author's compilation based on Namibian media sources.

backbench MP, who had raised criticism of the leadership's tight grip on party affairs. The party increasingly disapproved of critical voices.[54] This was particularly true of President Nujoma, whose information policy on cabinet appointments and reshuffles was minimal. In June 1995, a group of discontented party members formed an alternative party, SWAPO for Justice (SWAPO FJ). The formation of SWAPO FJ illustrates the dialectic relationship between Nujoma and his past followers: Although SWAPO FJ criticized the lack of intra-party democracy, it states that it would make Nujoma president for life in case it ever gained power.[55]

Nujoma's mini-reshuffle in September 1996 – which made Nangolo Mbumba (Ovambo) minister of finance and which consequently demoted Helmut Angula (Ovambo) to the ministry of agriculture, water, and rural development – was unexpected. It was Nujoma's first attempt to stop the rise of a potential successor.[56] Throughout the second part of 1996, speculation increased regarding whether or not Nujoma would seek a third term in office.[57] By 1998, speculations about the future presidential candidates were debated publicly. In the media, Prime Minister Hage Geingob (Damara), Minister for Trade and Industry Hidipo Hamutenya (Ovambo), and Minister for Fisheries and Marine Resources Hifikepunye Pohamba (Ovambo) circulated.[58] From the inception, Pohamba was seen as the favorite, mainly because of his personal and political proximity to Nujoma. Pohambe had served Nujoma all his life and had proven to be receptive to orders from above. Hamutenya's power base inside the party was comparatively small and reduced to his Ovambo subgroup, the Kwanyama. Geingob's disadvantage was his dominant personality and his abrasive leadership style. Both had bred hostility among the power brokers inside the cabinet. It had also alienated many party members and cost him the position of vice-presidency of the party. At the 1997 congress, Geingob lost against to Hendrik Witbooi (Nama), who won 58 percent of the delegates' vote.[59] At the same congress, Pohamba was elected secretary-general.[60] Garoeb's second disadvantage was his heritage: despite SWAPO's pan-tribal character, Nujoma's inner circle displayed a strong proclivity for an Ovambo candidate. Although Geingob was of mixed Damara/Ovambo heritage, he refused to reinvent

54 *Namibian*, August 2, 1996.

55 *Namibian*, June 2, 1995.

56 *Namibian*, September 13, 1996.

57 *Namibian*, December 5, 1996; *Namibian*, December 11, 1996.

58 *Namibian*, April 24, 1998.

59 *Namibian*, June 2, 1997.

60 As the ethnic composition of the party's leadership did not change in a manner that is significant for the context of this study, the congress is not discussed. Data on all leadership positions are with the author.

himself ethnically.[61] Nujoma's decision to seek a third term put a temporary end to speculations about his successor.

Nujoma's renewed bid for the presidency caused the first break-way from SWAPO. Ben Ulenga (Ovambo), a former Robben Island prisoner and Namibia's high commissioner to the United Kingdom, declared his resignation from his diplomatic post. In an open letter to the party leadership, he complained that the third term bill was an "unacceptable subjection of the national good as represented by the constitution to the personal circumstances and schemes of individuals."[62] Additional reasons for his resignation were SWAPO's lack of intra-party democracy and the government's military involvement in the Democratic Republic of Congo, which he saw as irreconcilable with SWAPO's intention to contribute to peace in Africa. Ulenga was immediately suspended from SWAPO's central committee.[63] In 1999, Ulenga founded the Congress of Democrats (CoD), which met the support of several former SWAPO ministers and high-ranking civil servants.[64]

The relationship between SWAPO and the free media worsened considerably. Nujoma's public appearances frequently ended with outbursts against the private media and in particular against *The Namibian*, the only newspaper that had openly supported SWAPO's struggle for independence. To the displeasure of Nujoma, the newspaper continued its independent coverage. When critical questions about the wisdom behind the purchase of a new presidential jet dominated Namibia's political discourse, Nujoma lashed out against what he perceived to be abuses against the principle of the freedom of the press.[65] In December 2006, Nujoma stated in a SWAPO-owned publication:

> The press in this country is reactionary. It is an enemy press. It must be denounced. This is not a Namibian press. It is foreigners who are leading the press here. They are either South African or have their own foreign tradition and culture. I am waiting for Namibians to take over the media and then they can talk about Namibia.[66]

When the donor community raised concern about the Epupa hydropower scheme, Nujoma warned the donors: "if you come with the aim of white superiority, we will get rid of you."[67] Even though these statements were directed at European donors, they were implicitly targeted at Namibia's

[61] Interview with Graham Hopwood, executive director of the Institute for Public Policy Research, July 24, 2008, Windhoek. The rejection of his Ovambo heritage was due to Geingob's father (who was Ovambo) having left the family at an early stage in Geingob's life.

[62] *Namibian*, August 28, 1998.

[63] *Namibian*, March 26 1999.

[64] *Namibian*, April 8 1995; *Namibian*, October 11, 1999.

[65] *Namibian*, May 5, 1995.

[66] Cited in *Namibian*, December 13, 1996, p. 6.

[67] Cited in *Namibian*, June 22, 1998, pp. 1–2. See also *Namibian*, September 8, 1999.

whites. On several occasions, Nujoma threatened to deport "foreigners" without defining who they were. Homosexuals became another popular target of Nujoma's eruptions.

In response to dissenting internal voices, SWAPO leaders called on the population to display unity in the face of Nujoma's contested third term bid. Those in favor of the constitutional term limit were denounced as traitors and the "dark forces" of the apartheid system.[68] The Council of the Churches in Namibia was accused of fostering "hidden agendas."[69] Otherwise, SWAPO regurgitated its merits in "the struggle" and the benefits its victory had brought to the people.

In contrast to the previous observation period, SWAPO was less occupied with defending itself against the opposition. Instead, it engaged in hazy reactions against those it regarded as having the potential to endanger its dominance. It kept all key characteristics of a catch-all party.

OBSERVATION PERIOD 3

Between 2000 and 2004, the SWAPO government introduced 10 bills, which found a wider audience. In particular, the 2000 Income Tax Amendment Bill and the 2003 Anti-Corruption Bill caused uproar in some quarters. The relationship between the different ethnic groups was not affected by any of the bills put forward; see Table 4.11.

The Democratic Turnhalle Alliance and Its Disintegration

There were no major differences between the DTA's 1994 and 1999 electoral campaigns. The campaign was slightly more targeted at specific regions and communities, as the party had lost its ability to campaign on a national scale. Accordingly, the party focused on regional issues. Once more, it stressed its merits for individual communities during the apartheid regime.

The programmatic content of the DTA election manifesto reached a new high: 59 percent of its manifesto content constitutes programmatic statements. In the two previous manifestos, this is due to an overemphasis of individual categories. Forty percentage points are statements in favor of categories 506 (Education Expansion: positive) and 504 (Welfare State Expansion: positive). In 1999, reports about declining standards in health and education determined the national discourse and were highlighted in the 1999 manifesto. The DTA was thus pragmatic when it come to the selection of issues it highlighted. The manifesto's effective number of programmatic statements (3.3) is far below the cross-national average (8.8). The DTA election manifesto, therefore, cannot be classified as programmatic. Other

[68] *Namibian*, April 20, 1999.
[69] *Namibian*, October 25, 1996.

TABLE 4.11. *Bills Passed by the National Assembly Between 1999 and 2004*

Name of Bill	Comment	Impact on Ethnic Relations
2000 Sales Tax Amendment Bill		no
2000 National Tourism Bill		no
2000 Income Tax Amendment Bill	introduction of taxation of fringe benefits	no. The bill caused great concerns in the business sector.
2000 Confiscation of Proceeds Bill		no
2000 Appropriation Bill		no
2000 Company and Employment Bill		no
2001 Trade and Business Facilitation Bill		no
2003 Anti-corruption Bill	the passing of the bill was stalled for several years.	no
2004 Additional Budget Bill		no
2004 Labor Act		no

Source: Author's compilation based on Economist Intelligence Unit, expert interviews, and the Namibian media. All data are with the author.

policy fields the party was keen on highlighting include the need for economic planning (6.7 percent) and the need of the government to intervene in the social-market economy (5.7 percent).

The party's strongholds remained in the South, in particular the Kavango and Herero areas. It yielded virtually no impact in the Ovambo-dominated North. See Table 4.12.

By 1999, the party's PNS and PDS are indicative of a mono-ethnic party. The PNS calculated on the basis of Afrobarometer data confirms the results derived from the DTA's electoral performance.

With its number of parliamentary seats reaching another low and its status as the official opposition seriously under threat by the newly formed CoD,[70] the DTA's ability to raise public attention declined further. Party life almost came to a complete standstill. In 2002, the combustive dynamics of the DTA resurfaced. Party divisions reflected a general sense of frustration over the ongoing state of decline. In May 2002, an internal memo by the administrative party secretary, Nico Smith – supported by Secretary-General

70 Both parties secured seven seats in the 1999 election, yet the Congress of Democrats secured slightly more votes. It was only due to SWAPO's aversion against the break-away group of Ulenga that the DTA managed to secure the status as official opposition.

TABLE 4.12. *Parties' Electoral Performance in 1999*

T3	SWAPO PDS	DTA PDS	Vote Share of Region
Caprivi	2%	2%	3%
Erongo	5%	6%	7%
Hardap	2%	8%	3%
Karas	3%	6%	4%
Kavango	8%	14%	9%
Khomas	11%	11%	13%
Kunene	1%	14%	3%
Ohangwena	17%	0%	13%
Omaheke	2%	15%	4%
Omusati	20%	1%	15%
Oshana	13%	1%	10%
Oshikoto	12%	2%	10%
Otjozondjupa	4%	20%	6%

PDS DTA: 96/ average diverging points across time and space: 52
PNS DTA: .51/ average PNS across time and space: .67
PNS DTA based on Afrobarometer data collected in 1999: .50/ average PNS across time and space: .72
PNS DTA based on Afrobarometer data collected in 2001: .50/ average PNS across time and space: .72
PDS SWAPO: 30/ average diverging points across time and space: 52
PNS SWAPO: .79/ average PNS across time and space: .67
PNS SWAPO based on Afrobarometer data collected in 1999: .80/ average PNS across time and space: .72
PNS SWAPO based on Afrobarometer data collected in 2001: .80/ average PNS across time and space: .72

Source: Author's compilation.

Venaani – leaked to the public. Smith and Venaani criticized the lax working attitude of several party functionaries and MPs:

When one considers that parliament only sits for some five months out of every 12, and the members clearly believe that the other seven months are holiday time for them, to run their own private business affairs, it is clear that you have developed an underserved over-inflated opinion of your own importance, but also a complete disregard of the interest of the party to which you own your position.[71]

The memo further stated that the party had failed to take the lessons of any electoral defeat since independence. This led to various rounds of infighting between Smith and party chairman Kaura. In the end, Smith resigned from the party.[72] In August 2003, Henk Mudge, Dirk Mudge's

[71] Cited in *Namibian*, May 3, 2002, pp. 1–2.

[72] *Namibian*, May 23, 2002, and *Namibian*, May 21, 2002.

son, announced the break-away of the Republican Party from the DTA.[73] Only one month later, Kuaimo Riruako resigned from the party, taking roughly half of the NUDO party with him.[74] Within the course of two months, the DTA had lost its two core ethnic constituents.

Its public statements reveal that the party failed to find a political niche in the post-apartheid state. In 2000, it called on the European Union to stop providing development aid to Namibia.[75] In parliament it continued to display African conservatism. Phillemon Moongo, in another debate on the domestic violence bill, accused Namibian women of bewitching their husbands with black magic so that their men could maintain an erection.[76] As previously, the party accused SWAPO of allocating money according to voting behavior. Various DTA leaders compared the government with the apartheid regime.[77] The ethnic tinges of the party remained visible. Kuaimo Riruako advocated a federal constitutional order that better reflected the political wishes of individual communities. In several speeches he stated that independence had only benefited the Ovambo.[78]

Although by virtue of its electoral performance, the DTA had declined to a mono-ethnic party, in general, the party did not undergo any major changes. It remained an ethnic alliance.

SWAPO: The Legacy of the Nujoma Succession

The incumbent's 1999 electoral campaign focused on the nascent CoD. The CoD represented a realistic threat to SWAPO's two-thirds majority. For the first time, it was challenged by a party whose founders had been part of the struggle for independence. In contrast to the DTA, the CoD's integrity was beyond doubt. The nomination of Ben Ulenga (Ovambo) as presidential candidate posed a real electoral threat to SWAPO's heartland.

At the start of the campaign, commentators expected SWAPO to change its previous campaign strategy. Ulenga, who had been at the forefront of the resistance struggle, appeared an unlikely target for accusations of being a stooge of the apartheid system. However, SWAPO followed its previous behavioral pattern. It decried Ulenga as traitor of the liberalization struggle. At rallies, SWAPO ministers insisted that Ulenga had provided the apartheid regime with information about SWAPO.[79] Nujoma warned the Namibian

73 *Namibian*, August 21, 2003.

74 *Namibian*, September 19, 2003. Riruako later registered his own party. Heated arguments between Riruako and DTA leader Kaura continued over which part of NUDO was the "real" NUDO.

75 *Namibian*, February 2, 2000.

76 *Namibian*, October 30, 2002.

77 *Namibian*, April 8, 2002; *Namibian*, September 9, 2003.

78 *Namibian*, August 15, 2003.

79 *Namibian*, November 11, 1999.

TABLE 4.13. *Ethnic Composition of Namibia's 1999 Cabinet*

Community	Number of Cabinet Ministers Allocated	Percentage of Cabinet Positions
Ovambo	15	67%
White	0	0%
Damara	2	9%
Kavango	2	9%
Herero	1	5%
Nama	1	5%
Caprivian	1	5%
Colored	0	0%
TOTAL	22	100%

Source: Author's compilation based on Namibian media sources.

electorate to be wary of new parties as these had been infiltrated by whites. The dangers associated with the CoD were compared with the achievements of SWAPO in office.[80] As in previous periods, the party stressed its merits – access to jobs, health, and education – and its tenacity during "the struggle." Domestic observers argued that because the CoD was a SWAPO breakaway, the governing party's campaign was more passionate and ardent than all previous ones.[81]

SWAPO's 1999 manifesto lacked programmatic content. Only 36 percent of all manifesto statements had a programmatic content. The manifesto emphasized categories 506 (Education Expansion: positive, 6.5 percentage points) and 506 (Welfare State Expansion: positive, 10.4 percentage points).

At the polls, SWAPO defended its two-thirds parliamentary majority. Its electoral support remained uncontested in the North and widespread in the South. As Table 4.12 demonstrates, the PDS decreased, whereas the PNS increased. Both changes were driven by the migration of Ovambo traders and workers from the North to the South.[82] However, the national character of SWAPO remains beyond doubt. Nujoma's third cabinet confirms this. See Table 4.13.

The total number of Ovambo ministers corresponds to the size of the Ovambo community. For several years, Nujoma had been under pressure to increase the number of Ovambo ministers, given their numerical strength and the dedication the community had shown during the fight against

[80] *Namibian*, November 29, 1999.

[81] Interview with Justine Hunter, executive director of Namibia Institute for Democracy, July 30, 2008, Windhoek.

[82] Interview with Gerhard Tötemeyer, former SWAPO deputy minister and member of the National Assembly, July 10, 2008, Windhoek.

apartheid.[83] The allocation of cabinet positions to the Damara included two key ministries, the office of the prime minister (Hage Geingob) and the foreign ministry (Theo-Ben Gurirab). These positions were traditionally reserved for non-Ovambos.[84]

For the first time since 1989, Namibia's whites were not represented at the cabinet table. It would be an oversimplification to accuse SWAPO of the deliberate political marginalization of Namibia's whites. Two factors must be taken into consideration. The first is the political attitudes of Namibia's whites toward SWAPO's land policy, which is generally seen as accommodating of white interests ("willing seller, willing buyer"). The land policy relied on the willingness of large-scale farmers to sell a minor part of their land to the Namibian government at current market prices. This rarely materialized. Jan de Wet, the chairman of Namibia's commercial farmer association and a life-long supporter of the principles of political apartheid, publicly appealed to white farmers to start contributing positively to land reform or face the consequences.[85] The second is the attitude of Namibia's white population toward SWAPO. Klaus Dierks, a former German-Namibian SWAPO MP, declared at his retirement from politics: "All I have had, from beginning to end, are smear campaigns from the Germans. I would not make that sacrifice again, being in politics for the German tribe."[86] He added that if white Namibians complained about marginalization, they had brought this situation on themselves. German political loyalty was directed first and foremost toward Germany. Most German-speaking Namibians remained convinced of their image of SWAPO as a terrorist organization (Tötemeyer 2004). White attitudes toward Namibian politics are characterized by apathy and lack of interest in politics.[87] The political marginalization of white Namibians is thus due to their failure to acknowledge Namibia's post-1989 condition and their subsequent unwillingness to constructively contribute to Namibian nation-building. Despite the decline of white participation in SWAPO, the party is regarded as catch-all.

With the Nujoma era drawing to a close, speculations about a suitable successor re-emerged. As previously, the three most widely circulated names included Prime Minister Geingob, Minister for Trade and Industry Hamutenya, and Nujoma's most trusted ally, SWAPO Secretary-General

83 Interview with Gerhard Tötemeyer, former SWAPO deputy minister and member of the National Assembly, July 10, 2008, Windhoek.

84 Interview with Andrew du Pisani, University of Namibia, July 21, 2008, Windhoek. Interview with Wolfgang Kleine, director of the Hans Seidl Foundation in Namibia, August 2, 2008, Windhoek.

85 *Namibian*, November 4, 2002.

86 *Namibian*, October 26, 1999.

87 Interview with Hans-Erik Staby, former DTA Member of the National Assembly, July 8, 2008, Windhoek.

Pohamba.[88] A first indication of Nujoma's own preference occurred in August 2002 when he proposed Pohamba to become Witbooi's successor as vice-president of the party.[89] Inside the Politbüro, factions formed around each candidate, each of which put forward suggestions for the new SWAPO leadership line-up. The Nujoma camp proposed Ngarikutuke Tjirange (Herero) as new secretary-general, whereas the Hamutenya faction supported Nashas Angula (Ovambo). The group around Geingob favored former cabinet member Ben Amathila (Ovambo). All factions were cross-cutting in terms of ethnicity. All individuals supported by Nujoma belonged to the party's old guard.[90]

In late August 2002, Nujoma sacked Geingob as prime minister and offered him the post as minister for local government, which Geingob rejected. His relegation was the result of his outspoken criticism of attempts to facilitate a fourth term of Nujoma – an option the president was contemplating.[91] Out of office, Geingob soon found himself voted out of the Politbüro.[92] After Nujoma declared publicly in April 2004 that he was not considering a fourth term, the Politbüro subsequently nominated three candidates for his succession. An extraordinary party congress should have the final say in the succession saga. The nominees included Hamutenya, Pohamba, and Angula. Pohamba's support based consisted of party functionaries. Hamutenya was backed by intellectuals and the business community. The nomination of Angula effectively split the Hamutenya camp.[93] Hamutenya and Pohamba emerged as front-runners.

A few days before the SWAPO congress – scheduled for late May 2004 – Hamutenya was dismissed from the cabinet without any explanation. The congress was held under dubious circumstance. Two days before the congress commenced, the location remained unknown to a large segment of SWAPO delegates.[94] Pohamba won the contest after a two-round contest with 341 to Hamutenya's 167 votes.[95] All but one vote for Angula went to Pohamba in the second round, which indicates some sort of agreement between the Angula and the Pohamba camp.[96] The question of how best to deal with the Nujoma legacy decided the outcome. A large number of

[88] *Namibian*, February 22, 2002.

[89] *Namibian*, August 6, 2002. Witbooi himself declared that he would no longer be available due to his ailing health.

[90] *Namibian*, August 9, 2002.

[91] *Namibian*, August 28, 2002.

[92] *Namibian*, September 16, 2002.

[93] *Namibian*, May 7, 2004.

[94] *Namibia*, May 27, 2004.

[95] *Namibian*, May 31, 2004. The results above are the result of the run-off. The results of the first round are Pohamba 213, Hamutenya 166 votes. The votes for Angula were not reported.

[96] *Namibian*, June 4, 2004.

delegates opted for Pohamba, as they feared that selecting the candidate not favored by the president would inevitably provoke a fourth Nujoma term.[97] The defeat of Hamutenya demonstrated that a coherent middle class that cherished technocratic leadership was unable to succeed.[98] Ethnic-strategic considerations were also at work. The Politbüro had nominated only Ovambo candidates. A non-Ovambo presidential candidate might not have found the same degree of support in the North when confronted by Ulenga's CoD. SWAPO as a whole remained national in terms of its composition: party factions were cross-cutting. SWAPO's leadership composition was now composed of Nujoma as president, Pohamba as vice-president, and Tjirange (Herero) as secretary-general. A closer look at the Politbüro reveals a significant number of representatives of the numerous smaller communities; the same is true of the party list of the candidates for the National Assembly.[99]

In the media, Nujoma's outbursts reached new heights. At the annual meeting of the National Union of Namibian Workers, Nujoma instructed them to work around the clock to protect the nation against anti-African forces.[100] His ongoing support for Zimbabwean President Mugabe followed the same reasoning:

> Today it is Zimbabwe, tomorrow it is Namibia or any other country. We must unite and support Zimbabwe. We cannot allow imperialism to take over our continent again. We must defend ourselves. (...) In Namibia we will not allow these lesbians and gays. We fought the liberation struggle without that. We do not need it in our country.[101]

The labeling of SWAPO "enemies" as homosexuals and alcoholics had become the norm. Ulenga supporters and SWAPO supporters opposed to his fourth term regularly became popular targets.[102] The SWAPO Youth League increasingly turned into a hotbed of the party's most radical members. Many of its members became de facto spokespersons for the Nujoma camp. Its chairman, Paulus Kapia, advocated that public appointments should only be granted to the party's most loyal members.[103] In line with Nujoma, the Youth League accused private newspapers of serving the interests of the Western world.[104]

97 *Namibian*, April 16, 2004.
98 *Namibian*, June 11, 2004. Interview with Andre du Pisani, University of Namibia, July 21, 2008, Windhoek.
99 *Namibian*, October 4, 2004.
100 *Namibian*, January 18, 2002.
101 Cited in *Namibian*, August 19, 2002, pp. 1–2.
102 *Namibian*, May 26, 2004.
103 *Namibian*, February 12, 2003.
104 *Namibian*, July 16, 2004. From September 2002 onward, SWAPO no longer advertised in *The Nambian*.

TABLE 4.14. *Bills Passed by the National Assembly Between 2004 and 2005*

Name of Bill	Comment	Impact on Ethnic Relations
2005 State-Owned Enterprise Council Bill	the government took over responsibility for the running of parastatals	no
2007 Labor Bill	the bill changed the procedures for resolving labor disputes through arbitration, and added a significant extension of employees' holiday and compassionate leave entitlement	no
2009 Communications Bill		no
2010 Financial Institutions and Markets Bill		no

Source: Author's compilation based on Economist Intelligence Unit, expert interviews, and the Namibian media. All data are with the author.

Government ministers refrained from these hostilities and focused their energy on outlining the challenges of the day. The technocratic content of the bills tabled in parliament shows that SWAPO in essence stuck to its catch-all character. Behind closed doors, cabinet members urged the donor community not to give too much weight to the former president's statements.[105] Large segments of the white business community remained in close contact with the party's hierarchy.[106] In most public appearances, the party stuck to the same rhetoric it had employed since independence and made extensive references to previous achievements.

SWAPO retained its catch-all character. Its support base remained national, its factions were ethnically diverse, it pursued technocratic policies, and it continued to form an all-inclusive government. Only the Nujoma wing cultivated its antiwhite discourse.

OBSERVATION PERIOD 4

Between 2005 and 2009, the SWAPO government introduced four bills, which became law. See Table 4.14. None of these had any impact on ethnic relations.

105 Interview with Wolfgang Kleine, director of the Hans Seidl Foundation in Namibia, August 2, 2008, Windhoek.

106 Confidential interview with a previously high-ranking member of the SWAPO Politbüro.

The Rise and Fall of the Congress of Democrats

Since its formation in 1999, the CoD included a variety of rank-and-file civil servants and former SWAPO members from all regions. The party formed out of frustration with Nujoma's third term, Namibia's involvement in the war in Angola, and general unhappiness about the visible lack of policies with the potential to move the country ahead. Neither its endless glorification of "the struggle," nor the technocratic approach was conducive to the mobilization of the country's growing youth (Tötemeyer 2004).

The CoD's initial leadership included Ben Ulenga (Ovambo) as party president, Rosa Namises (Herero) as vice-president, Tsudao Gurirab (Damara) as secretary-general, and Uli Eins (White) as treasurer.[107] Shortly after its first congress, divisions emerged between chairman Ulenga and the so-called "Concerned Group" led by Nora Schimming-Chase (Herero[108]). Schimming-Chase had narrowly lost the vote for the party's vice presidency and blamed her defeat on voting irregularities. In subsequent years, these divisions worsened over Ulenga's abrasive and erratic leadership. Ulenga had given up a secure position as Namibian diplomat and therefore felt he had sacrificed more than other CoD leaders. Consequently, he believed he should be given a greater say in determining the party's direction than anyone else.[109] The division between Ulenga and Shimming-Chase was largely personal and not driven by ethnic antagonism. It never led to the rise of an Ovambo or Herero faction. Members of the Concerned Group originated from all parts of the country. To accommodate their concerns, Schimming-Chase was elected chairperson of the party.

Relations inside the CoD remained strained. At the third party congress in 2004, Ulenga faced strong competition for the CoD presidency by Schimming-Chase and the recently elected Secretary-General Ignatius Shixwameni (Herero). The party overwhelmingly reelected Ulenga. Schimming-Chase was elected deputy president, and Tsudao Gurirab (Damara) was elected national chairperson. Kala Gertze (colored) was elected secretary general and Kavari Kavari treasurer.[110]

The CoD's 2004 campaign focused on SWAPO's neglect of democratic norms and SWAPO's rhetoric against those who criticized the government. In the months leading up to the 2004 election, the party highlighted the various corruption scandals SWAPO ministers had been involved in. With regard to the distribution of land, the CoD advocated the implementation of existing laws.[111] The CoD elections strategy was similar to the strategy

[107] *Namibian*, August 2, 1999.
[108] Nora Schimming-Chase is of mixed German-Herero heritage.
[109] Confidential interview with Western donors working closely with the CoD.
[110] *Namibian*, August 2, 2004.
[111] *Namibian*, October 22, 2004.

chosen by the DTA. However, it avoided the ethnic connotations of previous DTA campaigns. It criticized the governing party's conduct without insinuating that it favored one community over another. It did market itself to communal leaders, but it appealed to a small segment of the Namibian middle class, which previously had backed SWAPO.

It criticized the abuse of public funds by the government, but it vehemently rejected Nujoma's antiwhite and anti-Western oratory.[112]

An examination of its 2004 manifesto shows 41 percent of the manifesto content to be of programmatic content. Thirty percentage points are due to three policy categories: category 504 (Welfare State Expansion: positive, 18 percent of the overall content), category 506 (Education Expansion: positive, 6 percentage points), and category 606 (Social Harmony: positive, 6 percentage points). The number of effective policy statements (3.9) is very low. Therefore, the CoD manifesto is classified as nonprogrammatic.

Its electoral performance remained disappointing. The CoD performed well in traditional opposition areas of the Southern provinces. Its stronghold was the ethnically mixed Khomas region, which contains a significant segment of Herero and Ovambo voters. In the Northern regions, it underperformed, yet did slightly better than the DTA had done previously. See Table 4.15.

At first sight, its medium to high PDS and its medium to low PNS are indicative of an alliance party. These quantitative findings should not be taken at face value. Ulenga was Ovambo, yet the party fared comparatively well in the (non-Ovambo) South. The PNS calculated on the basis of Afrobarometer data confirms the national support base of the party. The party's ability to gain votes in the North was hampered because of sporadic violence organized by SWAPO supporters.[113] In terms of its electoral output, I classify the party as a catch-all party.

The party remained divided between the Ulenga camp and those appalled by his leadership. Ultimately, the party became dysfunctional. The National Executive Council called for an extraordinary national congress in 2007 to hold new party elections. The Schimming-Chase group rejected the move. Nevertheless, the congress took place and resulted in a walk-out by the Schimming-Chase camp, after their candidate for the presidency, Shixwameni (Herero), lost by only 15 votes. More than 50 ballots were declared void. The new leadership line-up consisted exclusively of Ulenga supporters. Alfred Chilinda (Caprivi) was elected vice-president, and Rosa Namises (Herero) was elected new secretary-general.[114] At the time of writing, the Namibian High Court has ruled a re-run of the 2007 congress.

112 *Namibian*, November 15, 2005; *Namibian*, October 7, 2004.

113 *Namibian*, November 11, 2004.

114 *Namibian*, May 7, 2007. Other leadership positions were not reported by the media. The party headquarter was not accessible given the ongoing legal uncertainty over the outcome of the party congress.

TABLE 4.15. *Parties' Electoral Performance in 2004*

T4	SWAPO PDS	CoD PDS	Vote Share of Region
Caprivi	3%	7%	3%
Erongo	6%	10%	8%
Hardap	3%	10%	4%
Karas	4%	12%	5%
Kavango	11%	8%	9%
Khomas	14%	32%	17%
Kunene	2%	2%	3%
Ohangwena	14%	1%	11%
Omaheke	2%	2%	4%
Omusati	15%	1%	12%
Oshana	11%	3%	9%
Oshikoto	10%	4%	8%
Otjozondjupa	5%	9%	7%

PDS CoD: 71 / average diverging points across time and space: 52
PNS CoD: .58/ average PNS across time and space: .67
PNS CoD based on Afrobarometer data collected in 2005:
.90/ average PNS across time and space: .72
PDS SWAPO: 24/ average diverging points across time and space: 52
PNS SWAPO: .84/ average PNS across time and space: .67
PNS SWAPO based on Afrobarometer data collected in 2005:
.76/ average PNS across time and space: .72

Source: Author's compilation.

In parliament, the CoD accused the government of corruption and criticized Pohamba for his dependency on Nujoma.[115] It played on the governing party's unresolved detainee question by tabling motions in parliament concerning the fate of SWAPO prisoners in Angola.[116] However, given its internal divisions, its small number of MPs, and its lack of a working infrastructure, it was hardly visible after the 2004 elections. The technocratic approach of the government toward policy making did not allow the opposition to throw a challenge.

I classify the CoD as a catch-all party. Its leadership bridged the country's dominant ethnic cleavage lines. Its motive of formation, its rhetoric, and the nature of its party factions were typical of a catch-all party. The party stayed clear of traditional leaders.[117] Afrobarometer data prove that the party could rely on nationwide support.

[115] *Namibian*, November 23, 2005.

[116] *Namibian*, October 11, 2006.

[117] In some policy fields the stance of the CoD was diametrically opposed to the view of traditional leaders. The health policy of the CoD, for example, foresaw compulsory HIV tests to demonstrate that the disease affected all sectors of society.

TABLE 4.16. *Ethnic Composition of Namibia's 2004 Cabinet*

Community	Number of Cabinet Ministers Allocated	Percentage of Cabinet Ministers Allocated
Ovambo	17	65%
White	0	0%
Damara	2	7%
Kavango	3	12%
Herero	3	12%
Nama	0	0%
Caprivian	1	4%
Colored	0	0%
TOTAL	**26**	100%

Source: Author's compilation.

SWAPO and Pohamba

For the first time since independence, SWAPO contested the parliamentary and presidential elections with a different presidential candidate. Despite this, the SWAPO campaign focused on Nujoma. It was not any different from any of the previous campaigns. Many inside and outside the party noted that the governing party found it difficult to justify its access to power.[118] The 2004 election manifesto displayed a slight decline of programmatic content from (36 percent to 34 percent). Neither its campaign nor its manifesto had noticeable programmatic undertones; the same is true for the relatively few bills the party proposed in parliament.

Once more, SWAPO secured a two-thirds parliamentary majority. Its PNS falls into the high to very high and its PDS into the low to very low category. Its PNS based on Afrobarometer survey data also remained high. The election illustrated that the party was virtually without competition, whatever its internal state.

Pohamba's first cabinet was dominated by Ovambo speakers, yet – as previously – smaller communities were represented according to their numerical strength (see Table 4.16).

Pohamba's impact on the party was low. SWAPO remained torn between a Nujoma and a Hamutenya faction.[119] In December 2005, the immediate former minister of trade and industry, Jesaya Nyamu (Ovambo), was expelled from the party. His expulsion constituted the latest in a long row of Nujoma-led purges. The root cause of Nyamu's dismissal was his intention to form an alternative party. Nyamu had considered this option in

118 Interview with Gerhard Tötemeyer, former SWAPO deputy minister and member of the National Assembly, July 10, 2008, Windhoek.

119 *Namibian*, March 9, 2005.

written form at the time of Hamutenya's expulsion from the cabinet one year earlier.[120] Under mysterious circumstances, his private notes had found their way to Nujoma supporters and subsequently to the public.

In November 2007, Nyamu and Hamutenya registered a new party, the Rally for Democracy and Progress (RDP).[121] Inside SWAPO, pro- and anti-Nujoma forces engaged in regional leadership battles. Many had to be resolved by the courts.[122] All over the country, party functionaries were asked to swear an oath of loyalty to SWAPO.[123] Several leaders from the second row, such as Ambassador Shapua Kaukungua and former Deputy Minister Michaela Hübsche, declared that intra-party democracy was more threatened ever before.[124] The drama reached a peak in October 2007, when Nujoma tried to initiate a mass purge. Had his initiative been successful, it would have caused the downfall of several senior cabinet ministers. Nujoma's initiative failed. The party leadership, in particular those who had remained a neutral stance in previous battles, dealt a blow to Nujoma further ambitions. SWAPO's independent wing called on Nujoma to resign from his position as party president.[125]

The party congress in late November 2007 elected Pohamba as new party president, former Prime Minister Hage Geingob (Damara) as vice-president, and Pendukeni Ithana (Ovambo) as (first female) secretary-general.[126] All previous leadership positions remained occupied by the same people. Commentators noticed the new leadership's conciliatory approach toward dissenting party voices. Geingob's political mini-comeback as prime minister was the most visible result.[127] New divisions inside the party occurred between the party's hierarchy and the women's wing, which at times fervently (yet unsuccessfully) demanded that 50 percent of all positions in the party's Politbüro should be allocated to women.[128] The party's youth wing remained Nujoma's loyal adjutant and organized various smear campaigns against Hamutenya and those allied with him.

Under President Pohamba, SWAPO's rhetoric altered conspicuously. Whereas previously there had been a mix of racialist and catch-all rhetoric, now the catch-all element prevailed. In his first few months in office, the new president highlighted the need to fight corruption, which he decried as the main cause for the underperformance of the Namibian economy.[129] His

[120] *New Era*, December 12, 2005.
[121] *New Era*, November 9, 2007; *Namibian*, November 9, 2007.
[122] *Namibian*, February 17, 2006; *Namibian*, May 11, 2006; *Namibian*, May 22, 2006; *Namibian*, July 27, 2006; *Namibian*, February 28, 2007.
[123] *Namibian*, November 13, 2007.
[124] *Namibian*, February 9, 2007.
[125] *Namibian*, October 2, 2007.
[126] *Namibian*, November 30, 2007. The position of party chairman remained dormant.
[127] *Namibian*, March 9, 2007.
[128] *Namibian*, September 15, 2006.
[129] *Namibian*, March 22, 2006.

other priorities included the need to ensure law and order and the provision of better education and health.[130] Statements critical of white Namibians were now pursued by second-rank politicians, in particular, representatives of the Youth League.[131]

After Pohamba's take-over as party president, SWAPO became slightly more accommodating of party critics. Nujoma's racialist rhetoric became less salient, although it was kept alive by the Youth League. In the period between 2004 and 2009, very little changed in comparison with previous periods. SWAPO, therefore, remained a catch-all party.

NAMIBIA AFTER THE 2009 ELECTIONS

The period after 2009 deserves some brief comments. The formation of the RDP did not usher in a new period of multiparty competition. SWAPO remained the dominant party, lacking a serious competitor for power. The RDP followed in the footsteps of previous opposition parties; it failed to formulate coherent policy alternatives. The party spent the better part between 2009 and 2012 trying to get the Namibian Supreme Court first to cancel and later to verify the 2009 election results. This proved futile. In terms of its rhetoric, the party highlighted policy deficiencies of the SWAPO government, particularly in the area of law and order. Thus far, the RDF has not fallen apart, which is indicative of ongoing harmonious ethnic relations inside the party. The RDF leadership is drawn from all corners of the country, with its top positions filled by Ovambo. Its main support remains the non-Ovambo South.

Inside SWAPO, the divide between the rhetorically radical Nujoma camp and the rest continues to haunt intra-party relations. The nomination of Utoni Nujoma, the son of the founding president, to the position of minister of foreign affairs raised the fear of many that SWAPO might fall back into the hands of the Nujoma family. Overall, however, the choice of ministers and the elections to the SWAPO national leadership showed clear signs of continuity. The leadership set-up and the cabinet maintained its ethnic balance. All party elections were carefully orchestrated by the party leadership. Recent months were characterized by the question of who will become the next SWAPO presidential candidate. Toward the end of 2011, it appeared evident that Hage Geingob is most likely to face SWAPO secretary-general Livula-Ithana in a leadership contest.

POLITICAL PARTIES IN AFRICA: FINDINGS FROM NAMIBIA

The salience of ethnicity in Namibian party politics is low. SWAPO has been a catch-all party from its inception. It has consistently managed to bridge

[130] *Namibian*, April 13, 2007.
[131] *Namibian*, June 22, 2006.

the country's dominant ethnic cleavages. At no point in time was SWAPO at risk of disintegrating into mono-ethnic parties, although the party faced a multiethnic alliance, the DTA, as main competitor.

Although in the pre-1989 period SWAPO was loosely affiliated with the Eastern bloc, it refrained from ideological statements or policies. The analyses of party manifestos and the examination of SWAPO-sponsored bills show that SWAPO was devoid of any programmatic convictions. In terms of its actual rhetoric, the party highlighted its achievements for Namibia. The party increasingly pursued a racialist rhetoric, denouncing white Namibians and those affiliated with the opposition as traitors of the liberalization struggle. However, this was only one aspect of its approach to the public. Its catch-all elements prevailed. Party factions emerged once a suitable successor for former President Nujoma had to be determined. Throughout the whole period under scrutiny, SWAPO managed to bridge Namibia's dominant cleavage lines. SWAPO could always rely on nationwide support. Although the Ovambo regions were its heartlands, it derived considerable support from the non-Ovambo regions. Between 1989 and 2009, very little changed inside the party. It is important to stress that SWAPO's relationship with intra-party democracy is complicated at best. Doubts remain regarding to what extent the party has managed to overcome its legacy as liberation army.

If SWAPO serves as the prototype of a catch-all party, the DTA is the prototype of an ethnic alliance. The party's internal division into numerous mono-ethnic parties and its failures to overcome these proved detrimental to its political survival. Its rhetoric had visible anti-Ovambo undercurrents. It maintained close links with all traditional leaders bar the Ovambo. Its electoral support never managed to reach Namibia's North. As SWAPO, its election manifestos and its rhetoric were free of ideological beliefs. In line with findings from Kenya, the historical evolution of DTA demonstrates that multiethnic alliances do not stand the test of time. Ultimately, the logic of ethnic politics leads to party fission.

The political stand-off between SWAPO and the DTA – a mixed-party system – eventually gave way to a new political constellation. With the rise of the CoD, the salience of ethnicity in party politics decreased further. The CoD resembled SWAPO in all aspects of party life – a national composition of leadership, a national support base, personalistic party factions, and a catch-all rhetoric. Table 4.17 summarizes all our results for the Namibian cases.

Although the DTA and the CoD both failed to qualify as relevant parties, the inclusion of the official opposition in each observation period provided a more thorough understanding of the Namibian party system. The transformation from a mixed to a nonethnic system could thus be illustrated. In Namibia, enduring party competition has led to more national parties.

TABLE 4.17. *Summary of Disaggregated Results for All Political Parties in Namibia*

Party:	Party Scoring Sheet										
SWAPO	Party Goals		Electoral Strategy		Organizational Structure			Social Base			
Observation Period	Motive of Formation	Rhetoric	Electoral Rhetoric	Content of Election Manifesto	National Coverage	Party Factions	Party Apparatus	Leadership Composition	Cabinet Composition	PDS and PNS	Classification
T1	pro-democracy/ catch-all	catch-all	promoting unity	low	n/a	None	not visible	bridging cleavages	bridging cleavages	medium to low; medium to high	catch-all
T2	pro-democracy/ catch-all	catch-all; anti-white	catch-all	low	n/a	based on individuals	Youth League and women's wing visible	bridging cleavages	bridging cleavages	low to very low; medium to high	catch-all
T3	pro-democracy/ catch-all	catch-all; antiwhite	catch-all; anti-white	low	n/a	based on individuals	Youth League and women's wing visible	bridging cleavages	bridging cleavages	low to very low; medium to high	catch-all
T4	pro-democracy/ catch-all	catch-all	catch-all	low	n/a	None	Youth League and women's wing visible	bridging cleavages	bridging cleavages	low to very low; high to very high	**catch-all**
Across Time	pro-democracy/ catch-all	catch-all	catch-all	low	n/a	based on individuals	Youth League and women's wing visible	bridging cleavages	bridging cleavages	low to very low; high to very high	**catch-all**

(*continued*)

TABLE 4.17 *(continued)*

Party	Party Scoring Sheet										
	Party Goals		Electoral Strategy		Organizational Structure			Social Base			
DTA Observation Period	Motive of Formation	Rhetoric	Electoral Rhetoric	Content of Election Manifesto	National Coverage	Party Factions	Party Apparatus	Leadership Composition	Cabinet Composition	PDS and PNS	Classification
T1	pro-democracy	catch-all	catch-all; ethnic	high due to overemphasis on individual policy categories	n/a	ethnic	individual ethnic parties in touch with respective elders	failing to bridge cleavages	n/a	medium to high; medium to high	ethnic-alliance
T2	pro-democracy	catch-all: statements dependent on SWAPO policy of the day; ethnic	catch-all; ethnic	high due to overemphasis on individual policy categories	n/a	ethnic	individual ethnic parties in touch with respective elders	failing to bridge cleavages	n/a	high to very high; medium to low	ethnic-alliance
T3	pro-democracy	catch-all: statements dependent on SWAPO policy of the day; ethnic	catch-all; ethnic	high due to overemphasis on individual policy categories	n/a	ethnic	individual ethnic parties in touch with respective elders	failing to bridge cleavages	n/a	high to very high; low to very low	ethnic-alliance
Across time	pro-democracy	catch-all	ethnic	high due to overemphasis on individual policy categories	n/a	ethnic	ethnic	failing to bridge cleavages	n/a	high to very high; low to very low	ethnic-alliance
Party: CoD Observation Period											
T4	pro-democracy' SWAPO break-away	catch-all	catch-all	low	n/a	based on individuals	not visible	bridging cleavage lines	n/a	medium to high; medium to low	catch-all

Source: Author's compilation.

In Kenya, ethnic parties are ubiquitous. In Namibia, a nonethnic party dominates the political landscape; ethnic and nonethnic parties coexist peacefully. In both countries, enduring multiparty competition does not lead to the hardening of ethnic relations. The next chapter examines political parties in Ghana, a country in which nonethnic parties are ubiquitous.

5

Ghana

The Ubiquity of Nonethnic Parties

In Kenya, ethnic parties dominate the scene. In Namibia, ethnic and nonethnic parties shape the political arena. My third case, Ghana, illustrates that in some African countries the political landscape is dominated by various nonethnic party types, including the catch-all party, the programmatic party, and the personalistic party. It is the only case in which the programmatic party and the personalistic party feature. Ghana has traditionally played a pivotal role in the study of African politics. Both in the immediate post-independence period and in the post–third wave period, the research community dedicated a lot of attention to Ghanaian politics.

After the return of multiparty democracy, political contest is dominated by two major parties, the National Patriotic Party (NPP) and the National Democratic Congress (NDC).

The NPP was in opposition between 1992 and 2000. In 2008, the NPP was voted back into opposition. Over time, the NPP transformed from a multiethnic alliance to a programmatic party. Once in government, it transformed into a catch-all party. The NDC was in government between 1992 and 2000, in opposition between 2000 and 2008, and was voted back into government in late 2008. The party started out as a personalistic party; subsequently it became a catch-all party. Thus, Ghana is the only country where the programmatic party type emerges. Both major parties display visible ideological predilections.

Historically, Ghanaian politics displays a comparatively uneven trajectory in which military dictatorship repeatedly succeeded over attempts to implement a sustainable parliamentary democracy until the inauguration of the Fourth Republic in 1992. The first section of this chapter looks at these previous attempts and displays how they are interwoven with the rise of ethnic cleavages. The main part of the chapter is dedicated to the two major political parties in Ghana's Fourth Republic, the NPP and the NDC. Table 5.1 summarizes the cases and observations examined in this chapter.

TABLE 5.1. *Overview of Ghanaian Cases and Observations*

Observation Period	Significant and/or Effective Party
Period 1 (1992–1996)	NPP
	NDC
Period 2 (1996–2000)	NPP
	NDC
Period 3 (1990–2004)	NPP
	NDC
Period 4 (2004–2008)	NPP
	NDC

Source: Author's compilation.

THE FIRST THREE REPUBLICS, ETHNIC CLEAVAGE LINES, AND POLITICAL PARTIES

Traditionally, party competition in Ghana has been structured around two major political traditions, Nkrumahism, "a little bit to the right," and Busiaism, "a little bit to the left" (Apter 1955, Nugent 1995). In the immediate pre- and post-independence period, the Nkrumahists were organized in the Convention's People's Party (CPP). The CPP advocated an immediate end to colonialism and stressed the plights of the socially and economically disadvantaged segments of Ghanaian society. The Busiaists, under the leadership of J.B. Danquah and later Kofi Busia, organized in the United Gold Coast Convention (UGCC) and later in the Progress Party (PP), represented the conventional elements of Ghanaian political society: wealthy farmers, lawyers, and all those who had received Western education. Although elections in the run-up to the First Republic (1951–1957) were regularly won by the CPP, the Second Republic (1969–1972) was dominated by the PP. Ghana's short-lived Third Republic (1979– 1981) saw a return to power by the Nkrumahist (Zollberg 1964, Rathbone 1973, Morrison 2004, Morrison and Hong 2006).

The military coups of Jerry J. Rawlings in June 1979 and in December 1981 introduced a third element to political party competition, whose relationship with the two conventional elements of Ghanaian politics is not easy to decipher. From its inception, Rawlings espoused a decidedly left-wing rhetoric. In his first address after his 1981 coup, Rawlings envisioned Ghana to replace elitist politicians with genuine representatives of the ordinary people.[1] This notwithstanding, the Rawlings administration

[1] "Fellow citizens of Ghana, as you noticed, we are not playing the national anthem. In other words this is not a coup. I ask for nothing less than a revolution (...) In other words, the people, the farmers, the police, the soldiers, the workers you – the guardians – rich or poor,

implemented large-scale economic reforms based on the recommendations of the International Monetary Fund and the World Bank. At first, the visible contradictions between his rhetoric and his actions endangered his presidency; however, the People's National Democratic Congress (PNDC) became ultimately associated with him (Ninsin 1987, Adedeji 2001). His outbursts against Ghana's ruling elites, his charismatic appeals to ordinary people, and his modest background have led many to refer to his military coup as "small-boy revolution."[2] Many members of the administration were inspired by the ideas of socialism, and a significant number of them had been part of the Nkrumahist movement (Nugent 1995, Oquaye 2004). Rawling's rejection of Ghana's two major political traditions led many to describe his impact on the political science as the "Rawlings factor" in Ghanaian politics.

Despite these ideological pursuits, Ghanaian party politics incorporated an ethnic dimension. Two cleavage lines emerged. First, an Akan/non-Akan divide and, in particular, a divide between the Akan and the Ewe. Second, a division between the country's Muslim-dominated North and the Christian South.

Historically, Akan societies regarded Ewe culture as inferior. In the precolonial era, the Ewe served as manual laborers for Akan farmers. Many Akan chiefs had Ewe servants. In the run-up to independence, the Ewe became seen as a threat to the territorial integrity of the Ghanaian state. Before the First World War, the Volta region (British Togoland) had been part of German Togoland. After the Second World War, significant segments of the Ewe population favored reunification with French Togoland (the former German Togoland). The Togoland Congress emerged and demanded the territorial reunification of the Ewe people. In a United Nations–led referendum, however, a slim majority voted against secession from Ghana. In the Southern section of the Volta region, a majority voted in favor of reunification with Togo.[3] Pan-Ewe nationalism rekindled at various stages in the 1960s and 1970s (Brown 1980, 1982, Austin 1963, Amenuemy 1989).

Akan-Ewe antagonism shaped the transition from military rule to the Second Republic (1966 and 1969). Under the leadership of General Emmanuel Kotoka (Ewe), the Ghanaian military overthrew Nkrumah in 1966 to facilitate a return to parliamentary democracy. Kotoka was killed

should be part of the decision-making process of this country." Rawlings cited in Oquaye 2004: 97. In his early speeches, Rawlings consistently referred to the need to establish a political system based on revolutionary socialism. See Adedeji 2001.

[2] What helped Rawlings were the particular manner in which his first military coup had come about and the way he treated former military rulers in the aftermath of his 1979 coup. For a historical insight, see Hansen and Collins 1980, where the term "Rawlings revolution" is used for the first time.

[3] A total of 93,095 votes were cast in favor of remaining a part of Ghana, 67,492 against (Austin 1963: 142).

in 1967 in a counter-coup led by Benjamin Arthur, an Akan from the Brong-Ahafo region. All of Arthur's collaborators were Akan. Subsequently, Arthur's counter-coup was portrayed as a conspiracy of the Akan against the Ewe. Political struggles in the run-up to the inauguration of the Second Republic exacerbated ethnic tensions. General Afrifa (Akan), Kotoka's successor as chairman of the military transitional government, cultivated a political friendship with Kofi Busia (Akyem/Akan). His two vice-chairmen, Harlley and Deku (both Ewe), supported K.A. Gbedemah (Ewe), the new figurehead of the Nkrumahist tradition. The 1969, electoral campaign played on cultural stereotypes. The complete lack of Ewe participation in Busia's 1969 cabinet was widely noticed and intensified the Akan/ Ewe divide (Chazan 1982, Baynham 1985a, 1985b, Danso-Boafo 1996, Asante and Gyimah-Boadi 2004).

An additional cleavage line exists between the country's Muslim-dominated North and the Christian-dominated South. The North does not constitute one monolithic cultural block. However, in Ghanaian political discourse, the North is culturally and economically distinct (Lentz and Nugent 2000). In the mid-1950s, the Northern People's Party represented the particularities of the Northern regions (Austin 1964). The cultural sensitivities of the North were greatly affected by the Alien Compliance Order of 1971. The Order required all residents who lacked appropriate documentation to leave the country. Thousands of Northern residents were forced into emigration. The Order thus complicated the relationship between the North and the Busiaist tradition (Peil 1974, Brydon 1985).

The political divisions between the Akan and the Ewe as well as between the North and the South are regarded as Ghana's dominant ethnic cleavage lines. As shown, this is an abstraction; yet it corresponds to the political divisions reflected in Ghana's political discourse. With regard to the North, it would be wrong to examine the relationship between individual Northern communities and the South at the level of political parties. On their own, these communities are politically insignificant. The situation is different among the Akan; the Ashanti on their own are numerically strong. However, adding an additional cleavage line (Ashanti versus Non-Akan or Ashanti versus the rest) would not alter the study's findings. The ethnic composition of Ghana is shown in Table 5.2, and the ethnic composition of Ghana provinces is shown in Table 5.3.

OBSERVATION PERIOD 1

In the late 1980s, opposition to the Rawlings dictatorship was coalescing. The key event that gave momentum to the democratization movement was Adu Boahen's J.B. Danquah lectures delivered at the British Council in Accra. Advocating an end to the "culture of silence," Boahen, professor of African history at the university of Legon, decried the PNDC regime as

TABLE 5.2. *Ethnic Composition of Ghana Nationwide*

Ethnic Group	Percentage of Population
Akan	49.1%
Mole-Dagbon (Northern)	16.5%
Ewe	12.7%
Ga-Adangbe	8%
Guan	4.4%
Gurma (Northern)	3.9%
Grusi (Northern)	2.8%
Mande-Busanga (Northern)	1.1%
Other	1.5%

Source: Ghana Statistical Service. 2002 Census data from Ghana.

having failed the country. Under pressure from donors, the democratization movement, and individuals inside the PNDC government, the Rawlings government initiated a program for the return of democratic rule. After several rounds of consultation with civil society about the future constitutional set-up, the government inaugurated a Consultative Assembly in 1991. The Assembly drafted a new constitution, which was subsequently put to the population in a referendum (Afari-Gyan 1995, Haynes 1995, Nugent 1995, Oquaye 2004).

A small selection of bills passed by the parliament of Ghana between 1992 and 1996 is outlined in Table 5.4. Neither of these bills affected ethnic relations.

The New Patriotic Party: In the Footsteps of the PP

The NPP held its first national congress on August 15, 1992. The congress confirmed Bernard da Rocha – the former secretary-general of the Progress Party – as chairman. In his acceptance speech, da Rocha stressed the NPP's ongoing commitment to the Busia legacy.[4] At its inception, the NPP served as an umbrella group for all advocates of democratic reform. The congress was also attended by K.A. Gbedemah, Nkrumah's first minister of finance, who had been one of Busia's greatest political rivals in the Second Republic.[5] The party constitution stressed its commitment to the rule of law and the creation of a democratic state. It confirmed its respect for the institution of chieftaincy and its desire to promote a free-market economy (NPP 1998).

A variety of individuals announced their intention to serve as NPP presidential candidates. The most prominent contestants were Adu-Boahen

[4] *People's Daily Graphic*, August 15, 1992; *People's Daily Graphic*, August 16, 1992.

[5] Gbedemah lost the founding (and only) election of Ghana's Second Republic to Busia. The campaign was one of the most aggressive ones in Ghanaian history.

TABLE 5.3. *Ethnic Composition of Ghana's Provinces*

Region	Ethnic Composition
Greater Accra	Akan: 39.8% Ga: 29.7% Ewe: 18%
Eastern	Akan: 51.8% Ga-Adangbe: 18.8% Ewe: 15.9% Guan: 7.2%
Western	Akan: 78.3% Mole-Dagbon: 7.6% Ewe: 5.9%
Ashanti	Akan: 77.9% Mole-Dagbon: 8.6% Ewe: 3.2%
Brong Ahafo	Akan: 62.7% Mole-Dagbon: 15.4% Grusi: 4.3%
Central	Akan: 82% Guan: 6.1% Ewe: 4.8%
Volta	Ewe: 68.5% Guan: 9.2% Akan: 8.5%
Northern	Mole-Dagbon: 52,2% Gurma: 21.8% Akan: 10% Guan: 8.7%
Upper East	Mole-Dagbon: 74.5% Grusi: 8.5% Mande-Busanga: 6.2%
Upper West	Mole-Dagbon: 75.7% Grusi: 18.4% Akan: 3.2%

Source: Ghana Statistical Service. 2002 Census data from Ghana.

(Akan/Ashanti[6]), Ghana's most outspoken campaigner for democratic rule, and Dr. Kofi Dsane-Selby (Akan/Fante), a founding father of the PP. Less established contenders included John Kufuor (Akan/Ashanti), a former deputy foreign minister under Busia, and Dr. K. Safo-Adu (Akan/Ashanti), Busia's former minister of agriculture.[7] The Boahen supporters stressed

[6] At times, Boahen is named as Akyem. His father was Akyem, his mother Ashanti.

[7] *People's Daily Graphic*, August 15, 1992; *People's Daily Graphic*, August 16, 1992.

TABLE 5.4. *Selection of Bills Passed in Ghana Between 1992 and 1996*

Name of Bill	Comment	Impact on Ethnic Relations
1992 Representation of the People Bill	provided for the Election of a President	no
1992 Chieftancy Bill	amended the Chieftaincy Law	no
1992 Refugee Bill	prohibited the expulsion of refugees	
1992 National Media Commission Bill	provided for the Establishment of a National Media Commission	no
1993 Local Government Bill	extended the period of existence of District Assemblies	no
1993 Civil Service Bill	continued the existing civil service	no
1993 Electoral Commission Bill	established the Electoral Commission	no
1993 Commission of Human Rights and Administrative Justice Act	established the Commission of Human Rights and Administrative Justice	no
1993 Local Government Bill	established the local government system	no
1995 Export and Import Bill	revised the laws relating to external trade	no
1996 National disaster Management Bill	established the National Disaster Management Organization	no
1996 Constitution of the Republic of Ghana Amendment Bill	amended the 1992 Constitution in numerous articles	no

Source: Author's compilation based on Economic Intelligence Unit, data provided by the Parliament of Ghana, the Africa Yearbook, expert interviews, and the Ghanaian media. All data are with the author.

Boahen's virtues as an advocate for multiparty democracy and denounced his younger challengers for their lack of experience. They criticized Kufuor for his involvement with the Rawlings government (Agyeman-Duah 2006). Boahen won the contest by a landslide, and he picked Alhaji Alhassan (Northern) as his running mate. Kwame Pianim (Akan/Ashanti) became his campaign manager.[8]

[8] Boahen: 1,121 votes, Dsane-Selby: 345, Kuffour: 326.

Courage Quashigah[9] (Ewe) and Ray Kakraba-Quashie (Ewe) became the image of the NPP face in the Volta region (Nugent 1995). Shortly after being elected, Boahen paid courtesy calls to all traditional Ewe leaders.[10] The NPP thus reached out beyond the traditional strongholds of the Busia-Danquah tradition. In the party leadership, Ewe membership, however, remained absent. At its 1995 congress, the NPP voted for a new leadership. The new line-up included Peter Adjetey (Ga) as chairman; Agbalno Wosi (Northern), Salifu Bawa Deyaka (Northern), and Ama Busia (Akan/Akyem) as vice-chairmen; Hackman Agyeman (Akan) as national treasurer; and Agyenim Boateng (Akan) as secretary-general (Agyeman-Duah 2006).

The greatest challenge for the NPP's 1992 electoral campaign was the reputation of Adu-Boahen as elitist and anti-Ewe. His intellectual credentials and his large urban support were a liability in the vast rural areas of the North. Opposition utterances referring to Rawling's mixed-race heritage (Ewe/Scottish) reminded many of Busia's Alliance Compliance Order. Boahen's reference to Rawlings as *akonta* ("brother-in-law") fostered his image as an Ashanti nationalist.[11]

NPP heavyweights focused on Rawling's dismal human rights record and decried the culture of intimidation.[12] The party stressed that every vote for the NPP was first and foremost a vote for freedom.[13] Much time was dedicated to the NPP's economic agenda and its allegiance to free-market values. Boahen's made extensive reference to macroeconomic theory, by which he again appeared elitist (Jeffries and Thomas 1993).

The NPP's 1992 manifesto contained a large share of programmatic statements (46 percent). The programmatic base was not due to an overemphasis on individual policy categories.

The most emphasized programmatic categories were category 401 (Free Enterprise: positive, 5.6 percentage points) and category 402 (Incentives: positive, 5.2 percentage points); see Table 5.5.

After the 1992 elections, the NPP continued to highlight its market-friendly outlook. The economic spokesman of the NPP's parliamentary party, Kofi Apraku, criticized various governments' budgets for failing the needs of the private sector.[14] Jones Ofori Atta, the chairman of the NPP finance committee, repeatedly complained about high taxation and Ghana's oversized government machinery.[15] The party further tried to portray itself as a national force. In the Volta and the Northern regions, NPP politicians

[9] Quashigah was Rawling's cousin. He had been accused of initiating a military coup against Rawlings in the 1980s.

[10] *Statesman*, September 27, 1992.

[11] *People's Daily Graphic*, August 16, 1992.

[12] *People's Daily Graphic*, October 19, 1992.

[13] *People's Daily Graphic*, November 2, 1992.

[14] *Daily Graphic*, January 13, 1993.

[15] *Daily Graphic*, May 22, 1993; *Statesman*, May 23, 1993.

TABLE 5.5. *Programmatic Content of Election Manifestos Across Countries*

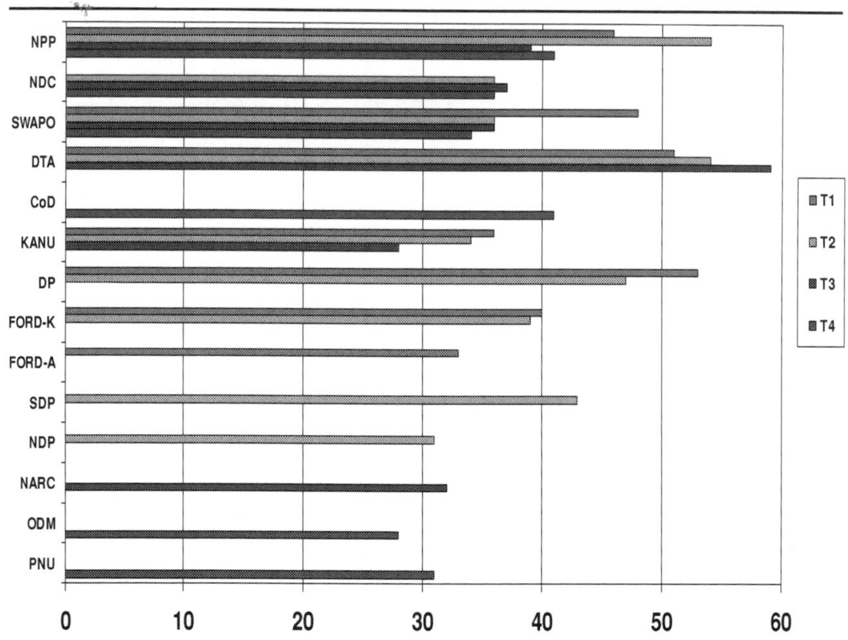

Source: Author's compilation. See also Elischer 2012.

such as Major Quashigah (Ewe) or Alhaji Alhassan (Northern) appealed to their communities to support the NPP.[16]

In terms of its electoral performance, Boahen performed over-proportionally strong in Ashanti, yet underperformed equally strong in the Volta and in the Northern regions (see Table 5.6). Due to the opposition boycott of the parliamentary elections, data from the presidential election are taken as proxy for the PDS and PNS of both parties.

The PNS and PDS are slightly below the catch-all threshold. It is noteworthy that the PNS of Busia's Progress Party in 1969 of .81 was thus significantly higher than the NPP equivalent in 1992.[17] Although political circumstances in 1969 favored Busia and those in 1992 favored Rawlings, the data indicate that the NPP vote spread is not distributed as equal as that of its predecessor.

After its boycott of the parliamentary election, divisions inside the NPP emerged over the party's future political strategy vis-à-vis the Rawlings administration. The faction led by chairman da Rocha was in favor of

[16] *Statesman*, September 6, 1992; *Statesman*, March 13, 1994; *Statesman*, May 15, 1994.

[17] Calculations are based on electoral data reprinted in *Legon Observer*, July 27, 1979.

TABLE 5.6. *Parties' Electoral Performance and Ability to Field Candidates in 1992*

	NPP		NDC		
T1	RNC[18]	PDS	RNC	PDS	Vote Share of Region
Greater Accra	n/a	16%	n/a	12%	17%
Eastern		15%		12%	12%
Western		7%		10%	10%
Ashanti		39%		10%	18%
Brong Ahafo		9%		10%	9%
Central		7%		10%	8%
Volta		1%		19%	10%
Northern		3%		9%	8%
Upper East		2%		5%	5%
Upper West		1%		3%	3%
TOTAL		100%		100%	100%

PDS Boahen: 48/ average diverging points across time and space: 52
PNS Boahen: .65/ average PNS across time and space: .67
PDS Rawlings: 26/ average diverging points across time and space: 52
PNS NDC: .88/ average PNS across time and space: .67

Source: Author's compilation based on data provided by the Electoral Commission of Ghana.

participating in consultations with the government.[19] The Boahen faction dismissed any kind of cooperation.[20] The division between the two sides mirrored the split between the two Busiaist parties of the Third Republic, the United Convention Party headed by Ofori Atta,[21] and the Popular Front Party led by Victor Owusu. The former supported the Boahen stance and the latter the views of da Rocha (Agyemen-Duah 2006). In the run-up to the 1996 elections, two factions emerged: the "Patriotic Club," which was supportive of a Kufuor candidacy, and "COMO," which backed Boahen. Both power blocs emerged from inside the Ashanti region.[22] Although both campaigned in favor of an Ashanti politician, Kufuor's power base was outside his Ashanti home region. His relationship with the NPP Ashanti regional chairman Donkor-Fordwoor – one of the party's main sponsors – was severely constrained.[23]

18 The Ghanaian Electoral Commission refused the release of the official results of the 1992 parliamentary elections.

19 The Rawlings government had offered consultation meetings as a parliamentary opposition was lacking.

20 *Africa Confidential*, November 19, 1993; *Statesman*, November 28, 1993.

21 Ofori-Atta formally suggested Boahen as NPP presidential candidate at the party's 1992 congress.

22 *The Statesman*, November 6, 1994.

23 *Statesman*, October 8, 1995.

At the NPP's 1996 national delegates' congress, numerous candidates applied to become the party's flag bearer; all candidates were Akan.[24] Both Kufour and Boahen tried to build nationwide coalitions of support. Kufuor managed to combine the votes of delegates from regions where the NPP and its predecessor parties traditionally underperformed: Northern, Upper East, Upper West, and the Volta region.[25] Boahen was less successful in rallying support outside the Akan-dominated regions. Boahen's defeat did not lead to party defections as observed in Kenya. Instead, all defeated candidates congratulated Kufuor and declared their support for him.[26]

The classification of the NPP in period 1 is not straightforward. Under Boahen, the party's Akan bias was more visible than in any subsequent period. His campaign rhetoric allowed for speculation of the party's national character. The NPP leadership did not include any Ewe representatives. Electoral indicators show that the party is slightly below the cross-national average for catch-all parties. Therefore, I classify the NPP as an ethnic alliance. After the Democratic Party in Kenya, the NPP is the second ethnic party with clearly visible programmatic foundations.

The National Democratic Congress: A Dictator Elected

The National Democratic Congress (NDC) was launched on June 11, 1992. It was made up of a number of pro-Rawlings associations, whose leaders had been beneficiaries of the Rawlings period.[27] The NDC's party statues referred to Rawlings as founder and leader of the party.[28] On September 17, 1992, Rawlings (Ewe) was unanimously nominated as NDC presidential candidate. There was no alternative candidate. The elections to all leadership positions followed the same modus operandi. For each position, there was one candidate. There was no secret ballot; individuals got their positions by acclamation. Issifu Ali (Northern) and A.A. Munufie (Northern) were "elected" as joint chairmen, and Prof. Yaw Twumasi (Akan/Ashanti), Harry Sawyer (Akan/Fante), and Joseph Caiquo (Akan/Fante) were elected as vice-chairmen. Huudu Yahaya (Northern) was given the position of secretary-general. With an Ewe as constitutionally prescribed party head, the NDC incorporated all major groups. Rawlings nominated A.K. Arkaah (Akan/Fante), the chairman of a smaller Nkrumaist party (National Convention Party), as his running mate.[29]

The NDC's 1992 election campaign stressed the party's national composition and portrayed the NPP as an Ashanti-based elitist club of corrupt

24 *Weekend Statesman*, March 7, 1996.

25 *Daily Graphic*, April 20, 1996. Kufuor gained 1,034 out of 2,000 votes against 7 candidates.

26 *Daily Graphic*, May 8, 1996; *Chronicle*, May 16, 1997.

27 *People's Daily Graphic*, June 11, 1992.

28 This was the case until 2001. See National Democratic Congress 2001.

29 *People's Daily Graphic*, October 1, 1992.

TABLE 5.7. *Ethnic Composition of Ghana's 1993 Cabinet*

Community	Number of Cabinet Ministers Allocated	Percentage of Cabinet Allocated
Akan	15	55%
Ewe	3	11%
Ga	2	7%
North	7	26%
TOTAL	27	100%

Source: Author's compilation based on Asante and Gyimah-Boadi 2004 and Ayensu and Darkwa 1999.

big-man politicians.[30] The NDC described Rawlings as the creator of true democracy, that is, democracy without the type of politicians that had necessitated his military coups. Rawlings decried the depravity of corrupt intellectuals who had betrayed the trust of the people.[31] Rawlings cultivated an informal campaign style, which included spontaneous walkabouts with farmers or manual laborers (Jeffries and Thomas 1993). The NDC thus contrasted Rawling's "humbleness" with Boahen's alleged elitism. Rawlings' achievements, such as the electrification of large parts of the North or improvements in infrastructure, also featured on the campaign trail. One of Ghana's leading newspapers, *The Chronicle*, filled its pages with pictures showing Rawlings opening new dams or inaugurating electrification projects in peripheral areas.[32] The NDC failed to produce an election manifesto.

Rawlings showed a solid performance in the three Northern regions and the Volta region. However, he also made significant inroads into the Akan regions, in particular in the Central region and in Brong-Ahafo. See Table 5.6. The Rawlings vote was spread more equally than the Boahen vote. Rawlings' electoral support is indicative of a nonethnic party, as the PNS falls into the medium to high and its PDS into the medium to low category.

The NDC cabinet comprised 27 ministries. See Table 5.7. It displayed a favoritism for the North in terms of the number of appointments. However, both the Akan and the Ewe received a share of the cabinet, which responded to the size of their population.

The legacy of Ghana's "culture of silence" and ongoing restriction on the free media means that not too much is known about diverging views

30 *People's Daily Graphic*, August 21, 1992.

31 *People's Daily Graphic*, October 19, 1992.

32 This is true of the *People's Daily Graphic*, who did so almost daily in the run-up to the presidential elections.

inside the party. The wide variety of individuals who had joined the "Rawlings revolution" caused a clash of ideological convictions, as Nkrumahists, technocrats, and military men often held diverging views regarding where the country should be headed. Factions did not emerge for as long as Rawlings was in charge.[33] Rawlings' dominance inside the NDC was paramount. Rawling's vice-president became the most prominent victim of the former dictator's notorious unwillingness to compromise. At one point, Rawlings physically attacked Arkah, after Arkah complained of being sidelined.[34]

Much of the party's rhetoric was dedicated to Rawlings' past achievements, his ongoing commitment to the nation, and the significance of his revolution.[35] Rawlings was the center of any NDC's action. In the summer of 1995, Accra was hit by severe flooding. Rawlings arrived at the scene and monitored the rescue activities. Subsequently, the media provided extensive coverage of yet another Rawlings intervention in the face of great adversity.[36] In the following weeks, the NDC provided the national media with thankful notes from Ghanaians abroad praising the president for his commitment to protect the city.[37] Although the opposition tried to impress with alternative budgets, the NDC portrayed Rawlings as the provider of shelter for the masses. The bills tabled in parliament were never debated in public – largely an outcome of the absence of a viable parliamentary opposition. None of the bills displayed any programmatic preferences, and most were technocratic in nature.

Rawlings frequently warned the media not to abuse the constitutionally guaranteed freedom of speech. On various occasions he threatened action against journalists or opposition politicians of inciting political discontent.[38] Although he continued to portray the NPP in ethnic colors, Rawlings himself – in great contrast to Daniel arap Moi – never raised fears of any group. The NDC as a whole decried tribalism and elitism, in particular the elitism of the democratic opposition.[39] The party leadership paid extensive visits to traditional elders of all communities. The combination of the NDC's national character combined with the domineering status of Rawlings – prescribed in the party's constitution and visible in political everyday life – makes the NDC a personalistic party.

33 Interview with John Mahama, NDC vice-presidential candidate 2008, April 10, 2008, Accra.

34 The punch-up took place on December 25, 1995, and was widely reported by the private media.

35 *Daily Graphic*, January 1, 1994; *Daily Graphic*, June 5, 1996.

36 *Daily Graphic*, July 6, 1995

37 *Daily Graphic*, July 26, 1995.

38 *Daily Graphic*, January 18, 1994; *Daily Graphic*, May 5, 1995. For Rawlings' implicit threats to the Ghanaian media, see Hasty 2005.

39 *Daily Graphic*, November 5, 1993; *Daily Graphic*, May 2, 1996.

TABLE 5.8. *Selection of Bills Passed in Ghana Between 1996 and 2000*

Name of Bill	Comment	Impact on Ethnic Relations
1996 Security and Intelligence Agency Bill	provided for National and Regional Security Agencies	no
1996 Ghana Health Service and Teaching Hospitals Bill	established the Health Service	no
1997 Import Bill	established higher taxes on imports	no
2000 Constitutional Amendment Bill	made it easier for the president to replace his deputy	no
2000 Public Sector Wage Bill	established a 20% wage increase for the public sector	no
2000 Industry Law Amendment Bill	strengthened the Security and Exchange Commission	no

Source: Author's compilation based on economic Intelligence Unit, data provided by the Parliament of Ghana, the Africa Yearbook, expert interviews, and the Ghanaian media. All data are with the author.

OBSERVATION PERIOD 2

In the second observation period, the NDC government passed fewer laws. As in the previous period, none affected ethnic relations (see Table 5.8). With the exception of the 2000 Wage Act, none indicated a ideological preference of the incumbent party.

The New Patriotic Party: Generation Kufuor

Under its new presidential flag bearer, the NPP approached the election campaign with essentially the same messages as in 1992. It highlighted human rights abuses – between 1992 and 1996 many opposition sympathizers had fallen victim to police shutdowns[40] – and the involvement of leading government figures in corruption affairs. It stressed the economic hardships Ghanaians were subjected to. Electricity and food supply shortages topped the political agenda. Although the content of the campaign remained the same, the style of the campaign changed. Kufuor was decidedly less academic and more inclusive than Boahen (Ayee 1998). Kufuor traveled

[40] Based on interviews with news editors of major private newspaper in Accra throughout the month of April 2008.

extensively through the North and to areas where the party had underperformed in 1992.

The programmatic content of its 1996 manifesto (54 percent) exceeded that of the previous one. The categories that the manifesto emphasized most reveal that the party tried to reach out more to ordinary Ghanaians. Category 504 (Welfare State Expansion: positive) increased from 2.5 percentage points of the overall content in 1992 to 5.2 percentage points; category 506 (Education Expansion: positive) increased from 4 percentage points to 9 percentage points; its commitment to category 701 (Labor Groups: positive) went up from 2 percentage points to 4.5 percentage points. The party's commitment to its core principles remained intact; the party highlighted category 414 (Economic Orthodoxy: positive, 6.6 percentage points) and category 401 (Free Enterprise: positive, 4.9 percentage points).

At the polls, the NPP slightly improved its vote share. Its electoral bias toward the Ashanti vote decreased. Despite its miserable performance in the Volta and the Northern region, its PDS was characteristic of a catch-all party. Its PNS remained below the cross-national average. The same is true for the PNS that is calculated on the basis of Afrobarometer data. In the Volta region and in some parts of the North, it remained unable to field candidates everywhere. Nevertheless, it was present in all parts of the country. See Table 5.9.

After its second defeat, the party experienced an intense debate about its future strategy. The most divisive issue was the question of whether or not its presidential candidate should automatically serve as the leader of the party – a scenario the NPP constitution proscribed. The NPP's establishment in the North and in the Volta region favored a solution in which the presidential candidate continued to be in charge of party affairs. This would create a stronger link between the party and rural voters.[41] The shift of attention from the presidential candidate to the party leader after the end of an election year was thought to be confusing for many semiliterate voters. The larger-than-life presidency of Rawlings, whose domineering style had succeeded twice, fostered the impression that political competition required strong and uncontested leaders. Supporters of a constitutional amendment were found among the party's youth wing, functionaries from regions where illiteracy levels were high, and the contemporaries of Kufuor, who were gaining the upper hand inside the party. Opponents criticized the proposed amendment as being at odds with the democratic tradition of the NPP.[42]

The party approached its 1998 congress in an atmosphere of tension and paralysis. The debate about the future role of its presidential candidate constrained party relations. In addition, there was an acute shortage

[41] *Statesman*, January 18, 1998.

[42] *Daily Graphic*, November 11, 1997; *Daily Graphic*, December 4, 1997.

TABLE 5.9. *Parties' Electoral Performance and Ability to Field Candidates in 1996*

	NPP		NDC		
T2	RNC	PDS	RNC	PDS	Vote Share of Region
Greater Accra	95%	20%	100%	15%	17%
Eastern	96%	14%	100%	11%	12%
Western	89%	7%	100%	10%	10%
Ashanti	100%	33%	100%	11%	18%
Brong Ahafo	95%	10%	100%	10%	9%
Central	94%	8%	100%	9%	8%
Volta	79%	1%	100%	16%	10%
Northern	74%	5%	100%	9%	8%
Upper East	67%	1%	100%	6%	5%
Upper West	100%	1%	100%	3%	3%
TOTAL	90%	100%	100%	100%	100%

PDS NPP: 42 / average diverging points across time and space: 52
PNS NPP: .65/ average PNS across time and space: .67
PNS NPP based on Afrobarometer data collected in 1999: .63/ average PNS across time and space: .72
PDS NDC: 20/ average diverging points across time and space: 52
PNS NDC: .89/ average PNS across time and space: .67
PNS NDC based on Afrobarometer data collected in 1999: .86/ average PNS across time and space: .72

Source: Author's compilation based on data provided by the Electoral Commission of Ghana.

of funds, causing several postponements of the congress.[43] Two candidates competed for the chairmanship; Professor F.T. Sai (Akan), whose generous donations had made the congress possible in the first place, and Odoi Sykes (Ga), the candidate of Kufuor's young Turks. Sykes' victory was historical in many ways. First, it cemented the hold of Kufuor over the party. Second, for the first time in the history of the Busiaist tradition, the chairman of the respective party was not Akan. The elected vice-chairmen were Ama Busia (Akan), Dr. Wayo Seini (Northern), and Dr. Kweku Afriyie (Akan/Ashanti). The party's new treasurer was Kwesi Brew (Akan/Fante). The election of Courage Quarshigah as national organizer meant that for the first time an Ewe held a position in the party's top leadership. Finally, Dan Botwe (Guan) was elected new secretary-general. The NPP's top leadership now brought together individuals from all major groups and many smaller communities.[44] The congress further decided to elect the new presidential candidate outside Accra, in Sunyani. The new location highlighted that the party was

43 *Daily Guide*, August 29, 1998.
44 *Statesman*, September 6, 1998.

serious about reaching out beyond its traditional strongholds.[45] The congress refused to change the NPP constitution and did not promote its presidential candidate to become the permanent party spokesman. At the Sunyani conference, Kufuor triumphed over Akufo-Addo (Akan/Akyem), who came in a distant second with 628 to Kufuor's 1,296 votes. Other challengers were Kofi Apraku, Malik Yakubu, Henry Mensah, and John Koduah. Yakubu was the first Northerner who attempted to claim the NPP most prestigious position.[46] Both Kufuor and Akufo-Addo had supporters from all main communities. Kufuor's renewed victory stemmed from the delegates' conviction that he would stand a better chance because he was already known to the electorate.[47] Ethnic calculations were not at work.

Between 1996 and 2000, the NPP fostered its image as the party of political and economic freedom.[48] Other themes were its commitment to constitutionalism and national reconciliation, that is, the need to come to terms with the severe human rights abuses of the Rawlings regime.[49] More than previously, Kufuor engaged in extensive tours to the Volta and the Northern regions, where he emphasized the national character of the party and promised that a future NPP government would not discriminate against any group.[50] He was particularly keen on visiting Ghana's rural areas to overcome the party's urban bias.[51] Other high-ranking NPP figures followed his line. Akufo-Addo on several occasions urged voters in the Volta region to trust the NPP and called on members of his own party to apologize for Busia's Aliens Compliance Act.[52] Numerous NPP leaders paid courtesy calls to the traditional leaders of communities, whose majority had voted for the NDC. In the urban areas, Kufuor organized public talks with Imams to woo the so-called Zongo communities.[53] Once more the party nominated a Northerner – Alhaji Aliu – as Kufuor's running mate.[54]

Although the electoral output of the NPP in observation period 2 is still partly indicative of an ethnic alliance, overall the party reached out to communities it had previously neglected. Combined with its high programmatic share, it is classified as programmatic party.

[45] *Statesman*, September 27, 1998.
[46] *Daily Guide*, October 19, 1998.
[47] *Daily Guide*, October 23, 1998.
[48] For examples, see *Daily Graphic*, August 11, 1997; *Daily Guide*, December 1, 1998; *Daily Graphic*, January 31, 2000.
[49] *Daily Graphic*, January 4, 1999.
[50] *Daily Guide*, August 1, 1998; *Daily Graphic*, March 1, 2000.
[51] *Statesman*, February 13, 2000. This was of particular importance as Akufo-Addo is a blood relative of Busia.
[52] *Daily Guide*, September 18, 1998.
[53] *Statesman*, March 21, 1999. The Zongos are Muslims from the North who migrated to Kumasi and Accra.
[54] *Daily Graphic*, September 8, 2000. Other potential running mates were Alhaji Iddrisu and Kweku Afriyie.

TABLE 5.10. *Ethnic Composition of Ghana's 1997 Cabinet*

Community	Number of Cabinet Ministers Allocated	Percentage of Cabinet Allocated
Akan	12	52%
Ewe	2	9%
Ga	3	13%
North	6	26%
TOTAL	23	100%

Source: Author's compilation based on Asante and Gyimah-Boadi 2004 and Ayensu and Darkwa 1999.

The National Democratic Congress: A Dictator Reelected

The NDC's 1996 election campaign was essentially a replay of the previous campaign. It associated the social welfare of Ghana with the political welfare of its head of state. In the run-up to the 1996 presidential elections, the *Daily Graphic* featured a story of a man on the street who had asked Rawlings to pass him some bread shortly after Rawlings had conducted his 1979 military coup. Rawlings was more than willing to hand over the bequest. The story concluded that "unless the educated men in the various political parties learn to break bread with the uneducated and the downtrodden, the latter will treat them with disdain and contempt when they approach them to solicit for their vote."[55]

In this manner, the party highlighted the personal charms of its leader and stressed his seemingly modest nature. Electrification and the improvements of infrastructure remained other leitmotifs, which were linked to the wisdom of Rawlings (Ayee 1998).

The programmatic content of the NDC election manifesto (36 percent) was below the cross-national average (40 percent). Among the coding scheme's programmatic categories, the party mainly stressed category 504 (Welfare State Expansion: positive, 9.8 percentage points of the overall content), category 506 (Education Expansion: positive, 5.2 percentage points), and category 606 (Social Harmony: positive).

The NDC's electoral performance mirrored its previous performance. See Table 5.7. The Volta region remained its stronghold, with Ashanti as the only region where it significantly underperformed. Its PNS is the highest score identified in this study. The composition of the second Rawlings cabinet is outlined in Table 5.10.

As in 1992, the cabinet included members of all major communities, although of the 12 ministries given to the Akan, only 2 were held by an

55 *Daily Graphic*, October 22, 1996, p.7.

Ashanti.[56] The marginalization of this subgroup is not accompanied by the exclusion of the Ewe or the Northern communities.

The NDC leadership also remained all-inclusive. In December 1998, the party held it second congress. As in 1992, preselected candidates gained their positions by acclamation. The new leadership included Alhaji Ali (Northerner) and A.A. Munifie (Akan) as co-chairmen; Professor Awonoor (Ewe), J.Y.A Kwoffie (Akan), Faustina Nelson (Akan/Fante), Shirley Ayittey (Ga), Kwaku Baah (Akan), and Yaw Boamah (Akan) as vice-chairmen; Alhaji Yahaya (Northerner) as secretary-general; and Dr. Sydney Laryea (Ga) as national treasurer.[57]

In June 1998, Rawlings unilaterally declared his vice-president Atta Mills (Akan/Fante) to be the party's next presidential candidate. To many inside the NDC establishment, Mills was a newcomer, who was not linked to any of the groups involved in the 1979 and 1981 coups.[58] Most functionaries therefore took issue with Rawlings' choice rather than the manner in which Rawlings had conducted his choice. Only a small number of party functionaries dared to publically criticize Rawlings' leadership style. These renegades gathered under the roof of the Reform Movement led by Goosie Tanoh (Akan).[59] In February 1999, the Movement issued a public statement criticizing the personality cult around Rawlings and the absence of any procedures by which the party leadership could be held accountable. The Reform Movement further accused Rawlings of equating the will of his party with his own and that of his wife, Nana Rawlings (Akan/Ashanti).[60] Nana Rawlings yielded significant influence over party and public appointments.[61] After the Reform Movement's failure to recruit a sizeable number of rebels, it left the party. At the NDC's special nomination, Mills was elected unopposed. In his speech, Rawlings referred to Mills as "my son in whom I am well pleased."[62] In his acceptance speech, Mills promised to consult Rawlings 24 hours a day if elected president.

The nomination of Mills' running mate proved more controversial. Initially, Mills favored Obed Asamoah (Ewe), Rawlings' long-term foreign minister. Rawlings refused his approval, as Asamoah belonged to the technocratic wing of the (P)NDC machinery. His resignation from the cabinet in the mid-1990s had been motivated by his conviction that the NDC lacked

[56] *Daily Graphic*, February 21, 2000.
[57] *Daily Guide*, December 13, 1998.
[58] *Daily Graphic*, February 2, 1999.
[59] *Daily Guide*, November 12, 1998.
[60] *Daily Graphic*, February 20, 1999.
[61] Interview with various newspaper editors in Ghana. All interviews were conducted in Accra in April 2008.
[62] *Daily Graphic*, January 19, 2000, p.1.

an intellectual backbone as a result of the personality cult around Rawlings.[63] His vice-presidential bid was heavily opposed in the North, which felt entitled to the position of the vice-presidential candidate.[64] Eventually, Mills submitted to Northern demands and appointed Martin Amidu as his running mate.[65]

Rhetorically, the party cultivated support among rural citizens and the underprivileged.[66] It stressed its commitment to equally opportunity[67] and highlighted that it had never discriminated against any region.[68] It reiterated its adherence to Rawlings' principles, the achievements of his military coups, and the centrality of the Rawlings legacy for the NDC.[69] Accordingly, it was Rawling's military intervention that ended Ghana's political and economic decay.[70] Several party heavyweights began to equate the party with the Nkrumahist heritage. Mills was now increasingly depicted as Nkrumah's disciple.[71]

Little changed inside the NDC. Rawlings was still the party's heart and mind. The Reform Movement failed to have a lasting impact. The party retained its national character. The NDC remained a personalistic party.

OBSERVATION PERIOD 3

In observation period 3, the NPP was elected into government for the first time in the Fourth Republic. A selection of bills that were passed in parliament is outlined in Table 5.11. None of the bills affected ethnic relations.

The New Patriotic Party in Power

The third multiparty elections resulted in the first democratic and peaceful transfer of power in Ghanaian history. Despite its change of fortune, the NPP's 2000 campaign resembled the previous one. The party emphasized its willingness to reach out to all groups and regions. Particular attention went to the Northern regions. During the run-off between Kufuor and Mills in December 2000, the NPP was keen on reinventing itself as the political home of the North. An NPP pull-out from the leading newspaper read:

63 *Daily Guide*, July 31, 1997.
64 *Chronicle*, April 3, 2000.
65 *Daily Graphic*, September 4, 2000.
66 *Daily Guide*, December 7, 1998.
67 *Daily Graphic*, January 21, 1999.
68 *Daily Graphic*, June 5, 1999.
69 *Daily Graphic*, August 6, 2000.
70 *Daily Graphic*, June 3, 1999; *Daily Graphic*, June 5, 1999.
71 *Daily Graphic*, April 28, 1999; *Daily Graphic*, September 28, 2000. Mills used to attend classes at the Kwame Nkrumah Institute when he was a young civil servant in the early 1960s.

TABLE 5.11. *Selection of Bills Passed in Ghana Between 2000 and 2004*

Name of Bill	Comment	Impact on Ethnic Relations
2002 Bank of Ghana Bill	gave the Bank of Ghana greater autonomy to pursue an independent monetary policy	no
2002 National Reconciliation Bill	established a Truth and Reconciliation Commission	no. The bill, however, was extraordinarily contested between NPP and NDC.
2003 National Health Insurance Bill	established a public health insurance scheme in every district	no
2004 Foreign Exchange Bill	brought foreign exchange regulations in line with international standards	no
2004 Long Term Saving Bill	provided the regulatory framework for a pension scheme	no
2004 Credit Union Bill	amended the regulatory framework for a pension scheme	no

Source: Author's compilation based on economic Intelligence Unit, data provided by the Parliament of Ghana, the Africa Yearbook, expert interviews, and the Ghanaian media. All data are with the author.

"Roots of NPP are deeply in the North" and "Let's join together to fight rural poverty."[72]

The classification of the NPP 2000 manifesto is not straightforward. It contained a programmatic share of 39 percent, slightly below the cross-national average (40 percent). The party emphasized category 405 (Welfare State Expansion: positive, 4.1 percentage points), category 605 (Law and Order: positive, 3.9 percentage points), and category 414 (Economic Orthodoxy: positive, 3.1 percentage points). Its effective number of programmatic categories (13.8) was above the cross-country average (8.8).

Table 5.12 shows the NPP's performance in the historic 2000 election. The party achieved its goal to become a nationwide political force. Its PDS decreased from 42 to 34. Its PNS increased from .65 to .73. In the 2000 elections, the NPP achieved the same national outreach as its main political rival. Its PNS based on Afrobarometer data increased from .63 to .79.

[72] *Daily Graphic*, December 23, 2000.

TABLE 5.12. *Parties' Electoral Performance and Ability to Field Candidates in 2000*

	NPP		NDC		
T3	RNC	PDS	RNC	PDS	Vote Share of Region
Greater Accra	100%	19%	100%	16%	17%
Eastern	100%	13%	100%	12%	11%
Western	100%	9%	100%	9%	10%
Ashanti	100%	31%	100%	11%	19%
Brong Ahafo	100%	10%	100%	9%	9%
Central	100%	8%	100%	9%	8%
Volta	100%	2%	100%	15%	9%
Northern	100%	5%	100%	10%	9%
Upper East	100%	2%	100%	5%	5%
Upper West	100%	1%	100%	4%	3%
TOTAL	100%	100%	100%	100%	100%

PDS NPP: 34/ average diverging points across time and space: 52
PNS NPP: .73/ average PNS across time and space: .67
PNS NPP based on Afrobarometer data collected in 2001: .79/ average PNS across time and space: .72
PDS NDC: 20/ average diverging points across time and space: 52
PNS NDC: .74/ average PNS across time and space: .67
PNS NDC based on Afrobarometer data collected in 2001: .76/ average PNS across time and space: .72

Source: Author's compilation based on data provided by the Electoral Commission of Ghana.

Ashanti remained its bastion, but it made headways in the North in terms of the absolute number of votes; it also achieved a slight improvement of its vote share in the Volta region. Its electoral performance is now fully in line with the criteria of a nonethnic party type.

The Busia government of 1969 lacked Ewe membership, which for long accounted for the reputation of the Busia-Danquah tradition as Akan- or Ashanti-only. Kufuor's 2001 cabinet displays a bias in favor of governing party's electoral stronghold (see Table 5.13). However, no community was excluded or drastically underrepresented.

Shortly after its success at the polls, many party heavyweights were promoted to the cabinet, which triggered the election of a new party leadership. The 2005 NPP congress elected Harrona Esseku as new chairman. Esseku was the first Fante to occupy the position. He won the leadership contest against Samuel Addae-Dua (Akan/Ashanti) and Mohammed Musah (Northerner). The new vice-chairmen were Stephen Ntim (Akan/Ashanti), Agnes Okudzeto (Ewe), and Edmund Annan (Ga). Lord Commey (Ga) was elected as new national organizer, and Dan Botwe (Guan) was confirmed as

TABLE 5.13. *Ethnic Composition of Ghana's 2001 Cabinet*

Community	Number of Cabinet Ministers Allocated	Percentage of Cabinet Allocated
Akan	22	69%
Ewe	2	6%
Ga	3	9%
North	5	16%
TOTAL	32	100%

Source: Author's compilation based on Asante and Gyimah-Boadi 2004 and Ayensu and Darkwa 1999.

secretary-general. The North left the congress empty-handed.[73] The Northern regions, however, were sufficiently represented in the cabinet. Delegates from the Volta region staged a walk-out in protest against the low number of Ewe ministers. The walk-out remained without consequences – party defections or any form of sustainable protest did not occur. The protest of delegates from the Volta region and the sidelining of the North in the party leadership shows that the nationalization of the party was still a work in progress. Kufuor's nomination as presidential flag bearer for the 2004 election was conducted by acclamation.[74]

In one of his first speeches, Kufuor appealed to his own community, the Ashanti, to understand that in the past they had often offended the sensibilities of other tribes.[75] He promised to work hard to increase the chances of his party in the Volta region. Throughout his first term, Kufuor remained in touch with the region's traditional leaders.[76] At the 10th anniversary of the party, Harrona Esseku reasserted the NPP's commitment to principles of the Danquah-Busia tradition:

> It is reasserted in our manifesto as the avowal of individual freedom in a liberal democratic state where the development of the individual and of society in a free political atmosphere, under the rule of the law are the principles of the state. Free enterprise, fundamental human rights and a vigorous pursuit of private initiative are its abiding principles. We must be proud that our philosophy had been vindicated worldwide today.[77]

73 *Public Agenda*, August 27, 2001. The inclusion of two Ga politicians in the NPP leadership did not go unnoticed in the Ghanaian media. The Ga appointments were a further indication of the national outreach of the party.
74 *Daily Graphic*, January 6, 2003.
75 *Daily Graphic*, February 19, 2001.
76 *Daily Graphic*, January 5, 2002. This is further based on interviews with numerous newspaper editors and the NPP 2008 campaign team in Accra. All interviews were conducted in April 2008.
77 *Accra Mail*, July 24, 2002.

Although Kufuor and the NPP leadership continued to hail the principles of Busiaism,[78] the party's public statements largely were dedicated to the worries of Ghana's Muslim communities[79] and the developmental needs of the Volta region.[80] The party was keen on highlighting its new grassroots structures in the Volta region.[81] NPP ministers spent most of their time explaining the virtues of many new government initiatives such as the National Health Insurance Scheme, Ghana's participation in the Heavily Indebted Poor Countries Initiative HIPC initiative,[82] or new measures against inflation.[83] In its day-to-day life, catch-all rhetoric had begun to replace ideological principles. None of the bills tabled in parliament showed any connection between the party's ideological roots and the policies it put forward.

Overall, the NPP's catch-all character is beyond doubt and visible in every indicator. The transformation clearly occurred at the expense of its ideological convictions.

The National Democratic Congress Falling Apart

The NDC's 2000 campaign theme was its long-term experience in government. It insinuated that a take-over by Kufuor would be dangerous due to the opposition's intellectual deficiencies.[84] Furthermore, the NDC called on Ghanaians not to forget the harsh tax regime of the Busia government. In that manner, the NDC reacted to the opposition's complaints about tax increase and a hike in living costs. Rawlings frequently stated that political changes in developing countries would be risky and expensive. The defection of Alhaji Inusah, a former NPP campaign manager, gave the NDC fear campaign a new momentum. On the NDC campaign trail, Inusah argued that the NPP was reaching out to the Muslim communities with the sole intention of compiling a list of Muslims it wished to expel from the country – just as the Progress Party had done in the 1970s.[85] Insuah demanded the arrest of the NPP leadership, as they had rigged various by-elections in their favor.[86] Mills promised an all-inclusive government, taking on board former

78 For an example see *Daily Graphic*, March 3, 2003.

79 *Daily Graphic*, August 26, 2003; *Daily Graphic*, November 26, 2003; *Daily Graphic*, August 6, 2004.

80 *Daily Graphic*, September 22, 2003; *Daily Graphic*, February 4, 2004; *Daily Graphic*, May 1, 2004; *Daily Graphic*, June 19, 2004.

81 Interview with Samuel Dzamesi, regional minister of the Volta Region and member of the Kufour cabinet, April 22, 2008, Ho.

82 *Daily Graphic*, January 8, 2004.

83 *Daily Graphic*, May 12, 2004.

84 *Daily Graphic*, November 10, 2000.

85 *Statesman*, July 30, 2000.

86 *Daily Graphic*, December 4, 2000.

NPP economic spokesperson and political heavyweight Kwame Pianim, who had left the NPP after being sidelined from its leadership.[87] Even though the NDC campaign still focused on Rawlings and his past achievements, the party began to look for alternative topics. On numerous occasions, it tried to claim the Nkrumahist heritage.

However, the manifesto's programmatic content increased very moderately (from 36 percent to 37 percent) and cannot be classified as programmatic. The MRG coding scheme distinguishes between left- and right-wing categories and thus facilitates an analysis of the overall content of left- and right-wing statements. The NDC's left-wing content decreased in comparison with the left-wing content in the previous election.[88] Therefore, its manifesto content moved from the left to the center and not to the left, as its self-portrayal suggested. Nkrumahist or socialist principles were not visible in the party's 2000 manifesto.

The NDC's electoral output remained characteristic of a catch-all party. Its surprisingly dismal performance in Central province shows that ethnicity matters rather little. Central province is the home province of Atta Mills. As previously, the NDC fielded candidates in all regions.

Its departure from government left the party in a state of confusion. In March 2001, the NDC commissioned a "Re-Organization Committee" under the leadership of Obed Asamoah (Ewe).[89] Asamoah's final report, tabled in April 2001, identified the party's lack of internal democracy and its tense relationship with the private media as the main causes of its defeat.[90] The report urged a discussion about the party's future presidential candidate.[91] Unsurprisingly, the report triggered strong reactions from those who regarded the "Rawlings factor" as sine qua no condition for the party's future.[92] The struggle for the future course of the party led to the rapid formation of two factions. The "traditionalists" supported the status quo and wanted Rawlings to remain the spiritual leader of the party. The "democratizers" demanded the NDC's emancipation from Rawlings; they proposed the separation between the party's leadership and the party's founder.

In December 2001, Asamoah declared his intention to stand as new party chairman and demanded an end to the practice of preselecting the party leadership. In addition, he called for a return of the Reform Movement and former cabinet ministers P.V. Obeng and Kwesi Botchwey, who had both left politics out of frustration over Rawlings' firm grip over party affairs.[93]

87 *Daily Graphic*, December 12, 2000.
88 This is outlined in greater detail in Chapter Six for all parties.
89 *Daily Graphic*, March 5, 2001.
90 *Daily Graphic*, April 9, 2001.
91 *Daily Graphic*, April 10, 2001.
92 *Daily Graphic*, June 14, 2001; *Daily Graphic*, November 21, 2001.
93 *Daily Guide*, December 12, 2001.

Asamoah was supported by the leader of the NDC Youth wing, Iddrisu Haruna (Northerner). Haruna advocated a new, more left-wing image of the party.[94] Mills remained absent from these debates, which indicates his marginal role within the party's hierarchy and his dependence on Rawlings' support at the time. In April 2002, the NDC National Executive Committee eradicated the co-chairmanship. The new chairman was now officially also the party leader – a key demand of the prodemocracy group and a first victory over Rawlings, who had argued fervently against these changes.[95]

At the 2002 NDC congress, the reformist wing triumphed again. Asamoah (Ewe) convinced the majority of the delegates to vote for him instead of Alhaji Iddrisu (Northerner), the candidate of the Rawlings camp.[96] Alhaji Yahaya (Northener), Nii Adamatio (Ga), Juliet Hilda Salifu Bolco (Northener), Kweku Baah (Akan), E.T. Mensah (Other), and Lee Ocran (Akan) were elected vice-chairmen. Nii Aryeh (Ga) was elected as new secretary-general, and Margaret Clarke-Kwesie (Fante) was made new national treasurer. Samuel Ampofo (Akan) obtained the position of national organizer.[97] Most functionaries had not occupied any leadership positions before and were either directly affiliated or silent supporters of the democratizers. The party leadership composition bridged Ghana's dominant ethnic cleavage lines. At the congress, the NDC publicly declared its commitment to social-democratic values.[98]

In August 2002, Kwesi Botchwey (Akan) declared his intention of becoming the new NDC presidential candidate. In his announcement, Botchwey broke ranks with the Rawlings group:

> I have been very much encouraged and heartened at the growing calls and appeals from within the party for an open and competitive and truly democratic process for electing the party's presidential and other candidate for national elections and for the conduct of the party's business generally (. . .) I have been an advocate of greater democracy and more openness and competition within our great party well before the last general elections.[99]

Botchwey underscored his candidature by suggesting that the party should be rebuilt around a social democratic platform and no longer serve as a political vehicle for the aspirations of individuals.[100] Shortly thereafter, Mills declared his intention to stand as presidential candidate. He highlighted

94 *Daily Guide*, December 20, 2001.
95 *Daily Graphic*, April 20, 2002; *Daily Guide*, April 23, 2002.
96 Asamoah obtained his position by a majority of two votes (334 over 332).
97 *Daily Graphic*, April 29, 2002.
98 *Daily Graphic*, July 19, 2002.
99 *Daily Graphic*, August 28, 2002.
100 *Daily Graphic*, October 10, 2002; *Daily Graphic*, October 28, 2002.

his experience as vice-president as justification for his bid.[101] As had been the case inside the NPP in the mid-1990s, party factions inside the NDC were driven by different conceptions about the future direction of the party. The reformist leadership of Asamoah (Ewe)/Botchwey (Akan/Ashanti) faced the status quo group headed by Rawlings (Ewe)/Mills (Akan/Fante). Both had nationwide support and were campaigning across the country.[102] In contrast to the previous congress, the status quo faction carried the day and dealt a humiliating defeat to Botchwey: Mills won by 1,116 of 1,310 votes.[103] Botchwey's catastrophic performance owed much to the harassment and intimidation attempts of the Rawlings group.[104] The circumstances that had led to the defeat of the democratizers led to further polarization. Asamoah demanded a redefinition of the role of the founder of the party – a direct attack on the preeminent role of Rawlings in the party. Asamoah interpreted several NDC defeats in by-elections as the result of Rawlings' intimidating personality.[105] In the run-up to the 2004 elections, Mills nominated Alhaji Mohammed Mumuni, a Northerner. For a long time, John Mahama, a Northerner with Christian roots, had been touted as an alternative. His political proximity to the Asamoah faction stood in the way of his candidacy.[106]

The ascendancy of the reformist wing affected the party's rhetoric. Whereas before the NDC commitment to social justice was linked to Rawlings' "humbleness" and his rejection of the corrupt political elite, now it was portrayed as part of its social democratic foundation. These changes were subtle and not immediately visible, as the ideological undertones of the "Rawlings revolution" had always been compatible with the political ideas of social-democracy. Both the "Rawlings factor" and left-wing rhetoric remained visible in the NDC's rhetoric. On some occasions, the party proclaimed the significance of the principles of the June 4 revolution[107]; on others, it stated that its 2004 manifesto would be based on the notion of democratic socialism.[108] Statements praising the June 4 revolution often came from Mills[109]; those in favor of democratic socialism came from Asamoah.[110]

101 *Daily Graphic*, September 11, 2002; *Daily Graphic*, October 21, 2002.
102 For example, in Ashanti, the NDC's regional leadership was split down the middle between the two camps. See *Daily Graphic*, January 27, 2003.
103 *Daily Graphic*, December 21, 2002.
104 *Daily Graphic*, March 13, 2003.
105 *Daily Graphic*, April 4, 2003.
106 *Daily Graphic*, September 24, 2004. In addition, Mumuni carried the support of the party's Zongo members among whom the NDC tried to increase its support.
107 *Daily Graphic*, June 6, 2001.
108 *Daily Graphic*, August 7, 2002.
109 *Daily Graphic*, June 4, 2004
110 *Daily Graphic*, May 20, 2004.

Under Asamoah's guidance, the party issued an apology to the private media and media practitioners for human rights abuses committed during its term in office.[111]

However, above all, the party was averse to anything the NPP was doing. It decried the various NPP budgets as "killer budgets,"[112] it criticized Ghana's participation in the HIPIC initiative,[113] and it regularly accused the Kufuor administration of corruption.[114] Catch-all rhetoric prevailed. As previously, the party leadership engaged in courtesy calls to various traditional leaders without showing any bias for any particular community.[115]

Over the course of the third observation period, the party type of the NDC changed: with the departure of Rawlings from the presidency, a group of party reformers entered the scene and advocated a pronounced social democratic agenda. Although their take-over was halted midway, the days in which the party was run by an individual were gone. The programmatic content of its manifesto remained below average and its rhetoric dominated by catch-all phrases. Thus the NDC transformed from a personalistic to a catch-all party.

OBSERVATION PERIOD 4

Between 2004 and 2008, very few bills were discussed at greater length by the political parties and the media. The 2006 Representation of the People Bill overshadowed the political debate. The bill allowed the Ghanaian diaspora to participate in parliamentary and presidential elections, a change widely seen to favor the incumbent NPP. Many politically conscious Ghanaians had left the country to flee the Rawlings dictatorship. Although the bill had strong partisan undertones, it did not affect ethnic relations in the country. See Table 5.14.

The New Patriotic Party in Its Second Term

The NPP made democratic progress its major 2004 campaign theme. The party stressed that Ghana had never before been more democratic.[116] Accordingly, a return to power of the NDC equaled a return to state-led

[111] *Daily Graphic*, October 7, 2003.

[112] *Daily Graphic*, February 28, 2003.

[113] *Daily Graphic*, June 3, 2004; *Daily Graphic*, March 19, 2004.

[114] *Daily Graphic*, February 3, 2004; *Daily Graphic*, September 7, 2004.

[115] *Daily Graphic*, July 8, 2004; *Daily Graphic*, July 31, 2004. If bias was visible at all, it was in favor of leaders whose communities had deserted the party, such as, for example, the Ga chiefs in Greater Accra.

[116] *Daily Graphic*, November 29, 2004.

TABLE 5.14. *Selection of Bills Passed in Ghana Between 2004 and 2008*

Name of Bill	Comment	Impact on Ethnic Relations
2004 Insurance Bill	improved the regulatory framework of the insurance industry	no
2006 Representation of the People Bill	enabled the diaspora to vote	no, but heavily contested bill between NPP and NDC.
2008 Government Wage Bill	increased the salaries of government workers	no
2008 Borrowers and Lenders Bill	positioned the financial sector to promote financial service	no

Source: Author's compilation based on Economist Intelligence Unit report, data provided by the Parliament of Ghana, the Africa Yearbook, expert interviews, and the Ghanaian media. All data is with the author.

harassment of the private and public sphere.[117] As previously, the party referred to its achievements in the fields of macroeconomic stability and infrastructural development.[118] A further campaign theme was its promise to propel Ghana to become a middle-income country.[119] The party, and in particular Kufuor, confirmed the NPP's ongoing commitment to be inclusive of all groups.[120] The Volta region received particular attention during the campaign; here the NPP highlighted various government-sponsored projects.[121] The NPP's programmatic foundations were less and less visible. This notwithstanding, the manifesto's programmatic content (41 percent) remained slightly above the cross-country average, as did its number of effective programmatic categories (9).

Kufuor's all-inclusive campaign strategy paid off. For the first time, the NPP achieved a higher PNS that the NDC. See Table 5.15. As in 2000, the party's electoral performance was characteristic of a nonethnic party type.

The 2005 cabinet allocated an eminent share of cabinet positions to the Akan. The Ewe and the Northern groups were numerically underrepresented. Yet, as a whole, the cabinet was inclusive of all major groups. See Table 5.16.

Party factionalism occurred as the question of who would succeed Kufour entered the agenda. The party's 2005 congress saw severe competition for

117 *Daily Graphic*, November 30, 2004.

118 *Daily Graphic*, December 6, 2004.

119 *Daily Graphic*, November 9, 2004.

120 *Daily Graphic*, November 27, 2004; *Daily Graphic*, October 12, 2004.

121 *Daily Graphic*, November 29, 2004; *Daily Graphic*, November 27, 2004; *Daily Graphic*, September 30, 2004; *Daily Graphic*, June 25, 2004.

TABLE 5.15. *Parties' Electoral Performance and Ability to Field Candidates in 2004*

	NPP		NDC		
T4	RNC	PDS	RNC	PDS	Vote Share of Region
Greater Accra	100%	20%	100%	22%	20%
Eastern	100%	13%	100%	10%	11%
Western	96%	9%	100%	9%	10%
Ashanti	100%	28%	100%	10%	18%
Brong Ahafo	100%	9%	96%	10%	9%
Central	95%	9%	100%	7%	8%
Volta	100%	3%	100%	14%	8%
Northern	100%	6%	100%	11%	9%
Upper East	100%	2%	100%	4%	4%
Upper West	90%	1%	100%	3%	3%
TOTAL	99%	100%	100%	100%	100%

PDS NPP: 26/ average diverging points across time and space: 52
PNS NPP: .80/ average PNS across time and space: .67
PNS NPP based on Afrobarometer data collected in 2005: .84/ average PNS across time and space: .72
PDS NDC: 22/ average diverging points across time and space: 52
PNS NDC: .68/ average PNS across time and space: .67
PNS NDC based on Afrobarometer data collected in 2005: .75/ average PNS across time and space: .72

Source: Author's compilation based on data provided by the Electoral Commission of Ghana.

the party leadership. Three candidates vied for the party chairmanship: the incumbent Harrona Esseku (Akan/Fante), Peter Mac Manu (Akan/Ashanti), and Steven Ntim (Akan/Ashanti). Ntim had the support of President Kufuor. Esseku's chances of reelection were slim. He had fallen out with the party's establishment over his criticism of Kufuor's failure to raise sufficient funds for the party. Kufuor was opposed to Mac Manu; he felt the elections of an Ashanti chairman could provide ammunition to those who depicted the party as ethnic.[122] Kufuor's endorsement of Ntim was detrimental for Ntim. Many party delegates perceived him to be dependent on the president.[123] Mac Manu stressed that in contrast to Ntim, he had gone through the mill of the party machinery.[124] Both Ntim and Mac Manu attempted to woo delegates nationwide. At the congress, Mac Manu was supported by a majority of delegates from Western, Central, Eastern, Upper East, and

[122] *Daily Dispatch*, November 28, 2005. The NPP was in great financial difficulties in late 2005 when it was unable to maintain several party offices across the country and incapable of paying the electricity bill of its party headquarter.

[123] *Statesman*, December 18, 2005.

[124] *Daily Graphic*, November 25, 2005.

TABLE 5.16. *Ethnic Composition of Ghana's 2005 Cabinet*

Community	Number of Cabinet Ministers Allocated	Percentage of Cabinet Allocated
Akan	20	69%
Ewe	2	7%
Ga	3	10%
North	4	14%
TOTAL	29	100%

Source: Author's compilation Based on Asante and Gyimah-Boadi 2004 and Ayensu and Darkwa 1999.

Upper West, whereas Ntim was backed by a majority of delegates from Brong-Aahafo, Volta, Ashanti, Greater Accra, and the Northern region. Eventually, Mac Manu secured a narrow victory.[125] As in previous contests, the ability to rally support on a national scale and across ethnic divides was characteristic of both contenders.[126] Other elected officials included the vice-chairmen Hawa Yakubu (Northerner), Agnes Okudzeto (Ewe), and Abdul-Rahman Musah (Northerner). Gifty Ayeh (Akan) was made national treasurer and Ohene Ntow (Akan) secretary-general. Lord Commey (Ga) was reelected as national organizer.[127]

The defeat of Ntim was the first setback for the Kufuor camp, whose time in power was drawing to a close. Akufo-Ado's ascendancy inside the party became visible. At the 2007 special congress, 17 candidates competed for the position of the presidential candidate. Only three stood a serious chance: Nana Akufo-Addo, Kufuor's long-term challenger and by now a well-established cabinet minister of various portfolios; Alhaji Mahama Aliu (Northerner), Ghana's vice-president; and Alan Kyerematen (Akan/Fante). Kyerematen had served as the former Ghanaian ambassador to the United States and had been a long-term confidante of Kufuor.[128] In the run-up to the congress, Kufuor left no doubt about his allegiance to Kyerematen.[129] The NPP's 2007 party congress again became the battleground between the Kufuor and the Akufo-Addo camp. Aliu's bid failed as the North divided its combined vote share among all major contenders irrespective of their ethnicity.[130] This narrowed the race to two contestants. The enormous wealth of his family, his long-term political connections – he is the son of Edward Akufo-Addo, Ghana's ceremonial President of

[125] *Statesman*, December 17, 2005. No region voted en bloc.

[126] *Statesman*, December 19, 2005. MacManu gained 711, Ntim 635 votes.

[127] *Accra Mail*, December 19, 2005.

[128] *Daily Graphic*, November 19. 2007.

[129] *Daily Graphic*, November 29, 2007; *Statesman*, December 29, 2007.

[130] Interview with Arthur Kennedy, communications director of the Akufo-Addo 2008 presidential campaign, April 3, 2008, Accra. *Statesman*, October 1, 2007.

the Second Republic, the grand nephew of J.B. Danquah, and the nephew of Ofori-Atta, the presidential candidate of the Busiaist movement in the short-lived Third Republic – but also the anger Kufuor's intervention in the process caused were crucial in securing Akufo-Addo's victory.[131]

Akufo-Addo nominated Dr. Mahamudu Bawumia from the North as his running mate. A significant segment of the party supported Gladys Asmah (Akan/Fante) for the vice-presidential slot to woo voters in Central province – which together with Greater Accra represents the region with most swing voters – to stick with the NPP.[132] Yet the party's aspiration to include the North in the nation's two most prestigious party positions prevailed.

Overall, the NPP remained a catch-all party. To become a serious contender for the leadership, candidates had to form nationwide alliances. Party factions remained structured around powerful individuals. The party's rhetoric did not change. Although the party manifesto was programmatic, the party as a whole was not.

The National Democratic Congress and Rawlings' Long Shadow

The NDC's 2004 election campaign was the first campaign after the takeover of the reformist wing, which had claimed to redefine the party along social-democratic lines. As a result, the 2004 campaign did have stronger programmatic undertones. The NDC leadership decried the Busiaists' notion of a "property-owning democracy" as a concept that was detrimental to economic inclusion and social justice.[133] Mills repeatedly portrayed the NDC as the NPP's social-democratic counterpart.[134] This notwithstanding, catch-all rhetoric prevailed. The Mills campaign made the abuse of public funds by the government another of its leitmotif. The Kufuor government was criticized for their "ostentatious lifestyles." Mills described the NDC leaders as trustworthy and humble.[135] For the first time, the party explicitly distanced itself from the military.[136] By 2004, the NDC campaign rhetoric was an eclectic mix of vague social-democratic catchphrases, catch-all slogans, and the mantra of the "Rawlings revolution." The catch-all element was the strongest element.

[131] *Daily Graphic*, December 24, 2007. Akufo-Addo gained 1,096 votes, Alan Kyerematen 738 votes. Kyerematen declared that he would not go into a second round and withdrew from the race. Alhaji Aliu Mahama received 146 votes.

[132] *Ghana News Agency*, August 2, 2008.

[133] *Daily Graphic*, October 25, 2004; *Daily Graphic*, December 6, 2004; *Daily Graphic*, November 12, 2004.

[134] *Daily Graphic*, November 1, 2004.

[135] *Daily Graphic*, November 12, 2004; *Daily Graphic*, November 22, 2004; *Daily Graphic*, October 4, 2004.

[136] *Daily Graphic*, September 27, 2004.

The NDC's 2004 election manifesto did not qualify as a programmatic manifesto. Its programmatic content stagnated at 36 percent. However, in contrast to the 2000 manifesto, the left wing content increased from 20 percent to 23 percent, whereas its right-wing content went down from 17 percent to 13 percent. The categories the party stressed most were category 504 (Welfare State Expansion: positive, 6.6 percentage points) and category 506 (Education Expansion: positive, 5.1 percentage points).

Election results once more pinpoint the party's nonethnic nature, although the party was losing some ground with regard to its PNS. Its PDS was far below the cross-country average. The party failed to regain Central and Greater Accra. As usual, it underperformed in Ashanti.

Following its second electoral defeat, factionalism between the Rawlings/Mills and the Asamoah/Botchwey camp intensified. Immediately after the election, the party's founder redirected his venomous attacks to his opponents inside the NDC. On several occasions, he disparaged their incompetence to lead.[137] The Asamoah camp blamed Mills and his inability to emancipate himself from Rawlings as the main cause for the party's failure to regain power.[138] The NDC's 2005 congress became a battleground of mutual accusations of incompetence and betrayal.[139] The Rawlings camp emerged victorious, as its candidate for the chairmanship, Kwabena Adjei (Ewe), beat Obed Asamoah (Ewe) by a landslide of 1,158 to 208 votes. Johnson Nketsia (Akan) was elected new secretary-general, Samuel Ampofo (Akan) national organizer, and Margaret Clarke Kwesie (Akan/Fante) national treasurer.[140]

The return of the Rawlings clique triggered a number of high-profile defections. The most prominent party defectors included Kwaku Baah, the former national vice-chairman; Frances Assiam,[141] the NDC's former national women's organizer; Emmanuel Nti Fordjour, the former chairman of the NDC in Ashanti[142]; and Obed Asamoah, the former chairman. Asamoah founded the Democratic Freedom Party (DFP).[143] All former defectors stated that before and during the congress they had been intimidated by the Rawlings faction. At the party's 2006 special congress, John Atta Mills was reelected as the NDC presidential candidate. Mills beat his closest rival, Ekow Spio-Garbrah (Akan/Fante), by a wide margin.[144]

137 *Statesman*, January 14, 2005; *Daily Graphic*, October 18, 2005.

138 *Daily Graphic*, December 2, 2005.

139 *Daily Graphic*, December 23, 2005.

140 *Daily Graphic*, December 24, 2005.

141 *Daily Graphic*, December 29, 2005.

142 *Daily Graphic*, January 15, 2006. In Ashanti province, the tension between the two camps was higher than elsewhere, as half of the regional party executive was aligned to Rawlings, whereas the other half was opposed to him.

143 *Daily Graphic*, April 8, 2006.

144 *Daily Guide*, December 22, 2006. Mills gained 1,362 votes over Spio-Garbrah's 146. Other candidates included Alhaji IdDRisu (137 votes) and Eddie Annan (28 votes).

However, the large-scale defection of the reformist wing and Mills' renewed candidature did not eradicate the reformist group from the ranks of the NDC. Mills himself was no longer a staunch supporter of Rawlings. Rawlings himself had started to complain about the ingratitude of his former disciple.[145] Mills' nomination of John Mahama, a Christian from the North – against the explicit wishes of Rawlings – confirms the growing rift between the two.[146] Mahama is known for his aspiration to strengthen the party's social democratic profile.[147]

In term of its general rhetoric, the party continued its campaign against Ghana's participation in the HIPIC initiative[148] and accused the government of being anti-rural. It heavily opposed the 2006 Representation of the People Bill.[149] At times, NDC leaders stressed the party's ideological differences to the NPP. They described the NDC as a party of the ordinary citizen, whereas the NPP made the rich richer and the poor poorer. As the NPP, the party stayed in permanent contact with traditional leaders across the country.[150] The populist element of its rhetoric symbolized by Rawlings also featured between the 2004 and the 2008 elections. The former dictator publicly compared Kufuor with Ataa Ayi, a convicted mass murderer.[151] At official visits in Germany and the United Kingdom, he called for the overthrow of the government. Many NDC MPs and party functionaries backed his statements.[152] In most instances, however, the party simply criticized the government for failing to initiate growth that benefits the masses.[153]

The NDC's transformation from a personalistic to a catch-all party consolidated in the fourth observation period. Programmatic undertones were visible, yet they failed to make sufficient headway in order for the party to be classified as programmatic.

GHANA AFTER THE 2008 ELECTIONS

Ghana's December 2008 elections ended with the surprise victory of the NDC. Hardly anyone had predicted that the governing NPP would have to engage in a second round of the presidential elections, let alone lose it; even less had foreseen the dramatic losses of the governing party in the

[145] Interview with John Mahama, NDC vice-presidential candidate 2008, April 10, 2008, Accra.

[146] *Daily Guide*, February 1, 2007.

[147] Interview with Kathrin Meissner, resident representative of the Friedrich Ebert Foundation in Ghana, April 2, 2008, Accra.

[148] *Daily Graphic*, March 19, 2004.

[149] *Daily Graphic*, June 3, 2004.

[150] *Daily Graphic*, July 31, 2004.

[151] *Statesman*, March 20, 2005.

[152] *Daily Guide*, November 6, 2006.

[153] For example, see *Daily Graphic*, March 2, 2005.

parliamentary elections. The NPP's achievements – its liberalization of the media landscape, the introduction of a national insurance health scheme, and sustainable economic growth – were encapsulated in its slogans "We are moving forward," "Ghana has never been as stable," and "Ghana has never been that free before."[154]

However, eight years in power had left its traces. Various shortcomings had begun to haunt the administration. A backlog in civil service salaries caused unease among public workers. The NPP's dismal performance in the Central region was caused by governmental inertia regarding the illegal presence of Chinese fishermen. First and foremost, however, there was a strong perception among the electorate that corruption was on the rise.[155] The NPP had obvious problems to justify why the electorate should provide it with a third term in office.

In the parliamentary elections, both parties lost several core constituencies. The Ghanaian electorate commonly referred to the elections as "Punishment Vote," in which the excessive self-confidence of Akufo-Addo and inept MPs from both parties were taught a lesson in public accountability. In great contrast to Kenya, the last Ghanaian elections were thus the culmination of the country's democratization efforts. Ethnicity did not feature in the campaign, and neither did it occupy the minds of the electorate during the count of the vote. Despite legal attempts by Akufo-Addo to stop the Electoral Commission from announcing a winner, leading NPP figures quickly called on their party to accept the outcome. Thus, for the second time, government and opposition changed hands in a peaceful and democratic manner. Table 5.17 outlines the two parties' respective PNS scores for the 2008 elections.

Since the inauguration of John Atta Mills as president, the dynamics of party competition remained unchanged. In both parties, the rivalry between factions perpetuated. Inside the NDC, Mills faced a torrent of criticism from the Rawlings camp, at times seriously questioning his capacity to govern. In July 2011, the NDC elected its new presidential candidate. After several months of bitter antagonism, analysts expected a narrow showdown between Konadu Rawlings amd Atta Mills. However, Mills secured his 2012 nomination with a dramatic landslide of 97 percent. The result underlines the decline of Rawlings' influence inside his former party. Mills' sudden death in the summer of 2012 just a few months before the 2012 elections did not alter the dynamics of Ghanaian party politics. Within days, John Mahama from the North, the new contender and president, nominated Amissah-Arthur from the Fante community to the position of vice-president. Inside the NPP, tensions between Akufo-Addo and Kyerematen/Kufuor worsened.

154 Based on the author's attendance of several NPP rallies in the Greater Accra region and in Ashanti in the run-up to the elections.

155 See Afrobarometer Briefing Paper 49.

TABLE 5.17. *Parties' Electoral Performance in 2008*

T5	NPP PDS	NDC PDS	Vote Share of Region
Greater Accra	17%	22%	20%
Eastern	12%	9%	11%
Western	9%	9%	10%
Ashanti	29%	10%	18%
Brong Ahafo	10%	9%	9%
Central	8%	9%	8%
Volta	3%	14%	8%
Northern	7%	11%	9%
Upper East	3%	4%	4%
Upper West	2%	3%	3%
TOTAL	100%	100%	100%

PDS NPP: 26/ average diverging points across time and space: 2
PNS NPP: .84/ average PNS across time and space: .67
PNS NPP based on Afrobarometer data collected in 2008: .76/ average PNS across time and space: .72
PDS NDC: 22/ average diverging points across time and space: 2
PNS NDC: .87/ average PNS across time and space: .67
PNS NPP based on Afrobarometer data collected in 2008: .72/ average PNS across time and space: .72

Source: Information compiled from Electoral Commission of Ghana 2008 (Provisional Results) as relayed by the private media.

Akufo-Addo secured the nomination of his party, securing 79 percent of the vote of all NPP delegates.

Both parties remained an ethnically balanced leadership. In terms of rhetoric, the NDC highlighted its commitment to the fight against corruption by instigating procedures against former NPP government personnel. The NPP laid into the opposition by accusing it of going for politically motivated prosecutions. In 2012, the Mills administration was hit hard by allegations of government payments to NDC supporter Alfred Woyome, allegations the Economic and Organized Crimes Office (EOCO) partly confirmed. Oil exportation and how to deal with its benefits garnered comparatively little attention. Although tensions between the two parties increased in the run-up to the 2012 elections, ethnicity did not become a major divisive issue in Ghanaian party politics (EIU 2009, 2010, 2011, 2012; Africa Yearbook 2009, 2010, 2011, 2012).

POLITICAL PARTIES IN AFRICA: FINDINGS FROM GHANA

The salience of ethnicity in Ghanaian party politics is low. Ghana's party system is a nonethnic party system. Throughout four observation periods, Ghanaian politics has shown remarkable stability. Party competition remained dominated by two political parties. Both changed their party types several times.

Although the NPP started out as an ethnic-alliance party, from its inception, the party aimed at becoming a nationwide political force. Its "integrative turn" from an ethnic alliance to a nonethnic (i.e., programmatic) party, which occurred in observation period 2, was accelerated by the fact that the incumbent party was a nonethnic party. While in opposition, the NPP had clearly distinguishable programmatic beliefs. These were visible in its manifestos and in its public statements. Once in government, the party was less explicit about its desire to create a free-market economy. Policy making was overshadowed by technocratic expediency. Kufour's main priority was to increase the vote share of the party in regions where the Busia-Danquah tradition fared poorly. Party factions were based on powerful individuals with cross-cutting support from all communities and regions. The Akan, and in particular the Ashanti, have dominated the party. All NPP chairmen and presidential candidates were Akan. Just like the Namibian SWAPO, the Ghanaian NPP is dominated by one ethnic group. However, just as SWAPO, the NPP as a whole has bridged its nation's dominant ethnic cleavage line. With the exception of the first observation period, the NPP leadership and its cabinets have always included representatives from the Ewe and the Northern communities. Over time, it managed to broaden its social base. Its electoral support has widened considerably. Overall, the NPP is a catch-all party with visible programmatic underpinnings. Although its ideological backbone grew weaker over time, the party never left any doubt about its programmatic heritage.

The NDC started out as a personalistic party. It was founded with the clear intention of keeping Jerry J. Rawlings in power. In the first two observation periods, the party was structured around him. Party elections did not take place. Populist rhetoric shaped its 1992 and 1996 campaign. This changed with the departure of Rawlings. The party began to portray itself as social-democratic/Nkrumahist party. The ideological preference of its political opponent played an important part in this. Rawling's status as the official party founder ensured him a long-term presence in the party leadership. Therefore, the change in strategy occurred incrementally and was not without setbacks for the reformers. The examination of the NDC manifestos and its campaign sound bites has shown that social-democratic ideas coexist with catch-all and pro-Rawlings oratory. The catch-all elements, however, prevail. Overall, the NDC transformed from a personalistic to a catch-all party. In terms of its composition and its electoral performance, it remained a nationwide force. Table 5.18 summarizes all findings of this chapter.

The analysis of parties in Namibia and Ghana thus reveals striking findings about party competition in Africa. In both countries, nonethnic parties prevail. Although in Namibia, ethnic and nonethnic parties coexist most

TABLE 5.18. *Summary of Disaggregated Results for Parties in Ghana*

	Party Scoring Sheet										
	Party Goals		Electoral Strategy		Organizational Structure			Social Base			
Party: NPP Observation Period	Motive of Formation	Rhetoric	Electoral Rhetoric	Content of Election Manifesto	National Coverage	Party Factions	Party Apparatus	Leadership Composition	Cabinet Composition	PDS and PNS	Classification
T1	ideas and catch-all	catch-all and programmatic	ethnic and programmatic	high	n/a	based around individuals	n/a	failing to bridge cleavages	n/a	medium to high; medium to low	ethnic alliance
T2	ideas and catch-all	catch-all and programmatic	catch-all	high	high	based around individuals	n/a	bridging cleavages	n/a	medium to low; medium to low	programmatic
T3	ideas and catch-all	catch-all	catch-all	high	high	none	n/a	bridging cleavages	bridging cleavages	medium to low; medium to high	catch-all
T4	ideas and catch-all	catch-all	catch-all	low	high	based around individuals	n/a	bridging cleavages	bridging cleavages	low to very low; high to very high	catch-all
Across Time	ideas and catch-all	catch-all and programmatic	catch-all	high in opposition, low in government	high	based around individuals	wings not visible	bridging cleavages	bridging cleavages	increasingly catch-all	catch-all
Party: NDC Observation Period											
T1	keep Rawlings in power	praising leader; populist-socialist	praising leader; populist	n/a	high	none	women's wing and youth wings visible	bridging cleavages	bridging cleavages	low to very low; high to very high	personalistic
T2	keep Rawlings in power	praising leader; populist-socialist	praising leader; populist	low	high	none	n/a	bridging cleavages	bridging cleavages	low to very low; high to very high	personalistic
T3	catch-all and ideas	catch-all and social-democratic	catch-all and social-democratic	low	high	based on individuals	youth wing visible	bridging cleavages	n/a	low to very low; medium to high	catch-all
T4	catch-all and ideas	catch-all and social-democratic	catch-all and social-democratic	low	high	based on individuals	n/a	bridging cleavages	n/a	low to very low; medium to high	catch-all
Across Time	catch-all and ideas	catch-all and social-democratic	catch-all and social-democratic	low	high	based on individuals	youth wing and women's wing at times visible	bridging cleavages	bridging cleavages	low to very low; medium to high	catch-all

of the time, in Ghana, ethnic parties are almost completely absent. The distinguishing features between the NPP and the NDC are their presidential candidates and their ideological predilections. Ghanaian politics thus strongly resembles politics in industrialized societies. In stark contrast to Kenya, the dominant political strategy in Ghanaian and Namibian politics has been to establish nationwide political forces and to define these forces by ideas and/or personalities.

Accordingly, both Ghana and Namibia falsify those who were skeptical about the feasibility of peaceful multiparty competition in Africa. Personal merit, the ability to mobilize voters in all regions, and, to a limited extent, party ideology prevail over the centrifugal tendencies of ethnicity. Neither in Namibia nor in Ghana did multiparty competition foster ethnic divisions. Instead, in both cases, the salience of ethnicity decreased over time. The next chapter illustrates this finding in greater depth and provides a comparative examination of all results.

6

The Diversity of African Party Politics

The previous three chapters applied the Diamond and Gunther (2001 and 2003) typology to Kenya, Namibia, and Ghana. This chapter summarizes the results from those chapters in a comparative manner. The primary finding emanating from the empirical analysis of parties in the three African countries is that the African political landscape is much more diverse than commonly assumed. Contrary to conventional scholarly wisdom, ethnic parties do not dominate the political scene in Africa. Instead, a wide variety of party types exist. In Namibia and Ghana – two of the three countries – nonethnic party types prevail. Only in Kenya do ethnic parties dominate the political contest. Multiparty competition in ethnically segmented societies does not harden communal relations but instead increases party outreach.

In reviewing the empirical results from Kenya, Ghana, and Namibia, the chapter notes a variation of political party types at two levels: at the level of individual parties (i.e., within countries) and between countries over time. This chapter focuses on variation within countries. It identifies context-specific factors responsible for this type of variation. Subsequently, the chapter compares and contrasts the programmatic content and the political orientation (left versus right) of parties. It also pays some attention to the role of programmatic orientations. Previous authors have dedicated little to no effort toward examining this dimension of African politics.

The small number of cases demands further verification of the results; particularly so because case selection was guided by the intent to illustrate diversity. However, the examination of an additional number of parties cannot be conducted with the same depth because the collection of even basic data on African parties is a cumbersome process. To facilitate a less labor-intense analysis, I first examine the discriminatory power of each indicator of the typology. In doing so, I identify a small selection of indicators that allow for a preliminary analysis of parties. Subsequently, I apply the indicators with the most discriminatory power to a number of politically significant parties in Tanzania, Botswana, Senegal, Malawi, Burkina Faso, Zambia, and Benin. The additional cases confirm the findings from the three in-depth cases. Ethnic parties exist in numerous countries, but they do not dominate political competition: nonethnic parties prevail in most countries. There is no country in which multiparty competition leads to a hardening of communal relations. Although the additional findings do not provide a representative sample of cases, they strengthen the results from the three in-depth cases significantly.

POLITICAL PARTIES IN KENYA, NAMIBIA, AND GHANA

The application of the amended Diamond and Gunther typology to three African countries exposes the striking diversity of African party politics. All five party types at the heart of this study – mono-ethnic parties, ethnic alliances, catch-all parties, personalistic parties, and programmatic parties – feature in the three countries under scrutiny. Table 6.1 summarizes all results. The detailed analysis of parties in the previous 3 chapters has covered 12 parties. As parties have changed their type on several occasions in Kenya and Ghana, the table includes 18 party types and 28 observations.

This study reveals 5 observations of the mono-ethnic party, 11 observations of the multiethnic alliance, 9 observations of the ethnic catch-all party, 2 observations of the personalistic party, and 1 observation of the programmatic party type. Of a total of 28 observations, 16 are ethnic parties (i.e., mono-ethnic and ethnic alliances), and 12 are nonethnic parties (i.e., catch-all, programmatic, and personalistic). All five party types feature at the heart of the Diamond and Gunther typology.

In purely numerical terms, ethnic parties are more frequent than nonethnic parties. Overall, the multiethnic alliance is the prevalent party type. Similar results emerge when turning to the second observation period: analyzing parties between 1989 and 2009. Of the 12 cases, 3 parties constitute mono-ethnic parties, 5 are ethnic alliances, and 4 are catch-all parties. The use of a different observation period changes the results in as far as personalistic and programmatic parties no longer feature. Both types are overtaken by the catch-all type.

Reviewing the cases in which the classification of parties was not straightforward diminishes the seeming dominance of ethnic parties. In three instances, the final classification of parties was not clear-cut: the NPP in the first observation period and KANU in the first two observation periods.

The difficulties of classifying the Ghanaian NPP derive from a lack of data. The analysis of the 1992 Ghanaian election relied on secondary literature. Newspaper coverage of opposition activities was limited. As a result of the NPP's boycott of the first election, no data existed to illuminate the extent to which the party was able to field candidates nationwide.

KANU was the most national of all Kenyan parties. Results indicate that overall, the party orients itself toward the interests of its core clientele, to

TABLE 6.1. *Results from the Application of the Amend(ed) Diamond Typology*

Country	Party	Observation Period	
Kenya	KANU	1992–1997	alliance
		1997–2002	alliance
		2002–2007	alliance
		across time	alliance
	FORD-K	1992–1997	alliance
		1997–2002	mono-ethnic
		across time	alliance
	FORD-A	1992–1997[1]	alliance
	DP	1992–1997	alliance
		1997–2002	mono-ethnic
		2002–2007	mono-ethnic
		across time	mono-ethnic
	SDP	1997–2002	mono-ethnic
	NDP	2007–2002	mono-ethnic
	NARC	2002–2007	alliance
Ghana	NPP	1992–1996	alliance
		1996–2000	programmatic
		2000–2004	catch-all
		2004–2008	catch-all
		across time	catch-all
	NDC	1992–1996	personalistic
		1996–2000	personalistic
		2000–2004	catch-all
		2004–2008	catch-all
		across time	catch-all
Namibia	SWAPO	1989–1994	catch-all
		1994–1999	catch-all
		1999–2004	catch-all
		2004–2009	catch-all
		across time	catch-all
	DTA	1989–1994	alliance
		1994–1999	alliance
		1999–2004	alliance
		across time	alliance
	CoD	2004–2009	catch-all

Source: Author's compilation.

which the rhetoric and involvement of leading Kenyan government politicians in ethnic clashes attest. The legacy of one-party rule under KANU must

[1] Where the analysis of a party is confined to one observation period, its classification across time equals its classification in the period in which the party was relevant.

,LE 6.2. *Party System Nationalization Scorcs (PSNS) for Ghana, Namibia, and Kenya*

	First Parliamentary Cycle	Second Parliamentary Cycle	Third Parliamentary Cycle	Fourth Parliamentary Cycle
Ghana	n/a	.70	.70	.74
Namibia	.80	.70	.67	.71
Kenya	.59	.54	.62	.42

Source: Author's compilation.

also be considered. KANU projected the manpower and the infrastructure that made it appear to be a national party.

Switching the unit of analysis from individual parties to party systems, however, not only diminishes but falsifies the assumption that ethnic parties dominate. Ethnic parties dominate in only one country: Kenya. The overall number of party types is biased in favor of a higher number of ethnic parties due to the proliferation of a high number of Kenyan parties, which are significant (Sartori 2005a) and effective (Laakso and Taagepera 1979). Nonethnic parties prevail in Ghana and Namibia. Namibia becomes a nonparty system with the onset of the fourth and Ghana a nonethnic party system with the onset of the second observation period. Already from its inception, the NPP in Ghana attempted to become a nationwide political force. The DTA never qualified as a significant and effective party; the study only included the DTA to analyze the dynamics of party competition. Thus in Ghana and Namibia, ethnicity matters very little.

PSNS outlined in Table 6.2 confirm the varying degrees to which ethnicity influences party systems.

Across all three countries, party competition becomes less ethnic over time. The Ghanaian NPP always attempted to include those communities outside its core clientele. In observation period 1, this strategy failed as a result of its presidential flag bearer. The arrival of "generation Kufour" in the highest echelon of the party triggered a transformation, first to a programmatic and later to a catch-all party. In Namibia, the DTA was replaced by the CoD as the official opposition. The DTA had consistently failed to make any inroads into the northern part of the country. In Kenya, the formation of nonethnic parties failed. Party competition remained driven by ethnic parties. This notwithstanding, Kenyan parties started to merge with other parties during the second observation period. This process reached its peak in the run-up to the third multiparty election in 2002. Today, party competition is characterized no longer by mono-ethnic but by multiethnic alliances. The bloody aftermath of the 2007 Kenyan elections demonstrates that despite parties' growing inclusiveness, ethnic violence continues to haunt the population at large. In all three countries, it appears that political competition reduces the impact of ethnicity on political parties rather than augmenting it. Democratization thus appears to decrease but not enhance communal tensions.

In Ghana and Namibia, the formation of nonethnic parties occurred against the background of a nonethnic incumbent party. In Ghana, the opposition NPP reached out to stand a better chance to claim power against the incumbent NDC. In Namibia, the opposition DTA did not stand the test of time and disintegrated because of the ethnic nature of its member parties. In Kenya, the rise of NARC occurred against the background of the formation of New KANU, which for a short time bridged the country's dominant cleavage lines. Unfortunately, the selection of cases does not allow a test of whether the same trends are observable if the party in government is ethnic. Yet one can clearly observe a "contagion effect" unfolding over time whereby all parties attempt to increase their national coverage.[2]

The following statements summarize the results of the application of the Diamond and Gunther typology to three African countries:

Mono-ethnic, alliance, catch-all programmatic, and personalistic parties exist in Africa's post–third wave democracies.

The most dominant party type is the ethnic alliance. Distinguishing between ethnic and nonethnic parties, ethnic parties prevail numerically over nonethnic ones.

Personalistic and programmatic parties are not sustainable over time.

The salience of ethnicity at the aggregate level of political parties decreases over the course of successive multiparty elections.

Although the application of the Diamond and Gunther typology has significantly advanced our understanding of African party politics, typologies are always rather static representations of the empirical world. Those African countries in which multiparty competition has become the norm are still in the process of democratization. Parties change their party type rather frequently in comparison with the more stable party types of the Western world. Nevertheless, the empirical analysis has covered party development over the course of 20 years. The systematic application of the typology thus revealed a general trend and has shown that African politics is anything but static. The following section analyzes changes in party types over time in greater detail.

Variation Within Countries: Some Observations

Differences in party types can be observed at two levels. First, at the party level over time, the Ghanaian NPP serves as an example that changes from

[2] The phrase "contagion effect" normally describes the contagion effect of European left-wing mass parties. Duverger (1954) was the first to observe the effect.

an ethnic alliance to a programmatic party between 1996 and 2000. Second, variation occurs between countries over time. Ghanaian parties and Namibian parties are predominantly nonethnic, whereas Kenyan parties are exclusively ethnic. This section focuses on variation at the party level.

The comparative political science literature observes changes in party types over the course of several decades. It discusses these changes in relation to political, economic, and societal transformations (Katz and Mair 1995, Miller 1996, Boix 1998, Mair et al. 2004, Lewis-Beck 2008). Parliamentary democracy in Africa is a fairly recent phenomenon and still at a nascent stage. To pinpoint where changes in party types have occurred, much shorter observation periods are at scholars' disposal. In the following, I briefly analyze which parties changed their type and which typology indicators were affected by this change.

This study notes four parties that undergo a change of type:

FORD-K changes from an alliance to a mono-ethnic party.
The DP changes from an alliance to a mono-ethnic party.
The NPP changes from an alliance to a programmatic and subsequently to a catch-all party.
The NDC changes from a personalistic to a catch-all party.

FORD-K and the DP remain ethnic parties. In the case of FORD-K, the transformation is due to changes in four indicators: national coverage, the nature of party factions, leadership composition, and electoral support (PNS and PDS). The remaining indicators either already signified a mono-ethnic party, could not be measured due to a lack of data, or do not discriminate between mono-ethnic parties and multi-ethnic alliances.[3] In the case of the DP, the transformation from an alliance to a mono-ethnic party occurs in three indicators: party factions, party apparatus, and leadership composition. Two indicators in the previous observation period (national coverage and electoral output) were already indicative of a mono-ethnic party. These changes reflect the Kenyan parties' tendency toward fission at the time. Both the transformation of the DP and the FORD-K occurred within the first observation period. Both parties are mono-ethnic with the start of the second observation period.

The Ghanaian NPP is the only party to undergo two changes: first, from an ethnic (i.e., alliance party) to a nonethnic type (programmatic party) and subsequently to another type of nonethnic party (catch-all party). Alterations between the first and the second observation period affect the NPP's electoral rhetoric, national coverage, leadership composition, and electoral output.

[3] Not all indicators discriminate between all party types. For example, the indicator "programmatic content" merely distinguishes programmatic from catch-all and personalistic parties. The same principle applies to a number of indicators. See Chapter Two.

However, even in the first observation period, a variety of indicators already alluded to a nonethnic character, including its motive of formation, general rhetoric, and the nature of its factions.

The change from a programmatic to a catch-all party occurs as the result of a decline in the programmatic content of party rhetoric and the programmatic content of its election manifesto. Both are key indicators for distinguishing programmatic from other nonethnic parties. These changes occur after the NPP claimed power and thus show that the decline of programmatic degree among governing parties is not a feature unique to established democracies.

The Ghanaian NDC changes from a personalistic to a catch-all party, which constitutes a change within the nonethnic types of the party typology. This alteration affects four indicators: motive of formation, party rhetoric, electoral rhetoric, and the nature of party factions. The focus on Jerry J. Rawlings faded as the party founder and leader came closer to political retirement. The characteristics of a catch-all party were visible slightly before the end of the second observation period.

As in Kenya, the changes of party types in Ghana are linked to country-specific factors, in particular, the nature of the Ghanaian political regime and its evolution between the late 1980s and early 1990s, when an authoritarian military dictatorship gave way to a multiparty democracy. Initially, a former military dictator was elected president on the ticket of a political party. Rawlings' political background explains the initial nature of the NDC. The closer the country approached the post-Rawlings period, the more urgent it became for the NDC to redefine its raison d'être. The most obvious option was to define itself in contrast to its political opponent, a catch-all party with visible programmatic underpinnings. The NDC adopted programmatic ideas to a greater extent than previously, although it never qualified as a programmatic party. The decade-old political division into Busiaism/Nkrumahism provided historically fertile ground to do so.

In general, African political parties change their type fairly frequently: of a total of 12 parties, 4 changed their type over a relatively short period of time. Party alterations occurred mainly within ethnic or nonethnic types and rarely between them. There is only one change from an ethnic to a nonethnic party: the NPP in Ghana. All changes in party types can be linked to interactions with other parties. FORD-K and the DP changed within a political framework characterized by the spread of mono-ethnic parties. The NPP and the NDC altered their type in relation to one another: the NPP broadened its support base to position itself to pose a serious electoral challenge to the NDC. The NDC redefined its purpose to remain a serious political competitor once its founder was constitutionally forced to leave active politics.

African Parties and Political Ideology: Some Observations

The question of party ideology in Africa deserves attention. For decades, scholars agreed that party ideology was absent from African politics (Elischer 2012). The coding of election manifestos has facilitated a quantitative measurement of the extent to which African parties care about programmatic ideas. Results for this exercise have been reported in the respective empirical chapters. The MRG coding scheme facilitates the measurement of a manifesto's overall programmatic content and the measurement of the political orientation of parties alongside a right-left–wing axis. The empirical chapters focused on the overall programmatic content of party manifestos; they were interested in the extent to which individual parties espouse right- and left-wing statements. In the following, I examine how African parties position themselves on a right-left–wing axis.

By subtracting the percentage share of a party's left-wing categories from the percentage share of its right-wing categories, the MRG scheme determines the political positioning of parties. If the result is positive, the party is biased toward the political left; if the result is negative, it favors the political right. Table 6.3 illustrates the findings for all parties. T1 indicates the date of the first election after the introduction of multiparty democracy. In the case of Kenya and Ghana, T1 is 1992; in the case of Namibia, T1 is 1989. T2 indicates the date of the second election. In the case of Kenya, T2 indicates 1997; in the case of Ghana, 1996; in the case of Namibia, 1994, and so forth.

Many scholars have argued that in the absence of an industrial revolution, ideological cleavages have not emerged in Africa (Lemarchand 1972, Randall and Svasand 2002, Randall 2007). Results from the coding exercise confirm their assumptions, revealing the majority of manifestos to originate from the moderate left. The average position for all parties is a positive value of nine.

The discussion of individual parties showed that all parties demand increases in health care and education spending. The policy issues parties stress most are nearly all devoid of ideology. Of the 28 party manifestos, 15 stress category 411 (Technology and Infrastructure: positive), 5 place their greatest emphasis on category 410 (Productivity: positive), 2 highlight category 304 (Political Corruption: negative), 2 are most interested in category 504 (Welfare State Expansion: positive), 2 give most preference to category 201 (Freedom and Human Rights: positive), 1 to category 605 (Law and Order: positive), and 1 to category 506 (Education Expansion: positive). With the exception of the last four categories, all categories lack ideological content.

The radical and contradictory positioning of the DTA in T2 and T3 and the strong left-wing stance of the CoD in T4 are results of their overemphasis of individual policy categories. The NPP and the DP are the only parties in which the high degree of programmatic content cannot be reduced to a

TABLE 6.3. *Political Positioning of Parties*

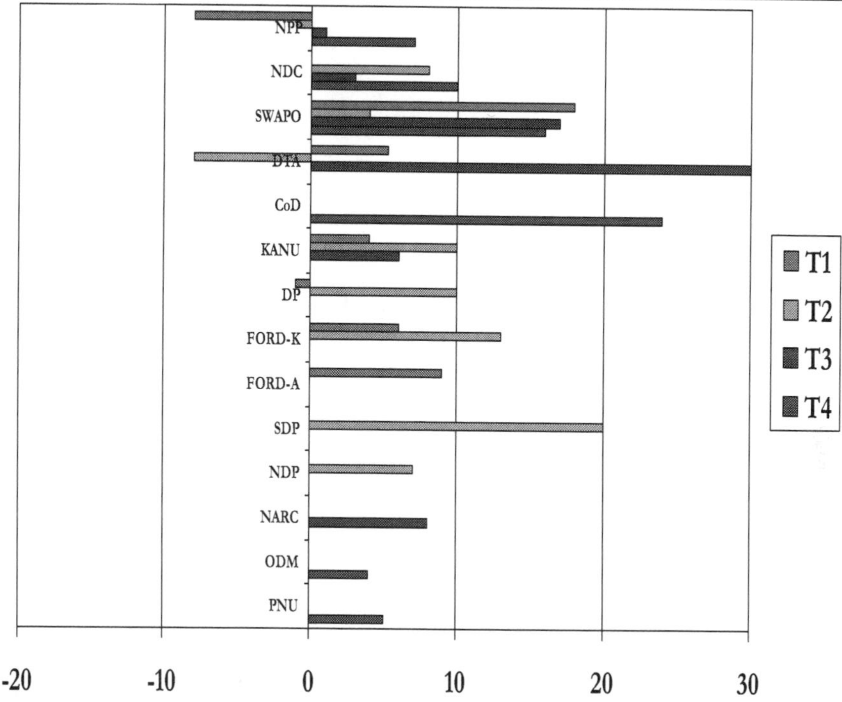

Source: Author's compilation. See also Elischer 2012.

few categories. They are also the only parties positioned on the political right. The DP and the NPP in observation period 1 are good examples showing that ethnic parties have ideological underpinnings. The right-wing programmatic underpinnings of the DP are derived from its core clientele, the Kikuyu community, which is known to be well situated in Kenya's economy. The same holds true for the Ashanti, the core clientele of the NPP.

This short outline of additional results from the coding of party manifestos raises thought-provoking questions for further research. Although overall, party ideology matters little, a few African parties have ideological convictions. The data gathered sets the stage for future comparisons between the ideological content of African party manifestos with manifestos from other regions.

TOWARD A NEW FRAMEWORK OF COMPARISON FOR AFRICAN PARTIES

This study has constructed a framework by which the salience of ethnicity on political parties can be assessed across countries. With 10 indicators, this has been an extensive task. Scholars interested in large-N studies might find the typology to be too labor-intensive. To facilitate a preliminary verification of the results from the three in-depth cases, I examine which indicators hold most discriminatory power to differentiate between party types. Thereby, my focus is on the distinction between ethnic and nonethnic parties.

Motive of Formation

Any analysis of political parties will have to deal with the conditions that surrounded their foundation. Therefore, this indicator is logically irreplaceable. Yet its purpose is limited. In 24 of 28 instances, parties have been founded for reasons that fall into the category of "catch-all": the main intention of their founders was to establish democratic rule and to better the living conditions of their populations. In very few instances did programmatic ideas supplement the process of party formation. Only a very few number of parties can be assumed to have started out with the explicit purpose to represent particular communities. This includes the Kenyan NDP and, to a lesser extent, the Namibian DTA. Against the background of these results, one therefore cannot conclude a party's type from its motive of formation.

Rhetoric

Of 28 observations, there are 18 instances in which parties' rhetoric is either purely catch-all or contains catch-all elements. Of these, nine observations turn out to be ethnic parties (mono-ethnic or ethic-alliance parties), whereas nine are nonethnic (catch-all or programmatic). In addition, I find eight observations in which parties' rhetoric contains ethnic elements. In all instances in which a party's rhetoric contained appeals to group solidarity, the party could be classified as mono-ethnic. Thus the nature of one type of ethnic party becomes visible in its statements: mono-ethnic parties do mean what they say. However, although overall figures indicate that African parties by and large talk the same talk, party rhetoric provides a good opportunity to identify mono-ethnic parties.

Electoral Rhetoric

Results show that in 21 of 28 observations, a party's electoral rhetoric contains catch-all elements. By and large, African parties approach elections in a similar manner, trying to increase its vote share by promoting ideas that large parts of the electorate like to hear. In eight instances, parties used ethnic statements either exclusively or as part of their larger campaign strategy. Again, in all eight instances the party classification scheme identified the party as ethnic. Despite great similarity in election campaigns, sound bites appealing to the benefits of individuals groups feature and thus can identify ethnic parties. However, although it is true that every party that espouses ethnic campaign rhetoric is an ethnic party, it is not true that every party classified as ethnic also espouses ethnic rhetoric. Of 15 observations of ethnic parties, only 8 displayed ethnic campaign rhetoric. Electoral rhetoric on its own therefore is insufficient to identify parties.

Ideology/Manifesto Content

The amended Diamaond and Gunther party typology applied a manifesto coding scheme that is derived from the historical experience of Western European parties. This might have raised the conventional criticism that "African parties are different" and cannot be compared with their Western counterparts; simultaneously, it has been the most innovative part of my framework. Contrary to criticism, the scheme has been found to be very applicable in an African context. Only 11.8 percent of all policy statements were identified as "uncodable," that is, did not fit any policy category put forward by the MRG coding scheme. I found only four instances in which manifestos displayed a genuinely high programmatic content (the Ghanaian NPP in T1 and T2 and the Kenyan DP in T1 and T2). Yet in three of these four cases, the party under scrutiny turned out to be an ethnic party. Thus although the scheme worked surprisingly well in an African context and has greatly added to our understanding of to what extent ideology matters in African politics, one cannot conclude the nature of the party from this indicator. Even parties with a high programmatic content can turn out to be ethnic parties.

National Coverage

A party's ability to field candidates nationwide is reduced to 18 observations as a result of the Namibian electoral system and a lack of data in the first observation period in Ghana. In 13 cases, our indicator displays medium to high values, indicating nonethnic parties. However, only six of these turn out to be nonethnic. In seven instances, we are left with ethnic parties. In five cases, this indicator displays a medium or low capacity to field candidates, and all five turn out to be ethnic. National coverage is another indicator that on its own cannot differentiate between ethnic and nonethnic parties.

Party Factions

Of our 27 observations for this indicator, 8 parties display ethnic party factions, 11 are characterized by factions based on individuals, 7 have no factions, and in 1 instance, factions were made up of members from one group. Even though my ideal type of a nonethnic party is defined by party factions based on individuals (relying on nationwide support), I find this condition to be met in six nonethnic and five ethnic parties. The same happens to the ideal type of the personalistic party, which is defined as having no factions. In seven of our observations, this condition is met, yet only two of these are personalistic, whereas two are ethnic and three are nonethnic parties.

Party Apparatus

Only in very few instances was data available for this indicator. The low institutionalization of parties means that not too much is known about party wings. A sufficient amount of data could not be collected to assess this indicator.

Leadership Composition

Data for this indicator are available in 26 of 28 observations. In 14 observations, a party's leadership was able to overcome dominant ethnic cleavage lines. In 12 of these instances, we are left with a nonethnic party; only twice does the result for this indicator diverge from my ideal type. These include KANU (Kenya) in observation period 1 and NARC in observation period 3. Both parties incorporate catch-all elements. KANU entered the period of multiparty competition as a party having dominated Kenya for almost three decades. The leadership that presided over the party was elected before the return of multiparty democracy and is not representative of the time period under scrutiny. NARC's leadership was also catch-all, yet only remained united for a short period of time. The party existed for a very short period and was born out of the electoral frustration of Kenya's opposition. The unique historical contexts in which both operate explain why disaggregated results for this indicator diverge from the aggregate classification of both parties. Apart from these two cases, results for this indicator match the aggregate results. This is also true for the 12 observations in which leadership composition does not bridge ethnic cleavages: all 12 turn out to be ethnic parties.

Cabinet Composition

By definition, data are only available for parties that managed to claim power. Case selection reduces that number to 11. In nine observations, respective cabinets managed to bridge cleavage lines, and only in one case – NARC in Kenya – the party was classified as ethnic. In two instances, the party failed to do so, and in both cases, the party was classified as ethnic. Therefore, both leadership and cabinet composition are comparatively well-suited to distinguish between ethnic and nonethnic parties.

Party Divergence Scores and Party Nationalization Scores

It has become commonplace to classify African parties according to their electoral performance. According to the typology, one can expect the PDSs of a nonethnic party to have a medium to low or a low to very low value. Fourteen observations display such scores, and yet in three instances, the overall classification is typical of an ethnic party. These include KANU (observation periods 2 and 3) and NARC (observation period 3). PDSs that fall into the medium to high and high to very high category indicate ethnic parties. In 13 instances, parties display such scores, and 11 of them turn out to be ethnic parties. The only observation whose final classification diverges is the Namibian CoD in observation period 4 – a party whose political significance is in doubt. Therefore, with the exception of very few instances, our PDS fairly accurately matches the final classification results.

The same is true of the PNS. Ethnic parties are characterized by medium to low or low to very low PNSs. Of 12 observations that match these criteria, 10 turn out to be ethnic parties, whereas 2 parties are eventually classified as nonethnic. These exceptions are the CoD in observation period 4 and the NPP in observation period 2. Nonethnic parties are characterized by a medium to high or a high to very high score. Of 15 observations that fulfill these criteria, 10 turn out to be nonethnic parties, whereas 5 are classified as ethnic. The exceptions include KANU in all three observation periods, NARC in observation period 1, and the CoD in observation period 4. Furthermore, there are three cases in which the PDS and the PNS point to different party types: KANU and SWAPO in observation period 1 and the NPP in observation period 2. Electoral indicators therefore are best suited to identify party types at least for the limited purpose of distinguishing between ethnic and nonethnic parties. Ideally such distinctions will be supplemented by data about their leadership and their cabinet composition.

The discussion about the relationship between results for individual indicator and parties' overall classification shows that no indicator can distinguish different party types on its own. This confirms that all parties constitute mixed types. Even though the Diamond and Gunther typology has worked well when applied empirically, the essence of political parties is difficult to capture, not only in Africa, but anywhere across the globe. The evaluation of the indicators used in this study shows leadership composition and indicators derived from electoral output to be best suited to arrive at a less labor-intensive identification of parties. However, this should occur over a period of time that covers at least two parliamentary cycles to account for contextual factors. These two indicators should therefore be at the heart of any large-N study using our amended typology.

VERIFICATION OF RESULTS: PRELIMINARY EVIDENCE FROM ADDITIONAL CASES

The in-depth application of the amended Diamond and Gunther party typology to three countries has revealed new and challenging findings about the political salience of ethnicity in Africa. Ethnic parties do not dominate party politics in the three countries under scrutiny. Multiparty competition also does not foster ethnic exclusion in the medium to long term. Because of the small number of countries under scrutiny, these findings call for verification with the help of additional cases (King, Keohane, and Verba 1994).The selection of Ghana, Kenya, and Namibia as case studies was based on the assumption that in these three countries, party competition is driven by diverse dynamics (Gerring 2006, Seawright and Gerring 2008). I aim to corroborate the major findings from my three in-depth cases with preliminary findings from as many additional cases as possible. The analysis of political parties in Kenya, Namibia, and Ghana required extensive field research. Applying the amended Diamond and Gunther typology to additional parties cannot be conducted in the same depth. The following section, therefore, establishes preliminary evidence on the basis of the secondary literature, which makes previous scholarly occupation with the respective parties a necessary selection criterion. Other criteria include that no civil war has taken place, that the country is neither a failing nor a failed state, that party competition has taken place for at least two to three parliamentary cycles, and that the country has at least temporarily been classified as an electoral democracy by Freedom House. As Chapter Seven demonstrates in detail, the analysis of parties in Kenya, Namibia, and Ghana finds the presence of a numerically dominant group to be conductive to the formation of nonethnic party types. To test this claim further, cases are also selected according to their ethnic composition.

The preliminary cases include a selection of politically significant parties from Tanzania, Botswana, Malawi, Senegal, Burkina Faso, Zambia, and Benin. Although Botswana, Senegal, and Burkina Faso include a numerically identifiable dominant ethnic group, Zambia, Malawi, Tanzania, and Benin are composed of several groups, none of which is numerically superior. In total, the preliminary cases include 22 parties from 7 countries. In contrast to the in-depth cases of Kenya, Namibia, and Ghana, the subsequent analysis does not cover every parliamentary period but rather focuses on the whole period under scrutiny (i.e., the period between the onset of multiparty contest and the present day) or on those periods for which reliable data are available. Systematic research on African parties is still in a nascent stage, and sufficient data are not readily available for an analysis of each parliamentary cycle.

I examine the additional cases with those indicators whose discriminatory power has proven sufficiently strong to arrive at an accurate classification of the party in question. These indicators include the party leadership composition, its rhetoric, party factions, and its electoral indicators. I confine the analysis of the additional cases to the politically most important parties in each country. The main aim of the additional cases is not to provide the same systematic analysis as in the previous chapters, but to provide preliminary evidence that African party politics is diverse and must not be confined to ethnic parties.

TANZANIA

Tanzania achieved independence in 1961. In 1964, mainland Tanzania merged with Zanzibar. In 1965, Tanzania officially became a one-party state under the leadership of Tanzania African National Union (TANU), which later became the Chama Cha Mapinduzi (CCM). Multiparty competition returned to Tanzania in early 1991. In contrast to neighboring Kenya, these changes were instigated by long-time president Nyerere and the governing CCM.

Ethnic relations between all communities are traditionally seen as amicable. This is not the case on the island of Zanzibar, which has constituted the theatre for violent religious conflict between the black African and the Arabic-African populations. The Zanzibar elections of 2000 were particularly violent (Chege 2007). My analysis covers the long-term governing party, CCM, and the former long-term official opposition, the Civic United Front (CUF), and the new official opposition, Chama cha Demokrasia na Maendeleo (CHADEMA). The observation period covers the period between 1995 and 2010 and thus three parliamentary cycles. Although the CCM continues to benefit from the legacy of one-party rule and has remained virtually without serious political competition, the CUF is a serious contender for power on the Zanzibar islands. Since 2010, CHADEMA has become the strongest opposition party in Tanzania.

Because dominant ethnic cleavages cannot be deciphered a priori for the country as a whole, the analysis of parties will pay particular attention to the relationship between the numerically strongest community, the Wasukuma, and the smaller groups, including the Nyamwezi, the Chagga, the Haya, and the Nyakusa. The Wasukuma constitute 13 percent and the smaller groups up to 5 percent of the population (Nyang'oro 2004). In addition, I regard the division between the communities on mainland Tanzania and the Zanzibar islands as a second dominant ethnic cleavage.

The Chama Cha Mapinduzi

From 1965 to 1991, Tanzania was a de jure one-party state under the leadership of TANU (the CCM), which pursued socialist economic policies. During the period of one-party rule, the CCM ensured the equal representation of all ethnic communities in the cabinet and in the party. After the introduction of multiparty democracy, the party's national executive committee maintained representatives from all ethnic groups.[4] After 1991, the CMM also retained its parallel leadership structure for Zanzibar, with a special secretary-general and a special executive national committee responsible for matters affecting the island. Throughout the period under scrutiny, the CCM presidential candidate came from mainland Tanzania, and its vice-presidential candidate from Zanzibar (Mmuya 1998). Cabinets have remained national in scope, with several key ministries reserved for Tanzania's numerous minority communities (Nyang'oro 2004). Nothing indicates that these dynamics have changed in recent years or are about to change in the near-to-medium future (Reith 2010).

The party's electoral rhetoric has been shaped by the party's new approach toward the free-market economy and its break with its socialist past. The 2000 and 2005 election campaigns proved apt examples. The party vigorously defended the various privatization campaigns it had initiated. It strongly contested those who publically stated that international companies were making profits at the hands of the ordinary Tanzanian. Its election campaign in 2010 focused mainly on government achievements in the past.[5]

Since 2000, the party's main line of division has run between those in favor of free-market reforms and those who maintain a strong affinity for Nyerere's particular brand of socialism. Both former president Benjamin Mkapa and current president Jakaya Kikwete supported economic liberalization but had to face up to strong intra-party opposition by the supporters of socialist economic principles.[6] In 2007, factionalism became driven by the involvement of senior party figures in corruption scandals. Two factions emerged: on the one hand, CCM-Mafisadi, which included party leaders tarnished by corruption such as former Prime Minister Edward Lowassa, the former Infrastructure Minister Andrew Chenge, and the current secretary-general of the party, Yusuf Makamba; and on the other hand, CCM-Safi, led by the speaker of the National Assembly, Samuel Sitta. The campaign against CCM-Mafisadi was supported by Kikwete, who saw this as a convenient means of getting rid of powerful intra-party opponents.[7]

Although there has always been talk about the danger of the CCM falling apart into ethnic wings, any evidence for this assumption is lacking.[8] There is a numerically strong bloc of Zanzibar politicians inside the CMM; however, the group does not lobby for Zanzibar candidates but rather serves as a

[4] Data compiled with the help of media coverage and expert interviews. All data are with the author.
[5] Economist Intelligent Unit, various issues between 2000 and 2010.
[6] Economist Intelligent Unit, various issues between 1998 and 2007.
[7] Economist Intelligence Union, 2009 to 2011.
[8] Africa Year Book, 2001 to 2010.

TABLE 6.4. *Party Nationalization Scores – Tanzania*

Party	CCM	CUF
PNS	1995: 0.91	
	2000: 0.94	2000: 0.61
	2005: 0.94	2005: 0.66
	2010: 0.92	2010: 0.54
PNS based on Afrobarometer	2008: 0.93	2008: 0.51
PNS across time and space (in-depth cases)	0.67	
PNS across time and space (all cases)	0.68	

Source: Compiled by the author on the basis of election results by the National Electoral Commission of Tanzania and Afrobarometer.

platform for party candidates to introduce their views to the most prominent functionaries from the islands (Mmuya 1998).

Throughout the observation period, the CCM fielded candidates in every constituency. Its PNSs are outlined in Table 6.4. The party can undoubtedly rely on nationwide support; data from Afrobarometer confirm this. Preliminary evidence thus suggests that the CCM is a catch-all party with seemingly weak programmatic foundations. The party is national in composition, its factions nonethnic, its rhetoric catch-all, and its PNS[9] far above the cross-country average of this study.

The Civic United Front

The Civic United Front (CUF) was Tanzania's strongest opposition party between 1991 and 2005. The party was created in the early 1990s by former chief minister of Zanzibar, Shariff Hamad, who had been expelled from the CCM in the late 1980s due to allegations that he had committed treason. The CUF is led by a general governing body consisting of 45 delegates: 25 delegates represent the mainland, and 20 delegates represent Zanzibar (Shayo 2005). On the one hand, the CUF has stressed its commitment to improving the living standard of low-income people. On the other hand, the party has highlighted that the island of Pemba was its stronghold and that it represented first and foremost the interest of the Pemba people (Oloka-Onyango and Nassali 2003).

The CUF is characterized by ethnic factionalism. The mainland CUF only exists in some pockets in the coastal areas and is confronted by a much stronger Pemba wing led by Maalim Hamad. Hamad is the secretary-general and the de facto leader of the party. The party has witnessed several attempts at rebuilding the party exclusively around the needs of the Pemba people (Mmuya 1998). On various occasions, Hamad has been accused of

[9] All PNS for the preliminary cases are outlined in Annex H.

seeking the support of Islamic fundamentalists and of trying to Arabize the party (Muye and Chaligha 1994). Domestic and international analysts see the CUF as Islamic leaning and as favoring Zanzibar's Arab Africans over black Africans.[10] Over the course of the last two decades, the party has contested fewer and fewer constituencies. In 1995, it fielded candidates in 75 percent of all seats. In 2000, that number declined to 60 percent. In the last two elections, the share of contested constituencies declined to 50 percent (Nyang'oro 2004).

Its electoral indicators also give evidence of the ethnic nature of the party. The CUF has clearly identifiable strongholds in the coastal areas of the mainland. On Zanzibar, it traditionally gains roughly 50 percent of the vote. Its PNS is below the cross-country average. The PNS derived from Afrobarometer confirms its narrow electoral support. The CUF is therefore classified as an ethnic alliance.

CHADEMA

The CHADEMA (Chama cha Demokrasia na Maendeleo; Party for Democracy and Progress) party was established in 1993 by Edwin Mtei, a former minister of finance. Mtei was of Chagga origin. Frequently, the party is regarded as a Chagga party. Although CHADEMA has failed to become a national party, it clearly is not confined to one ethnic community.

Ever since its formation, it has been seen as the party of property and capital. At times the party leadership argued that members without property could not qualify as members of the national party executive (Mmuya 1998, Shayo 2005). Some members have accused the party leadership of running the party like a company and for behaving like senior executives (Nyang'oro 2004). In 2010, the party contested the elections with Dr. Willibrod Slaa as its presidential candidate. Slaa is a Catholic priest, who became famous in 2007 when he published a "list of shame" outlining the names of ministers and CCM functionaries who were allegedly involved in corrupt activities. Slaa made the fight against corruption the main theme of his election campaign.

Although ethnicity does not feature inside the party nor in the party rhetoric, the party's national coverage has remained limited. In 2010, it contested 52 percent of all constituencies. CHADEMA is virtually nonexistent in Zanzibar but has clearly identifiable strongholds in Arusha and Dar-es Salaam. Its strong urban bias indicates its multiethnic nature, but this should not detract from the fact that it has not (yet) become a national party. Its PNS derived from election results and Afrobarometer data both attest to that. CHADEMA therefore is classified as an ethnic alliance.

[10] Africa Yearbook, 2006 to 2010.

BOTSWANA

Since its independence from the United Kingdom in 1966, Botswana has been seen as the model African country, both in terms of its economic performance and in terms of its competitive party system. Ethnic relations are seen as amicable (Posner 2004, Hodler 2005). In terms of its ethnic setup, 79 percent of the population are Tswana, 11 percent Kalanga, and 3 percent Basarawa. I regard the division between Tswana and Kalanga as the dominant ethnic cleavage line. My analysis includes the long-time governing Botswana Democratic Party (BDP) and the long-time opposition, the Botswana National Front (BNF). The observation period covers the period from the 1999 election until the most recently concluded 2009 elections.

The Botswana Democratic Party

The BDP has been the ruling party of Botswana since 1965; since independence, it has been undefeated in elections. Like SWAPO in Namibia, it was formed as a national liberation movement. The BDP was initially composed primarily of one group: the Tswana. However, the party has a long tradition of reaching out to Botswana's many smaller communities and has consistently included them in its leadership.

This is reflected in the ethnic composition of its various cabinets since independence. From the outset of political competition, the BDP incorporated Kalangas into the cabinet. High-ranking ministers from both the Tswana and the Kalanga appointed assistant ministers from the respective other group. An ethnic breakdown of both communities shows that in the last decade and a half, the Tswanas made up roughly half the cabinet, which means they are underrepresented numerically. The Kalanga were allocated between 15 percent and 20 percent of all cabinet positions; the remaining positions were allocated to the smaller communities (Selolwane 2004, Robinson and Parsons 2006, Economist Intelligence Unit 2009, Subudubudu 2009).

During election campaigns, the party focused on past achievements. It consistently portrayed itself as a national political force. In doing so, it tried to deflect attention from the numerous corruption scandals the BDP has been involved in since the 1990s.

During the 1990s, factionalism emerged between president Festus Mogae and high-ranking party functionaries. The root cause of the tension was Mogae's unwillingness to stick to basic principles of intra-party democracy. Under his successor, President Ian Khama, the relationship between the president and the rank-and-file deteriorated further. Currently, the party is split between the Merafhe/Nkate faction (also known as "A-Team") and the Kwelagobe/Kedikilwe faction. Despite the support of President Kharama, the "A-Team" suffered severe setbacks at the 2009 party convention, when

TABLE 6.5. *Party Nationalization Scores – Botswana*

Party	BDP	BNF
PNS	1999: 0.86 2004: 0.83 2009: 0.68	1999: 0.71 2004: 0.63 2009: 0.68
PNS based on Afrobarometer	Afrobarometer 2005: 0.90 Afrobarometer 2009: 0.93	Afrobarometer 2005: 0.77 Afrobarometer 2009: 0.80
PNS across time and space (in-depth cases)	0.67	
PNS across time and space (all cases)	0.68	

Source: Author's compilation on the basis of data provided by the Electoral Commission of Botswana and Afrobarometer.

none of its members were elected into leadership positions. President Khama subsequently appointed his loyalists to party positions he had created in the aftermath of the congress. These highly personalized factions are rooted in Botswana's economic malaise. Various recent government policy initiatives failed to initiate sustained and effective growth. In addition, President Kharma has recruited many party functionaries from the military, which has deepened concerns over intra-party democracy. Ethnic divisions do not characterize the party (Lotshwao 2011).

Throughout the observation period, the BDP has contested all constituencies. Its PNS values outlined in Table 6.5 display its national outreach. I classify the BDP as a catch-all party.

The Botswana National Front

The Botswana National Front (BNF) has been the country's principal opposition since the late 1960s. At its foundation, its main goals were to change the country's economic orientation toward the West, reorient free-market principles to a socialist economy, and pursue a foreign policy of nonalignment. At the beginning, the party was a loose alliance of tribal leaders from all parts of the country, who cooperated with dedicated socialists. The party was formed by Kenneth Koma, who belonged to the latter (Selololwane 2004, Subudubudu and Molutsi 2009).

In the 1970s and 1980s, the BNF highlighted ethnic inequalities between the Kalanga and the Tstwana. This did not constitute a political bias in favor of the Kalanga but was the result of a careful economic analysis of income distribution. At the time, the Tstwana regions enjoyed a significantly higher standard of living than the rest of the country; any party who had the intention of fighting social inequality would have had to focus on the economic neglect of the Kalanga. The strategy of focusing on income disparities between different ethnic groups did not pay off, as the vote of the Kalanga remained divided between the BNF and the BDP (Selolwane 2002).

The party subsequently focused its rhetoric on the plight of the poor in general. In the last two decades, it has consistently portrayed itself as the only political force that cares for the economically marginalized in general and the rural poor in particular. It further stressed its commitment to good governance. The party leadership has consistently included representatives of the Tswana, the Kalanga, and the country's many smaller communities (Swatak 1999, Mokopakgosi and Molomo 2000).

In terms of factionalism, the party experienced turbulent times. In 1994, the young socialist faction accused Koma of not being radical enough in fighting for social justice. This led to two splits: the formation of the United Socialist Party, which included the radical (mainly young) members of the party, and the formation of the Social Democratic Party, a conglomerate of disgruntled losers in the BNF's primaries (Oswei-Hwedie 2001). Koma's domineering party management style greatly contributed to these breakaways. The simmering conflict between Koma and those in favor of a more open and transparent party eventually culminated in the gravest conflict in the party's history. The 1998 BNF congress led to stone throwing and open violence between the Koma wing and its opponents, the so-called Concerned Group. The congress was aborted, and the BNF central committee was dissolved. Koma's continuous refusal to surrender the leadership of the party led to the breakaway of the Botswana Congress Party a few months later (Lotshwao 2011, Oswei-Hwedie 2001). Koma's retirement from the party leadership in 2001 refuelled divisions: at the 2001 BNF congress, Otsweletse Moupo faced Peter Woto for the chairmanship of the party. Moupo was the candidate of the Concerned Group, and Woto the candidate of the so-called Party Line, the faction supported by Koma. Moupo won by a landslide, and the pro-Koma camp subsequently departed from the BDF and formed the National Democratic Front (Makgala 2005).

Over the course of the last 15 years, the BNF has contested all seats in parliament. Its PNSs indicate the national scope of the party (see Table 6.5). The BNF is therefore classified as a catch-all party.

SENEGAL

Senegal became independent from France in 1960. From 1966 to 1974, Senegal was a one-party state under the leadership of the Union Progressiste Sénégelaise (UPS). After social unrest, limited party pluralism was reintroduced in 1974. Initially, the number of parties was limited to three, each representing one major political ideology. The governing UPS (later renamed the Parti Socialiste International, PS) covered the social-democratic spectrum, the Parti Africain de l'Idépendance (PAI) was constructed as a Marxist-Leninist party, and the Parti Démocratique Sénégalais represented the liberal-democratic middle. The PS continued to remain in power. In 1983, after more social unrest, all restrictions on party formations were lifted under president Diouf (Hartmann 2010).

The subsequent analysis covers the formerly governing PS, which lost power in the 2000 elections, and the former long-term opposition and current governing party, the Parti Démocratique Sénégalais. The period under scrutiny covers the period from the 1993 election until today. As in Tanzania, dominant ethnic cleavages cannot be deciphered, given that Senegal is one of the few African countries where open ethnic conflict has been absent. Because the Wolof group is the dominant ethnic group, my analysis uses the division between the Wolof community and all other communities as the (potentially) dominant ethnic cleavage line (Stavenhagen 1996, Kwang Johnson 2004).

Parti Socialiste

Since its formation in the precolonial period, the PS (and its predecessor party, the UPS) has managed to build a nationwide political machinery bridging all ethnic and regional boundaries. Of great importance was the support of Muslim brotherhoods (marabouts) and in particular the support of the Mouride brotherhood. The Mouride brotherhood is led by the Wolof, but it has always been open to non-Wolof speakers. Since its formation, the party has kept close relations with all marabouts and socioeconomic interest groups (Moegenburg 2002, Creevy et al. 2005, Treydte et al. 2005).

The party leadership and all PS cabinets of the 1990s reflected the ethnic setup of the Senegalse state (Hartmann 2010, Osei 2010). The election of Ousmane Dieng as secretary-general of the party illustrated the inclusion of minority groups in the leadership setup. Dieng is a member of the Griots, a minute community beset with many prejudices (Treydte et al. 2005).

While in power, the PS made extensive reference to the basic principles of socialist ideology, thus reflecting the long-term legacy of its founder, Léopold Senghor. Since being voted into opposition in 2000 and especially since the current president, Abdoulaye Wade, has refused to step down after two terms in office, the PS has espoused good-governance rhetoric. It has further highlighted the need to fight corruption in the country. Each electoral has campaign focused strongly on the party's presidential candidate (Osei 2010).

Intra-party rivalry is characterized by powerful individuals competing for party positions. In the early 1990s, former supporters of the late president Senghor (barones) had to compete with the young technocrats (Dioufistes) close to president Diouf (Moegenburg 2002). This remained the case throughout the 1990s and beyond. Given the declining economic conditions, president Diouf increasingly lost grip over his party. In 1998, Diouf's former minister of the interior, Djibo Ka, formed his own party, the Union

TABLE 6.6. *Party Nationalization Scores – Senegal*

Party	PS	PDS
PNS	1993: 0.92	1993: 0.87
	1998: 0.90	1998: 0.78
	2001: 0.84	2001: 0.90
PNS based on Afrobarometer	2005: 0.87	2005: 0.95
	2009: 0.87	2009: 0.95
PNS across time and space (in-depth cases)	0.67	
PNS across time and space (all cases)	0.68	

Source: Author's compilation on the basis of data provided by Hartmann (2010), Osei 2010, and Afrobarometer data.

pour le Renoveau Démocratique (URD). Not long after, Diouf's former foreign minister, Moustapha Niasse, formed the Alliance des Forces du Progrés. After the 2000 elections, party factions continued to be personalistic in nature (Creevy et al. 2005, Hartmann 2010).

The party's PNSs are outlined in Table 6.6. The national support for the PS is confirmed by Afrobarometer data from 2005 and 2009. Overall, the PS is classified as a catch-all party.

The Parti Démocratique Sénégalais

The Parti Démocratique Sénégalais was founded in 1974 by Abdoulaye Wade. From its inception, it included members from all communities in its leadership (Osei 2010). Although the PDS was initially obliged to be a liberal-democratic party, it always had many members who agreed with the socialist ideology of the governing PS but who had joined the opposition because they felt the country needed a change of government. This often led to contradictory party statements. The party frequently called for cutbacks and supported austerity measures. However, at the same time, other members demanded economic measures that benefitted the poor (Moegenburg 2002, Treydte 2005). In the 1990s, the Parti Démocratique Sénégalais increasingly focused on the economic failures of the incumbent party (Hartmann 2010).

In 2000, the Parti Démocratique Sénégalais achieved the first democratic handover of power in the history of Senegal. All Parti Démocratique Sénégalais cabinets included representatives from all regions and all communities. Although the party allocated cabinet positions to those regions where it performed best, this allocation mechanism did not lead to the marginalization of any group.[11] The national setup of the party remained in place

[11] Economist Intelligence Unit, various reports in 2000, 2005, and 2010.

throughout the whole period under observation, despite extensive cabinet reshuffles and intra-party turmoil.

The main cause for party divisions was Wade's intolerance of dissenting views. Wade used reshuffles to get rid of potential opponents for the presidency. In the first five years of his presidency, the government underwent eight cabinet reshuffles, most of which were directed against the technocratic wing of the government. In April 2004, Wade sacked Prime Minister Seck, at the time the second in command of the Parti Démocratique Sénégalais; Wade subsequently pursued a policy of "Desecktisation." In 2005, Wade let go of one of the coalition members that had brought him to power: the Ligue Démocratique/Movement pour le Parti du Travail (LD/MPT). The LD/MPT had criticized the conduct of several Parti Démocratique Sénégalais ministers.

Wade sacked Decentralization Minister Arminata Tall in March 2006, after Tall highlighted various shortcomings the government had failed to address. Maky Sall, the successor of Seck in the office of the prime minister, was sacked in 2007 after publically stating that the president's son, Karim Wade, had been involved in the financial mismanagement of funds allocated to organize the summit of the Islamic Conference. Wade's intention to contest the presidential election for a third time cemented the divisions into a pro- and an anti-Wade camp.[12]

The PNSs of the Parti Démocratique Sénégalais display the national nature of the party. Due to its national leadership, its developmentalist rhetoric, its personalist factions and its nationwide political support, the Parti Démocratique Sénégalais is classified as a catch-all party.

MALAWI

Malawi gained independence from the United Kingdom in 1964. In 1966, the country turned into a one-party dictatorship. Between 1964 and 1995, it was governed by Dr Hastings Banda and the Malawi Congress Party (MCP). Social unrest gave way to multiparty democracy in 1994.

In Malawi, ethnicity exercises great salience. Former president Banda received his main support from his own Chewa community (located in the Central region), which received extensive state funding during the period of one-party rule. In 1968, Banda decided that the official national language of Malawi was to be Chichewa, a Chewa dialect. Other tribal languages were disallowed. The North, composed of numerous smaller communities, in particular suffered economic stagnation and state harassment (Kaspin 1995).

[12] The data on party factions have been compiled with the help of Economist Intelligence Unit reports between 2000 and 2011. All data are with the author.

Party competition in Malawi is said to be driven by ethno-regional factors, with the three provinces, North (dominated by the Tumbuka), South (dominated by the Yao and the Lomve), and Central (dominated by the Chewa) overwhelmingly voting for one particular party. The Chewa constitute 32.6 percent of the population, the Tumbuka 8.8 percent, the Yao 13.5 percent, and the Lomwe 19 percent.[13] I take the divisions into the Yao/Lomwe, the Chewa, and the Tumbuka as the dominant ethnic cleavage lines. Only parties that unite groups across these communities will be seen as nonethnic parties (Osei-Hwedie 1998, EISA 2002).

The subsequent analysis covers the United Democratic Front (UDF), the governing party between 1994 and 2008; the Malawi Congress Party (MCP), the governing party between 1964 and 1994; the Alliance for Democracy (AFORD); and the Democratic Progressive Party (DPP), which claimed power in 2009. The observation period for the MCP and the UDF covers the period between 1995 and 2009. The observation period for AFORD covers the period between 1995 and 1999. Subsequently, AFORD became politically irrelevant. The DPP is a recent party. I analyze the DPP between 2005 and 2009.

The Malawi Congress Party

The formerly unitary party, the MCP, formed in the late 1950s. Its main purpose was "to link on a non-ethnic basis African associations, independent churches and other groups of educated Africans" (EISA 2002: 15). The MCP emerged as the decisive winner of the 1961 elections. In 1971, Banda was declared president for life (EISA 2002).

In the run-up to the 1994 election campaign, the party could still rely on its legacy as a former unitary party. The party continued to include Northerners such as Chisiza Du and Danton Mhandawine in high-ranking leadership positions. Both belonged to the party's national executive committee. Soon after the first elections, Northern participation in the top leadership became nonexistent (Van Donge 1995). The party maintained leaders from the South, most notably Gwanda Chakuamba, who was the general secretary of the party, Banda's vice-presidential candidate in the 1994 elections, and president of the party after Banda's death. The MCP never espoused ethnic rhetoric (Ott et al. 2000).

Intra-party relations suffered extensively. After the death of Banda, Chakuamba won the 1995 presidential nomination against John Tembo from Central province. Chakuamba was an advocate of an alliance with the AFORD party, a strategy Tembo detested. The division came to a head in August 2001, when both factions held separate party congresses. The

[13] The data is taken from the Malawi 2008 national population and housing census. See Republic of Malawi 2008.

Chakuamba faction held its congress in Southern province and the Tembo faction in Central province. According to the party statue, the congress should have been held in the South. The Tembo faction, however, feared that if the congress were to be held in the stronghold of an opponent, its candidates would not stand a fair chance of winning. Chukuamba refused to switch the location for the same reason. The August 2001 crisis demonstrated that Tembo was in command of the MCP parliamentary party (all of whom were from Central province), whereas Chukuamba was in charge of the party outside parliament. This clearly illustrates the ethnic dimension of the MCP factions (Chisinga 2006 Maroleng 2004). The Malawian high court ultimately declared the congress of the Tembo faction to be the legitimate congress. Chakuamba and his wing broke away and formed the Republican Party. In the 2004 elections, the MCP again offered a Central-South ticket, with Tembo as presidential candidate and Brown Mpinganjiro as vice-presidential candidate. Most of the party's leading functionaries were by then exclusively drawn from Central province (Gloppen et al. 2006).

The declining outreach of the party is also visible in the percentage of the constituencies the party contested. In the 1994 elections, the MCP contested 100 percent of all constituencies; in 1999, the party still had a national outreach and contested 97 percent; in 2004, the number declined to 87 percent and omitted large parts of the North. After the formation of the DPP in 2005 and after several break-aways, the party could field candidates in only 37 percent of all constituencies. All of these were located in Central province.[14]

The PNSs (Table 6.7) confirm the view that the MCP continuously declined in scope and outreach over time. The party performed poorly in the 1994 election, which was due to its unpopular presidential candidate, former dictator Banda. After Banda's departure, the party did better in 1994. Due to the breakaway of the party's support base in the North and the South, it regressed into a mono-ethnic party, the main basis of which is the Chewa. Data from Afrobarometer confirm this. Outside the Chewa community, the party has no political base.

The United Democratic Front

The UDF was launched in 1992. Prior to that it had operated as a clandestine anti-MCP movement. Its leader and presidential candidate, Bakili Muluzi, had been a leading member of the MCP. At its inception, the party stressed its commitment to transparency and constitutionalism and its compliance with international human rights standards. In later campaigns, the UDF

[14] The analysis is based on data provided by the Electoral Commission of Malawi and CMI 2006.

TABLE 6.7. *Party Nationalization Scores – Malawi*

Party	MCP	UDF	AFORD	DPP
PNS	1994: 0.58 1999: 0.76 2004: 0.47 2009: 0.45	1994: 0.57 1999: 0.65 2004: 0.66 2009: 0.64	1994: 0.48 1999: 0.42	2009: 0.92
PNS based on Afrobarometer	1999: 0.69 2005: 0.51 2009: 0.42	1999: 0.72 2005: 0.70 2009: 0.52	1999: 0.26 2005: 0.22	2009: 0.89
PNS across time and space (in-depth cases)	0.67			
PNS across time and space (all cases)	0.68			

Source: Author's compilation on the basis of data provided by the Malawi Electoral Commission, EISA data, CMI 2006, and Afrobarometer.

was a vocal supporter of International Monetary Fund and World Bank programs (Ihonvbere 1997).

Little information can be extracted from the party leadership setup, as no party convention took place between 1993 and 2004. The party's national executive committee was handpicked by Muluzi. Apart from President Muluzi, the governor of South province, David Kapito, was the most influential power broker inside the UDF (Chinsinga 2003). The party always had two vice-presidents, one from the North and one from the center. Muluzi himself was from the South. All UDF cabinets were national in terms of composition. President Muluzi appointed his vice-president from the center; several high-ranking government positions such as the finance minister were reserved for individuals from the North (van Donge 1995). All UDF cabinets were national in composition (Economic Intelligence Unit Reports 1995 to 2005).

For the better part of its time in government (1995–2009), the party maintained internal discipline. After Muluzi's attempt to extend his presidential term failed, he named Binga wa Muthuarika (from Southern province) as his presidential successor. Cassim Chilumpa (from Central province) was named as the UDF's next vice-presidential candidate (EISA 2009). The UDF was rocked by factionalism after newly elected president Muthuarika engaged in anticorruption drives against several former UDF ministers and heavyweights. In February 2009, president Mutharika announced his resignation from the UDF and formed the Democratic Progress Party, which secured his re-election in 2009.

In the 1994 and 1999 elections, the party contested 100 percent of all constituencies; in 2004, the percentage of contested seats declined to 85 percent; in the recently concluded 2009 elections, the party was still able

TABLE 6.8. *Party Nationalization Scores – Burkina Faso*

Party	CDP	ADF/RA
PNS	2007: 0.87	2007: 0.52
PNS based on Afrobarometer	2009: 0.93	2009: 0.78
PNS across time and space (in-depth cases)	0.67	
PNS across time and space (all cases)	0.68	

Source: Author's compilation on the basis of data provided by the Electoral Commission of Burkina Faso and Afrobarometer.

to contest 83 percent of all seats. Its electoral indicators, outlined earlier (see Table 6.8), do not allow for an easy classification of the party. PNS values derived from official election results indicate that its support base was confined to its core region, Southern province. However, it ought to be noted that independent parliamentarians (i.e., elected parliamentarians not affiliated with any party) constituted the second strongest force in the country's National Assembly between 1999 and 2009. In most cases, independent candidates are disgruntled UDF members who failed to make it in the primaries (CMI 2006). The PNS calculated on the basis of ethnic groups with the help of Afrobarometer data further displays a more equal spread of support for the UDF than its election results suggest. The decline in 2009 is due to the rise of the DPP, which became a serious political contender in all parts of the country.

At the time of writing, the UDF has been reduced to a party of Southern province, its original heartland. Viewed over the entire period between 1995 and 2009, party factions were not based on ethnic divisions, and the party's leadership and its cabinet setup were national. The party further refrained from ethnic rhetoric. Overall, I classify the UDF as a catch-all party.

The Alliance for Democracy

The AFORD started off as a grassroots organization protesting the autocratic Banda regime. Chakufwa Chihana, a veteran trade unionist and human rights activist, led the party. In the pre-1995 period, Chihana had spent several years in prison for offending the president. He was in exile until the early 1990s (Ihonvbere 1997).

From its inception, AFORD failed to create the image of a national party. In the run-up to the 1995 election, AFORD appointed Justin Malewezi from the Center region as treasurer and Peter Kaleso from the South as vice-presidential candidate. Both had been appointed in absentia; both quit their positions in a matter of days. Other party functionaries from the South and the Center resigned from the party within weeks (van Donge 1995). AFORD's leadership thus remained confined to the Tumbuka community throughout the observation period. Although the party spoke out for more democratic rights, it failed to address the wider social and economic issues of the country, which was detrimental to its ability to build a national base (Ihonvbere 1997).

A further burden on the party was the idiosyncratic leadership style of Chihana, who clearly overshadowed the rest of his party. At times, Chihana aligned AFORD with the governing UDF and at times with the long-term MCP opposition. In no instance was his position backed by a party congress. Party factions emerged in 2001 when the open term bill – foreseeing a third term for president Muluzi – was widely discussed. Although the faction surrounding Party Chief Whip in Parliament Greenwell Mwamondwe and the majority of ordinary party members rejected the bill, Chihana supported it. A majority of the AFORD party congress rejected it (Chinsinga 2003, CMI 2006). Chihana subsequently left AFORD and joined the UDF.

Over time, the party contested fewer and fewer constituencies. In 1995, AFORD managed to field candidates in 90 percent of all constituencies; in 1999, it contested 39 percent of all seats; in 2004 and 2009, it was only able to contest 21 percent of all seats.[15] All of the contested constituencies are located in the North or in areas with larger segments of the Tambuka population. The electoral performance confirms AFORD's narrow social base. Outside the Tumbuka population, the party enjoys little to no support. Its leadership is confined to one major group, its factions are personalistic (with both leaders coming from the same community), its rhetoric geared toward the Northern region, and its electoral support confined to the major group that makes up its leadership. I classify it as a mono-ethnic party.

The Democratic Progressive Party

The recently created DPP is a breakaway from the formerly governing UDF. Given its short lifespan, it can only be discussed cursorily. The party was formed by president Binga wa Muthuarika, who broke away from the UDF after he fell out with the DPP heavyweights over his fight against corruption. All DPP cabinets included members of all major communities. The same can be said for the DPP leadership. Party factions have emerged, although these are structured around personalities.[16] With regard to its electoral performance, the DPP was the first party to not have a clearly identifiable stronghold. The 2009 election – the first election the DPP contested – broke the previous pattern of regional voting (EISA 2009). The party's PNS clearly confirm this. The party is classified as a catch-all party.

[15] The data are based on CMI 2006 and the Election Commission of Malawi.

[16] Based on recent press coverage by the Malawi Voice.

BURKINA FASO

Burkina Faso gained independence from France in 1960. Since its independence, it has experienced five military coups. The last coup in 1987 was executed under the leadership of Capitain Blaise Compaoré. Comparé noted the proliferation of groups opposed to military rule. By 1988, he formed the Organisation pour la Démocratie Populaire/Mouvement du Travail (ODM/MT), which in the mid-1990s became the Congress pour le Démocratie et le Progrès (CDP).[17] Thus when multiparty democracy was restored in 1991/1992, the incumbent regime already had a political party in place (Otayek 1992, Santiso and Loada 2003).

My analysis covers two parties, the incumbent CDP and its long-term opponent, the Rassemblement Democratique Africain – l'Alliance pour la Democratie et la Federation (ADF-RDA). The observation period for both parties is the last two parliamentary cycles, that is, the period between 2002 and 2010.

Dominant ethnic cleavages are not easy to decipher because the country has not experienced major ethnic conflict (Stroh 2011). No reliable data exist on the ethnic composition of the population. The Mossi are estimated to constitute half of the population (Scarritt and Mozaffar 1999). Accordingly, I use the division between Mossi and non-Mossi as the potential dominant ethnic cleavage line.

The Congrès pour le Démocratie et le Progrès

The CDP has been the leading party in Burkina Faso since the first multiparty elections in 1992. With the exception of the legislative period between 2002 and 2007, the CDP has been the dominant party in the legislature. It formed from a wide patchwork of political and civil society organizations seeking state patronage. Since its inception, it has included numerous socioeconomic groups as well as interest groups from all sections of society.

Since its formation, the CDP has included Mossi and non-Mossi leaders alike; numerous smaller communities have all been represented in the cabinets since 1992 (Hagberg 2002, Stroh 2011).[18] The same applies to leadership positions inside the party (Stroh 2011).

The CDP has consistently stressed its commitment to developing the country and has highlighted the role of incumbent president Comparé. In particular, during the civil war in Ivory Coast, the party stressed the image of Comparé as defender of the nation. Ethnicity has never featured in any election campaign (Bleck and van de Walle 2010).

[17] In the following, I refer to the governing party as CDP.

[18] These findings are confirmed by data on cabinet setups provide by the Economist Intelligence Unit (various reports between 1992 and 2010).

Due to very scant information about politics in Burkina Faso in general and political parties in particular, only sporadic evidence regarding party factions is available. Factions are centered around four people: party chairman, Roch Kaboré; party deputy chairman, Salif Diallo; the brother of the president, François Comparé; and the mayor of Ouagadougou, Simon Comparé. The faction led by Kaboré does have a programmatic tinge, given that it espouses liberal economic policies; the Diallo wing stresses its commitment to socialist policies. Roch Kaboré is known to be a political moderate. Following the murder of the investigative journalist Robert Zongo in December 1998, the Kaboré faction advocated new elections given the loss of legitimacy of the government.[19] Ultimately, all factions aim at increasing support for the individual in charge of the faction (Harsch 2009, Stroh 2011).

The CDP contested all 45 constituencies in the most recently concluded 2007 election. In the 2002 election, regions were used as constituencies. Constituencies were thus much larger. The CDP again contested all of them (Stroh 2011). The PNS could only be derived for the most recently concluded 2007 election. They display a national spread of electoral support. This is confirmed by Afrobarometer data. Other studies on political preferences in Burkina Faso confirm my findings (Bleck and van de Walle 2010, Stroh 2010, Basedau and Stroh 2012). Overall I classify the CDP as a catch-all party. It refrained from ethnic rhetoric and has a national leadership, nonethnic factions, and national electoral support.

The Rassemblement Démocratique Africain – l'Alliance pour la Démocratie et la Fédération

Burkina's long-standing parliamentary opposition is much older than the governing CDP. The RDA was founded in 1946 in Dakar as the RDA for the whole of francophone West Africa. Between 1960 and 1966, the RDA was the ruling party of Burkina Faso (Upper Volta at the time). In 1998, it merged with the ADF. The main motive behind the formation of both parties was to protest the authoritarian government of Comporé. In the post-transition phase, it sought cooperation with the government. In 2005, the ADF-RDA supported Comporé in the presidential elections (Monsch 2008).

The party leader, Gilbert Ouédraogo, is known to have close family ties with Mossi chiefs and is at times regarded as the top political representative of the Mossi. As a whole, however, the party included Mossi and non-Mossi functionaries. The leadership composition does not indicate any ethnic bias (Stroh 2011). In its election campaigns, the ADF/RA is surprisingly precise. In its manifestos and rallies, the party named quantitative goals of what

[19] The "Zongo murder" is the most widely published political event in the political history of Burkina Faso. For details, see Harsch 2009, Hilgers 2010, and Hagberg 2002.

achievements it would like to see implemented. There is no information about party factions (Stroh 2011).

The ADF/RDA contested the 2003 and 2007 elections in all constituencies (Carlos and Loada 2003, Monsch 2008). The PNS derived from election results indicates a multiethnic alliance, whereas the PNS derived from Afrobarometer data indicates a more equal spread of the vote. Even if Afrobarometer data were not available, the ADF/RDA would be classified as a catch-all party. The available information demonstrates that its leadership setup and its rhetoric is free from any ethnic bias.

ZAMBIA

Zambia achieved independence from the United Kingdom in 1964. Since then it has experienced three republics. Between 1964 and 1972, a multiparty system was in place. Between 1972 and 1991, the country was under one-party rule and the reign of the United National Independence Party (UNIP). The political protests directed against the autocratic one-party rule of its president, Kenneth Kaunda, ushered in the third republic and the return of multiparty democracy in 1991. The elections of 1991 saw a change of power from the UNIP to the Movement for Multiparty Democracy (MMD). The MMD has remained in power ever since.

Compared with other African countries, Zambian politics has been discussed in detail in the political science literature. Drawing on this literature, I regard the division between Bemba and Lozi as well as between Bemba and Tonga as Zambia's dominant ethnic cleavage lines (Osei-Hwedie 1998, Carey 2002, Posner 2005, Scarritt 2006).

My analysis includes the incumbent MMD, the formerly governing UNIP, and the Patriotic Front (PF). The PF is currently the major opposition party. The observation period covers the period from 1991 to the unexpected death of former president Levy Mwanawasa in 2008.

The Movement for Multiparty Democracy

The MMD was formed as a loose protest movement against Banda's one-party state. It contained numerous socioeconomic groups of different political persuasions, intellectuals, the urban elite, and the churches. Beyond the goal of removing the autocratic UNIP from power, these groups had very little in common. The MMD was led by Frederick Chiluba, a Bemba who was formerly head of the Zambia Congress of Trade Unions. Chiluba won the race for the presidential candidacy of the MMD against Arthur Wini, a Lozi. The vice-presidential candidate was Levi Mwanawasa from the Lenje minority group (Baylies and Szeffel 1992, Osei Hwedie 1998, Rakner and Svasand 2004).

The Kaunda regime has often been accused of pursuing ethnic nepotism in favor of the president's Bemba community. Critics of Kaunda frequently contrast his approach with the approach taken by his predecessor, who distributed government positions among all major ethnic groups. In his first three years in office, the president sacked 17 ministers and deputy ministers in total. Most of the victims of Chiluba's wrath were technocrats. Those allowed to stay were politicians whose political rise can be traced back to the period of the unitary state (Rakner 2003). In the local media, the victims of these reshuffles were seen as ethnic leaders of the Lozi and Tonga. A detailed breakdown of cabinet positions invalidates these accusations. All major communities remained part of the cabinet. None of the three major communities became politically marginalized. The Zambian political elite does not regard ethnicity as a driving political force inside the MMD (Hulterström 2004, 2007, Rakner and Svasand 2004). Chiluba's successor, Levy Mwanawasa, was from a minority community in the Central region. He also appointed ministers from all major communities. The composition of the party's national executive committee similarly fails to indicate an ethnic bias in favor of any one community (Erdmann and Simutanyi 2006).

The MMD was formed in March 1991, just prior to the first Zambian elections in November. This did not provide sufficient time to build a coherent party structure. As a result, the party was heavily internally divided along ethnic lines. After Arthur Wini lost the race to become the party's presidential candidate, relations between the Lozi and Bemba functionaries declined. Following the election of Banda to office, the so-called Caucus for National Unity (CNU; the faction was also known as the Young Turks) formed. It demanded more Lozi in party leadership positions and publically criticized the political dominance of the Bemba within the MMD. The CNU quit the party after the 1993 cabinet reshuffle, and its leading figures reorganized into the National Party (NP). Most of the NP's leading members were Lozi and Tonga (Rakner 2003). The division between the pro-Banda wing and the formation of the CNU was thus largely driven by ethnic considerations.

In 1995, the Zambia Democratic Congress (ZDC) split from the MMD. The ZDC was formed by two MMD ministers from the Bemba community: Dean Mung'omba and Derrich Chitala. Both were dismissed from the cabinet in 1995 after declaring their intention to contest the presidency on an MMD ticket. In 1997, the Republican Party – led by MP Ben Mwila (Bemba) – broke away, yet remained confined to support from Bemba areas. In the run-up to the 2001 elections, the MMD congress expelled 50 MPs, among them 8 ministers and 13 deputy ministers. The expelled individuals formed a number of political parties; all of these remained irrelevant. During the presidency of Mwanawasa, intra-party divisions revolved around supporters of the new president and supporters of Chiluba; the latter was

TABLE 6.9. *Party Nationalization Scores – Zambia*

Party	MMD	UNIP	PF
PNS	1991: 0.95 1996: 0.90 2001: 0.80 2006: 0.84	1991: 0.81 2001: 0.62	2006: 0.51
PNS based on Afrobarometer	2005: 0.78 2009: 0.83	2004: 0.44	2005: 0.43 2009: 0.59
PNS across time and space (in-depth cases)		0.67	
PNS across time and space (all cases)		0.68	

Source: Author's compilation on the basis of data provided by the Electoral Commission of Zambia and Afrobarometer.

known as the "true blue movement." Both factions included members from all major communities (Erdmann and Simutanyi 2006).

The MMD fielded candidates in all constituencies throughout the period under observation. The party's PNSs clearly display national electoral support. The PNS value for the 1991 election is exceptionally high. Zambians from all walks of life were desperate for change in 1991. Since then, the spread of support has remained at a high level. Afrobarometer data confirm this (see Table 6.9).

I classify the MMD as a catch-all party. Its national leadership bridged Zambia's dominant ethnic cleavage lines. The party was internally divided along both ethnic and personalistic lines; in the early 1990s, it experienced several breakaways. However, Bemba, Lozi, and Tonga representatives continued to remain inside the party. The MMD has contested all elections in all constituencies. Without doubt, the party can rely on nationwide support.

The United National Independence Party

The UNIP was the governing party during Zambia's period of one-party rule. It became the main opposition between 1991 and 1996; it boycotted the subsequent 1996 elections. In 2006, it joined an electoral alliance with various smaller parties.

Throughout the period of the one-party state, the party provided for national cabinets. Several high-ranking cabinet positions were reserved for non-Bembas; between 1973 and 1991, there were six prime ministers, of whom four were Lozi and two were Tonga. The party leadership included representatives of all major ethnic groups. Although Kaunda's family background cannot be traced back to one particular community (parts of his family are from Malawi), he is often considered a Bemba.

Since the reintroduction of multiparty democracy, the party has highlighted its commitment to basic developmental goals. It has encouraged MMD policies but called for more transparency and accountability. Like most African opposition parties, it portrayed itself as a party dedicated to the principles of good governance (Carey 2002 Rakner and Svasand 2004).

Factions inside the party have been heavily personalistic. Following the 1991 elections and the party's relegation into opposition, Kaunda resigned from active politics. Henceforth, the party was divided between Kaunda loyalists and party reformers. The loyalists were led by the party's vice-president, Malimba Masheke, a Lozi and Kaunda's last prime minister. The reformers were headed by Kebby Musokatwana (Tonga), Kaunda's successor as party president and also one of Kaunda's former prime ministers. In 1995, Kaunda staged a political comeback against Musokatwana and regained the party's leadership. The party has remained divided between these two camps. In more recent years, the reformers have been led by Malimba Masheke, the former head of the loyalists who fell out with his former camp. The loyalists are led by Secretary-General Sebastian Zulu. The main goal of the loyalists is to install the sons of Kaunda in leadership positions and for Wezi Kaunda to become the party's presidential candidate. The reformers wish to rejuvenate the party. The party's leadership positions continue to be drawn from all over the country (Erdmann and Simutanyi 2006; Burnell 2001).

Until the 2006 elections, UNIP fielded candidates in all constituencies. Although in 1991, its vote spread was distributed fairly equally, in 2001, its PNS indicates a multiethnic alliance. Afrobarometer data and a descriptive analysis of election results[20] show that UNIP support is heavily confined to the Eastern region. Its support among the Lozi, Tonga, and Bemba is very low.

Overall, I classify the party as a catch-all party. Although its electoral support is restricted, its leadership is from all parts of the country. Ethnicity is certainly not the driving force behind its political appeals. Its internal divisions might run deep; however, they are free of ethnic-strategic considerations.

The Patriotic Front

The PF was formed as a result of the expulsion of 22 MPs and 8 ministers from the MMD in the run-up to the 2001 elections. The party emerged as the official opposition after the 2006 elections. The PF was formed by Michael Sata (Bemba). Initially, Sata had been a leading supporter of president Chiluba's attempt to change the constitution to extend his presidential

[20] All data are with the author.

term in office. He quit the MMD when he failed to become the MMD presidential candidate after Chiluba's third-term bid fell through. Sata had been one of the MMD's leading figures and its national secretary. Unfortunately, nothing is known about the PF leadership setup.

In the 2001 election, the party's rhetoric was heavily pro-Bemba. Sata (Bemba) tried to win votes from disappointed MMD core voters. In the 2006 elections, Sata changed tune and pursued a pro-poor and anti-Chinese agenda. His main intention was to gain the support of the urban poor from all ethnic communities. In contrast to 2001, he held mass rallies in all provinces.

Nevertheless, even in 2006, the party fielded virtually no parliamentary candidates in the North-Western and the Western regions. Although the North-Western region is home to a variety of minority communities, the Western region is the home province of the Lozi. In the Southern region, the home region of the Tonga, the party contested less than half the seats. The PF's PNSs indicate a narrow support base. Afrobarometer data show that the support for the PF is growing outside its core clientele. A descriptive analysis of the 2006 elections shows that Sata has won many constituencies in urban non-Bemba areas. In rural areas, his support has remained confined to Bemba regions (Cheeseman and Hinfelaar 2010).

Overall, I classify the PF as a multiethnic alliance. The party has consistently failed to bridge the country's dominant ethnic cleavages. It lacks any support in Lozi and Tonga areas.

BENIN

Benin gained independence from France in 1960. Its post-independence history was characterized by numerous military coups and several attempts to reestablish multiparty democracy. After years of communist one-party rule under Mathieu Kérékou, sustainable multiparty democracy returned in 1991.

Ethnicity is seen as a major factor in the country's political history. The country's dominant ethnic cleavage lines run between the Fon in the South (39 percent of the population), the Adja (15 percent) and Bariba (9 percent) in the North, and the Yoruba in the South-Eastern part of the country. Only a party that bridges the divide between these three communities will be regarded as a nonethnic party (Battle and Seely 2007, Battle and Seely 2010, Basedau et al. 2011, Stroh 2011).

The analysis of political parties in Benin is a particularly challenging enterprise, as very little has been published on political parties in Benin. What makes this endeavor even more difficult is the great instability of the party system. My analysis includes the Parti Social-Démocrate (PSD) between 1991 and 2011, the Parti du Renouveau Démocratique (PRD) between 1991 and 2007, and the Front d'Action pour le Renouveau et le

Développement (FARD-Alafia) between 1995 and 2003. These parties either constituted major opposition parties or were part of the government. I further analyze the Alliance pour une Dynamique Démocratique (ADD) between 2007 and 2011, the L'Union pour le Bénin du Future (UBF) between 2007 and 2011, and the Forces Cauris pour un Bénin Emergent (FCBE) between 2003 and 2011.

The Parti Social-Démocrate

The PSD formed in the run-up to the first multiparty elections in 1991. It included many individuals who opposed the existing autocratic regime. The party's leading figure and presidential candidate in the first three presidential elections was Bruno Amoussou (Adjia).

The PSD leadership included personnel from the Adja and the Mina communities. Although the PSD did not openly campaign in favor of one specific community, it focused on the home region of its leadership, the North. Throughout the observation period, the party remained overshadowed by its presidential candidate. Internally, the party was shaken by personal antagonisms between Amoussou and various opponents; all actors involved in these divisions were from the Adjia community (Stroh 2011, Engels 2005a).

Benin's party law allows parties to forge alliances at the national and the regional level. Both occur frequently. On the ballot paper, candidates appear under the name of the alliance and never under the name of the party they belong to. This makes it impossible for research to identify how many regions a party is contesting. In the 1991 and 1995 elections, the PSD contested the elections together with the Union Nationale pour la Solidarité et le Progrès. In 1999, it contested the elections on its own. In 2003, the PSD was part of the L'Union pour le Bénin du Future (UBF) and in 2007 part of the Forces Cauris pour un Bénin Emergent (FCBE). Its leadership, its personalistic factions, and its alliances with other parties indicate a mono-ethnic nature.

The PSD's electoral performance (see Table 6.10) confirms this. Its PNSs are indicative of a mono-ethnic party. A descriptive analysis of Afrobarometer data shows that outside the Adjia community, the PNS has little to no support.[21] I classify the PSD as a mono-ethnic party.

The Parti du Renoveau Démocratique

The PRD was formed in 1990 with the intention of ending the autocratic Kérékou regime. In 1991, 1995, and 1999, the party regularly emerged as one of the three strongest parties in parliament. In 2006 and 2011, its

[21] All data are with the author.

TABLE 6.10. *Party Nationalization Scores – Benin*

Party	PSD	PRD	FARD-Alafia	ADD	UBF	FCBE
PNS	1991: 0.44	1991: 0.67	1995: 0.31	2003: 0.56	2003: 0.65	2007: 0.72
	1995: 0.49	1995: 0.50				
		2003: 0.32				
PNS based on Afrobarometer	2005: 0.31	2005: 0.58	2005:0.31			
	2009: 0.26	2009: 0.53				
PNS across time and space (in-depth cases)		0.67				
PNS across time and space (all cases)		0.68				

Source: Author's compilation on the basis of data provided by the Electoral Commission of Benin, Afrobarometer, and Creevy and Vengroff 2005.

presidential candidate Adrien Houngbédji became the runner-up in the presidential elections.

The PRD was founded by Yoruba exiles living in France. The PRD expressed greater support for economic-friendly policies than any other party. The party's electoral rhetoric was initially characterized by prodemocracy slogans; subsequently, it adjusted the content of its statements to whether or not it was part of the coalition that formed the government. In government, the PRD stressed governmental achievements; in opposition it called for improvements in living conditions (Creevy et al. 2005, Stroh and Never 2006, Olodo and Sossou 2008).

From its inception, its leadership was dominated by the Yoruba. In contrast to most other parties in Benin, the PRD is not beset by internal factions. In 1997, several of its leading figures left the party for the MADEP, which was founded to challenge the PRD in its stronghold (Engels 2005, Stroh 2011).

The PRD was one of the few parties that contested the 2003 elections with its own list. Its 1991 PNS is fairly high.[22] The values declined rather drastically after the 1995 elections. A descriptive analysis of Afrobarometer data[23] shows that the party's support is not confined to the Yoruba, but extends to the Fon community. Yet the party lacks Northern support. The PRD is certainly not a national party. I classify the PRD as a multiethnic alliance.

The Front d'Action pour le Renouveau et le Développement

The FARD-Alafia was formed in 1994 to counterbalance the governing party at the time. Its founding members came mainly from Benin's North and were drawn from the pre-1991 autocratic Kérékou regime. From its inception, the party had very close links with the chiefs and ethnic welfare organizations from the Northern part of the country (Engels 2005b). Its electoral campaigns were characterized by the praise of President Kérékou, who was reelected as president in 1996 and in 2001. In 2001, Kérékou was reelected on the ticket of FARD-Alafia. Intra-party factions hardly existed. After Kérékou's resignation from politics, the election of the presidential candidate in 2006 passed without any major debate. The party chose Daniel Tawéma, Kérékou's former minister of the interior (Stroh 2011).

The electoral support of FARD-Alafia is unambiguous. Election results and Afrobarometer data clearly indicate a mono-ethnic party. This coincides with data from its leadership composition. I classify the party as a mono-ethnic party.

[22] In 1991, the PRD was in an alliance with the PNPD. The effect of the PNPD on the PNS scores can safely be neglected.

[23] All data are with the author.

Alliance pour une Dynamique Démocratique, l'Union pour le Bénin du Future, and Forces Cauris pour un Bénin Emergent

I discuss all three alliances in brevity, as their main components have already been analyzed. They constitute political responses to Benin's political history, as all three tried to combine the regional and ethnic strongholds of various individual parties.

The ADD consisted of the PSD, the MADEP, and the Parti de la Renaissance du Benin (PR), the party of former president Nicéphore Soglo (1991–1996). The ADD openly claimed to be the party of the South. It tried to present itself as the regional-ethnic alternative to the Northern-focused UBF. Its main sound bite in the 2003 campaign was that Benin was in acute danger of falling back into the hands of autocratic rule (Qurban and Engels 2007, Stroh 2008). The ADD was a conglomeration of ethnic parties failing to bridge the country's dominant ethnic cleavage lines. Its PNS outlined in Table 6.10 confirms this. I classify the ADD as a multiethnic alliance.

The UBF formed in the run-up to the 2003 elections and included FARD-Alafia and the PSD. For a long time, MADEP and numerous smaller parties seemed to be willing to join this alliance but opted out at the last minute. In contrast to the ADD, the UBF had a coherent party structure and did not allow its members to campaign independently. The mastermind behind its formation was Bruno Amoussou. The UDF was characterized by heavy infighting due to the ethnic nature of its constituent parts. Accordingly, it was short-lived. Like the ADD, it is classified as a multiethnic alliance. Both its self-portrayal as the alliance of the South and its PNS confirm this (Lötzer 2003, Stroh 2008).

The FCBE formed in the run-up to the 2007 elections with the main purpose of electing Yayi Boni to office. The FCBE is a conglomeration of more than 25 political parties, among them FARD-Alafia and the UDS.[24] All of its member parties can safely be classified as ethnic party types. The FCBE regards itself as an alliance of these parties and not as a party in its own right. Since its formation, no stable party structures have emerged. I therefore also classify the FCBE as a multiethnic alliance, although its constituent parties are drawn from all over the country. Of all parties in Benin, it is the only party with the potential to evolve into a national party. Its PNS indicates that it is by far the most national party in Benin.

SUMMARY OF THE PRELIMINARY CASES

The previous section applied a variety of indicators from the Diamond and Gunther typology to seven additional countries. The empirical evidence from the seven additional cases is thus only of a preliminary nature. My intention

[24] Data are with the author

TABLE 6.11. *Results from the Application of Party Typology to Preliminary Cases*

Country	Party	Observation Period	Preliminary Result
Tanzania	CCM	1995–2010	catch-all
	CUF	1995–2010	ethnic alliance
	CHADEMA	1995–2010	ethnic alliance
Botswana	BDP	1995–2009	catch-all
	BNF	1995–2009	catch-all
Senegal	PNS	1993–2009	catch-all
	PS	1993–2009	catch-all
Malawi	UDF	1995–2009	catch-all
	AFORD	1995–2005	mono-ethnic
	MPC	1995–2009	mono-ethnic
	DPP	2005–2009	catch-all
Burkina Faso	CDP	2002–2010	catch-all
	ADF-RDA	2002–2010	catch-all
Zambia	MMD	1991–2008	catch-all
	UNIP	1991–2008	catch-all
	PF	2000–2008	ethnic alliance
Benin	PSD	1991–2010	mono-ethnic
	FARD-A	1995–2003	mono-ethnic
	PRD	1991–2007	ethnic alliance
	ADD	2003–2007	ethnic alliance
	UDF	2003–2007	ethnic alliance
	FCBE	2003–2010	ethnic alliance

Source: Author's Compilation.

was to test whether nonethnic parties are as frequent as the analysis of the three in-depth countries suggests. Table 6.11 outlines the results from the preliminary cases.

The results generated from the application of the party typology to 25 parties from 7 additional cases are in line with the results from the three in-depth cases.

First, results show that the typology can be applied to numerous other countries. Only in a few instances was the classification not straightforward. In all instances, however, the distinction between the ethnic and nonethnic party types could be ascertained. Numerous parties call for a more in-depth analysis of the role of programmatic content. In Tanzania, Botswana, and Senegal, political ideology appears to matter for the nature of the parties. Party factions and party statements display strong ideological undertones. Due to reasons of space and resources, this study could not identify the extent to which this is the case. The preliminary cases show clearly that any systematic and holistic analysis of African parties ought to take the ideological aspects of party life into consideration.

Second, of 22 parties, I find 4 mono-ethnic parties and 9 multiethnic alliances, that is, 13 ethnic party types. Twelve parties correspond to the catch-all type and constitute nonethnic party types. These numerical results strongly resemble the findings from the application of the typology to the three in-depth cases. Ethnic parties exist, yet they hardly dominate African politics.

Third, at the level of party system, I find only one party system to be an ethnic party system (Benin), three party systems to include ethnic and nonethnic parties (Tanzania, Malawi, and Zambia), and three nonethnic party systems (Botswana, Senegal, and Burkina Faso). With regard to the salience of ethnicity, the preliminary cases also show variation within and between countries. The nonethnic and mixed-party systems constitute the majority. Again, this finding is in line with the results from the three in-depth cases. In two of the three mixed systems – Tanzania and Zambia – nonethnic parties clearly dominate political competition. In Tanzania, neither the CUF nor CHADEMA pose a serious threat to the incumbent CCM. The governing party of Zambia is a catch-all party. Only since 2001 has the main opposition party been a multiethnic alliance (between 2001 and 2006, the main opposition party was the UPND; since 2006, the main opposition is the PF); before 2000, the main opposition party was a catch-all party (between 1991 and 1996, the main opposition was the UNIP; between 1996 and 2001, it was the ZDC).

Fourth, among the preliminary cases, there is only one ethnic party system: Benin. Yet in contrast to Kenya – the only in-depth case with an ethnic party system – political contest in Benin is free from endemic ethnic violence. Ghana and Benin are the only two African countries that have experienced two peaceful hand-overs of power between government and opposition. In contrast to Kenya, state stability is clearly not at stake, despite the prevalence of ethnic parties. Democracy and ethnic parties thus appear to be compatible – in Africa as elsewhere.

Fifth, my previous finding that parties and party systems become less ethnic the longer party competition endures deserves closer examination. In Malawi, the party system was initially characterized by one catch-all and two mono-ethnic parties. In the recent 2009 election, the party system saw the emergence of a new party, the DPP, which claimed power; the emergence of the DPP has led to a decrease of the salience of ethnicity. In Botswana, the main opposition, the BNF, pursued partially ethnic rhetoric in the 1970s; today, party competition is free from ethnic consideration. Zambia and Tanzania both contain ethnic and nonethnic parties; however, in both countries, the salience of ethnicity is decreasing. Tanzania's CHADEMA has been classified as an ethnic alliance; however, the party does not appeal to specific communities. So far, it has failed to build up a party structure that allows it to contest elections on a nationwide basis. This is very different from the CUF, which explicitly regards itself as a party of the Zanzibar islands.

In Zambia, the current main opposition, the PF, started out as an ethnic party. In recent years, the PF has demonstrated its aspiration to increase its outreach.

Even in Benin, where ethnicity shapes party competition to a much greater extent than in any other country, the formation of multiethnic alliances (e.g., the ADD and the UBF), and in particular the formation of the FCBE, shows that parties have a tendency to increase their outreach over time. The number of significant parties in parliament is decreasing over time (Stroh 2008). Overall, it seems fair to say that there is reason to believe that regular competition decreases the salience of ethnicity; although the evidence provided by the additional cases is only preliminary, nothing suggests that multiparty competition fosters ethnic divisions over time.

POLITICAL PARTY TYPES IN AFRICA

This chapter has summarized results from the application of the Diamond and Gunther typology to 3 African countries and 14 political parties in a comparative manner. These results were verified with the help of 7 additional countries and 25 additional parties. The additional parties could only be analyzed in a preliminary manner. The findings unsettle conventional assumptions about political competition in nonindustrialized societies. Although ethnicity is an important factor in African politics, African party politics must not be confined to ethnic loyalties. In Africa's multiparty democracies, a plethora of party types feature, including mono-ethnic parties, multiethnic alliances, catch-all parties, programmatic parties, and personalistic parties.

In simple numerical terms, the in-depth analysis of parties in Kenya, Namibia, and Ghana identified mono-ethnic and multiethnic alliances to be the prevalent party types. Furthermore, a large number of nonethnic parties was identified. Most nonethnic parties in Africa constitute catch-all parties. Even programmatic parties could be found, although – like personalistic parties – programmatic parties are not sustainable over time. Interestingly, some ethnic parties have visible programmatic underpinnings. The attention to this neglected aspect of African party competition deserves future attention. Although overall ethnic parties constitute the (slim) majority of party types identified, in two of three countries, nonethnic parties have become the norm. Over time, African parties are keen on increasing their outreach. They become less ethnic and more national the longer multiparty competition endures. Enduring political competition does not lead to the hardening of communal relations.

To examine a greater number of parties in a less labor-intense manner, I applied a selection of indicators of the Diamond and Gunther typology to 25 parties in 7 additional countries. The selection of indicators was based on an analysis of their discriminatory power. Despite this shortcut procedure, the analysis of the additional parties was not possible in the same depth as in

Kenya, Namibia, and Ghana. Basic data were often not available given the nascent stage of party research in Africa. The principal goal was to determine whether nonethnic parties are really as frequent as the results from the three in-depth countries indicated.

The examination of 25 parties in Tanzania, Botswana, Senegal, Malawi, Burkina Faso, Zambia, and Benin confirmed that ethnic parties indeed do not dominate African party politics. Among the seven countries, there is not a single one where multiparty contest has led to an increase in the salience of ethnicity at the level of political parties. All ethnicity-based parties instead tried to increase their outreach over time. Although the preliminary cases need to be examined in greater detail – many parties, for example, demonstrate the need to examine the role of programmatic content in much greater depth – they challenge the notion that party contest in Africa is first and foremost ethnic. Twenty years after the introduction of multiparty contest, political diversity, not uniformity, is characteristic of African parties. The systematic analysis of parties in three counties supplemented with the preliminary analysis of parties in seven additional countries thus has led to a much more nuanced view of African parties.

The political salience of ethnicity differs within countries. Although all parties in Kenya across time are ethnic, Ghana and Namibia were initially characterized by the coexistence of ethnic and nonethnic parties. Subsequently, ethnic parties transformed into nonethnic parties – in the case of Ghana – or are replaced by nonethnic opponents – in the case of Namibia. In the case of Ghana, the formerly ethnically based opposition transformed into a nonethnic party within one parliamentary cycle. In the case of Namibia, the opposition lacks political significance. Country-specific factors such as strategic considerations are largely responsible for these changes.

However, the salience of ethnicity also differs at the country level. Both the in-depth cases and the preliminary cases demonstrated this. Ethnicity clearly exercises more salience in Kenya than in Ghana and Namibia. Ethnicity has little to no effect on parties in Botswana, Senegal, Burkina Faso, and Tanzania. By contrast, in Malawi, Zambia, or Benin, ethnicity shapes party contest. These differences between countries are stark and require further examination. The political science literature thus far cannot explain why in some nonindustrialized democracies ethnic parties prevail, whereas in others nonethnic parties have become the norm. The next chapter tries to identify which variables might account for differences between countries.

7

Explaining the Formation of Nonethnic Parties

Africa's party systems are characterized by great diversity. In some countries, nonethnic parties dominate. In other countries, ethnic parties are prevalent. In a third group, ethnic and nonethnic parties coexist. The previous chapter illustrated that ethnicity exercises a significantly higher salience in Kenya than in Namibia or Ghana. The preliminary cases showed that ethnicity exercises high salience in Benin but has little effect on parties in Botswana, Senegal, and Burkina Faso. In three countries, Tanzania, Zambia, and Malawi, neither ethnic nor nonethnic parties prevail. These countries contain mixed-party systems. The political salience of ethnicity thus varies between countries.

This chapter examines the inter-country variation between ethnic and nonethnic party types in greater detail. It tries to explain why in some countries ethnicity matters more than in others. Despite the inclusion of a larger number of additional cases, the number of cases is too small to formulate a theory, which explains why ethnic parties dominate in some countries but not in others. In 7 of 10 countries, the findings are only preliminary. The intention of this chapter, therefore, is considerably more modest. It examines the explanatory power of individual variables that affect the political salience of ethnicity. The chapter constitutes the first attempt to identify a number of variables that affect party formation in nonindustrialized societies. Systematic comparative research on party types in nonindustrialized societies is virtually nonexistent. Scholars more or less assume that ethnic parties dominate political party contest in nonindustrialized societies. Although the previous chapters have falsified this assumption, the current study cannot achieve more than outlining a few variables that future studies with a more explanatory approach should take into consideration.

I proceed in two steps. In a first step, I outline and examine a number of variables the literature regards as suitable to account for diverging party types between countries. These include economic conditions, the electoral system, democratic quality, party laws, path dependence, and the ethnic composition of countries. I analyze the explanatory value of these variables on the basis of the results generated by the three in-depth cases. I find a correlation between ethnic structure and the salience of ethnicity: ethnic parties and party systems occur in countries that lack a core ethnic group and in which the ethnic fractionalization is high; nonethnic parties and party systems occur in countries that have a core ethnic group and where the ethnic fractionalization index is low. Subsequently, I analyze whether this finding holds for the preliminary cases. Results show that in 8 of 10 countries, the hypothesized relationship holds. Although overall, no variable on its own can explain the formation of nonethnic parties, scholars should pay greater attention to the importance of ethnic structure when accounting for the rise in party types.

VARIANCE BETWEEN COUNTRIES

Economic Variables

Economic Growth and Human Development at the National Level

I expect political grievances to be sharpened in countries in which growth remains stagnant or absent and in which human development deteriorates. Ethnicity might be one channel through which such grievances are raised. I measure economic growth and human development with a variety of indicators: the gross domestic product (GDP) per capita (expressed in U.S. dollars [USD]), real GDP percentage growth, human development trends, and the national Gini coefficient. Although the GDP per capita and real GDP percentage growth are conventional ways of measuring economic progress, human development index trends are derived from development indicators that measure various dimensions of individual well-being – including longevity (measured by life expectancy), level of knowledge (measured by a combination of literacy and duration of school attendance), and standard of living (measured by purchasing power adjusted to local circumstances). The Gini coefficient provides insights into the degree of inequality within countries. Tables 7.1 and 7.2 outline each country's GDP per capita and economic growth rates between the early 1990s and the most recently available data.

With regard to the GDP per capita, one can see roughly the same level of economic development in Ghana and Kenya yet significantly higher figures for Namibia. The average income per capita over the whole period of time is USD 413 in Ghana, USD 498 in Kenya, and USD 2,191 in Namibia. Although Ghana and Kenya show similar performances over the whole period, both have produced very different types of parties and party systems. The case of Ghana illustrates that nonethnic parties are not contingent on economic growth rates. In recent years, Kenya and Ghana have experienced sustainable increases in GDP per capita, which have not led to any changes in party types in either of the two countries.

TABLE 7.1. *GDP Per Capita (in USD in Current Prices)*

	1990	1991	1992	1993	1994	1995	1996	1997	1998	1999	2000	2001	2002	2003	2004	2005	2006	2007	2008
Ghana	463	500	449	387	343	398	416	404	427	430	270	281	318	384	436	513	594	690	786
Kenya	517	474	453	307	358	444	437	472	479	438	409	423	419	467	490	561	661	780	891
Namibia	2,068	1,966	2,005	1,863	2,032	2,121	2,051	2,071	1,881	1,826	1,803	1,668	1,596	2,253	2,816	3,193	3,474	3,672	3,805

Source: IMF World Economic Surveys.

TABLE 7.2. *Real GDP Growth as a Percentage*

	1990	1991	1992	1993	1994	1995	1996	1997	1998	1999	2000	2001	2002	2003	2004	2005	2006	2007
Ghana	3	5	4	5	3	4	5	4	5	4	4	4	4	5	6	6	6	6
Kenya	4	1	−1	0	3	4	4	0	3	2	0	4	1	3	5	6	6	7
Namibia	2	8	7	−2	7	4	3	4	3	3	3	2	7	3	7	5	3	6

Source: World Bank.

TABLE 7.3. *Human Development Index (HDI) Trends*

	1990	1995	2000	2005
Ghana	0.52	0.54	0.57	0.55
Kenya	0.56	0.54	0.53	0.52
Namibia	n/a	0.70	0.66	0.66

Source: United Nations Development Program Human Development Reports.

Statistical figures for economic growth confirm these findings. Over the entire period under scrutiny, the Ghanaian economy has seen an average growth of 5 percent, Kenya an average growth of 3 percent, and Namibia an average growth of 4.4 percent. Although Kenya is clearly lagging behind and is the only country of the three with recurring periods of zero growth, these figures alone cannot account for the different dynamics between Kenya on the one side and Ghana and Namibia on the other.[1]

A more appropriate mean for the assessment of individual human development is the human development index (HDI) trend (see Table 7.3).

The closer the HDI trends are toward the numerical value of 1, the higher the degree of human development. Again, we see fairly similar values for Ghana and Kenya, which excludes the possibility that diverging degrees of human development account for the rise of ethnic party types. Namibia produces higher HDI values than Ghana and Kenya yet the same type of (nonethnic) political parties as Ghana. The extended analysis of the Namibian party system demonstrated that ethnic parties feature in the Namibian political system; comparatively high levels of economic development can, therefore, also produce ethnic parties.

Finally, the inequalities within countries also need to be considered. Social exclusion can be expected to foster a climate of communal politics. Table 7.4 outlines the aggregate Gini coefficient for all three cases. The closer the coefficient is to 1, the higher the degree of inequality; the closer the coefficient is to 0, the higher the degree of equality.

The available data show stark differences between Namibia on the one side and Ghana and Kenya on the other. Kenya's and Ghana's respective coefficients over time have been relatively close, which confirms our previous finding: there is no correlation between different levels of economic growth or development at the national level and the political party or party system types.

Economic Growth and Human Development at the Regional Level

Examining the regional economic differences within countries necessitates the stipulation of an important caveat: regions or districts serve as weak

[1] A comparison of countries across individual time periods would have yielded the same results.

TABLE 7.4. *Gini Coefficient for Ghana, Kenya, and Namibia*

	1992	1993	1994	1997	1998	1999	2007
Ghana	0.59	n/a	n/a	n/a	0.57	0.41	0.41
Kenya	0.57	n/a	0.44	0.42	n/a	0.56	0.43
Namibia	n/a	0.74	n/a	n/a	n/a	n/a	0.74

Source: World Income Inequality Database.

proxies for ethnic groups; in Africa, as elsewhere, ethnically homogenous regions rarely exist. Unfortunately, in almost all countries, data are collected at the level of regions and not at the level of communities. As a result, findings have to be cross-checked with the ethnic composition of regions, as outlined in the respective previous chapters. To measure development, I use regional HDI and regional rates of the human poverty incidence (HPI) rate. These are the most frequently employed instruments by the United Nations in its examination of any developmental discrepancies within countries. In the case of Ghana, regional HDI data are not available. Therefore, I analyze regional economic outputs with the help of HPI rates and the social exclusion index (SEI). In Namibia, differences in the regional developmental outputs are examined with the help of HPI rates. Namibia is the only country in my sample where data collection has been conducted at the level of language groups.

In Kenya, the case with the highest salience of ethnicity, we find significant developmental differences between regions (see Tables 7.5 and 7.6).

In 2001, human development was most advanced in Nairobi. The only other region above the national average HDI was the Kikuyu-dominated Central province. Poorly performing regions include the North Eastern, Coast, Nyanza, and Western province; these four regions display HDI values that fall into the category of low development countries, whereas the rest fall into the category of medium development countries (United Nations

TABLE 7.5. *HDI Across Kenya's Regions*

Province	HDI Index 2001	HDI Index 2006
Kenya	0.54	0.53
Nairobi	0.78	0.77
Central	0.60	0.64
Coast	0.47	0.52
Eastern	0.54	0.51
Rift Valley	0.51	0.53
Nyanza	0.44	0.47
Western	0.45	0.52
North Eastern	0.41	0.29

Source: United Nations Development Program 2001, 2006.

TABLE 7.6. *HPI Rates as a Percentage Across Kenya's Regions*

Province	HPI 2001	HPI 2006
Kenya	34.5	n/a
Nairobi	32.4	29.9
Central	30.7	32.3
Coast	37.5	42.5
Eastern	39.8	40.0
Rift Valley	36.8	40.5
Nyanza	44.3	37.4
Western	41.1	36.1
North Eastern	44.8	50.5

Source: United National Development Program 2001, 2006.

Development Program 2001). HPI rates in 2006 strongly resemble the previous findings, with the North Eastern province dramatically lagging behind the rest of the country, followed by the Nyanza and Western provinces. Although the Central province and Nairobi are still home to a large share of people living in poverty, HPI rates are significantly lower there than in the other provinces. An analysis of the 10 richest and poorest districts by the United Nations in 2001 – as well as of the 20 richest and poorest constituencies – confirms these findings, as displayed in Tables 7.7 and 7.8.

These statistics underline one of the traditional undercurrents of Kenyan political discourse: the economically advantageous position of the Kikuyu. Whether this has occurred as a result of deliberate economic policy benefiting the Kikuyu or as an outcome of climatic and other factors – the prevalence of various diseases such as malaria in the Western and Nyanza provinces – is irrelevant. The analysis of ethnic cleavages in Kenya has shown these cleavages to be structured around the Kikuyu. Political party competition has been equally influenced by the "Kikuyu question."

In the case of Ghana, data measuring the economic inequalities between regions occur with the help of HPI rates as well as the SEI. Table 7.9 outlines HPI by region. Table 7.10 outlines the degree of social exclusion measured by the SEI.

As in Kenya, there are striking differences between regions. The North (consisting of the Northern, Upper East, and Upper West) is lagging far behind the national average figures. Despite the economic division between north and south, both major Ghanaian parties have consistently incorporated Northern politicians into their respective leadership structures. The political division between Ewe and Akan has proven much stronger than the division between the north and the rest of the country. The Volta region also continues to lag behind the average HPI rates, yet to a much lesser

TABLE 7.7. *UN 2001 District Ranking by HDI*

Top 10 Districts			Bottom 10 Districts		
District	HDI Value	Population	District	HDI Value	Population
Nairobi	0.78	32.4% Kikuyu 16.5% Luhya 18.5% Luo	Tana River	0.38	37% Pokomo 32.9% Orma
Tharaka Nithi	0.66	89% Meru	Homa Bay	0.38	76.5% Luo 9.6% Basuba
Mombassa	0.65	27.9% Mijikenda 13.9% Luo 12.5% Kamba 9.3% Luhya	Migori	0.36	77% Luo
Nyeri	0.62	97% Kikuyu	Wajir	0.35	97.5% Somali
Kiambu	0.62	88% Kikuyu	Busia	0.35	61.4% Luhya
Embu	0.61	61% Embu 7.1% Kamba 5.5% Kikuyu	Kwale	0.33	82.6% Mijikenda
Murang'a	0.61	96% Kikuyu	Samburu	0.26	74.7% Samburu
Nyandarua	0.60	96% Kikuyu	West Pokot	0.24	85.2% Kalenjin
Nakuru	0.59	59.7% Kikuyu 15% Kalenjin 7.4% Luhya	Turkana	0.20	94.5% Turkana
Meru	0.58	89% Meru	Marsabit	0.19	28.2% Marsabet 23.4% Gabra 18.3% Rendile 9.7% Somali

Source: United Nations Development Program 2001. The population figures are taken from Schröder (1998) and are based on the Kenya 1989 census. The data for Tharaka Nithi, Homa Bay, and Migori are approximations, as these districts did not exist in 1989.

extent degree than it did previously. In terms of its social exclusion, the region has traditionally done better than the national average. Today, the Ewe-populated Volta region is performing neither significantly better nor worse than other regions.

The data reveal two things: first, that the bridging of the developmental gap between the Volta region and the rest of the country has not made the ethnic cleavages existing between the Akan and the Ewe disappear. Voting behavior in the Volta and in the Ashanti regions remains diametrically opposed. Second, Ghana illustrates the point that stark economic differences between regions and groups do not inevitably lead to the formation of ethnic parties. Ghanaian parties have successfully bridged the gap between the Ewe and the Akan.

TABLE 7.8. *Kenya's 20 Richest and Poorest Constituencies Based on HPI Rates*

Richest			Poorest		
Constituency	Poverty Incidence as %	Province Majority Population	Constituency	Poverty Incidence as a%	Province Majority Population
1. Kabete	17	Central Kikuyu	210. Ganze	84	Coast Mijikenda
2. Kiambaa	19	Central Kikuyu	109. Kuria	81	Nyanza Kuria
3. Limuru	22	Central Kikuyu	208. Kitui South	76	Eastern Kamba
4. Mathira	24	Central Kikuyu	207. Kinano	75	Coast Mijikena Kamba Luo
5. Githunguri	25	Central Kikuyu	206. Kaloleni	74	Coast Mijikenda
6. Ndaragwa	25	Central Kikuyu	205. Bonchari	74	Nyanza Kisii
7. Othaya	27	Central Kikuyu	204. Rarieda	74	Nyanza Luo
8. Kieni	28	Central Kikuyu	203. Ndhiwa	73	Nyanza Luo
9. Kibaru	29	Central Kikuyu	202. Kitui Central	72	Eastern Kamba
10. Mathioya	29	Central Kikuyu	201. Rangwe	72	Nyanza Luo
11. Bura	31	Coast Oromo-Orma Pokoma Somali	200. Kasipul-Kabondo	72	Nyanza Luo
12. Gatundu South	31	Central Kikuyu	199. Ikolomani	72	Western Luhya
13. Lari	31	Central Kikuyu	198. Karachuonyo	72	Nyanza Luo
14. Kigume	31	Central Kikuyu	197. N. Mugirango-Borabu	71	Nyanza Kisii
15. Westlands	31	Nairobi Kikuyu Luhya Asian	196. Wajir North	71	North Eastern Somali
16. Mukurwe	31	Central Kikuyu	195. Bondo	70	Nyanza Luo
17. Kangema	31	Central Kikuyu	194. Butula	70	Western
18. Teta	32	Central Kikuyu	193. Kisumu Rural	70	Nyanza Luo
19. Ndia	32	Central Kikuyu	192. Budalange	70	Western Luhya
20. Keugoya	33	Central Kikuyu	191. Funyula	70	Western Luhya
TOTAL		18 Central 1 Coast 1 Nairobi	TOTAL		10 Nyanza 4 Western 3 Coast 2 Eastern 1 North Eastern Province

Source: Republic of Kenya 2008 and Schröder (1998), based on the 1989 population census in Kenya.

TABLE 7.9. *HPI as a Percentage in Ghana Across Regions*

Region	HPI 1991/1992	HPI 1998/1999	HPI 2005/2006
Ghana	51.7	39.5	28.5
Western	59.6	27.3	18.4
Central	44.3	48.4	19.9
Greater Accra	25.8	5.2	11.8
Volta	57.0	37.7	31.4
Eastern	48.0	43.7	15.1
Ashanti	41.2	27.7	20.3
Brong Ahafo	65.0	35.8	29.5
Northern	63.4	69.2	52.3
Upper East	66.9	88.2	70.4
Upper West	88.4	83.9	87.9

Source: Ghana Statistical Service 2007.

The case of Namibia confirms this finding. Table 7. 11 outlines the HPI rates in Namibia across regions. Table 7.12 outlines the HPI by language group.

Within Namibia, poverty affects the Ovambo-dominated regions (Ohangwena, Oshikoto, Omusati, and Omaheke) as well as the Ovambo community as a whole. However, thus far, no political party has formed that focuses exclusively on the well-being of the Ovambo. Rather, the major opposition party – the DTA – lacked for most of its existence any Ovambo participation.

TABLE 7.10. *Degree of Social Exclusion as a Percentage in Ghana Across Regions*

Region	SEI 1992	SEI 1999	SEI 2006
Ghana	52	40	29
Western	42	21	11
Central	26	29	12
Greater Accra	16	3	7
Volta	34	23	19
Eastern	29	26	9
Ashanti	35	12	12
Brong Ahafo	40	18	18
Northern	37	32	32
Upper East	40	43	43
Upper West	53	51	54

Source: UNDP 2007.

TABLE 7.11. *HPI in Namibia Across Regions*

Region	HPI 1993/1994	HPI 2008
Namibia	52.8	27.6
Khomas	16.8	6.3
Erongo	29.1	10.3
Oshana	68.8	19.6
Karas	32.1	21.9
Kunene	63.2	23.0
Otjozondjupa	35.3	27.8
Caprivi	73.0	28.6
Omaheke	52.0	30.1
Omusati	70.5	31.0
Hardap	34.1	32.1
Oshikoto	69.9	40.8
Ohangwena	82.7	44.7
Kavango	62.6	56.5

Source: Namibia Household Income and Expenditure Survey 1993, cited in van Rooy et al. (2006) and by the Republic of Namibia (2008).

On the basis of these results, any economic inequalities between groups cannot be seen as a sufficient condition for the formation of ethnic parties. In all three countries, stark economic differences between regions and groups exist, yet it is only in Kenya that ethnic parties have emerged. This is not to deny that economic differences matter politically. The allegedly privileged position of the Kikuyu continues to resurface in Kenya and undoubtedly has

TABLE 7.12. *HPI in Namibia Across Language Groups*

Language Group	HPI
Oshiwambo	50.6
Rukavango	18.4
Nama/Damara	14.2
Otjiherero	5.4
Caprivian	4.7
Afrikaans	3.0
Setswana	0.2
German	0.0
English	0.0

Source: Republic of Namibia (2008).

contributed to the ethnicization of Kenyan politics. The dismal economic situation in Ghana's north is a major factor that makes the north a distinct political entity. However, across countries, economic differences at the regional level cannot account for the rise of ethnic parties.

ELECTORAL SYSTEMS AND POLITICAL PARTIES

Political scientists have long recognized the importance of electoral systems for shaping the nature of political competition. Electoral systems translate votes into legislative seats, structure the arena of political competition (party systems), and provide incentives to political actors to adjust their behavior. Majoritarian systems are associated with stable two-party systems and the ability of the elected to rule without having to take the political demands of coalition partners into consideration ("governability"). In agrarian societies, majoritarian systems are said to provide a closer link between political representatives and the electorate (Barkan 1995). Systems of proportional representation are associated with a higher degree of representative fairness and higher voter turnout (Blais 2006, Kuenzi and Lambright 2007). In the scholarly literature, a large body of work exists that discusses the effects of various electoral systems on party systems, proportionality of vote transfer, and coalition politics (for just some examples, see Grofman and Lijphart 1986, Lijphart 1994, Reilly and Reynolds 1999, Sartori 2001). The return of democratic competition to large parts of the Third World inevitably caused a debate about which system might be better suited to accommodate the interests of ethnic groups in a manner that is conducive to democratic stability and peace. Several scholars used the nascent question of the political future of post-apartheid South Africa to debate which electoral system was best suited to accommodate the potential for ethnic divisions in ethnically segmented societies.

Thus the essential question underlying the debate about electoral systems in nonindustrial societies is less directly concerned with questions of fairness. Instead, authors have been concerned with whether or not a particular electoral system predisposes parties to seek ethnic inclusion and intergroup compromise. From the inception of this debate, Andrew Reynolds and Arend Lijphart have argued in favor of proportional representation (PR). They stress the historical raison d'être of PR in Europe: the provision of sufficient and balanced minority representation to counteract threats to national unity. Because PR facilitates minority interest articulation – or, in the case of Africa, the interests of all those who do not belong to the numerically superior tribes – it is inclusive. Because in the vast majority of African countries no ethnic group represents more than half of the population, PR either leads to power-sharing in the form of consociational arrangements or in the form of multiethnic parties or multiethnic governments that consist of various ethnic parties. In short, PR accommodates a maximum amount of groups and in return leads to "ethnic compromise." It further ensures the inclusion of potential "spoilers" into the parliamentary realm. All of these foster an atmosphere of cooperation, which is conducive to the consolidation of democracy (Lijphart 1991, Barkan 1995, Reynolds 1995).

Horowitz warned against expecting too much from PR systems. He argued that in ethnically divided societies, ethnic coalitions – both at the level of government and at the level of political parties – are frequently formed yet are rarely sustained: they are coalitions of convenience. Instead of fostering compromise, ethnic coalitions have the potential to generate ethnic antagonism, as they are most likely to fall apart over ethnic issues. Using the examples of Northern Ireland and Malaysia, Horowitz demonstrated that the formation of nonethnic parties is not primarily related to the electoral system in place. The 1970s elections to the National Assembly in Northern Ireland were conducted under the single transferable vote system, an abridged version of PR. Even though vote pooling occurred, radical ethnic parties succeeded by opposing political accommodation. By contrast, in Malaysia, which conducts its elections under a first-past-the-post (FPTP) system, an interethnic coalition emerged, which Horowitz traced back to specific political circumstances at the time of its formation. More recent analyses of the racial nature of political campaigning in South Africa have confirmed the view that ethnically based parties continue to feature in proportional representation systems (Davis 2004). Horowitz argued in favor of the Alternative Vote (AV), as it provides an incentive for parties to form inter-ethnic coalitions before the elections. Parties that campaign on an ethnically inclusive ticket will benefit from second preferences (Horowitz 1992).

Electoral Systems and Parties in Kenya, Ghana, and Namibia

All voices involved in the debate about electoral systems stress the need for inter-ethnic compromise and inter-ethnic voting. Given the omnipresence of multiethnic parties (in our case, the multiethnic alliance and the multiethnic catch-all party) and the fact that, by and large, African electorates always vote across ethnic lines to at least some extent, a quick review of the ideal case scenario that electoral systems should produce is necessary. Lijphart advocates PR on the basis of the following:

> Divided societies, both in the West and elsewhere, need peaceful coexistence among the contending ethnic groups. This requires conciliation and compromise, goals that in turn require the greatest possible inclusion of representatives of these groups in the decision-making process. Such power-sharing can be arranged much more easily in parliamentary and PR systems than in presidential and plurality systems. (Lijphart 1991: 81)

Accordingly, PR electoral systems aim at the inclusion of as many groups as possible in government, as all parties in ethnically segmented societies are assumed to be ethnic parties. Horowitz (1992) never defined explicitly under which condition group accommodation is achieved. Yet the examples that he discussed (Cyprus, Malaysia, Nigeria, and Northern Ireland) indicate that this is best achieved when parties can rely on the vote sharing of the main ethnic communities of their respective countries. Thus what Horowitz (1992) is mainly interested in is the vote pooling of diverse communities. As the major voices in the debate aim at the highest degree of inclusion possible, I regard the catch-all, the programmatic, and the personalistic party as types that represent situations in which these conditions are met.

Following Reynolds (Reilly and Reynolds 1999) and Lijphart (1991), we could expect there to be a greater degree of accommodation in Namibia (PR system) than in Kenya and Ghana (majoritarian/FPTP systems). Namibia initially confirms the assumption that PR systems contribute to the formation of inclusive politics. The only significant and effective party in Namibia – SWAPO – corresponds to our ideal type of the catch-all party. However, lowering the threshold of significant and effective parties, my examination of the Namibian party systems reveals that there is a wide variety of ethnic parties. This is true of the official opposition and of the many smaller parties that managed to secure legislative representation in Namibia's National Assembly. At different periods in time, these included the Herero-based National Unity Democratic Organization (NUDO), the Damara-based United Democratic Front (UDF), and two white-based parties, the Republican Party (RP) and the Monitor Action Group (MAG). Although the NUDO was briefly discussed in the context of the fourth observation period in Namibia and identified as the Herero wing of the DTA, the UDF, the RP, and the MAG have not been part of our analysis. The sparse secondary literature about these parties clearly indicates their ethnic nature. Their respective PNSs that are outlined in Table 7.13 confirm this conclusion.

Scholars identify a connection between the PR system and the electoral survival of small mono-ethnic parties (Le Beau 2005). This illustrates that, at the level of smaller parties, PR can actually have the opposite than desired impact: it encourages ethnic politics, although at a level that is not threatening to national unity. The in-depth analysis of the Namibian parties provided in Chapter Four reveals additional arguments, and ones that question the effect of the electoral system on party formation. The party's nonethnic nature predates the introduction of the electoral system. SWAPO formed long before parliamentary democracy, and its electoral rules appeared to be a realistic option in and for Namibia. A variety of other factors are responsible for its national character: SWAPO was founded against the background of brutal racial oppression and, as such, was in the position to espouse goals that all communities could associate with. By providing it with the

TABLE 7.13. *PNS of Namibian Parties Not Considered Significant*

Party/Election	PNS
UDF 1994	.34
UDF 1999	.32
UDF 2004	.36
DTA 2004	.45
NUDO 2004	.26
RP 2004	.47

Source: Author's own compilation, based on Lodge (1999) and EISA (2005).

status of the sole and authentic representative of the Namibian people, the international community implicitly enforced a national character on to the movement (Ansprenger 1984, Pütz et al. 1990).

After all, the greatest weapon of SWAPO's domestic opponents was their portrayal of SWAPO as a radical Ovambo-based movement that, if elected to power, would put Namibia's southern communities at great disadvantage. Once independence had been achieved, its national setup proved an electoral asset. The implementation of PR can thus be seen as less relevant. As further discussed in the chapter about Namibian parties, the transformation of the official opposition from an alliance to a catch-all party was the outcome of the formation of a SWAPO break-away group, whose exit was brought about by factors germane to the Namibian political context. The "contagious effect" discussed in Chapter Six – the imperative to provide a nonethnic opposition in the face of a nonethnic party in government – also contributed to the success of the CoD in taking over the mantle of the official opposition from the DTA.

Thus although Namibia on its own provides initial evidence for the appeasing effect of PR systems, two qualifications are necessary: at the level of politically significant parties (SWAPO), the PR system had no effect. At the level of politically insignificant parties, Namibia has witnessed the proliferation of ethnicity-based parties. Both developments can be said to disprove the alleged impact of the PR system.

The divergence of party types in Kenya and Ghana provides even stronger evidence for excluding the respective electoral systems as the explanatory variable. Ghana is the country where the salience of ethnicity for parties is the lowest in this study, and Kenya is the country where the salience of ethnicity is the highest. I have found that majoritarian systems in Africa can produce both ethnic and nonethnic parties, whereas PR cannot be assumed to have significantly contributed to the formation of nonethnic parties or nonethnic voting in Namibia. African political parties thus defy the consequences that have been attached to particular electoral systems.

DEMOCRACY AND POLITICAL PARTIES

What is the impact of democratic quality on the formation of political parties? A regime that deliberately manipulates elections might do so to keep the ruling elite in power, whose membership is confined to specific communities. These elites might engage in election campaigns that insinuate an "all-or-nothing" character and in which some communities are pitched against others. Ethnic campaigns combined with electoral manipulation might thus become part of the "menu of manipulation" (Schedler 2002). If the incumbent party incorporates an ethnic bias and the regime displays a low content of democratic quality, this might lead opposition parties to either engage in ethnic politics themselves or to a process of fission to "throw the ethnic rascals out." If the incumbent party is national in its setup and the democratic quality is low, this might cause equally diverse reactions. Politicians might choose to build ethnic opposition blocs as the main pillars of political protest, or they might engage in cross-ethnic cooperation. The same alternatives are available to politicians if full democratic rights are provided and actors respect democracy as "the only game in town" (Przeworski 1991). Therefore party strategies cannot be predicted *ex ante*.

In a first step, the relationship between regime quality and political parties are examined – independent of the type of political party in government. To measure democratic quality, I use Freedom House values ranging from the early 1990s to the present day. Freedom House aggregate scores differentiate between regimes that are free (F), partly free (PF), and not free (NF). Table 7.14 outlines the Freedom House classifications for our three countries across time.

Kenya is classified as not free between 1992 and 2001, with the sole exception of 1992 (partly free) – the year of the first multiparty elections. From 2002 to 2008, it is classified as partly free. In addition, Freedom House does not classify Kenya as an electoral democracy except between 2002 and 2006, in other words, during the first Kibaki term. Of the three countries, it has the lowest degree of democratic quality. Comparing Kenya with Ghana and Namibia over the period as a whole suggests a relationship between the spread of ethnic parties and a low degree of democratic quality. Ethnic parties dominate Kenyan politics; simultaneously, it is the only country in which regime quality overall is never rated free. In Ghana and Namibia, nonethnic parties prevail, and regime quality is either rated as free (Namibia) or as constantly improving from partly free to free (Ghana).

An examination of the evolution of party types for each observation period discards this assumption: within Kenya, the increase in democratic quality from not free to partly free does not lead to a change in the ethnic composition or dynamics of Kenyan party politics. Although Kenyan politics

TABLE 7.14. *The Quality of Democracy Across Three to Four Observation Periods*

Period 1	1990	1991	1992	1993	1994	1995	1996	1997
Kenya	n/a		PF	NF	NF	NF	NF	NF
Ghana			PF	PF	PF	PF	PF	n/a
Namibia	F	F	F	F	F	n/a		
Period 2	**1995**	**1996**	**1997**	**1998**	**1999**	**2000**	**2001**	**2002**
Kenya	n/a		NF	NF	NF	NF	NF	PF
Ghana			PF	PF	PF	F	n/a	
Namibia	F	F	F	F	F	n/a		
Period 3	**2000**	**2001**	**2002**	**2003**	**2004**	**2005**	**2006**	**2007**
Kenya	n/a		PF	PF	PF	PF	PF	PF
Ghana	n/a	F	F	F	F	n/a		
Namibia	F	F	F	F	F			
Period 4	**2005**	**2006**	**2007**	**2008**				
Ghana	F	F	F	F				
Namibia	F	F	F	F				

Source: Author's own compilation based on Freedom House scores.

became driven by processes of fusion from the second observation period onward, and although Kenya witnessed the formation of (unsustainable) nonethnic parties in the run-up to the 2002 elections, the impact of democratic quality on these phenomena can be doubted. At the time of the party merger into New KANU and NARC, Freedom House scores for Kenya display values of 5.5 (2001) and 4.0 (2002). When NARC disintegrates, Freedom House scores display a value of 3.0 (2003). Kenya is classified as an electoral democracy between 2002 and 2006 (the highest quality of democracy Kenya has ever achieved), which is the time period when parties disintegrated.

Analyzing the processes of party formation weakens the supposed link between a low level of democracy and the spread of ethnic parties. Observations from Ghana further render this assumption powerless. Ghana is initially rated as partly free (between 1992 and 1999); from 2000 onward, it is regarded as free. The NPP changes from an ethnic to a nonethnic party with the arrival of Kufuor as the NPP president and his new party leadership in 1996. Given that the quality of democracy stays at the same level, changes in party types cannot be attributed to changes in the quality of democracy. Between 1996 and 1999, Ghana displays the same Freedom House values as Kenya between 2002 and 2007, yet the dynamics of party competition vary significantly. Eventually, Namibia – the only case in which regime can be classified as free throughout the entire period – illustrates that a high level of democratic quality can produce both ethnic as well as nonethnic parties. No causal relationship between the salience of ethnicity at the aggregate level of political parties and the democratic quality of the regime can be established. Ethnic parties can occur in free, partly free, and non-free regimes, whereas nonethnic parties equally emerge in free, partly free, and non-free regimes.

To verify these findings, party types are correlated with the quality of parliamentary elections. This is done with the aid of a database composed by Lindberg (2006) that evaluates the quality of elections in all Sub-Saharan African countries. Results confirm the findings derived from Freedom House: in Ghana and Namibia, all parliamentary elections are classified as free and fair, and yet in both we find ethnic and nonethnic parties. In Kenya, the first two elections are classified as elections with irregularities, whereas the third one is classified as free and fair. Yet – as outlined – Kenyan politics has consistently been shaped by ethnic parties.

In a second step, the interplay between the incumbent party type and the quality of the regime is analyzed. In Kenya, one can distinguish between two periods. Between 1992 and 1999, the regime quality was classified as not free and the incumbent party was ethnic. During that time, the opposition was in a constant process of ethnic fragmentation. Between 2000 and 2008, the regime quality was classified as partly free, and the party in government was again ethnic. During that time, the opposition parties also remained ethnic. In Ghana, we can also distinguish between two periods. Between 1992 and 1999, the regime was classified as partly free, and the party in government was nonethnic. The opposition underwent a transformation from an ethnic to a nonethnic party. Between 2000 and 2008, the incumbent party was again nonethnic, and the regime quality was classified as free. Namibia's political regime was free throughout its existence, and yet both ethnic and nonethnic opposition parties emerged. No definite conclusions can be drawn from these results, as Kenya is the only country with an ethnic party in government. All other countries remain governed by nonethnic parties.

THE LEGAL DIMENSION: PARTY LAWS AND POLITICAL PARTIES

Although the literature on African politics mentions, at times, the existence of party laws that legally proscribe the formation of ethnic parties, until recently these bans have not been analyzed systematically. A variety of scholars have tried to fill that gap (e.g., Basedau et al. 2007).[2] Party bans can have various impacts. First, ethnic party bans can force parties to change strategy and organize along other cleavages. In that case, party bans fulfill their purpose. Second, party bans have no impact on party formation either, because parties are successful in building up "alibi structures" (members, offices, and candidates for public office) in areas they implicitly or explicitly do not desire to represent or because state regulations cannot adequately

[2] See also the special issue of *Democratization* 17(4).

be enforced because of capacity shortage or a lack of political will. Authors thus far have focused on the question of whether or not party bans are conducive to conflict resolution and democratic stabilization (Becher and Basedau 2008). Unfortunately, they have not addressed the more proximate question of whether or not party bans have an effect on the type of party in place. This gap in research is likely to have been caused by a lack of agreement on how to classify African parties.

In Ghana, laws proscribing ethnic parties have a long tradition and date back to the Nkrumah area (Apter 1955, Austin 1963, Crabbe 1975). The current constitution does not permit parties to be based on ethnicity, religion, gender, professional groups, or a variety of other backgrounds. The Ghanaian state defines a party as nonethnic if it includes one member from each region in the party's National Executive, each district has at least one party member at the moment of its foundation, and the party has branches in all regions and offices in at least two-thirds of the districts in each region.

By contrast, until recently, Kenya had no legal mechanism in place that forbade the prescription of ethnic parties. Since July 2008, a new party law has been in place that prescribes that a party needs at least 200 members in each region, one member from each province in the governing body, and one founding member from each district. Namibia since independence has proscribed parties that discriminate on the basis of color, ethnicity, and race; however, no criteria have been formulated by which this regulation is enforced.

Can this explain the variance in the outcome variable? Once more, the classification of parties in each parliamentary cycle – in conjunction with lowering our definitional standards of what constitutes significant parties – sheds greater light on the effects of potential causal factors. Despite the comparatively strict party regulations in Ghana, the NPP has been classified as ethnic during the first observation period. In Namibia, the official opposition has for several periods been identified as an ethnic party. In addition, the overview of other several smaller parties in the Namibian legislature (see Table 7.3) illustrates that a wide variety of ethnic parties continues to feature in Namibia's political system. This indicates that ethnic party bans have a very limited overall effect on party systems. The differences between party types cannot, therefore, be linked to any legal proscriptions.

POLITICAL PARTIES AND THE TYPE OF INDEPENDENCE MOVEMENT

In the context of European party history, Lipset and Rokkan (1967) noted that the political configurations that shaped political party systems in late nineteenth-century Europe were still in place several decades later (Karvonen and Kuhnle 2001). In recent years, the long-term effects of foundational moments have been increasingly recognized by scholars associated with historical institutionalism. Accordingly, a particular path taken at "critical junctures" can have a long-term impact on countries' historical pathways. Historical institutionalists have been particularly successful in accounting for continuities in politics and in directing scholarly attention to the mechanisms that produce continuity. The latter is often described as path dependence or positive feedback (Collier and Collier 1991, Mahoney 2001, Mahoney and Rueschemeyer 2003, Pierson 2004, Capoccia and Kelemen 2007).

The run-up to independence in Africa qualifies as a critical juncture. The foundations of the future nature of national politics were laid in that period. At no other time did African leaders have the leverage to shape the political setup of their soon-to-be independent nations than in the immediate pre- and post-independence periods.[3] Simultaneously, the pre-independence period led to the first politicization of Africans on a large scale. In analyzing the nature of independence movements across countries, I intend to examine to what extent the ethnic cleavage lines that have shaped democratic competition in the 1990s were already in place.

Many studies have been written about the immediate pre- and post-independence politics; however, these are either reduced to individual case studies or to comparative studies that do not capture the extent to which these movements pursued a national outlook. Instead, historians emphasized the conflict of interests between traditional leadership and an allegedly emerging African middle class (Hodgkin 1956, Morgenthau 1961, Rotberg 1966). African historians have not yet filled this gap in the research. Using a historical variable exposes our findings to accusations of subjectivity. This problem is known to social scientists who draw on historical accounts. The daunting question is how to choose the sources of data without permitting correspondence between the chosen data and the questions the data are supposed to answer. The longer and the richer the historiographical tradition covering a particular topic, the lower the likelihood that bias can occur. Other solutions include the presentation of various historical accounts and the construction of a historical master narrative that is supplemented by alternative interpretations (Lustick 1996). Unfortunately, African historiography is anything but long and rich. Despite these substantial shortcomings, a provisional comparison of the nationalist movements of the three countries under scrutiny is still feasible.

The analysis of Namibia's independence movements is already complete, as the parties that fought for independence (SWAPO and, to a much lesser extent, the DTA) are still the same parties that were present at the beginning of the observation period. Our historical analysis therefore focuses on Ghana and Kenya and then compares the nature of the independence movements in all three countries. By "independence" or "nationalist movement," our

[3] I use the terms "immediate pre- and post-independence" period and "nationalist period" interchangeably.

study includes those major political parties that explicitly called for an end to colonialism/apartheid.

Ghana: The United Front

The first political movement in Ghana was the United Gold Coast Convention (UGCC), under the leadership of J. B. Danquah. Its formation was facilitated by the increasing radicalization of a young and aspiring intelligentsia, the moderately educated, and the indigenous trading community. Their increasing political alienation from British colonial rule was particularly strong in Ashanti (today, Ashanti province and Brong Ahafo) and the Colony (today, the Central, Western, and Eastern provinces). A particularly latent source of conflict with the colonial rulers was the price of cocoa. Between the two World Wars, prices for cocoa were heavily fluctuating, leading to several seller holdups. After the outbreak of the Second World War, prices for commodity goods increased dramatically between 1939 and 1941. Ghana's contribution to a European war further increased the political tensions.

With the exception of the north (today, the Upper West, Upper East, and Northern provinces), which was still caught in tribal and clan politics, the Gold Coast was full of political anxiety (Apter 1955, Austin 1964, Rathbone 2000). Against the background of these events, the UGCC formed on April 4, 1947. Right from its inception, the party understood itself as a nationwide movement and a bridge between the chiefs and the people – although its relationship with the traditional leaders was complicated at best. Its founding organizations were occupational interest groups such as the Colony's Farmer Union or the Ex-Servicemen Union. The immediate background to its formation was the independence of Burma, Ceylon, and India. Its leading members were A. G. Grant (chairman), R. S. Blay (vice president), J. B. Danquah (vice-president and the unofficial leader), R. A. Williams (treasurer), W. E. Ofori Atta, E. A. Akufo Addo, J. W. de Graft Johnson, and Obetsibi Lamptey. With the exception of Lamptey (Ga), all of its members were of Akan origin. The north at the time was still beset by a traditional lifestyle and nonparticipation in the national political life. The Ewe community was not excluded from involvement in the party; Komla Gbedemah (Ewe) was initially selected as the UGCC's secretary-general; however, he declined to take that position.[4] The UGCC soon fell apart, largely because of its fateful decision to call on Kwame Nkrumah to return from London and to become its secretary-general.[5]

[4] Gbedemah was offered the position as secretary-general after the UGCC had fallen out with Nkrumah.

[5] Detailed information is drawn from Austin (1961). Austin had exclusive access to the UGGC's minute book, on which his historical account is based.

There were three main causes that led to the split between the UGCC's "old guard" and Nkrumah. The first is the riots of February 1948 and Nkrumah's (wrongful) acknowledgment that the UGCC had been actively involved in them. Nkrumah intended to make the party appear more radical than it was. The second is the agreement by the UGCC to become an active member of the Coussey Commission, which had been inaugurated by the imperial government to formulate a new constitution for the Gold Coast. Cooperation with the colonial authorities led to a loss of prestige and was subsequently harshly criticized by Nkrumah. The third is the visit of Sir Sydney Abrahams to the Gold Coast arranged by the UGGC's old guard, an occurrence that Nkrumah decried in the press (Austin 1961). His formation of the Convention's Youth Organization – which anticipated the formation of the Convention's People's Party (CPP) – was based on the belief that a more radical force fighting British colonialism would better be able to capture the mood of the colony. Austin, who had unique access to internal UGCC memos dating from that period, concluded that:

> The broad nationalist front started under the UGCC leadership fractured quickly along moderate versus radical lines – it is probably fair to add along the lines of economic and social interest. (Austin 1961: 296)

The economic and social interest referred to were Nkrumah's more radical approach to independence and his socialist predilections. Nkrumah's frequent use of the term "comrade," his close connection to the openly socialist Western African National Secretariat, and his decade-long acquaintance with socialist pan-African thinkers – such as George Padmore – had long been sources of intense conflict between the business-minded UGCC leadership and its secretary-general (Geiss 1974). Nkrumah's CPP, which soundly defeated the UGCC in the 1952 elections, managed to create a nationwide movement with party branches covering the whole of the Gold Coast. Nkrumah's deputy was Gbedemah (Ewe), and his secretary-general was Kojo Botsio (Apter 1955, Austin 1961, Austin 1970, Hettne 1980). Thus the transformation of Ghana's nationalist movement from the UGCC to the CPP – as the prevailing political actor – was driven by increasing radicalism and different ideological conceptions about the future independent Ghanaian state. Ethnicity was clearly not the divisive issue between the UGCC and the CPP.

By contrast, the second split that occurred between the pre-independence African government of 1954 and a new opposition group – the National Liberation Movement (NLM) – had strong ethnic undercurrents. Opposition to the CPP emerged in the late summer of 1954, in Ashanti. Nkrumah's finance minister, Gbedemah, had introduced the Cocoa Duty and Development Funds Bill, which set a ceiling for the prices paid to cocoa farmers for a period of four years. The bill was designed as a precautionary measure to curb inflation. As the world market price at the time was significantly higher than the price fixed by the state, this step led to protests in Ashanti, where in the 1952 elections the CPP had gained 18 of 21 seats. Under the leadership of Kusi Ampofo, Osei Mensah, and E. Y. Baffoe (all Ashanti), demands for farmer interests soon transformed into demands for a federal structure for the Gold Coast. In speeches and rallies, the notion of an "Ashanti nation" featured extensively. This found support among the chiefs and most significantly attracted the support of the Ashantehene, who provided considerable financial resources to the NLM.

The party was officially founded on September 19, 1954, in Kumasi. The founding occurred among large crowds singing ancient war songs of the Ashanti. Bafour Osei Akoto – a senior linguist of the Ashantehene – was sworn in as the chairman of the party, whereby he had to swear the Great Oath of the Ashanti. The NLM drafted an alternative version of the constitution, which foresaw the Ashantehene to be the head of the Ashanti nation (Howe 1958, Austin 1970, Apter 1972, Goldsworthy 1973). In a reactionary turn against Nkrumah's radicalism, the chiefs in the province now realigned with their former opponents. Interestingly, the farmers of the colony – largely Fante or Ga – did not join the NLM, even though their political interests were identical to those of their Ashanti contemporaries (Rathbone 1973). According to Austin, "the NLM was a Kumasi-centered, Ashanti movement, which appealed for support in the name of the Ashantehene, the Golden Stool, Ashanti interest, Ashanti history, and Ashanti rights" (Austin 1970: 265).

The reaction of the CPP to the political onslaught of the NLM is noteworthy. Throughout the period of ethnic agitation inside Ashanti, the CPP retained a visible presence in the region. Those Ashanti whose family origins did not allow for their social progression continued to support the CPP. Traders who depended on government contracts and who could expect financial benefits from a strong central government also remained within the CPP (Austin 1970). The CPP's most prominent politician in Ashanti, Krobo Edusai, had close family ties to various Ashanti chiefs and stayed inside the party. To maintain a sizable segment of support, the CPP fostered its political support among the chiefdoms located further away from Kumasi, among those who had traditionally been skeptical of the domineering role of the Ashantehene. The government rewarded their loyalty with the creation of the Brong Ahafo region, where the CPP managed to claim the majority of seats in the 1956 elections (Austin 1970, Apter 1972, Hettne 1980). In the 1956 elections, the CPP won 44 percent of the popular vote in Ashanti, although its seat share declined from 18 (of 21) to 8 (of 21), whereas the NLM managed to win 54 percent.[6] Even though the high vote share was contingent on support from among non-Ashanti minorities – in particular, in the urban areas of Kumasi – these figures illustrate that the

[6] *Legon Observer*, February 16, 1979.

CPP remained a serious political contender among the Ashanti. The fact that the CPP managed to field candidates in all Ashanti constituencies underlines this point (Davidson 2007). Nationally, the CPP would triumph once more, taking 71 seats over the 33 combined seats of the overall opposition. Only in Ashanti and in the north did the CPP not emerge as the strongest political force. As in Ashanti, the CPP could claim a visible political presence in the north too: in the 1956 elections, it carried 44.6 percent of the popular vote and gained 11 of 26 seats.[7] Finally, both the CPP as well as the various pre-independence Nkrumah governments contained representatives from all communities (Asante and Gyimah-Boadi 2004).

The Ghanaian independence movement – initially represented by the UGCC and later by the CPP – was national in character: the breakup of the UGCC was not motivated or precipitated by ethnic undercurrents. The exclusion of the north from high-ranking UGCC party positions was an outcome of the sociopolitical realities of the north at the time. The formation of an ethnic opposition in Ashanti was not succeeded by the ethnic fragmentation of the CPP.

Kenya: Ethnic Disunity from the Start

In Kenya, the process of party formation followed a distinctly different pattern. The alienation of the Kikuyu from fertile land by the British led to a stratification of Kenyan society. Due to their loss of land, yet their proximity to Nairobi and missionary education, the Kikuyu developed a political consciousness at an earlier stage than other Kenyan communities (Holmquist and Ford 1994, Throup 1987). Political agitation – albeit at a low level, at least compared with later periods – started in the 1920s with the formation of the East African Association, which was initially led by Henry Thuku. Later it was succeeded by the Kikuyu Central Association (KAU) led by Jomo Kenyatta. For Kala, these early attempts at political protests illustrated that "Kenyan nationalism was in fact Kikuyu nationalism, an outcome of their mounting grievances" (Kala 1979: 99). The declining economic and social conditions of the Kikuyu led to a radicalization of Kikuyu activity that increasingly challenged Kenyatta's authority, who, by 1947, had become the president of the Kenya African Union (KAU). Kenyatta's strategy was to increase the support for the KAU among other communities. However, he had only limited success due to the lack of educated leaders living outside of the Central province (Arnold 1974). The early 1950s saw the radicalization of the Kikuyu protests, which had taken a violent turn in the form of the Mau Mau uprising (Throup 1987). Inside the KAU, Bildad Kaggia and his Forty Group advocated for the organization to take a more aggressive outlook. The closeness of prominent Mau Mau members to

[7] *Legon Observer*, February 16, 1979.

the KAU leadership resulted in the dissolution of the organization and the imprisonment by the British of Kenyatta, Kaggia, and several other Kenyan political leaders (Kyle 1999).

From 1955 onward, political parties were permitted at the district level – with the exception of in the Central province, given the Kikuyu nature of the Mau Mau (Throup 1987, Berman and Lonsdale 1992, Wrong 2008). The year 1959 saw the formation of two parties that tried to reach out nationally. First is the Kenya National Party (KNP), led by Masinde Muliro (Luhya), Daniel arap Moi (Kalenjin), J. K. ole Tipis (Masai), and Ronald Ngala (Mijikenda/Coastal). Shortly after its formation, however, it was dissolved, as other parties had constantly disrupted its activities. In Nairobi, for example, the KNP was unable to hold meetings, as Odinga's Luo-based Nairobi's People's Convention Party (NPCP) frequently disturbed its rallies. These were early examples of the high frequency and salience of political conflict. In June 1960, the founding members of the KNP and several other smaller parties came together under the umbrella of the Kenya African Democratic Union (KADU).

All of the KADU's founding elements were ethnic-based parties or associations – including Tipsis' Masai United Front, Moi's Kalenjin Political Alliance, Osman Araru's Somali National Association, the North Nyanza District Congress, the Coast African Political Union, and the Kilifi African People's Union. Ngala served as its president, Muliro as vice-president, Moi as chairman, and Martin Shikuku as secretary-general. The KADU's formation was driven by the fear of Kenya's smaller communities of the Kenya African National Union (KANU), which had formed in May 1960. In the KANU, the two largest tribes – the Kikuyu and the Luo – had united. British anti–Mau Mau propaganda had established a general sense of mistrust toward the Kikuyu, which was augmented by their numerical superiority and their comparatively well-educated background as a group. Increasing Luo participation in the urban labor market further deepened the fear of those communities that would initiate the KANU (Anderson 2005). The formation of the KANU had been anticipated in 1959 by the formation of the Kenya Independent Movement (KIM). Jomo Kenyatta was elected president; James Gichuru (Kikuyu) was elected as acting president while Kenyatta remained in prison. Oginga Odinga was elected vice-president, and Tom Mboya was elected as secretary-general. Initially, Ngala and Moi were elected as treasurer and deputy treasurer, respectively, in absentia. Both refused to remain part of the KANU because the founding KANU Congress demanded the dissolution of member parties (Teubert-Seiwert 1987). In contrast to the KANU, the KADU lacked nationalist aspirations and assumed tribalism to remain a prevailing feature of Kenyan politics (Anderson 2005).

Ethnicity was also the major point of contention inside both parties. Inside the KANU, the election of Mboya (Luo) as secretary-general caused apprehension among the Kikuyu delegates. Mboya's election as Nairobi delegate to the colonial Legislative Council had been facilitated by the disfranchisement of the Kikuyu due to the state of emergency in the colony. To mitigate these tensions, the KANU's acting president, Gichuru, created the additional position of organizing secretary and filled it with a Kikuyu individual. In the run-up to the 1961 elections, the Kikuyu wing of the KANU fielded an alternative candidate, Wayaki, against Mboya. Mboya won despite the ethnic odds against him (Kyle 1999, Goldsworthy 1982). In anticipation of the 1963 election, Kamba leader Paul Ngei broke away from the party and formed the African's People Party because of the KANU's refusal to give him a higher rank inside of the party.

Inside the KADU, the so-called Kitale issue showed the dilemma of a party that was built around ethnic interest groups. Several communities that helped to make up the party claimed to have the right to settle in the areas around Kitale. Tensions over this question came to the forefront openly at the Lancaster House Conference (Sanger and Nottingham 1964, Anderson 2005). Outside of the two parties, ethnic political unions formed that tried to unite communities under the roof of one party, such as the Luo Political Movement, the Kikuyu Political Movement, and the Baluhya Union (Teubert-Seiwert 1987).

Although both parties contested the 1961 election with almost identical platforms, in 1963 the ethnic cleavage between the KANU and the KADU – smaller nomadic groups versus larger agricultural communities – was clearly visible in their respective attitudes toward federalism ("majimboism") and the federal constitution that was drawn up at Lancaster House. From September 1961 onward, the KADU aggressively promoted devolution. By creating a strong federal setup, the party aimed to prevent the advent of Kikuyu dominance after independence (Sanger and Nottingham 1964, Teubert-Seiwert 1987). Candidates of the KADU mobilized voters by insinuating that once in power the KANU would quickly forget about the well-being of Kenya's smaller communities. The KANU contributed to this fear by campaigning against the drawn-up independence constitution and future federalism, which it portrayed as the KADU's attempts to create small ethnic kingdoms. The electoral contest and the result were telling: the KADU contested 59 of 177 constituencies. The number of constituencies contested by the KANU is not yet known, but was also far below the total number of constituencies. Although the KADU took the Rift Valley, Western, and Coastal provinces, the KANU took the Central, Nyanza, and Eastern provinces (Geertzel 1970, Wandiba 1996, Kyle 1999).

COMPARING AFRICAN INDEPENDENCE MOVEMENTS

Where does this leave the debate about the correlation between African nationalist movements and ethnic party politics? Table 7.15 outlines the historical features of all three cases scrutinized here.

TABLE 7.15. *Overview of Independence Movements*

Independence Movement		Participating Communities	Founding Elements	Background of Formation and Goals	Classification
Ghana	UGGC	largely Akan, yet not exclusionary	intellectuals professional groups	protest against privileged role of traditional leaders; protest against injustices of colonial system	national
	CPP	all	radical elements of UGGC	break-away from CPP; call for faster independence	national
	NLM	Ashanti	Ashanti farmers	Ashanti break-away from CPP;call for federalism	ethnic
Kenya	KANU	large tribes	ethnic district parties	protest against injustices of colonial system; strong centralized state	ethnic
	KADU	small tribes	ethnic district parties	protest against injustices of colonial system; federal state structure	ethnic
Namibia	SWAPO	all	workers	protest against labor conditions and apartheid; independence	national
	DTA	smaller communities	ethnic parties	supported and financed by South Africa; protest against petty apartheid	ethnic

Source: Author's own compilation.

Ghana and Namibia witnessed the rise of ethnically united independence movements. Ghana was led to independence by the CPP; in Namibia, SWAPO dominated the political scene. In both countries, the independence movement faced political competition by an alternative movement whose support was based on ethnicity. In Ghana, this was the NLM; in Namibia, this was the DTA. These movements were not strong enough to challenge their competitors in earnest. More importantly, both the NLM and the DTA were too weak to cause the ethnic fragmentation of their opponents. By contrast, the independence movement in Kenya was, from its inception, divided into two ethnic alliances: the KANU and the KADU.

Even though these results correspond with the data for each country's contemporary party system, some doubts still remain about the extent to which the type of independence movement can explain the political dynamics of party politics in the contemporary era. In Kenya, the immediate pre- and post-independence periods can account for the cleavage into Kikuyu and Kalenjin, but not for the cleavage between the Kikuyu and the Luo, which occurred after independence. The alliance between Raila Odinga and the coastal communities in the run-up to the 2007 elections – which was fought in favor of majimboism – shows how the political stance of the Luo leadership on the issue had changed. Whatever the causes behind this – genuine policy considerations or ethnic-strategic maneuvering, or both – it shows the limited explanatory power of independent movements as a variable in its own right. In addition, it must again be emphasized that any interpretation of pre-independence politics rests on thin historiographical ground if compared with those events of other regions. Finally, as with all historical explanations, questions remain regarding why a certain phenomenon appeared in the first place. Knowing that political dynamics were very similar in the nationalist period does not provide a general answer regarding why divisions occurred at that time. The political dynamics of the nationalist period might instead be an outcome of a structural variable.

ETHNIC FRACTIONALIZATION AND POLITICAL PARTIES

The ethnic heterogeneity of African states is frequently the subject of economic and political analyses. Economists see in the ethnic fractionalization of the continent a major reason why economic growth rates are lagging behind the rest of the world (Easterly and Levine 1997). In political science, ethnic diversity is also seen as a burden rather than as a source of enrichment. The literature on the allegedly negative consequences of ethnic heterogeneity is potentially endless. Although there is scholarly agreement that the multiethnic setup poses challenges to African nationhood and democratic consolidation, only a limited number of scholars have tried to outline the political consequences of the different degrees of heterogeneity.

Those who have approached the topic have done so from very different angles and with different research agendas in mind. In his analysis of the group relations between Chewas and Tumbukas in Zambia and Malawi, Posner shows that it is the size of a group that accounted for the rise of an ethnic cleavage in Malawi. In Malawi, both groups were large enough to be part of a potentially winning ethnic coalition and as a result have become political competitors. In Zambia, both groups are numerically insignificant; accordingly, no ethnic cleavage has emerged between them (Posner 2004).[8]

This is a first – and very general – indication that what matters for ethnic cleavages to emerge is the size and scope of the communities involved. Scholars who work on conflict resolution have arrived at more specific ideas of the effect of particular ethnic setups (Collier and Hoeffler 1998, 2004). Collier et al. (2001) distinguish between two types of ethnic fractionalization: "Dominance," a situation in which one group constitutes a majority, and "fractionalization," in which many smaller groups coexist. Basing their research on rational choice assumptions, they argue that in societies in which one group is dominant, the majority group has both the ability and the incentive to exploit other communities. In societies in which groups are fragmented, there is a lack of ethnic cohesion, which makes joint political action more cumbersome. Accordingly, a situation of "dominance" increases the conflict potential, whereas "fractionalization" makes societies safer.

The literature on ethnofederalism also regards political units with a higher degree of fractionalization to be less prone to ethnic antagonism. Hale (2000, 2004) examined the causes for state survival and collapse. His analysis finds that the presence of a core ethnic region makes state collapse more likely. A core ethnic region is defined as a region that either contains an outright majority of a particular community or in which a particular ethnic group makes up at least 20 percent more of the whole region's population than does the second largest group. The presence of one core ethnic region can contribute to ethnic conflict or secession due to a variety of factors. First, core ethnic regions have the potential to help organize a rival claim to sovereignty and are of sufficient scope to make any such challenge meaningful. Leaders of core regions might have allocation interests that are different from those of peripheral or other regions. Second, core ethnic regions can be perceived as threatening to smaller groups or regions, which undermines cooperation and thereby provokes conflict. Finally, and in conjunction with the preceding points, the existence of a core ethnic region makes the idea that the core ethnic groups can exist apart from, and independent of, the state more conceivable (Hewitt 1977, Hale 2004, 2000).

The few existing analyses on the consequences of a particular ethnic setup reveal a distinct preference for a high degree of ethnic fractionalization if political conflict is to be avoided. Even scholars who have not engaged in empirical research share this assumption (Temelli 1999). The sparse findings from the literature on ethnic conflict and ethnofederalism will, in the following, be tested in the context of political parties. For this purpose, I draw

[8] For a similar argument in Eastern Europe, see Stroschein 2011.

on the findings of the literature outlined in this section. I construct two possible scenarios: balancing and bandwagoning. In the former scenario, ethnic groups try to counterbalance each other and political competition remains structured around ethnic cleavage lines. In these societies, ethnic parties prevail. In the latter scenario, ethnic groups try to cooperate. Politics is, in this model, not structured around ethnic cleavages. Nonethnic parties prevail. A priori, nothing indicates which of the two will be the prevailing strategy.

Scenario 1: Balancing

This scenario is derived from some of the commonly held assumptions in the literature. In states where core ethnic groups – defined as groups that contain either an outright majority of the population or a group that makes up at least 20 percent more of the country's population than the second largest group (Hale 2004) – exist, ethnicity exercises high salience in party politics. The same reasoning as in the debate about ethnofederalism applies: core ethnic groups have a powerful incentive to play on group solidarity because their numerical superiority in conjunction with ethnic unity would allow them to grasp power easily. This condition is particularly prevalent in cases where core ethnic groups suffer from economic grievances. Their numerical superiority further allows them to avoid any coordination problems. The closer a core ethnic group is to an outright majority, the smaller the amount of groups it will co-opt into its alliance. Numerically large groups will therefore organize either in mono-ethnic parties or in multiethnic alliances. Due to the numerical superiority of the core ethnic group, trust and the potential for cooperation between communities are undermined. The remaining smaller communities – or at least those that are not part of the multiethnic alliance led by the large group – will fear political dominance and form alliances with peer groups. Thus mono-ethnic and alliance parties will be dominant, with potentially destabilizing effects on democratic consolidation. By contrast, in societies that contain many small groups of similar sizes, group leaders will aim at the formation of parties including a maximum amount of groups, because one's own community will never be sufficiently large to secure access to political power. In short, in countries with a core ethnic group, communities form mono-ethnic parties or multiethnic alliances to counterbalance each other, or, in ethnically fractionalized societies, the structural conditions are more conducive to the rise of nonethnic parties.

Scenario 2: Bandwagoning

This scenario is unlikely to occur according to the literature. Due to their numerical superiority, core groups are aware that they can yield significant political power. Groups that are close to an outright majority are further aware that ethnic unity is difficult to achieve for practical reasons – such as logistics or political apathy. Given their significant size, the group will produce several leaders aspiring to the highest political office the country has to offer, which makes ethnic unity on election day improbable. This will have two consequences. The dominant group will probably be represented in all major parties, or at least in more than one. Consequently, its respective leaders will reach out to as many other communities as possible as they are aware of the potential strength of their intra-ethnic competitors (representatives from the same groups aiming for electoral victory). Their strategy of "reaching out" will be particularly poignant in societies in which numerous smaller communities share roughly the same size and influence. Thus leaders from the dominant group have a strong political incentive to seek inter-group cooperation. In addition, their dominant status generally facilitates cooperation with other groups more easily, as their inclusion in top leadership positions is ensured. Simultaneously, small communities will choose bandwagoning over balancing as the dominant strategy and seek cooperation with the core ethnic group. This might occur out of ulterior motives – if you cannot beat them, join them – or out of the fact that the core group has produced more than one leader, who offers co-optation into a potentially winning coalitions. If the latter is the case, it appears likely that peripheral groups will also divide themselves among several parties. Such a scenario appears most conducive to the formation of nonethnic parties. In short, in countries with a core group, smaller communities are likely to engage in a strategy of bandwagoning, which in turn fosters the formation of nonethnic parties.

Core Groups and Political Parties: Empirical Evidence

To measure the ethnic fractionalization of countries, I use a new database by Scarritt and Mozaffar (1999) that distinguishes between ethnic cleavages at the national, middle, and lower levels (Posner 2004). It acknowledges that not every ethnic cleavage is mirrored at the national level of politics and thus takes note of only those cleavages that matter more than others. Using the Scarritt and Mozaffar database for my three case studies, I recalculate the ethnic fractionalization index based on the Herfindahl concentration formula. The results of this calculation are displayed in Table 7.16.

Results evidence roughly the same degree of fractionalization in Ghana and Namibia. Kenya maintains a much higher degree of ethnic fractionalization. This is not surprising, as both Ghana and Namibia contain a core ethnic group – the Akan and the Ovambo communities, respectively. According to prevalent thinking in the literature, we could have expected the salience of ethnicity to be more prevalent in Ghana and Namibia.

However, the party classification exercise proves the opposite: in countries in which ethnic fragmentation is low and that contain a core ethnic group, ethnicity features less at the aggregate level of political parties than

TABLE 7.16. *Ethnic Fractionalization Index Based on Scarritt and Mozaffar*

Country	Fractionalization of National Cleavage Lines
Kenya	.85
Namibia	.62
Ghana	.63

Source: Author's own compilation.

in countries that display a high ethnic fractionalization index. Thus, scenario 2 has been confirmed. Contrary to commonly held assumptions, balancing against the largest group does not take place in Ghana or Namibia. Neither does the respective largest group exclude others politically, even though in the Namibian case, the largest group is disadvantaged in terms of economic well-being. Instead, both the Akan and the Ovambo communities have forged sustainable political alliances across the dominant ethnic cleavages of their respective countries. As predicted in scenario 2, all significant and effective parties are either led by or include representatives of the core ethnic group.

Accordingly, ethnic unity among the core group is not sustainable. As a result, in more homogeneous African societies, the threshold for forming nonethnic parties is lowered significantly. By contrast, in countries that lack an ethnic core and that are less homogeneous, there is generally a higher sense of uncertainty over who might lay claim to power. This uncertainty – combined with the smaller size of groups – poses an imperative for groups to seek unity. This increases the threshold for the formation of nonethnic parties.

This corresponds to the empirical reality also found in the individual cases. The political history of the three countries shows that in Ghana, historically, ethnic parties were only of a temporary nature: in the 1950s, a variety of mono-ethnic parties existed – such as the Northern People's Party or the NLM (Apter 1955, Austin 1964) – all of which failed to become sustainable political forces. The same is true of party politics in the early Second Republic, when voting behavior displayed great divisions between the Ashanti and the Ewe and political campaigning had ethnic undertones. At the beginning of the Fourth Republic, ethnicity also featured briefly. Yet ethnicity has proven to be neither a winning strategy nor an enduring feature of party politics. The same is true in Namibia, even though the ethnically based opposition endured much longer. This shows that in less fractionalized states, ethnic parties feature, albeit only temporarily. The experiences of Ghana's First and Fourth Republics – as well as the all-embracing victories of SWAPO after Namibian independence – are very likely to have instilled some degree of political learning among politicians that ethnic parties rarely yield political victory. Ethnic parties are thus unattractive in these kinds of contexts if the goal is to seek power.

By contrast, in Kenya, post-independence politics had, from its inception, strong ethnic undercurrents, even during the period of the one-party state (Widner 1992, Throup and Hornsby 1998). After the return of multiparty politics, it was the ability of politicians to provide a sizable ethnic vote share that made them attractive for political mergers: Raila Odinga's ability to bring in his Luo vote share made him attractive to both the New KANU and the NARC. The same is true of Ngilu's Kamba support and Wamalwa's Luhya backing. Musyoka's support of the Kamba in 2007 – and Uhuru Kenyatta's potential to become the next Kikuyu leader – have recently made them the most promising contenders for the next Kenyan presidency, together with William Ruto (Kalenjin) and Raila Odinga (Luo). The political uncertainty that a highly fractionalized society produces explains the constant appeals of Kenyan politicians to their group members to provide a strong ethnic front.

Nonethnic parties only emerged briefly (and were unsustainable) in the run-up to the 2002 elections, when Kenya's largest ethnic group was divided between two presidential aspirants. This shows that the logic of our second scenario can temporarily feature in societies in which ethnic fragmentation is low. However, sooner or later, balancing will eventually eclipse bandwagoning.

VERIFICATION OF HYPOTHESIS WITH PRELIMINARY CASES

The analysis of the causes of variation between countries has discussed a number of variables the literature regards as crucial in affecting the formation of party types. At the outset, no key explanatory variable could be isolated due to the lack of systematic research on parties in ethnically segmented societies.

I identified the ethnic setup of countries to account for the rise of a particular party type in ethnically segmented societies. This finding is confirmed over time, as a review of political parties in the post-independence period has shown. Thus countries without a core ethnic group and a high ethnic fractionalization index appear to be conducive to the formation of ethnic parties. Countries lacking a core ethnic group and whose ethnic fractionalization index is low appear to be conducive to the formation of nonethnic parties. By virtue of the limited number of in-depth cases, this study cannot arrive at a theory of ethnic party formation; however, it can make an initial contribution of which factors a theory of ethnic party formation ought to take into consideration. The preliminary analysis of the seven additional cases enable a provisional analysis if the alleged relationship between party type and ethnic structure is robust.

TABLE 7.17. *Party Types and Ethnic Structure in 10 African Countries*

Country	Ethnic Fractionalization Index (Scarritt and Mozaffar 1999)	Party Type Assumed to Be dominant	Party Type Actually Dominant	Verification of Hypothesis
In-depth cases				
Kenya	0.85	ethnic		hypothesis-generating case
Namibia	0.62	nonethnic		
Ghana	0.63	nonethnic		
Preliminary cases: Nonethnic Party Systems				
Botswana	0.34	nonethnic	nonethnic	confirmed
Senegal	0.18	nonethnic	nonethnic	confirmed
Burkina Faso	0	nonethnic	nonethnic	confirmed
Preliminary Cases: Mixed-Party Systems				
Zambia	0.73	ethnic	mixed	partially confirmed
Malawi	0.62 (no ethnic core group)	nonethnic	mixed but less ethnic over time	confirmed
Tanzania	0.94 (no ethnic core group)	ethnic	largely nonethnic over time	not confirmed
Preliminary Cases: Ethnic Party Systems				
Benin	0.21 (based on 2002 census)	ethnic	ethnic	confirmed

Source: Author's Compilation.

The examination of the variation between countries used Scarritt and Mozaffar's (1999) dataset on ethnic cleavages and ethnopolitical groups to determine the ethnic structure of a country. The dataset focuses on ethnic cleavages that occur at the national level. Table 7.17 summarizes the findings from the classification of parties in the 10 countries under scrutiny. Using data from the Scarrit and Mozaffar database, it examines in which cases the hypothesized relationship between the ethnic structure of a country and the formation of a particular party type is confirmed and in which cases it is falsified.

Botswana (Tsawana 80 percent), Senegal (Wolof 82 percent), and Burkina Faso (Mossi 50 percent) all have ethnic core groups; their ethnic fractionalization index is below the fractionalization index of Ghana and Namibia. Therefore, I expect nonethnic parties to prevail. This is the case in all three countries. Neither in Botswana nor in Senegal nor in Burkina Faso does ethnicity affect party competition at the national level. Preliminary cases with a nonethnic party system, that is, cases in which all political parties were nonethnic parties, confirm the findings from the in-depth cases.

Results from the three mixed-party systems provide a more ambivalent picture. The first case, Zambia, does not have an ethnic core group, and its fractionalization index is higher than in Ghana and Namibia. I therefore expect ethnic parties to dominate party politics. As the analysis of a selection of Zambian parties has shown, this is only partially the case. Zambia's governing party, the MMD, is a catch-all party; among the numerous opposition parties, ethnic parties (the PF and the UPND) and nonethnic parties (the ZDC and the PF) can be found. However, Zambia also shows that the saliency of ethnicity does not decrease over time. Although nonethnic parties carry more political weight, ethnicity has continued to exercise political salience.

The fractionalization index of Malawi resembles the indexes of Ghana and Namibia. The dominant ethnic cleavage lines run between the country's Southern (51 percent), Central (41 percent), and Northern (8 percent) communities. Thus one numerically dominant group exists, which however cannot be seen as a core ethnic group.[9] Due to the low fractionalization index and the existence of a numerically dominant group, I expect nonethnic parties to form. Although for a long time the Malawian party system was characterized by both ethnic and non-ethnic parties, in the long run, nonethnic parties become prevalent. Therefore, the Malawian case confirms the hypothesized outcome.

Tanzania has neither a core ethnic group nor a numerically superior group. The fractionalization index calculated by Scarritt and Mozaffar (1999) is misleading. Scarrit and Mozaffar used the division between mainland Tanzania and the Zanzibar communities as the dominant national ethnic cleavage. My analysis has included the divisions between the numerous communities on the mainland. Calculating the Herfindahl concentration index on the assumption that numerous potentially dominant ethnic cleavage lines exist on the mainland, I arrive at a Herfindahl concentration index of 0.94, which indicates a very fragmented society. Accordingly, I expect ethnic parties to dominate party competition. Tanzania is the first case that refutes the assumption that a high fractionalization index is conducive to the formation of ethnic parties. Tanzania has a mixed-party system, and yet its nonethnic component (the CCM) clearly dominates the political scene. This might be due to context factors. First, in contrast to Kenya, the Tanzanian one-party state did not discriminate against specific communities. Second, the CMM initiated the return to multiparty democracy, whereas its counterpart KANU for the longest time resisted any kind of change. Be that as it

[9] As outlined earlier, a core ethnic group is a group that constitutes 50 percent and is at least 20 percent larger than the second largest group.

may, the case of Tanzania shows that the alleged correlation between a high fractionalization index and ethnic parties does not always apply.

Benin is the only preliminary case with an ethnic party system in place. Relying on numerous anthropological sources from the 1990s and previous periods, Scarrit and Mozaffar (1999) estimated that 55 percent of the population belongs to the Fon. Various Benin experts have taken issue with this number and argued that the Fon community does not represent more than 25 percent of the population (Battle and Seely 2007, Ferree 2010). The most recent national census undertaken in 2002 (Republic du Benin 2002) confirms these views. The ethnic breakdown provided by the census shows that Benin does not have an ethnic core group. Accordingly, the Fon constitute 39 percent, the Adja 16 percent, the Bariba 9 percent, and the Peul 7 percent of the population. Calculating the ethnic fractionalization at the national level with the help of the 2002 Benin census (Republic du Benin 2002), I end up with an ethnic fractionalization score of 0.80. The ethnic fractionalization score of Benin thus greatly resembles the fractionalization index of Kenya. Accordingly, I expect ethnic parties to dominate, which is the case. As in Kenya, parties have increased their outreach and turned into multiethnic alliances. However, as in Kenya, nonethnic parties are still to emerge.

I find in 8 of 10 countries a straightforward relationship between the ethnic composition of a country and the political salience of ethnicity. A high ethnic fractionalization index fosters ethnic parties, whereas a low fractionalization leads to the prevalence of nonethnic parties. In two countries, this relationship is not straightforward or falsified. On the basis of Zambia's ethnic structure, I expected Zambian politics to be dominated by ethnic parties. This is not the case, as ethnic and nonethnic parties coexist. Tanzania corresponds even less to the alleged relationship between ethnic structure and party type in place.

The empirical evidence provided by the additional cases suggests that the ethnic setup has at least some effect on the type of party in place. However, the extent to which ethnicity exercises political salience clearly must not be reduced to a mono-causal relationship. Context-specific factors are likely to play an important role in the extent to which ethnicity becomes politicized. In the case of Tanzania, it is likely that the heritage of the one-party state still matters for the dynamics of party competition. In contrast to Kenya, the CCM not only adjusted to the political liberalization process of the early 1990, but also brought this process about. Finally, it should be stressed that the robustness test of the hypothesis has been conducted with the help of preliminary cases. The outcome of this exercise should be regarded as such. Future research should start by providing an in-depth analysis of the seven additional cases to see which causal paths can explain the formation of party types.

TOWARD A THEORY OF THE FORMATION OF ETHNIC PARTIES

Drawing on findings from the application of the amended Diamond and Gunther typology to 10 countries, this chapter analyzed the explanatory power of a variety of variables that the literature regards as important in accounting for the formation of party types. Table 7.18 outlines these variables and their respective impact on party formation in the three in-depth cases. Economic growth at the national level, economic inequality at the regional level, the electoral system, democratic quality, and the party system cannot explain why nonethnic parties have formed.

There are doubts about the impact of ethnic party bans on the formation and types of parties, because ethnic parties have featured in Ghana and Namibia for a considerable period of time, even though party bans have been in place since both countries' independence. The salience of ethnicity at the starting point of African party politics corresponds to the salience of ethnicity in the contemporary period. However, the dynamics of party politics in the nationalist period cannot on their own explain why ethnicity carries more weight in Kenyan than in Ghanaian or Namibian politics.

The three in-depth cases indicated that the ethnic structure of a country might provide the missing causal link. Although the related literature on conflict resolution and ethnofederalism predicts ethnic conflict to be prevalent in countries that display a high degree of ethnic fractionalization, I initially found the opposite to be true with regard to the prevalence of ethnic parties: in countries in which ethnic core groups exist and in which ethnic fragmentation is low, ethnicity exercises a lower degree of political salience. Instead of fostering ethnic exclusion, core groups are internally divided among several parties, which provides smaller groups with an incentive to bandwagon with them rather than to try and balance against them. Evidence from the preliminary cases, however, only partially confirmed this finding. In 8 of 10 countries the finding is confirmed, in 1 case it is partially confirmed, and in 1 case the alleged relationship between the ethnic structure of a country and the party type in place is refuted.

This chapter arrived at a first contribution of which variables a future theory of ethnic party formation should take into account. More in-depth research is necessary to establish robust inferences about the joint impact of several variables. The three in-depth cases, for example, suggest that the historical pathways of countries should be considered. The same is true for country-specific variables. Due to the limitation of this study to a small number of cases, all this chapter could do was identify variables that future explanatory studies should take into consideration. This shortcoming notwithstanding, this chapter at least enables a more theory-driven approach to the future study of ethnic and nonethnic parties.

TABLE 7.18. *Summary of the Dependent and Independent Variables*

Country	Dependent Variable	Economic Performance	Economic Inequalities Between Groups	Electoral System	Democratic Quality	Ethnic Party Bans	Independence Movement	Social Structure
Kenya	dominance of ethnic patties	GDP pc: USD 499 Growth: 2.8%	stark	FPTP	low to medium	no law	divided	core ethnic group
Ghana	dominance of non-ethnic parties	GDP pc: USD 430 Growth: 3.9%	stark	FPTP	low to medium to high	law	united	core ethnic group
Namibia	dominance of non-ethnic parties	GDP pc: USD 2219 Growth: 4.2%	stark	PR	High	law	united	core ethnic group

Source: Author's own compilation.

Conclusion

Political Parties in Africa

THE EMERGENCE OF NONETHNIC POLITICS

African independence did not produce viable democratic states. From the early to mid-1960s, African nations underwent a rapid transformation to various forms of autocratic rule. Then, against the economic odds, multiparty democracy made a stunning and unpredicted comeback. Since the early 1990s, multiparty democracy has become the norm in many African countries. Nevertheless, there has been little conceptual and no comparative work on African parties or, indeed, parties in nonindustrialized democracies. Due to the silence on African parties, the scholarly community has missed the entry point to research how nonindustrialized countries democratize. The neglect of the study of individual African parties served as the point of departure for this study. The findings of this book shatter dominant assumptions about party politics in ethnically segmented societies. Ethnic parties are neither inevitable nor ubiquitous. The African landscape is more diverse than conventionally assumed.

After a concise review of the major argument, the present chapter elaborates on the democratization potential of African parties. Parties are the inevitable byproduct of democratization, yet the reverse relationship is rarely, if ever, analyzed. Only a few works exist. All highlight the deficiencies of African parties amid democratic consolidation. These studies frame their evaluations in terms of the European mass party of the 1960s. The European mass party, however, has outlived itself both in Europe and elsewhere. Comparative politics scholars have failed to propose alternative normative criteria by which the democratization potential of parties can be evaluated. Due to the lack of alternative criteria, I deliberately highlight the positive effects of African parties on democratization. A systematic analysis of parties is labor-intensive, and accordingly, the scope of this study is confined to a few cases. Accordingly, the findings of this book call for more comparisons between African parties, but also for future comparisons with parties elsewhere. Scholars interested in other regions of the globe can take the operationalization of the Diamond and Gunther (2001) typology as a starting point for the comparisons of parties in their region of interest. The final part of the conclusion outlines some basic insights that international aid practitioners can draw from this study.

AFRICAN POLITICAL PARTIES: THE MAIN ARGUMENT

For a long time, political science had very little to say about the nature of African parties. Parties were alleged to be ethnic parties and, as such, taken to be detrimental to democratic consolidation (Bratton and van de Walle 1997, Kaplan 1997, Horowitz 2000). In recent years, more scholars have dedicated greater attention to parties outside the Western world. Conceptual work, however, remained absent. Diamond and Gunther (2001) advanced the only party typology suitable for examining parties outside established democracies. Although the typology has not been applied empirically, the comparative political science literature offers numerous indicators of how the typology can be put to work. The operationalization of the typology offers two opportunities. First, it allows systematic comparisons of African parties. This step forms the major scholarly thrust of the present volume. Second, the typology makes African parties comparable to parties in other nonindustrialized countries. The analytical value of the typology in other regions must yet be examined by scholars who wish to build on the present work, which aims to provide some structure for the future debate about party types in nonindustrialized societies and as such serve as a comparative tool for the comparative politics literature.

The results from the application of the Diamond and Gunther typology to three African countries – Kenya, Ghana, and Namibia – proved the African landscape to be considerably more diverse than dominant conceptions of African political competition concede. That is, there is much more to the story than ethnic parties. To be sure, in Africa's multiparty systems, ethnic parties undoubtedly exist. The empirical evidence from Kenya shows ethnic parties to be ubiquitous in some countries. In line with the predications of Horowitz's (2000) seminal study, *Ethnic Groups in Conflict*, ethnic parties aggravate communal tensions and are conducive to electoral violence. The extremely violent 1992, 1997, and 2007 Kenyan elections vividly bore out this expectation. However, the empirical evidence gathered in this book indicates these dynamics to be the exception, not the rule.

In Namibia and Ghana, nonethnic parties clearly prevail. The coexistence of ethnic parties does not lead to the disintegration of nonethnic parties. Namibia's incumbent party, SWAPO, is the prototype of an African catch-all party. For some time, Namibia's official opposition, the DTA, was a multiethnic alliance. Namibia's catch-all party did not disintegrate in the face of an ethnic opposition; it endured over time. It was Namibia's ethnic opposition party that was replaced by a nonethnic party, the CoD.

In Ghana's two-party system, ethnic parties are almost completely absent. Only right after the inception of party competition did the NPP constitute a multiethnic alliance. It soon transformed into a programmatic party. Once in government, the NPP changed its type to a catch-all party. Its opponent, the NDC, started out as a personalistic party that in opposition turned into a catch-all party with visible programmatic undercurrents. Ghana and Namibia both illustrate that over time, multiparty competition makes party politics less ethnic. Nonethnic parties not only feature but also become more frequent over time. In Ghana's and Namibia's mixed-party systems, the presence of ethnic parties and state stability are congruent outcomes and must not be treated as opposites. Ongoing multiparty competition in ethnically segmented societies therefore does not lead to ethnic polarization; rather, it causes parties to widen their social base. These dynamics are also visible in Kenya, where after an initial period of party fragmentation, mono-ethnic parties transformed into multiethnic alliances. Nonethnic parties, however, failed to materialize.

These vexing results called for verification with the help of additional cases. On the basis of the empirical application of the party typology to three countries, I identified a selection of indicators with sufficient discriminatory power to ensure an accurate but less labor-intense classification of party types. A smaller number of indicators were subsequently applied to 25 politically significant parties in 7 additional countries: Tanzania, Botswana, Senegal, Burkina Faso, Malawi, Zambia, and Benin. The classification of these 25 additional parties generated preliminary evidence that verified findings from the in-depth analysis of parties in Kenya, Namibia, and Ghana.

Again, the findings show that ethnic parties do not dominate African politics. Among the additional cases, there is no country in which multiparty democracy leads to a hardening of ethnic relations, that is, an increase in the number of ethnic parties. Enduring multiparty competition either leads to an increase of nonethnic parties or to enduring peaceful coexistence between ethnic and nonethnic parties.

In the literature, the formation of ethnic parties is frequently blamed on the lack of industrial revolutions and the ethnic diversity of nations. This proposition no longer holds, because in some countries, ethnic parties dominate, whereas in others, nonethnic parties have become the norm. This study has sought to identify variables that might explain why ethnic parties form. Surprisingly, economic differences between groups and regions do not account for the formation of communal-based parties. Equally, the electoral system and the existence of ethnic party bans have no impact on the political salience of ethnicity. Instead, the existence of a core ethnic group correlates with the existence of nonethnic parties, whereas the lack of a core ethnic group is conducive to the formation of ethnic parties. In countries with a core ethnic group, communities engage in a political strategy of bandwagoning with the core group. In countries without a core ethnic group, communities balance against each other. These phenomena persist over time. The salience of ethnicity in contemporary multiparty politics corresponds to the salience of ethnicity in the period of the immediate pre- and post-independence era.

The seven additional cases by and large confirmed the hypothesized relationship between ethnic structure and dominant party type. Parties in Tanzania, however, clearly do not correspond to this logic. Thus the explanatory part of this study did not arrive at definite results, which is not surprising given the small number of cases at hand. Purely structuralist explanations, rarely, if ever, hold (Kitschelt 1993, 1994). Future explanatory research should focus on the ethnic structure of countries and examine its interplay with other variables. These studies should pay greater attention to agency variables, such as how ethnic relations were handled in the aftermath of independence. There were critical junctures that often set countries on a particular political path. The discussion of Tanzania indicates that the amicable communal relationships that characterize Tanzanian politics (with the exception of Zanzibar) have their origins in the manner in which the one-party state managed ethnic relations after independence.

Overall, this book argues that although many things in Africa are not right, not everything is going wrong. Artificially created, ethnically diverse states are capable of producing political contests that represent more than ethnic census. With the exception of Kenya, ethnicity actually matters rather little in day-to-day political life. Parties instead highlight shortcomings in the consolidation of democracy, stress government involvement in corruption affairs, and are keen on improving health care, education, and infrastructure. Hence, I argue that the democratization potential of African parties might often be frowned upon, but it is hardly ever evaluated vis-á-vis the political reality of the African predicament.

AFRICAN PARTIES AND DEMOCRATIC CONSOLIDATION

This study started out by outlining the potentially detrimental effect of ethnic parties on democratic consolidation. The empirical analysis of parties and the outcome of that analysis warrant a few remarks on the relationship between African parties and the democratic project. Although parties are the inevitable byproduct of democratization, the effect of parties on democratization is rarely examined (van Biezen 2004). Whenever the democratization potential of individual parties is analyzed, the European mass party of the post-1945 period serves as the standard normative yardstick (van Biezen 2003, Mair 2005). As outlined in Chapter Two, the European mass-based parties enjoyed large-scale and active party membership. They represented a clearly defined segment of the population and entertained organizational linkages with numerous interest groups. At the heart of policy formulation were clearly formulated ideological beliefs that mass parties promoted among their members. They were highly organized and institutionalized entities with firm roots in society. In short, mass parties represented citizens, educated citizens, and aggregated citizens' opinions. Contemporary scholars are overly pessimistic about whether parties in new democracies can emulate the basic functions of mass parties (Bratton and van de Walle 1997, Diamond and Gunther 2001, Randall and Svasand 2002, van Biezen 2004, Webb and White 2007, Manning 2008).

Taking the mass-based party as blueprint for the democratization potential of parties is highly problematic. As Chapter Two demonstrated, even Western parties have failed to live up to its ideals. Party membership has been in perennial decline, as have the ideological roots of parties. More than ever, European parties focus on the party's candidate(s) rather than their convictions once elections are approaching. Parties are more inclined to take a political stance on the basis of focus group discussions rather than their members. Politics has become professionalized; it is no longer the domain of "the people." New means of communications, in particular, television and the internet, have further marginalized the organizational backbone of parties. Ties with auxiliary organizations have been loosened to remain less committed to a particular cause of action, as a certain imprecision tends to suit a wider swath of voters. The major goal of parties is no longer to include citizens in the political process or to educate their members in the art of political persuasion, but to maximize votes. As a result, Western parties are no longer well institutionalized, no longer preside over deep roots in society, and are no longer the home of distinguishable political beliefs (Diamond and Gunther 2001, Gunther et al. 2002, van Biezen 2003, 2004, Mair 2005; for the same lament about American parties, see Wattenberg 1998). In sum, in the West: "Parties are not what they once were" (Schmitter 2001: 76).

The replacement of mass parties by catch-all and/or cadre parties has bereft them of their representative and integrative functions. Even the European left, in previous decades the homestead of the much-adored mass party, has become Americanized (for many European scholars, the ultimate failure) and dissolved into catch-all entities (Lipset 2001b, Puhle 2002, van Biezen 2003, 2004, Mair 2005, Satori 2005a). The emergence of new actors, in particular new social movements, and a visible antiparty attitude in many democracies were the consequences (Diamond and Gunther 2001, Mair 2005). Apathy and rising nonparticipation in party politics have created a "democracy without the demos" (Mair 2005: 24). The intellectual blueprint of the democratization potential is thus not only deeply Eurocentric, it has also become somewhat irrelevant in the region from which it derived.

As such, new criteria are required for the assessment of the potential of African parties to foster democratization. The following considerations are drawn from the empirical finding of this study and, as such, are tentative.

First and in the most general sense, in Africa, ethnic parties feature much less prominently than scholars have predicted. With regard to Africa's catch-all, programmatic, and personalistic parties, we can thus say that their integration potential, however weak it might be, is higher than the integration potential that is conventionally allocated to African parties. From a strictly empirical point, political integration in Africa is less concerned with the integration of large and clearly defined segments of the population. Instead, it relates to the ability of the party to reflect the multiethnic composition of the African state. Parties do not provide this representation function by incorporating "the people" at large, but by incorporating powerful individuals from the major communities that make up the state. A large number of parties fulfills this "integrative function" and thus contributes positively to nation-building.

Second, the comparative political science literature traditionally regards the ability of parties to aggregate interests and passions as essential (Schmitter 2001). Scholars working on African parties frequently criticize that parties fail to provide the aggregation function.

All parties in my sample engage in a political discourse in which programmatic ideas either do not feature or feature rarely. This is a major reason why scholars regard the democratization potential of African parties to be low (Bratton and van de Walle 1997, Randall and Svasand 2002, Manning 2008). Ghana has proven to be an exception, but even in Ghana, programmatic ideas do not dominate the political debate. To what extent the lack of programmatic ideas might be "bad" for democratization is puzzling to anyone who ever had the privilege to gain a first-hand experience of the economic challenges that African nations are facing. The ideologies of the post-1945 European world simply matter less (if they ever mattered at all), just as they were found to matter rather little in the Southern European democracies that emerged in the post-1974 period (Schmitter 2001). The African electorate can *ex ante* reasonably be expected to be first and foremost interested in better roads, better schools, health care, and sustainable economic growth. The willingness of parties to aggregate their citizens' aspirations cannot be denied. The empirical chapters have clearly shown that these ideas shape African party politics. African parties dedicate significant efforts in communicating these interests to their citizens. Starting from a more modest, and indeed more realistic basis, I argue that parties in Africa do aggregate the interests of their citizens.

Third, although parties derive their legitimacy from their representative functions (Sartori 2005b), their ability to structure electoral competition remains their primary function, especially in young democracies, where consolidation has not yet occurred (Schmitter 2001). The empirical chapters have shown that African party politics is dominated by powerful individuals, not by ordinary party members. Informal elite arrangements are the key to becoming the leader of a party. Some examples in this book include the formation of NEW KANU under Moi, the nomination of Uhuru Kenyatta as Moi's successor in Kenya, the nomination of John Atta Mills as Rawlings' successor in Ghana, and the presidential nomination process inside SWAPO in Namibia. Nomination procedures in opposition parties are no less contentious. In many instances, especially among multiethnic alliances, nomination contests cause splits and breakaways. The lack of truly democratic nomination procedures does not take away from the fact that electoral structuration takes place in Africa. African parties provide their electorates with a choice between alternative sets of leaders. They structure the electoral process by nominating candidates for office at regular intervals and as such clearly fulfill a key aspect of democratization.

Fourth, although only one of three in-depth cases is dominated by ethnic parties, no robust claim can be made about the relationship between ethnic party systems and democratic consolidation. The findings at least indicate an ambivalent role of ethnic parties in the process of democratic consolidation. The in-depth analysis of ethnic parties in Kenya shows that ethnic parties aggravate already communal tension, they make the formation of nonethnic parties impossible, and they make ethnic violence around election time likely. Ethnic parties in numerous other countries – in particular, in countries where ethnic parties coexist with much stronger nonethnic parties – do not follow these dynamics. Similarly, there are no indications that the ubiquity of ethnic parties in Benin, for example, stands in the way of democratic consolidation. As stated previously, this finding necessitates further in-depth research into countries where ethnic parties are prevalent. More detailed research must verify whether ethnic parties are really that much more detrimental to democratization than other party types (see also Ishiyama and Breuning 2011).

All of the preceding are tentative considerations deliberately highlighting the democratization potential of African parties – which the previous literature denies outright. The spread of multiparty democracy to hitherto autocratic polities calls for more innovative criteria of the democratization potential of parties. The stringent and outdated normative assumptions, derived from the European mass party, are no longer obtainable, either outside and inside the Western world. In the past, empirical research on parties has developed largely in isolation from normative research on democratization theory, which accounts for the lack of suitable criteria that a party has to fulfill to be seen as conducive to democratization (van Biezen 2005). Research on political parties therefore requires a new and more global agenda.

FUTURE RESEARCH ON (AFRICAN) PARTIES

The findings of this book raise provocative new questions about the role of ethnicity in Africa and other nonindustrialized societies. Given the small sample of countries, the major claim of this study is simply that African party politics is more diverse than assumed. As a consequence, African parties deserve closer and more systematic attention. Future research should take the Diamond and Gunther typology as a point of departure and analyze parties in other parts of the continent in greater depth and scope. The analytical tools in the hands of comparative political science research are suitable for the examination of African party politics. They should be employed across the continent.

Future studies on African parties should ask critical questions about the prevalence of ethnic parties in Africa and under which conditions they form. Related to this question are the implications of ethnic parties for stability and peace. A growing literature indicates that ethnic parties should not be equated with ethnic conflict, let alone ethnic violence (Newman 1996, Ishiyama and Breuning 1998, Chandra 2005, Birnir 2007, Ishiyama 2009, Basedau 2011, Ishiyama and Breuning 2011). This book has put forward a framework that allows studies to examine the ambivalent relationship between ethnicity and democracy in Africa. After all, the lacuna of research on the role of ethnic parties also reflects the absence of what constitutes an ethnic party. Thus far, no scholarly agreement exists regarding when a party qualifies as ethnic (Elischer 2008, Chandra 2011).

The ambivalent role of ethnic parties leads to the broader issue of the relationship between party types and their respective democratization potential. As argued earlier, the "mass party paradigm" is ill-suited for the assessment of democratic potential parties. There is a dire need to establish criteria by which African parties can be assessed in a more realistic manner. Such analysis can only be achieved with a much higher number of observations.

In addition, the Diamond and Gunther typology offers the opportunity to structure research on political parties in other post–third wave areas. Scholars can build on the operationalization of this work. They will most likely add and subtract some of the indicators suggested in this book. Whether they make the same choices is their decision and will be largely determined from the quality of data that can be extracted from their respective region of interest. Working with the universal typology of Diamond and Gunther, however, provides the only way to analyze parties around the world in a systematic and cumulative manner. Cross-regional comparisons of political parties have never been undertaken. Comparisons between regions generally are rare, especially when it comes to comparisons between Africa and other areas of the globe (for a notable exception, see Beissinger and Young 2002). Working with a global party typology could advance significantly the comparative politics research agenda. It holds the potential to shed new light on the political dynamics in ethnically segmented societies.

The application of a global typology to different world regions will unleash greater cooperation between area studies and disciplinary political science. The democratization of the "global South" has caused many scholars to search for a synthesis of the imperative to examine regional particularities and the imperative to contribute to theory formulation (Bates 1997, Katzenstein 2001, Basedau and Köllner 2007, Graham and Kantor 2007, Ahram 2011). Small-n comparisons are in the best position to advance a research agenda that fulfills both imperatives. Comparing countries at the meso-level offers the possibility of incorporating incremental changes to the typology that the political particularities of any world region might require. In this manner, important patterns of the political heterogeneity of regions can be highlighted and incorporated at the same time.

STRANGE BEDFELLOWS: ACADEMIC RESEARCH AND INTERNATIONAL PARTY ASSISTANCE

International party research and international party assistance both have been under the normative shadow of the mass party. For comparative researchers, the mass party represents an outdated entity. For aid practitioners, the mass party represents an intellectual blueprint. Carothers (2006) *Confronting the Weakest Link* was the first study to openly identify the strong effect of the so-called "mythic party model" on international party aid. The mythic model is the idealized version of the European mass party, that is, a party that is internally democratic, transparent in its financial dealings, managed in a nonpersonalistic fashion, highly inclusive of minorities, ideologically coherent and committed to its grassroots (Carothers 2006: 123).

The heavily Eurocentric approach is surprising for at least two reasons. First, it is striking that American party foundations – the National Democratic Institute and the International Republican Institute – have designed programs geared toward the creation of a European party type. The evolution of political parties in the United States shows vividly that the European mass party is not a requirement for democratic consolidation (see Epstein 1980, Carothers 2006). Second, as Chapter Two has shown in greater depth, very little is known in the academic community about non–Western parties.

It appears puzzling that the research departments of aid agencies themselves have not become drivers of change in party research. After all, they have the privilege of engaging with non-Western parties on a regular basis. Of course, research and aid programming follow different imperatives. Academic research requires in-depth and long-term occupation with a particular outcome of interest. By contrast, the work environment of international aid agencies is characterized by frequently shifting priorities, high staff turnover, and little regional expertise. Much of the nitty-gritty work on the ground is done by consultants, whose local expertise is limited (Kumar 2004). Insufficiently contextualized strategies and a lack of methodological effectiveness have given rise to phrases such as "party assistance tourism" and "management by helicopter" by frustrated practitioners.

The weaknesses of international party aid have been widely noted. Numerous scholars have argued that those engaged in party assistance ought to pay more attention to political party research to identify better the needs of parties in individual countries (see, e.g., Kumar 2004, Caton 2007, Burnell and Gerrits 2010, Erdmann 2010). This book has contributed new insights into the nature of parties on which the donor community can draw. First, the Diamond and Gunther typology itself can become a useful tool for in-depth research into potential future recipient parties. The typology allows for systematic and comparative research of those aspects of party life that are at the heart of the donor agenda. The typology facilitates research on the role of ethnicity, parties' willingness to be inclusive of minorities, parties' dedication to politically salient issues (whether programmatic or not), and parties' relationship with one another. If donor agencies want to "go deeper" (Carothers 2006: 213), they must know more about the nature of non-Western parties. The Diamond and Gunther typology enables the kind of in-depth research on which international party assistance can draw.

Second, the results from this study indicate that ethnic party bans are highly inefficient. An examination of the effect of ethnic party bans on party formation in Ghana and Namibia revealed that these bans have little to no impact. Party laws prescribe the existence of party offices and members in a certain number of administrative units or party bodies. Of course, the construction of offices around the country does not mean that these offices reach out to the communities residing nearby, although that link is frequently insinuated and, indeed, hoped for. Any observer of African politics will note that party offices frequently fulfill a variety of functions unrelated to political life: they are converted to hair salons, shops, or other economic activities that require a building. In other instances, offices are empty or dilapidated, and their main purpose is to fulfill party registration requirements on paper. It does not come as a surprise that ethnic parties continue to feature on the African landscape. As shown in the introduction, all African governments have implemented such bans with great rigor. On the basis of the findings of this book, there are doubts regarding to what extent party bans can create nonethnic parties.

Third, aid programming ought to take note of the existence of numerous catch-all parties in Africa. The catch-all party type stands in a positive relationship with democratic consolidation. Instead of fostering an ideological agenda, the donor community could actively strive to create catch-all parties. As shown, many African parties transform into catch-all parties over time. Donor agencies could help parties to increase their social base by prescribing the corporation of individuals from all major ethnic communities into the highest decision-making body of the party. The inclusion of popular leaders takes notice of the fact that party politics in Africa is leadership-driven – more so than in other parts of the globe.

Two criticisms will be imminent. First, the imposition of such strict criteria constitutes a direct infringement on intra-party decisions and thus an infringement of their democratic rights. Second, the only side effect will be "ethnic window-dressing": members from specific communities become part of the party's leadership, yet their actual influence will be very limited. Both criticisms have merit and cannot be rejected completely or out of hand. To force parties to provide a national leadership is a democratic infringement. The danger of "alibi leaders" certainly looms large in a patrimonial system. In most cases, the formation of a national leadership will be facilitated by informal deals among the strongmen of the party and the representatives of the community where the party underperforms – representation on paper in exchange for personal favors. This scenario cannot be ruled out. The effects of party laws, however, are contingent on how competing parties make use of this criterion. If one or several parties genuinely try to increase their performance with the help of community members who are underrepresented in the party, pressure will increase on the party system as a whole to become more nationalized. Genuine reforms ideally will take place inside the governing party. The prerequisite to open party offices in a selection of districts has clearly failed to have a lasting impact, and there is no reason why an alternative approach should not be tested.

Fourth, the requirement to engage more thoroughly and more systematically with the empirical reality on the ground should lead to more lenient criteria with regard to the selection of partners. Frequently, only parties with a nationwide presence qualify for external aid (Norris 2005, Caton 2007). However, as we have seen, ethnic parties frequently strive to become nationwide parties, yet simply lack the resources to move beyond their traditional stronghold. If ethnic parties are dedicated to follow constitutional norms and are not driven by cultural irredentism, there is no reason not to incorporate them. In reality, Western party organizations have long cooperated with ethnic parties.[1] There is no reason, therefore, why ethnic or other particularistic parties should not be explicitly entitled to receive funding.

Finally, this study calls for more institutionalized cooperation between the academic world and party aid agencies. It calls for more than the odd and badly attended workshop or seminar. It should be driven by the joint commitment systematically to collect and share basic data on parties. The nascent literature on parties shows that systematic data on African parties are still hard to come by. Systematic work on African parties is still a very labor-intensive process. With their presence and decade-long experience in the respective recipient countries, party foundations hold the organizational capacity to collect data on the ground. Academic researchers could make use of these facilities and generate these data, including membership figures,

[1] An example is the cooperation of the German Konrad Adenauer Foundation with the Civil United Front in Tanzania. For other examples, see Weissenbach 2010.

data on party financing, manifesto data, and historically grounded material on party formation and on party motives. Cumulative and collaborative datasets must become a top priority. Findings could be used to arrive at a better selection of recipients in return. Party aid agencies lack institutional memory (Carothers 2006). Academic research lacks basic data. There is no reason why the two should not combine their strength to eradicate their weaknesses.

COMPARATIVE POLITICS AND AFRICAN PARTIES

For the better part of the twentieth century, political parties outside Western Europe have been the stepchild of comparative politics. The lack of democratic norms and procedures outside the Western world, by virtue of definition, made the Northern hemisphere the main theatre of comparative research. The intrinsic Western bias in concept formation is a corollary of the long-term absence of democracy in today's third-wave democracies.

The intellectual prevalence of analytical frameworks, the content of which derives from the study of Western European societies, has led to a division between the discipline – political science – and area studies. At academic conferences and other gatherings, area specialists frequently accuse mainstream political science of fostering a research agenda that is as regional specific as their own ("Western European area studies"), although scholars on Western Europe rarely take note how confined their findings might be. This accusation carries some weight, as Chapter Two has shown. Leading lights in the field, such as Katz and Mair, Duverger, the numerous scholars working within the framework of Kirchheimer's catch-all party, and so forth, consistently fail to discuss or even mention the regional confinements of their concepts. However, the heavily Eurocentric state of the literature is also the result of the *longe dureé* of autocratic rule in Africa and, maybe even more so, a result of the inertia of "Africanists," "Latin Americanists," and "Asianists" to engage in concept formation in their regions.

Of all world regions, Africa has certainly received the least attention by adherents of a disciplinary approach. Once the scholarly preoccupation with questions of modernization ebbed, comparative politics approaches more or less departed from the continent. For a long while, African politics seemed too unique – too poor, too erratic, too personalistic, too patrimonial, and too authoritarian – to contribute substantial insights into those issues that are at the heart of political science. The third wave fundamentally altered the research landscape. However, scholars on African politics adjusted very slowly to these changes. Even today, there are still those who refuse to acknowledge that Africa has entered a new chapter in its history (see, e.g., Bayart 1993, Chabal and Daloz 1999, Chabal 2005, Chabal and Daloz 2006). Slowly but steadily, however, the disciplinary attention to African politics is growing. Political science concepts increasingly find their application to African politics (e.g., Bratton and van de Walle 1997, Reynolds 1999, Posner 2005, Lindberg 2006, LeBas 2011). This book has contributed to this growing trend. It provides a new analytical tool to the study of parties worldwide. Its results have far-reaching implications for the study of parties in nonindustrial societies.

The study of parties is one of the research fields at the heart of comparative politics. This book has established a new analytical instrument for the study of parties. To do so by analyzing parties located on the "periphery" is a new and timely approach, which takes note of the post-1990 political environment. Diamond and Gunther were the first to note that conventional political science concepts no longer speak to the empirical reality of the early twenty-first century. This book has followed their lead, and hopefully, many more studies will do so. The applicability of the typology to regions outside of Africa cannot be taken for granted. However, this study hopes to structure the future debate of political parties in post–third-wave democracies.

In the academic hierarchy, those scholars who focus on non-Western countries are still trailing those who concentrate on Western countries (Chege 1997, Engel 2003, Chabal 2005, Lonsdale 2005). Twenty years after the first round of multiparty elections, democracy in Africa remains fragile. The structural conditions in which African parties strive are still conducive to the survival of nondemocratic norms. However, in contrast to previous periods, multiparty democracy today appears to be sustainable in a number of countries. This book has demonstrated that the systematic study of African politics can reveal enormous lessons for comparative political science research in general. Never before in history has Africa provided such a fertile ground for political science research. The discipline as a whole should make greater use of the lessons that Africa and other world regions hold for the study of political science.

Annex A: Operationalization of Secondary Party Types

	Party Indicator and Characteristics									
	Party Goals		Electoral Strategy		Organizational Structure			Social Base		
Party Type	Motive of Formation	Rhetoric	Electoral Rhetoric	Content of Election Manifesto	National Coverage	Party Factions	Party Apparatus	Leadership Composition	Cabinet Composition	PNS and PDS
class-mass	promotion of worker's interest	supportive of workers	pro-working class; catch-all	high left-wing content prevailing	high	structured around individuals	important role of trade unions	bridging ethnic cleavage lines unions and professional organizations	bridging ethnic cleavage lines	medium to high/ very high PNS medium to low or very low PDS
Leninist	promotion of worker's interest	supportive of workers; reference to communist works	radical pro-working class; catch-all	high left-wing content is dominant	high	→ structured ideological splinter groups	→ important role of trade unions	→ bridging ethnic cleavage lines unions and professional organizations	bridging ethnic cleavage lines	medium to high/ very high PNS medium to low or very low PDS
religious-fundamentalist	promotion of religious ideas	supportive of religious groups; reference to religious leaders and tents	in favor of religious ideas (e.g. Sharia)	low	high	important role of clergy men	important role clergy men	representatives of one particular religious group	failing to bride religious cleavage	low/ very low PNS high/ very high PDS

Annex B: The Standard MRG Coding Frame

Domain 1 External Relations	Domain 2 FreedoSm and Democracy	Domain 3 Political System	Domain 4 Economy	Domain 5 Welfare and Quality of Life	Domain 6 Fabric of Society	Domain 7 Social Groups
101 Foreign Special Relationships: Positive	201 Freedom and Human Rights: Positive	301 Decentralisation: Positive	401 Free Enterprise: Positive	501 Environmental Protection: Positive	601 National Way of Life: Positive	701 Labor Groups: Positive
102 Foreign Special Relationships: Negative	202 Democracy: Positive	302 Centralisation: Positive	402 Incentives: Positive	502 Culture: Positive	602 National Way of Life: Negative	702 Labor Groups: Negative
103 Anti-imperialism: Positive	203 Constitutionalism: Positive	304 Political Corruption: Negative	403 Market Regulation: Positive	503 Social Justice: Positive	603 Traditional Morality: Positive	703 Farmers: Positive
104 Military: Positive	204 Constitutionalism: Negative	305 Political Authority	404 Economic Planning: Positive	504 Welfare State Expansion: Positive	604 Traditional Morality: Negative	704 Middle Class and Professional Groups: Positive

105 Military: Negative	405 Corporatism: Positive	505 Welfare State Limitation: Positive	605 Law and Order: Positive	704 Underprivileged Minority Groups: Positive
106 Peace: Positive	406 Protectionism: Positive	506 Education Expansion: Positive	606 Social Harmony: Positive	705 Non-economic Demographic Groups: Positive
107 Internationalism: Positive	407 Protectionism: Negative	507 Education Limitation: Positive	607 Multiculturalism: Positive	
108 European Integration: Positive	408 Economic Goals		608 Multiculturalism: Negative	
109 Internationalism: Negative	409 Keynesian Demand Management: Positive			
110 European Integration: Negative	410 Productivity: Positive			

(*continued*)

Domain 1 External Relations	Domain 2 FreedoSm and Democracy	Domain 3 Political System	Domain 4 Economy	Domain 5 Welfare and Quality of Life	Domain 6 Fabric of Society	Domain 7 Social Groups
			411 Technology and Infrastructure: Positive			
			412 Controlled Economy: Positive			
			413 Nationalism: Positive			
			414 Economic Orthodoxy: Positive			
			415 Marxist Analysis: Positive			
			416: Anti-growth Economy: Positive			

Source: Budge et al. (2001) and Klingemann et al. (2006).

Programmatic Manifesto Categories

The MRG coding scheme displays the following categories as left and right:

Left

103: Anti-Imperialism: Positive
105: Military: Negative
106: Peace: Positive
107: Internationalism: Positive
202: Democracy: Positive
403: Market Regulation: Positive
404: Economic Planning: Positive
406: Protectionism: Positive
412: Controlled Economy: Positive
413: Nationalization: Positive
504: Welfare State Expansion: Positive
506: Education Expansion: Positive
701: Labor Groups: Positive

Right

104: Military: Positive
201: Freedom and Human Rights: Positive
203: Constitutionalism: Positive
305: Political Authority: Positive
401: Free Enterprise: Positive
402: Incentives: Positive
407: Protectionism: Negative
414: Economic Orthodoxy: Positive
505: Welfare State Expansion: Positive
601: National Way of Life: Positive
603: Traditional Morality: Positive
605: Law and Order: Positive
606: Social Harmony: Positive

Annex C: Number of Effective Programmatic Categories

		Amount of Effective Programmatic Categories
NPP	T1	12.3
	T2	10.9
	T3	13.8
	T4	9
NDC	T1	n/a
	T2	7.3
	T3	13.3
	T4	11.2
SWAPO	T1	8.3
	T2	6.1
	T3	6.6
	T4	7.7
DTA	T1	8.9
	T2	6.3
	T3	3.3
CoD	T4	3.9
KANU	T1	12.5
	T2	9.9
	T3	9.8
DP	T1	11
	T2	10.8
FORD-K	T1	8.6
	T2	7.7
FORD-A	T1	4.9
SDP	T2	6.4
NDP	T2	9.2
NARC	T3	7.8
PNU	T4	11.7
ODM	T4	9.4
average total	T1-T4	8.8
average genuine programmatic	T1-T4	11.3
average with policy overstretch	T1-T4	5.8

Annex D: Summary of Party Nationalization Scores (PNS) and Party Divergence Scores (PDS)

PNS across Time and Space

Country	Party	PNS	Observation Period
Kenya	FORD-K	.56	1
	FORD-A	.60	
	DP	.61	
	KANU	.68	
	FORD-K	.45	2
	DP	.57	
	SDP	.42	
	NDP	.48	
	KANU	.76	
	NARC	.84	3
	KANU	.73	
	PNU	.66	4
	ODM	.70	
	ODM-K	.49	
national average		.61	
Ghana	NPP	.65	1
	NDC	.88	
	NPP	.65	2
	NDC	.89	
	NPP	.73	3
	NDC	.74	
	NPP	.80	4
	NDC	.68	
national average		.77	
Namibia	SWAPO	.74	1
	DTA	.81	
	SWAPO	.77	2
	DTA	.60	
	SWAPO	.79	3
	DTA	.51	
	SWAPO	.84	4
	CoD	.58	
national average		.71	
total average		.67	

PDS Across Time and Space

Country	Party	Diverging points	Observation Period
Kenya	FORD-K	83	1
	FORD-A	62	
	DP	58	
	KANU	52	
	FORD-K	80	2
	DP	58	
	SDP	84	
	NDP	110	
	KANU	40	
	NARC	24	3
	KANU	42	
	PNU	46	4
	ODM	62	
	ODM-K	86	
national average		63	
Ghana	NPP	48	1
	NDC	26	
	NPP	42	2
	NDC	20	
	NPP	34	3
	NDC	20	
	NPP	26	4
	NDC	22	
national average		30	
Namibia	SWAPO	47	1
	DTA	65	
	SWAPO	30	2
	DTA	90	
	SWAPO	28	3
	DTA	96	
	SWAPO	24	4
	CoD	71	
national average		56/27 (SWAPO only)	
total average		52	

Average total across time and space

Kenya	63
Ghana	30
Namibia	56/ 27 (SWAPO only)
total	**52**

Criteria and Classification

PDS
high to very high: 82–110 (mono-ethnic)
medium to high: 52–81 (alliance)
medium/average: 52
medium to low: 52–36 (catch-all, programmatic, personalistic)
low to very low: 36–20

PNS
high to very high: .78–.89
medium to high: .67–.78 (catch-all, programmatic, personalistic)
medium/average: .67
medium to low: .67–.55 (alliance)
low to very low: .55–.42 (mono-ethnic)

Annex E: Result for MRG Coding Scheme

Country	Party	Genuine Programmatic
Ghana national average: 41%	NPP Average across time: 45%	programmatic in T1 and Z2 not programmatic otherwise
	NDC Average across time:36%	not programmatic
Namibia national average: 45%	SWAPO Average across time: 39%	not programmatic
	DTA Average across time: 55%	not programmatic
	CoD Average across time: 41%	not programmatic
Kenya national Average: 37%	DP Average across time: 50%	yes in T1 and T2
	FORD-K Average across time: 40%	not programmatic
	KANU Average across time: 33%	not programmatic
	SDP Average: 43%	yes
	NDP Average: 31%	not programmatic
	NARC Average: 32%	not programmatic
	PNU Average: 31%	not programmatic
	ODM Average: 28%	not programmatic
total average across countries and time: 40%		

Annex F: PNS Calculated on the Basis of Afrobarometer Data

PNS of parties across dominant cleavage lines

Country	Party	PNS	Afrobarometer Round
Kenya	NARC	.93	2003
	KANU	.66	
	NARC	.69	2005
	KANU	.52	
national average		.70	
Ghana	NPP	.63	1999
	NDC	.86	
	NPP	.79	2002
	NDC	.76	
	NPP	.84	2005
	NDC	.75	
	NPP	.76	2008
	NDC	.72	
national average		.76	
Namibia	SWAPO	.80	1999
	DTA	.50	
	SWAPO	.80	2001
	DTA	.50	
	SWAPO	.76	2006
	CoD	.90	
national average		.73 (.79 SWAPO alone)	
total average		.72 (.75 SWAPO alone)	

Source: Afrobarometer data.

Notes on Afrobarometer data:

Due to the small number of respondents at the level of individual communities, PNS values derive from communities that are part of a dominant cleavage line. In Namibia, the dominant ethnic cleavage line includes the Ovambo, the white, and the Herero community. As both Afrikaans and English are spoken by a variety of communities, the number of white respondents could not be isolated. Therefore, data for the Namibian PNS values from Namibia are confined to the political preferences of Ovambo and Herero speakers. The author also has calculated PNS results for all Southern Namibian communities (Herero, Nama, Damara) and results are almost identical (the data are with the author).

In Ghana, PNS values derive from the Akan, the Ewe, and the various Northern communities.

In Kenya, PNS values derive from Kikuyu, Luo, or Kalenjin speakers. Afrobarometer data in Kenya have been collected in 2003 and 2005, shortly after the formation of NARC. Unfortunately, the Kenyan data are not very representative, as in these two years, Kenya was in possession of a national party (which proved unsustainable).

The number of respondents who do not feel close to any party constitute a significant part of those surveyed. The percentage share of those respondents who do not feel close to any political party is as follows:

Percentage of those who feel not close to any party

Country	Community	Round 1/1999	Round 2/2002	Round 3/2005	Round 4/2008
Kenya	Kikuyu	n/a	31%	30%	n/a
	Kalenjin	n/a	30%	35%	n/a
	Luo	n/a	32%	28%	n/a
Ghana	Akan	35%	31%	35%	41%
	Ewe	34%	43%	32%	36%
	"Northern"	28%	32%	20%	25%
Namibia	Ovambo	28%	21%	n/a	11%
	Herero	38%	38%	n/a	27%
	"Southern"	42%	42%	n/a	27%

Source: Based on Afrobarometer data.

Annex G: Scope of Party Systems Covered

Country	Observation Period	Parties	Electorate Covered
Kenya	1	KANU FORD-K FORD-A DP	96%
	2	KANU FORD-K DP NDP	90%
	3	KANU NARC	76%
Ghana	1	NPP NDC	n/a
	2	NPP NDC	85%
	3	NPP NDC	84%
	4	NPP NDC	88%
Namibia	1	SWAPO DTA	86%
	2	SWAPO DTA	92%
	3	SWAPO DTA	86%
	4	SWAPO CoD	81%

Source: Based on data provided by the respective electoral commission.

Annex H: Party Nationalization Scores (PNS) of the Preliminary Cases

Country	Party	PNS	Observation Period
Tanzania	CCM	0.91	1995
		0.94	2000
		0.94	2005
		0.92	2010
	CUF	0.61	2000
		0.66	2005
		0.54	2010
	CHADEMA	0.58	2010
Botswana	BDP	0.86	1999
		0.83	2004
		0.68	2009
	BNF	0.71	1999
		0.63	2004
		0.68	2009
Senegal	PS	0.92	1993
		0.90	1998
		0.84	2001
	PDS	0.87	1993
		0.78	1998
		0.90	2001
Malawi	MCP	0.58	1994
		0.76	1999
		0.47	2004
		0.45	2009
	UDF	0.57	1994
		0.65	1999
		0.66	2004
		0.64	2009

(*continued*)

Country	Party	PNS	Observation Period
	AFORD	0.48	1994
		0.42	1999
	DPP	0.92	2009
Burkina Faso	CDP	0.87	2007
	ADF/RDA	0.52	2007
Zambia	MMD	0.95	1991
		0.90	1996
		0.80	2001
		0.84	2006
	UNIP	0.81	1999
		0.62	2001
	UPND	0.58	2001
	ZDC	0.79	1996
	PF	0.51	2006
Benin	PSD	0.44	1991
		0.49	1996
	PRD	0.67	1991
		0.50	1996
		0.32	2003
	MADEP	0.32	2003
	FARD-Alafia	0.31	1995
	ADD	0.56	2003
	UBF	0.65	2003
	FCBE	0.72	2007
Cross country average	0.68		

Source: Author's own calculations.

Bibliography

Acemoglu, Daron, Simon Johnson, and James Robinson. 2002. "An African Success Story: Botswana." Department of Economics; Centre for Economic Policy Research, No. 3219.

Adams, James, Michael Clark, Lawrence Ezrow, and Garrett Glasgow. 2006. "Are Niche Parties Fundamentally Different from Mainstream Parties? The Causes and the Electoral Consequences of Western European Parties' Policy Shifts, 1976–1998." *American Journal of Political Science* 50 (3): 513–529.

Adedeji, John. 2001. "The Legacy of J.J. Rawlings in Ghanaian Politics." *African Studies Quarterly* 5 (2). http://web.africa.ufl.edu/asq/v5/v5i2a1.htm.

Afrobarometer. 2009. "How Ghanaian Rate the Performance of the NPP Administration." Afrobarometer Briefing Paper 49.

Afari-Gyan, Kwadwo. 1995. *The Making of the Fourth Republican Constitution of Ghana.* Friedrich Ebert Foundation.

Agyeman-Duah, Ivor. 2006. *Between Faith and History. A Biography of John A. Kufuor.* Chatham.

Ahluwalia, Davinder. 1996. *Post-Colonialism and the Politics of Kenya.* Nova Science Publishers.

Ajulu, Rok. 2002. "Politicized Ethnicity, Competitive Politics and Conflict in Kenya: A Historical Perspective." *African Studies* 61 (2): 251–268.

Amenumey, D.E.K. 1989. *The Ewe Unification Movement. A Political History.* Ghana Universities Press.

Anderson, David. 2005. "Yours in Struggle for Majimbo: Nationalism and the Party Politics of Decolonization in Kenya, 1955 to 1964." *Journal of Contemporary History* 40 (3): 547–564.

Angell, Harold. 1987. "Duverger, Epstein and the Problem of the Mass Party: The Case of the Parti Québécois." *Canadian Journal of Political Science* 20 (2): 363–378.

Ansprenger, Franz. 1984. *Die SWAPO: Profil einer afrikanischen Befreiungsbewegung.* Mathias-Grünewald-Verlag.

Asante, Richard, and Emmanuel Gyimah-Boadi. 2004. *Ethnic Structure, Inequality and Governance of the Public Sector in Ghana.* United Nations Research Institute for Social Development.

Apter, David. 1955. *The Gold Coast in Transition*. Princeton University Press.
Apter, David. 1972. *Ghana in Transition*. Princeton University Press.
Apter, David. 1986. *Africa Repartitioned?* Centre for Security and Conflict Studies.
Ahram, Ariel. 2011. "The Theory and Method of Comparative Area Studies." *Qualitative Research* 11 (1): 69–90.
Arnold, Guy. 1974. *Kenyatta and the Politics of Kenya*. Dent and Sons.
Arter, David. 1999. "From Class Party to Catchall Party? The Adaptation of the Finnish Agrarian-Center Party." *Scandinavian Political Studies* 22 (2): 157–180.
Austin, Dennis. 1961. "The Working Committee of the United Gold Coast Convention." *Journal of African History* 2 (2): 273–297.
Austin, Dennis. 1963. "The Uncertain Frontier: Ghana-Togo." *Journal of Modern African Studies* 1 (2): 139–145.
Austin, Dennis. 1964. *Politics in Ghana 1946–1960*. Oxford University Press.
Austin, Dennis. 1970. *Elections in Ghana 1969*. Indian Council for Africa.
Ayee, Richard. 1998. *The 1996 General Elections and Democratic Consolidation in Ghana*. University of Legon.
Ayee, Richard. 2008. "The Evolution of the New Patriotic Party." *South African Journal of International Affairs* 15 (2): 185–214.
Ayensu, K.B., and S.N. Darkwa. 1999. *The Evolution of Parliament in Ghana*. Sub-Saharan Publishers.
Badejo, Babafemi. 2006. *Raila Odinga. An Enigma in Kenyan Politics*. Yintab Books.
Bannon, Alicia, Edward Miguel, and Daniel Posner. 2004. "Sources of Ethnic Identification in Africa." Afrobarometer Working Paper 44.
Barkan, Joel. 1995. "Elections in Agrarian Societies." *Journal of Democracy* 6 (4): 106–116.
Bartolini, Stefano. 1999. "Collusion, Competition and Democracy." *Journal of Theoretical Politics* 11 (4): 435–470.
Bartolini, Stefano. 2000. "Collusion, Competition and Democracy: Part II." *Journal of Theoretical Politics* 12 (3): 33–65.
Basedau, Matthias. 2003. *Erfolgsbedingungen von Demokratie im subsaharischen Afrika*. Opladen.
Basedau, Matthias, Matthijs Bogaards, Christof Hartmann, and Peter Niesen. 2007. "Ethnic Party Bans in Africa: A Research Agenda." *German Law Journal* 6 (1): 617–634.
Basedau, Matthias, Gero Erdmann, and Andreas Mehler. 2007. *Votes, Money and Violence. Political Parties in Sub-Saharan Africa*. Elanders Gotab.
Basedau, Matthias, Patrick Köllner. 2007. "Area Studies, Comparative Area Studies, and the Study of Politics: Context, Substance, and Methodological Challenges." *Zeitschrift für Vergleichende Politikwissenschaft* 1 (1): 105–124.
Basedau, Matthias, and Alexander Stroh. 2008. "Measuring Party Institutionalization in Developing Countries: A New Research Instrument Applied to 28 African Political Parties." German Institute of Global and Area Studies Working Paper 69.
Basedau, Matthias. 2008. "Democracy and Elections in Africa by Staffan Lindberg." *Journal of Modern African Studies* 46 (3): 518–519.
Basedau, Matthias and Alexander Stroh. 2009. "Ethnicity and Party Systems in Francophone Sub-Saharan Africa." German Institute of Global and Area Studies Working Paper 100.

Basedau, Matthias, Gero Erdmann, Jann Lay, and Alexander Stroh. 2011. "Ethnicity and Party Preference in sub-Saharan Africa." *Democratization* 18 (2): 462–489.

Basedau, Matthias. 2011. "Managing Ethnic Conflict: The Menu of Institutional Engineering." German Institute of Global and Area Studies Working Paper 171.

Basedau, Matthias and Alexander Stroh. 2012. "How Ethnic Are African Parties Really? Evidence from Francophone Africa." *International Political Science Review* 33 (1): 5–24.

Bates, Robert. 1981. *Markets and States in Tropical Africa: The Political Basis of Agricultural Policies.* University of California Press.

Bates, Robert. 2007. "Area Studies and Political Science: Rupture and Possible Synthesis." *Africa Today* 44 (2): 123–131.

Bates, Robert. 1997. "Area Studies and the Discipline: A Useful Controversy?" *Political Science and Politics* 30 (2): 166–169.

Battle, Martin, and Jennifer Seely. 2007. It's All Relative: Competing Modes of Vote Choice in Benin. Afrobarometer Working Paper.

Battle, Martin, and Jennifer Seely. 2010. "It's All Relative: Modelling Candidate Support in Benin." *Nationalism and Ethnic Politics* 16 (1): 42–66.

Bayart, Jean-Francois. 1979. *L'Etat au Cameroun.* Presses de la Fondation Nationale des Sciences Politiques.

Bayart, Jean-Francois. 1993. *The State in Africa: The Politics of the Belly.* Longman Group.

Baylies, Carolyn, and Morris Szeffel. 1992. "The Fall and Rise of Multi-Party Politics in Zambia." *Review of African Political Economy* 19 (54): 75–91.

Baynham, Simon. 1985a. "Divide et Impera: Civilian Control of the Military in Ghana's Second and Third Republics." *Journal of Modern African Studies* 23 (4): 623–642.

Baynham, Simon. 1985b. "Civil-Military Relations in Ghana's Second Republic." *Journal of Contemporary African Studies* 4 (1/2): 71–88.

Becher, Anika and Matthias Basedau. 2008. "Promoting Peace and Democracy Through Party Regulation? Ethnic Party Bans in Africa." German Institute of Global and Area Studies Working Paper 66.

Beissinger, Mark, and Crawford Young. 2002. *Beyond State Crisis? Postcolonial Africa and Post-Soviet Eurasia in Comparative Perspective.* Woodrow Wilson Center Press.

Bekker, Simon, Martine Dodds, and Meshak Khosa. 2001. *Shifting African Identities.* Human Sciences Research Council.

Bendix, Reinhard. 1964. *Nation-Building and Citizenship: Studies of Our Changing Social Order.* Wiley.

Bendix, Reinhard. 1987. *Kings or People: Power and the Mandate to Rule.* University of California Press.

Bennett, Andrew, and Colin Elman. 2006. "Qualitative Research: Recent Developments in Case Study Method." *Annual Review of Political Science* 9: 455–476.

Bennett, George, and Carl Rosberg. 1961. *The Kenyatta Election: Kenya 1960–1961.* Oxford University Press.

Berg-Schlosser, Dirk. 1984. *Tradition and Change in Kenya: A Comparative Analysis of Seven Major Ethnic Groups.* Schönigh.

Berman, Bruce, Dickson Eyok, and Will Kymlicka. 2004. *Ethnicity and Democracy in Africa*. Oxford University Press.

Berman, Bruce, and John Lonsdale. 1992. *Unhappy Valley. Conflict in Kenya and Africa. Book One: State and Class*. Currey.

Bienen, Henry. 1967. "What Does Political Development Mean in Africa?" *World Politics* 20 (1): 128–141.

Birnir, Johanna. 2007. *Ethnicity and Electoral Politics*. Cambridge University Press.

Bjornlund, Eric, Michael Bratton, and Clark Gibson. 1992. "Observing Multiparty Elections in Africa: Lessons from Zambia." *African Affairs* 91: 405–431.

Blais, Andre. 2006. "What Affects Voter Turnout?" *Annual Review of Political Science* 9: 111–125.

Bleck, Jaimee, and Nicolas van de Walle, Nicolas. 2010. *Parties and Issues in Francophone West Africa. Towards a Theory of Non-Mobilization*. Cornell University, Center for International Studies.

Blyth, Mark, and Richard Katz. 2005. "From Catch-All Politics to Cartelization: The Political Economy of the Cartel Party." *West European Politics* 28 (1): 33–62.

Boas, Morten. 2001. "Liberia and Sierra Leone – Dead Ringers? The Logic of Neopatrimonial Rule." *Third World Quarterly* 22 (5): 697–723.

Bogaards, Matthijs. 2003. "Electoral Choices for Divided Societies: Multi-Ethnic Parties and Constituency Pooling in Africa." *Commonwealth and Comparative Politics* 41 (3): 59–80.

Bogaards, Matthijs. 2004. "Counting Parties and Identifying Dominant Party Systems in Africa." *European Journal of Political Research* 43 (2): 173–197.

Bogaards, Matthijs. 2005. Power-Sharing in South Africa: The African National Congress as a Consociational Party? In *From Power-Sharing to Democracy: Post-Conflict Institutions in Ethnically Divided Societies*, ed Toronto, Noel, 164–183. McGill University Press.

Bogaards, Matthijs. 2007. Electoral Systems, Party Systems, and Ethnicity in Africa. In *Votes, Money and Violence. Political Parties and Elections in Africa*, ed. Basedau, Matthias, Gero Erdmann, and Mehler, Andreas, 168–193. Elanders Gotab.

Bogaards, Matthijs. 2009. "How to Classify Hybrid Regimes? Defective Democracy and Electoral Authoritarianism." *Democratization* 16 (2): 399–423.

Bogaards, Matthijs, Matthias Basedau, and Christof Hartmann. 2010. "Ethnic Party Bans in Africa: An Introduction. *Democratization* 17 (4): 599–617.

Boix, Charles. 1998. *Political Parties, Growth and Equality: Conservative and Social Democratic Economic Strategies in the World Economy*. Cambridge University Press.

Boucek, Francoise. 2009. "Rethinking Factionalism. Typologies, Intra-Party Dynamics and Three Faces of Factionalism." *Party Politics* 15 (4): 455–488.

Brancati, Dawn. 2009. *Peace by Design: Managing Intrastate Conflict Through Decentralization*. Oxford University Press.

Brancati, Dawn. 2008. "The Origins and Strength of Regional Parties." *British Journal of Political Science* 38 (1): 135–159.

Branch, Daniel, Nic Cheeseman, and Leigh Gardner. 2010. *Our Turn to East*. LIT Verlag.

Bratton, Michael, and Nicholas van de Walle. 1997. *Democratic Experiments in Africa. Regime Transitions in Comparative Perspective.* Cambridge University Press.

Bratton, Michael, Ravi Bhavnani, and Tse-Itsin Chen. 2011. "Voting Intensions in Africa: Ethnic, Economic or Partisan." Afrobarometer Working Paper.

Braumoeller, Bear, and Gerry Goertz. 2000. "The Methodology of Necessary Conditions." *American Journal of Political Science* 44 (4): 844–858.

Bremmer, Ian. 2006. *The J Curve: A New Way to Understand Why Nations Rise and Fall.* Simon and Schuster.

Breusers, Mark, Suzanne Nederlof, and Teunis van Rheenen. 1998. "Conflict or Symbiosis? Disentangling Farmer-Herdsmen Relations: The Mossi and Fulbe of the Central Plateau, Burkina Faso." *The Journal of Modern African Studies* 36 (3): 357–380.

Brown, David. 1980. "Borderline Politics in Ghana: The National Liberation Movement of Western Togoland." *Journal of Modern African Studies* 18 (4): 575–609.

Brown, David. 1982. "Who Are the Tribalists? Social Pluralism and Political Ideology in Ghana." *African Affairs* 82 (322): 37–69.

Brown, Stephen. 2009. "Donor Responses to the 2008 Kenyan Crisis: Finally Getting it Right?" *Journal of Contemporary African Studies* 27 (3): 389–406.

Budge, Ian, Hans-Dieter Klingemann, and Richard Hofferberg. 1994. *Parties, Policies and Democracy.* Westview Press.

Budge, Ian, Hans-Dieter Klingemann, Andreas Volkens, Judith Bara, and Eric Tanenbaum. 2001. *Mapping Policy Preferences.* Oxford University Press.

Bunce, Valerie. 1995. "Should Transitologists Be Grounded?" *Slavic Review* 54 (1): 111–127.

Burin, Frederic. 1969. *Politics, Law and Social Change: Selected Essays on Otto Kirchheimer.* Columbia University Press.

Burnell, Peter. 1995. "The Politics of Poverty and the Poverty of Politics in Zambia." *Third World Quarterly* 16 (4): 675–690.

Burnell, Peter. 2001. "The Party System and Party Politics in Zambia: Continuities Past, Present and Future." *African Affairs* 100: 239–263.

Burnell, Peter. 2002. "Zambia's 2001 Elections: The Tyranny of Small decisions, 'Non-Decisions,' and 'Not-Decisions.'" *Third World Quarterly* 23 (6): 1103–1120.

Burnell, Peter. 2007. Different, Functional and Dynamic? Reflections on Gero Erdmann's Party Research: Western European Bias and the "African Labyrinth." In *Votes, Money and Violence. Political Parties and Elections in Sub-Saharan Africa*, ed. Basedau, Matthias, Gero Erdmann, and Andreas Mehler, 65–82. Elanders Gotab.

Burnell, Peter, and Andre Gerrits. 2010. "Promoting Party Politics in Emerging Democracies." *Democratization* 17 (6): 1065–1084.

Brydon, Lynne. 1985. "Ghanaian Responses to the Nigerian Expulsion of 1983." *African Affairs* 84 (337): 561–586.

Capoccia, Giovanni, and Daniel Kelemen. 2007. "The Study of Critical Junctures. Theory, Narrative and Counterfactuals in Historical Institutionalism." *World Politics* 59 (4): 341–369.

Caramani, Daniele. 2004. *The Nationalization of Politics. The Formation of National Electorates and Party Systems in Western Europe*. Cambridge University Press.

Carey, Sabine. 2002. "A Comparative Analysis of Political Parties in Kenya, Zambia and the Democratic Republic of Congo." *Democratization* 9 (3): 53–71.

Carothers, Thomas. 2006. *Confronting the Weakest Link. Aiding Political Parties in New Democracies*. Carnegie Endowment for International Peace.

Cartwright, John. 1983. *Political Leadership in Africa*. Croom Helm.

Caton, Matthias. 2007. *Effective Party Assistance. Stronger Parties for Better Democracy*. International IDEA.

Chabal, Patrick, and Jean-Pascal Daloz. 1999. *Africa Works. Disorder as Political Instrument*. International African Institute.

Chabal, Patrick. 2005. "Area Studies and Comparative Politics: Africa in Context." *Africa Spectrum* 40 (3): 471–484.

Chabal, Patrick, and Jean-Pascal Daloz. 2006. *Culture Troubles: Politics and the Interpretation of Meaning*. UK: Hurst and Company.

Chandra, Kanchan. 2004. *Why Ethnic Parties Succeed*. UK: Cambridge University Press.

Chandra, Kanchan. 2005. "Ethnic Parties and Democratic Stability." *Perspectives on Politics* 3 (2): 235–252.

Chandra, Kanchan. 2006. "What is Ethnicity and Does it Matter?" *Annual Review of Political Science* 9: 397–424.

Chandra, Kanchan. 2011. "What is an Ethnic Party?" *Party Politics* 18 (2): 151–169.

Chazan, Naomi. 1982. "Ethnicity and Politics in Ghana." *Political Science Quarterly* 97 (3): 461–485.

Cheeseman, Nicholas, and Robert Ford. 2007. "Ethnicity as Political Cleavage." Afrobarometer Working Paper.

Cheeseman, Nicolas, and Marja Hinfelaar. 2010. "Parties, Platforms, and Political Mobilization: The Zambian Presidential Elections of 2008." *African Affairs* 109 (434): 51–76.

Chege, Michael. 1997. "The Social Science Area Studies Controversy from the Continental African Standpoint?" *Africa Today* 44 (2): 133–142.

Chege, Michael. 2007. *Political Parties in East Africa: Diversity in Political Party Systems*. International Institute for Democracy and Electoral Assistance.

Chhibber, Pradeep, and Mariano Torcal. 1997. "Elite Strategy, Social Cleavages, and Party Systems in a New Democracy." *Comparative Political Studies* 30 (1): 27–54.

Chhibber, Pradeep, and Ken Kollman. 1998. "Party Aggregation and the Number of Parties in India and the United States." *American Political Science Review* 92 (2): 329–342.

Chinsinga, Blessings. 2003. "Lack of Alternative Leadership in Democratic Malawi: Some Reflections Ahead of the 2004 General Elections." *Nordic Journal of African Studies* 12 (1): 1–22.

Chisinga, Blessings. 2006. *Voter Apathy in Malawi: A Critical Appraisal*. Netherlands Institute for Multiparty Democracy.

Cliffe, Lionnel. 1994. *The Transition to Independence in Namibia*. Lynne Rienner.

Coleman, James, and Carl Rosberg. 1964. *Political Parties and National Integration in Tropical Africa*. University of California Press.

Collier, David, and James Mahon. 1993. "Conceptual "Stretching" Revisited: Adapting Categories in Comparative Analysis." *American Political Science Review* 87 (4): 845–855.

Collier, Paul, and Anke Hoeffler. 1998. "On Economic Causes of Civil War." *Oxford Economic Papers* 50 (4): 563–573.

Collier, Paul, Patrick Honohan, and Karl Moene. 2001. "Implications of Ethnic Diversity." *Economic Policy* 16 (32): 129–166.

Collier, Paul, and Anke Hoeffler. 2004. "Greed and Grievance in Civil War." *Oxford Economic Paper* 56 (4): 563–595.

Collier, Ruth, and David Collier. 1991. *Shaping the Political Arena. Critical Junctures, the Labor Movement and Regime Dynamics in Latin America*. Princeton University Press.

Cooper, Allan. 2001. *Ovambo Politics in the Twentieth Century*. University of America Press.

Coppedge, Michael. 1997. "A Classification of Latin American Political Parties." Kellogg Institute Working Paper.

Cowan, L. 1969. "Ten Years of African Studies." *African Studies Bulletin* 12 (1): 1–7.

Cowen, Michael, and Liisa Laakso. 2002. *Multi-Party Elections in Africa*. Currey.

Cox, Thomas. 1976. *Civil-Military Relations in Sierra Leone. A Case Study of African Soldiers in Politics*. Harvard University Press.

Crabbe, V.C.R.A.C. 1975. *The Electoral Commission. In Politicians and Soldiers in Ghana 1966–1972*, ed. Austin, Dennis and Robin Luckham, 140–163. Frank Class.

Croissant, Aurel. 2008. "Die Parteiensysteme neuer Demokratien in Ostasien: Merkmale, Typen und Institutionalisierungsgrad." *Zeitschrift für Vergleichende Politikwissenschaft* 2 (1): 70–98.

Creevy, Lucy, Paul Ngomo, and Richard Vengroff. 2005. "Party Politics and Different Paths to Democratic Transitions: A Comparison of Benin and Senegal." *Party Politics* 11 (4): 471–492.

Daadler, Hans. 2002. Parties: Denied, Dismissed, or Redundant? A Critique. In *Political Parties. Old Concepts and New Challenges*, ed. Richard Gunther, Jose Ramon-Montero, and Juan Linz, 39–57. Oxford University Press.

Daddieh, Cyril, and Jo Ellen Fair. 2002. *Ethnicity and Recent Democratic Experiments in Africa*. African Studies Association Press.

Dalton, Russell, Paul Beck, and Scott Flanagan. 1984. Electoral Change in Advanced Industrial Democracies. In *Electoral Change in Advanced Industrial Democracies. Realignment or Dealignment*, eds. Russell Dalton, Paul Beck, and Scott Flanagan, 47–71. Princeton University Press.

Danso-Boafo, Kwaku. 1996. *The Political Biography of Dr. Kofi Abrefa Busia*. Ghana University Press.

Davidson, Basil. 2007. *Black Star: A View of the Life and Times of Kwame Nkrumah*. James Currey.

Davis, Gavin. 2004. "Proportional Representation and Racial Campaigning in South Africa." *Nationalism and Ethnic Politics* 10 (2): 297–324.

Decalo, Samuel. 1976. *Coups and Army Rule in Africa. Studies in Military Style*. Yale University Press.

Diamond, Larry. 2002. "Thinking about Hybrid Regimes." *Journal of Democracy* 13 (2): 21–35.

Diamond, Larry, and Richard Gunther. 2001. Types and Functions of Parties. In *Political Parties and Democracy*, ed. Larry Diamond and Richard Gunther, Richard, 1–39. The Johns Hopkins University Press.

Dion, Douglas. 1998. "Evidence and Inference in the Comparative Case Study." *Comparative Politics* 30 (2): 127–145.

Dix, Holger. 1999. *Parlamentswahlen in Benin*. Konrad Adenauer Stiftung.

Dix, Holger. 2007. *Parlamentswahlen in Benin*. Konrad Adenauer Stiftung.

Dowd, Robert, and Michael Driessen. 2008. "Ethnically Dominated Party Systems and the Quality of Democracy: Evidence from sub-Saharan Africa." Afrobarometer Working Paper.

Downs, Anthony. 1957. "An Economic Theory of Political Action in a Democracy." *Journal of Political Economy* 65 (2): 135–150.

Dulani, Boniface, and Jan Kees van Donge. 2004. A Decade of Legislative-Executive Squabble in Malawi, 1994–2004. In African Parliaments. Between Government and Governance, ed. Ma Mohammed Salih, 201–224. Palgrave Macmillan.

Duverger, Maurice. 1954. *Political Parties. Their Organization and Activity in the Modern State*. London: Methuen.

Easterly, William, and Ross Levine, Ross. 1997. "Africa's Growth Tragedy: Policies and Ethnic Divisions." *Quarterly Journal of Economics* 112 (4): 1203–1250.

Eifert, Ben, Edwart Miguel, and Daniel Posner. 2007. "Political Sources of Ethnic Identification in Africa." Afrobarometer Working Paper.

Eifert, Ben, Edward Miguel, and Daniel Posner. 2010. "Political Competition and Ethnic Identification in Africa." *American Journal of Political Science* 54 (2): 494–520.

EISA. 2005. *EISA Regional Observer Mission. Namibia Presidential and National Assembly Elections 15–16 November 2005*. South Africa: EISA.

EISA. 2007. *EISA Observer Mission Report 2006*. Zambia: EISA.

EISA. 2009. *EISA Observation Mission Report. Malawi Presidential and Parliamentary Elections*. Johannesburg: EISA.

EISA. 2002. Malawi: The Colonial Period (1891–1964). http://www.eisa.org.za/WEP/maloverview9.htm.

Elischer, Sebastian. 2012. "Measuring and Comparing Party Ideology in Nonindustrialized Societies: Taking Party Manifesto Research to Africa." *Democratization* 19 (4): 642–667.

Elischer, Sebastian. 2008. "Do African Parties Contribute to Democracy? Some Findings from Kenya, Ghana and Nigeria." *Afrika Spectrum* 43 (2): 175–201.

Ellis, Stephen. 2005. "How to Rebuild Africa." *Foreign Affairs* 84 (5): 135–148.

Emminghaus, Christoph. 2003. *Politische Parteien im Demokratisierungsprozess. Struktur und Funktion Afrikanische Parteiensysteme*. Leske und Budrich.

Engel, Ulf. 2003. "Gedanken zur Afrikanistik. Zukunft und Zustand einer Regionalwissenschaft in Deutschland." *Afrika Spectrum* 38 (1): 111–123.

Engels, Jan Niklas. 2005a. *Parteien und Parteiensystems in Afrika*. Bonn: Friedrich Ebert Stiftung.

Engels, Jan Nikklas. 2005b. Benin vor den Wahlen. Kann der Primus der afrikanischen Demokratie einen legitimen Machtwechsel vollziehen? Friedrich Ebert Stiftung.

Enlow, James, and Melvin Hinich. 1990. *Advances in the Spatial Theory of Voting*. Cambridge University Press.

Epstein, Leon. 1980. *Political Parties in Western Democracies*. Praeger.

Erdmann, Gero, and Neo Simutanyi. 2006. "Factionalism in an African Party System: The case of Zambia." Paper presented at the Seminar Series for the Research Group on 'Issues in Democratization,' Department of Comparative Politics, University of Bergen.

Erdmann, Gero. 2004. "Party Research: Western European Bias and the "African Labyrinth." *Democratization* 11 (3): 63–87.

Erdmann, Gero. 2007a. Party Research: Western European Bias and the African Labyrinth. In *Votes, Money and Violence. Political Parties and Elections in Sub-Saharan Africa*, ed. Matthias Basedau, Gero Erdmann and Andreas Mehler, 34–65. Elanders Gotab,

Erdmann, Gero. 2007b. "Ethnicity, Voter Alignment and Political Party Affiliation–an African Case: Zambia." German Institute of Global and Area Studies Working Paper 45.

Erdmann, Gero, and Ulf Engel, Ulf. 2007. "Neopatrimonialism Reconsidered: Critical Review and Elaboration of an Elusive Concept." *Commonwealth and Comparative Politics* 45 (1): 95–119.

Erdmann, Gero. 2010. "Political Party Assistance and Political Party Research: Towards a Closer Encounter?" *Democratization* 17 (6): 1275–1296.

European Union. 2002. *Kenya General Elections 27 December 2002*. European Union.

Evans, Geoffrey, and Stephen Whitefield. 1993. "Identifying the Bases of Party Competition in Europe." *British Journal of Political Science* 23 (4): 521–548.

Ferree, Karen. 2010. "The Social Origins of Electoral Volatility in Africa." *British Journal of Political Science* 40: 759–779.

Forestiere, Carolyn. 2009. "Kirchheimer Italian Style. Catch-All Parties or Catch-All Blocs." *Party Politics* 15 (5): 573–591.

Fridy, Kevin. 2007. "The Elephant, Umbrella, and Quarrelling Cocks: Disaggregating Partisanship in Ghana's Fourth Republic." *African Affairs* 106 (423): 281–305.

Fukui, Haruhiro. 1985. *Political Parties of Asia and the Pacific*. USA: Greenwood Press.

Galvan, Dennis. 2001. "Democracy without Ethnic Conflict." Paper presented at the 94th Annual Meeting of the American Political Science Association.

Geddes, Barbara. 2003. *Paradigms and Sand Castles. Theory Building and Research Design in Comparative Politics*. University of Michigan Press.

Geertzel, Cheery. 1970. *The Politics of Independent Kenya*. East African Publishing Hose.

Geingob, Hage. 2004. "State Formation in Namibia: Promoting Democracy and Good Governance." PhD thesis. University of Leeds.

Geiss, Imanuel. 1974. *The Pan-African Movement*. Africana Publication.

Gerring, John. 1994. "A Chapter in the History of American Party Ideology: The Nineteenth-Century Democratic Party." *Polity* 26 (4): 729–768.

Gerring, John. 2004. "What is a Case Study and What Is It Good For." *American Political Science Review* 98 (2): 341–354.
Gerring, John. 2006. *Case Study Research*. Cambridge University Press.
Gerring, John. 2007. "Is There a Viable Crucial – Case Method?" *Comparative Political Studies* 40 (3): 231–253.
Glickman, Harvey. 1963. "Introducing Political Africa." *Journal of Modern African Studies* 1 (2): 229–236.
Gloppen, Siri, Edge Kanyongolo, Nixon Khembo, Nandini Petel, Lise Rakner, Lars Svasand, Arne Tostensen, and Mette Bakken. 2006. *The Institutional Context of the 2004 General Elections in Malawi*. Christian Michelsen Institute.
Goerz, Gary. 2005. *Social Science Concepts: A User's Guide*. Princeton University Press.
Goldthorpe, John. 1997. "Current Issues in Comparative Macrosociology: A Debate on Methodological Issues." *Comparative Social Research* 16 (1): 1–26.
Goldsworthy, David. 1973. "Ghana's Second Republic: A Post-Mortem." *African Affairs* 72 (286): 8–25.
Goldsworthy, David. 1982. *Tom Mboya: The Man Kenya Wanted to Forget*. Heinemann.
Good, Kenneth. 1968. "Kenyatta and the Organization of KANU." *Canadian Journal of African Studies* 2 (2): 115–136.
Graham, Loren, and Jean-Michel Kantor. 2007. "'Soft' Area Studies versus 'Hard' Social Science: A False Opposition." *Slavic Review* 66 (1): 1–19.
Grignon, Francois. 2001. Breaking the "Ngilu Wave": The 1997 General Elections in the Meru and Embu Regions. In *Out for the Count. The 1997 General Elections and Prospects for Democracy in Kenya*, ed. Marcel Rutten, Alamin Mazrui and Francois Grignon, Francois, 315–347. Fountain Publishers, 315–347.
Grusky, David, and Ravi Kanbur. 2006. *Poverty and Inequality*. Stanford University Press.
Gunther, Richard, José Ramón, and Juan Linz. 2002. *Political Parties: Old Concepts and New Challenges*. Oxford University Press
Gunther, Richard, and Larry Diamond. 2003. "Species of Political Parties. A New Typology." *Party Politics* 9 (2): 167–199.
Hagberg, Sten. 2002. "Enough is Enough: An Ethnographic Account of the Struggle against Impunity in Burkina Faso." *Journal of Modern African Studies* 40 (2): 217–246.
Hale, Henry. 2000. "The Parade of Sovereignties: Testing Theories of Secession in the Soviet Setting." *British Journal of Political Science* 30 (1): 31–56.
Hale, Henry. 2004. "Divided We Stand. Institutional Sources of Ethnofederal State Survival and Collapse." *World Politics* 56 (2): 165–193.
Halpern, Manfred. 1966. "Politics in the Congo, Decolonization and Independence by Crawford Young." *American Political Science Review* 60 (1): 118–119.
Hansen, Emmanuel, and Paul Collins. 1980. "The Army, the State and the 'Rawlings Revolution in Ghana.'" *African Affairs* 79 (314): 3–23.
Harmel, Robert, and Kenneth Janda. 1994. "An Integrated Theory of Party Goals and Party Change." *Journal of Theoretical Politics* 6 (3): 259–287.
Harneit-Sievers, Axel. 1984. *SWAPO of Namibia*. Hamburg: Institut für Afrika-Kunde.

Harneit-Sievers, Axel. 1990. *Wahlen zur Verfassungsgebenden Versammlung 1989*. Germany: Institut für Afrika-Kunde.

Harris, Peter, and Ben Reilly. 1998. *Democracy and Deep-Rooted Conflict: Options for Negotiations*. Stockholm: International IDEA.

Harsch, Ernest. 1999. "Trop, c'est Trop. Civil Insurgence in Burkina Faso 1998–1999." *Review of African Political Economy* 26 (8): 395–406.

Harsch, Ernest. 2009. "Urban Protest in Burkina Faso." *African Affairs* 108 (431): 263–288.

Hartmann, Christof. 2010. "Senegal's Party System: The Limits of Formal Regulation."*Democratization* 17 (4): 769–786.

Hasty, Jennifer. 2005. *The Press and Political Culture in Ghana*. Indiana University Press.

Haynes, Jeff. 1995. From Personalistic to Democratic Rule. In *Democracy and Political Change in Sub-Saharan Africa*, ed. John Wiseman, 91–115. Routledge.

Hepburn, Eve. 2009. "Re-conceptualizing Sub-state Mobilization." *Regional and Federal Studies* 19 (4–5): 477–499.

Hepburn, Eve. 2011. "Citizens of the Region: Party Conceptions of Regional Citizenship and Immigrant Integration." *European Journal of Political Research* 50 (4): 504–529.

Herbst, Jeffrey, and Greg Mills. 2009. "There Is No Congo." *Foreign Policy*, Web Exclusive.

Hettne, Björn. 1980. "Soldiers and Politics: The Case of Ghana." *Journal of Peace Research* 17 (2): 173–193.

Hewitt, Christopher. 1977. "Majorities and Minorities: A Comparative Survey of Ethnic Violence." *Annals of the American Academy of Political and Social Science* 433 (1): 150–160.

Hilgers, Matthieu. 2010. "Evolution of Political Regime and Evolution of Popular Representation in Burkina Faso." *African Journal of Political Science and International Relations* 49 (9): 350–359.

Hodgkin, Thomas. 1956. *Nationalism in Tropical Africa*. Fredrick Muller.

Hodgkin, Thomas. 1961. *African Political Parties. An Introductory Guide*. Penguin Books.

Hodler, Roland. 2006. "The curse of natural resources in fractionalized countries." *European Economic Review* 50: 1367–1386.

Homlquist, Frank, and Michael Ford. 1994. "Kenya: State and Society the First Year after the Election." *Africa Today* 41 (4): 5–25.

Hopkins, A.G. 1978. "An Economic History of West Africa: A Further Comment." *African Economic History* 6 (Autumn): 139–144.

Hopwood, Graham. 2007. *Guide to Namibian Politics*. National Institute for Democracy.

Hornsby, Charles. 2012. *Kenya. A History Since Independence*. I.B. Tauris.

Horowitz, Donald. 1991. *A Democratic South Africa? Constitutional Engineering in a Divided Society*. University of California Press.

Horowitz, Donald. 2000. *Ethnic Groups in Conflict*. University of California Press.

Hönnige, Christoph. 2007. *Verfassunsgericht, Regierung und Opposition. Die vergleichende Analyse eines Spannunsdreiecks*. Germany: Verlag für Sozialwissenschaften.

Howe, Russell. 1958. "Ghana: The First Year." *Phylon Quarterly* 19 (3): 277–285.

Huber, John, and Ronald Inglehart. 1995. "Expert Interpretations of Party Space and Party Locations in 42 Societies." *Party Politics* 1 (1): 73–111.

Hulterström, Karolina. 2004. Ethnic Politics: Parties and Policies in Kenya and Zambia. Acta Universitatis Upsaliensis.

Hulterström, Karolina, Yamin Kamete, and Henning Melber. 2007. *Political Opposition in African Countries: The Case of Kenya, Namibia, Zambia and Zimbabwe.* Nordic Africa Institute.

Human Rights Watch. 1993. *Divide and Rule. State-Sponsored Ethnic Violence in Kenya.* Human Rights Watch.

Human Rights Watch. 2007. *Criminal Politics. Violence, Godfathers and Corruption in Nigeria.* Human Rights Watch.

Human Rights Watch. 2008. *Ballots to Bullets. Organized Political Violence and Kenya's Crisis of Governance.* Human Rights Watch.

Hunter, Justine. 2008. *Die Politik der Erinnerung und des Vergessens in Namibia: Umgang mit schweren Menschenrechtsverletzungen der Ära des bewaffneten Befreiungskampfes 1966 bis 1989.* Peter Lang.

Hunter, Justine, and Robin Sherbourne. 2004. *On the Record: Political Party Representatives Challenged.* Konrad Adenauer Foundation.

Huntington, Samuel. 1968. *Political Order in Changing Societies.* Yale University Press.

Ihonvbere, Julius. 1997. "From Despotism to Democracy: The Rise of Multiparty Politics in Malawi." *Third World Quarterly* 18 (2): 225–247.

Ishiyama, John, and Marijke Breuning. 1998. *Ethnopolitics in the New Europe.* Lynne Rienner.

Ishiyama, John. 1999. "Sickles into Roses: The Successor Parties and Democratic Consolidation in Post-Communist Politics." *Democratization* 6 (4): 52–73.

Ishiyama, John, and Krystal Fox. 2006. "What Affects the Strength of Partisan Identity in Sub-Saharan Africa?" *Politics & Policy* 34 (4): 748–773.

Ishiyama, John. 2009. "Do Ethnic Parties Promote Ethnic Minority Conflict?" *Nationalism and Ethnic Politics* 15 (1): 56–83.

Ishiyama, John, and Marijke Breuning. 2011. "What's in a Name? Ethnic Party Identity and Democratic Development in Post-Communist Countries." *Party Politics* 17 (2): 233–241.

Ishiyama, John. 2012. "Explaining Ethnic Bloc Voting in Africa." *Democratization* 19 (4): 642–667.

Jackson, Robert, and Carl Rosberg. 1982. *Personal Rule in Black Africa. Prince Autocrat, Prophet, Tyrant.* University of California Press.

Jeffries, Richard, and Clare Thomas. 1993. "The Ghanaian Elections of 1992." *African Affairs* 92 (369): 331–366.

John, Daniel. 1999. *Voting for Democracy: Watershed Elections in Contemporary Anglophone Africa.* Ashgate.

Jones, Mark, and Scott Mainwaring. 2003. "The Nationalization of Parties and Party Systems." *Party Politics* 9 (2): 139–166.

Jonyo, Fred. 2003. The Centrality of Ethnicity in Kenya's Political Transition. In *The Politics of Transition in Kenya. From KANU to NARC*, ed. Walter Oyugi, Peter Wanyande, Peter and C. Ochiambo-Mbai, 155–179. Heinrich Böll Foundation.

Kabemba, Claude. 2004. *Elections and Democracy in Zambia.* South Africa: EISA.

Kadima, Denis, and Felix Owuor. 2006. The National Rainbow Coalition. In *The Politics of Party Coalitions in Africa*, ed. Denis Kadima, Denis, 179–221. Konrad Adenauer Foundation.

Kagwanja, Peter. 2006. "Power to Uhuru: Youth Identity and Generational Politics in Kenya's 2002 Elections." *African Affairs* 105 (418): 51–75.

Kala, A.S. 1979. Nationalism in Kenya before Independence. In *Economic and Political Development of Kenya*, ed. Priya Mutalik-Desai, 93–112. Himalaya Publishing House.

Kalipeni, Ezekiel. 1997. "Regional Polarization in Voting Pattern: Malawi's 1994 Elections." *African Journal of Political Science* 2 (1): 152–167.

Kandeh, Jimmy. 1992. "The Politicization of Ethnic Identities in Sierra Leone." *African Studies Review* 35 (1): 81–99.

Kandeh, Jimmy. 2003. "Sierra Leone's Post-Conflict Elections of 2002." *Journal of Modern African Studies* 41 (2): 189–216.

Kanyinga, Karuti. 2003. Limitations of Political Liberalization: Parties and Electoral Politics in Kenya, 1992–2002. In *The Politics of Transition in Kenya. From KANU to* NARC, ed. Walter Oyugi, Peter Wanyande, Peter and C. Ochiambo-Mbai, C, 180–211. Heinrich Böll Foundation.

Kaplan, Robert. 1997. *The end of the Earth: From Togo to Turkmenistan, from Iran to Cambodia. A Journey to the Frontier of Anarchy*. Vintage.

Kariuki, Samuel. 2008. "'We've been to hell and back . . . ': Can a Botched Land Reform Program Explain Kenya's Political Crisis? (1963–2008)." *Journal of African Elections* 7 (2): 135–172.

Karvonen, Lauri, and Stein Kuhnle. 2001. *Party Systems and Voter Alignments Revisited*. Routledge.

Kasara, Kimali. 2011. "Separate and Suspicious: Local, Social and Political Context and Ethnic Tolerance in Kenya." Afrobarometer Working Paper.

Kasfir, Nelson. 1976. *The Shrinking Political Arena: Participation and Ethnicity in African Politics with a Case Study of Uganda*. University of California Press.

Kaspin, Deborah. 1995. "The Politics of Ethnicity in Malawi's Democratic Transition." *The Journal of Modern African Studies* 33: 595–620.

Katz Richard. 2002. The Internal Life of Parties. In: *Political Parties in the New Europe. Political and Analytical Challenges*, ed. Richard Kurth Luther and Ferdinand Müller-Rommel, 87–118. Oxford University Press.

Katz, Richard, and Peter Mair. 1992. *A Data Handbook on Party Organizations in Western Democracies, 1960–1990*. UK: Sage Publications.

Katz, Richard, and Peter Mair. 1995. "Changing Models of Party Organization and Party Democracy. The Emergence of the Cartel Party." *Party Politics* 1 (1): 5–28.

Katz, Richard, and Peter Mair. 2009. "The Cartel Party Thesis: A Restatement." *Perspective on Politics* 7 (4): 753–766.

Katzenstein, Peter. 2001. "Area and Regional Studies in the United States." *Political Science and Politics* 34 (4): 789–791.

Keffer, Philip. 2010. "The Ethnicity Distraction? Political Credibility and Partisan Preferences in Africa." Afrobarometer Working Paper.

Kenig, Maria. 1978. "The Shrinking Political Arena: Participation and Ethnicity in African Politics with a Case Study from Uganda by Nelson Kasfir." *Journal of the International African Institute* 48 (4): 417–418.

Khapoya, Vincent. 1979. "The Politics of Succession in Africa: The Case of Kenya." *Africa Today* 26 (3): 7–20.

Kilson, Martin. 1966. *Political Change in a West African State: A Study in the Modernization Process in Sierra Leone*. Harvard University Press.

Kilson, Martin. 1976. Cleavage Management in African Politics: The Ghana Case. In *Cleavage Management in African Politics*, ed. Martin Kilson, 85–98. Harvard University Press, 85–98.

Kindiki, Kithure, and Osogo Ambani. 2005. *Selected Analyses of the 2004 Draft Constitution of Kenya*. Claripress.

King, Gary, Robert Keohane, and Sidney Verba. 1994. Designing Social Inquiry: *Scientific Inference in Qualitative Research*. Princeton University Press.

Kirchheimer, Otto. 1966. The Transformation of the Western European Party Systems. In *Political Parties and Political Developmen*, ed. Joseph LaPalombara and Myron Weiner, 177–201. Princeton University Press.

Kitschelt, Herbert. 1993. "Social Movements, Political Parties, and Democratic Theory." *Annals of the American Academy of Political and Social Science* 528 (1): 13–29.

Kitschelt, Herbert. 1994. *The Transformation of European Social Democracy*. Cambridge University Press.

Kitschelt, Herbert. 2000. "Linkages Between Citizens and Politicians in Democratic Polities." *Comparative Political Studies* 33 (6–7): 845–879.

Kitschelt, Herbert, Kirk Hawkins, Juan Luna, Guillermo Rosas, and Elizabeth Zechmeister. 2010. *Latin American Party Systems*. USA: Cambridge University Press.

Klingemann, Hans-Dieter, Andrea Volkens, Judith Bara, Ian Budge, Michael McDonald. 2006. *Mapping Policy Preferences II*. Oxford University Press.

Koole, Ruud. 1996. "Cadre, Catch-All or Cartel? A Comment on the Notion of the Cartel Party." *Party Politics* 2 (4): 507–523.

Kopecky, Petr. 1995. "Developing Party Organizations in East Central Europe." *Party Politics* 1 (4): 515–534.

Köllner, Patrick, Matthias Basedau, and Gero Erdmann. 2006. *Innerparteiliche Machtgruppen. Faktionalismus im internationalem Vergleich*. Campus.

Krouwel, A.P.M. 1999. "The Catch-All Party in Western Europe 1945–1990. A Study in Arrested Development." PhD thesis. Free University of Amsterdam.

Krouwel, A.P.M. 2003. "Otto Kirchheimer and the Catch-All Party." *West European Politics* 26 (2): 23–40.

Kuenzi, Michelle, and Gina Lambright. 2007. "Voter Turnout in Africa's Multiparty Democracies." *Comparative Political Studies* 40 (6): 665–690.

Kumar, Krishna. 2004. *International Political Party Assistance. An Overview and Analysis*. Netherlands Institute of International Relations 'Clingendael.'

Kwang Johnson, Nancy. 2004. "Senegalese into Frenchman or Peasants into Senegalese?: The Politics of Language, Culture and Assimilation: A Colonial and Post-Independence Critique (Senegal)." Paper presented at the annual meeting of the International Studies Association, Montreal, Quebec.

Kyle, Keith. 1999. *The Politics of the Independence of Kenya*. Macmillan.

Laakso, Markku, and Rein Taagepera. 1979. "'Effective' Number of Parties: A Measure with Application to West Europe." *Comparative Political Studies* 12 (1): 3–27.

Lambert, Michael. 1998. "Violence and the War of Word: Ethnicity v. Nationalism in the Casamance." *Africa* 68 (4): 585–602.

Larmer, Miles, and Alastair Fraser. 2007. "Of Cabbages and King Cobra: Populist Politics and Zambia's 2006 Elections." *African Affairs* 106 (425): 611–637.

Lauth, Hans-Joachim. 2000. "Informal Institutions and Democracy." *Democratization* 7 (4): 21–50.

Lauth, Hans-Joachim, Gert Pickel, and Christian Welzel. 2000. *Demokratiemessung. Konzepte und Befunde im Internationalen Vergleich.* Opladen.

Lawson, Letitia. 1999. "External Democracy Promotion in Africa: Another False Start?" *Commonwealth and Comparative Politics* 37 (1): 1–30.

Le Bas, Adrienne. 2011. *From Protest to Parties: Party-Building and Democratization in Africa.* Oxford University Press.

Le Beau, Debie. 2005. "Multiparty Democracy and Elections in Namibia." *Journal of African Elections* 4 (1): 1–26.

Lekorwe, Mogopodi. 2005. Organisation of Political Parties. In *40 Years of Democracy in Botswana: 1965–2005*, ed. Zibani Maudeni, 122–146. Mmegi Publishing House.

Lemarchand, Rene. 1972. "Political Clientelism and Ethnicity in Tropical Africa: Competing Solidarities in Nation-Building." *American Political Science Review* 66 (1): 68–90.

Lemarchand, Rene. 2007. "Consociationalism and Power Sharing in Africa: Rwanda, Burundi, and the Democratic Republic of the Congo." *African Affairs* 106 (422): 1–20.

Lentz, Carola and Paul Nugent. 2000. *Ethnicity in Ghana: The Limits of Invention.* Macmillan.

Levitzky, Steven, and Lucan Way. 2002. "The Rise of Competitive Authoritarianism." *Journal of Democracy* 13 (2): 51–65.

Lewis, Peter. 2011. "Nigeria Votes: More Openness, More Conflict." *Journal of Democracy* 22 (4): 60–74.

Lewis-Beck, Michael. 2008. *The American Voter Revisited.* University of Michigan Press.

Leys, Collin, and John Saul. 1994. "Liberation without Democracy? The SWAPO Crisis of 1976." *Journal of Southern African Studies* 20 (1): 123–147.

Leys, Colin, Paul Saul, and Susan Brown. 1995. *Namibia's Liberation Struggle. The Two-Edged Sword.* James Currey.

Lieberson, Stanley. 1991. "Small N's and Big Conclusions: An Examination of the Reasoning in Comparative Studies Based on a Small Number of Cases." *Social Forces* 70 (2): 307–320.

Lijphart, Arend. 1971. "Comparative Politics and the Comparative Method." *American Political Science Review* 65 (3): 682–693.

Lijphart, Arend, and Bernard Grofman. 1984. Choosing an Electoral System: *Issues and Alternatives.* Praeger.

Lijphart, Arend. 1991. "Constitutional Choices for New Democracies." *Journal of Democracy* 2 (1): 72–84.

Lijphart, Arend. 1999. *Patterns of Democracy: Government Forms and Performance in Thirty-Six Countries.* Yale University Press.

Lindeke, William, Winnie Wanzala, and Victor Tonchi. 1992. "Namibia's Election Revisited." *South African Journal of Political Studies* 19 (2): 121–138.

Lindberg, Staffan, and Minion Morrison. 2008. "Are African Voters Really Ethnic or Clientelistic? Survey Evidence from Ghana." *Political Science Quarterly* 123 (1): 95–122.

Lindberg, Staffan. 2007. "Institutionalization of Party Systems? Stability and Fluidity Among Legislative Parties in Africa's Democracies." *Government and Opposition* 42 (2): 215–241.

Lindberg, Staffan. 2006. *Democracy and Elections in Africa.* John Hopkins University Press.

Lipset, Seymour, and Stein Rokkan. 1967. *Party Systems and Voter Alignments: Cross National Perspectives.* Free Press.

Lipset, Seymour. 2001a. Cleavages, Parties and Democracy. In *Party Systems and Voter Alignments Revisited*, ed. Lauri Karvonen and Stein Kuhnle, 2–8. Routledge.

Lipset, Seymour. 2001b. The Americanization of the European Left. In *Political Parties and Democracy*, ed. Larry Diamond and Richard Gunther, 52–66. The Johns Hopkins University Press, pp. 52–66.

Lister, Gwen. 1981. "Political Parties and Tribal Groups in Namibia." Paper Prepared for a Seminar on Namibia held by the Scandinavian Institute of African Studies.

Loade, Augustin, and Carlos Santiso. 2002. *Landmark Elections in Burkina Faso.* International IDEA.

Lodge, Tom. 1999. "The Namibian Elections of 1999." *Democratization* 8 (2): 191–230.

Lofchie, Michael. 1985. *Zanzibar: Background to Revolution.* Princeton University Press.

Lonsdale, John. 2005. "African Studies, Europe & Africa." *Afrika Spectrum* 40 (3): 377–402.

Lotshwao, Kebapetse. 2011. "The Weakness of Opposition Parties in Botswana: A Justification for More Internal-Party Democracy in the Dominant Botswana Democratic Party (BDP)." *African Journal of Political Science and International Relations* 5 (2): 103–111.

Lötzer, Klaus. 2003. *Benin: Parlamentswahlen vom 30.03.2003.* Konrad Adenauer Stiftung.

Luckham, Robin. 1994. "The Military, Militarization and Democratization in Africa: A Survey of Literature and Issues." *African Studies Review* 37 (2): 13–75.

Lush, David. 1993. *Last Steps to Uhuru.* New Namibia Books.

Lustick, Ian. 1996. "History, Historiography, and Political Science: Multiple Historical Records and the Problem of Selection Bias." *American Political Science Review* 90 (3): 605–618.

Lynch, Gabrielle. 2006. "The Fruits of Perception: 'Ethnic Politics' and the Case of Kenya's Constitutional Referendum." *African Studies* 65 (2): 233–270.

Lynch, Gabrielle. 2007. "Kenyan Politics and the Ethnic Factor: The Case of the Kalenjin." PhD thesis. Oxford University.

Lynch, Gabrielle. 2008. "Courting the Kalenjin: The Failure of Dynasticism and the Strength of the ODM Wave in Kenya's Rift Valley Province." *African Affairs* 107 (429): 541–568.

MacIvor, Heather. 1996. "Do Canadian Political Parties Form a Cartel?" *Canadian Journal of Political Science* 29 (2): 317–333.

McCain, James. 1975. "Ideology in Africa: Some Perceptual Types." *African Studies Review* 18 (1): 67–87.

Mahoney, James. 1999. "Nominal, Ordinal and Narrative Appraisal in Macrocausal Analysis." *American Journal of Sociology* 104 (4): 1154–1196.

Mahoney, James. 2000. "Strategies of Causal Inference in Small-N Analysis." *Sociological Methods and Research* 28 (4): 387–424.

Mahoney, James. 2001. "Path-Dependent Explanations of Regime Change: Central America in Comparative Perspective." *Studies in Comparative International Development* 36 (1): 111–141.

Mahoney, James, and James Rueschemeyer. 2003. *Comparative Historical Analysis in the Social Sciences*. Cambridge University Press.

Mainwaring, Scott, and Timothy Scully. 1995. *Party Systems in Latin America*. Stanford University Press.

Mair, Peter. 2005. "Democracy Beyond Parties." CSD Working Paper.

Mair, Peter, Wolfgang Müller, and Fritz Plasser. 2004. *Political Parties and Electoral Change: Party Reponses to Electoral Markets*. SAGE.

Mair, Peter, and Ingrid van Biezen. 2001. "Party Membership in Twenty European Democracies: 1880–2000." *Party Politics* 7 (5): 5–21.

Mair, Stefan. 1994. *Kenias Weg in die Mehrparteiendemokratie: Von Uhuru über Harambee und Nyago erneut zu Uhuru*. Germany: Nomos.

Makgala, Christian John. 2005. "The Relationship between Kenneth Koma and the Botswana Democratic Party 1965–2003." *African Affairs* 104 (415): 303–323.

Mann, Michael. 2005. *The Dark Side of Democracy: Explaining Ethnic Cleansing*. Cambridge University Press.

Manning, Carrie. 2008. *The Making of Democrats*. Palgrave Macmillan.

Markowski, Radoslaw. 1997. "Political Parties and Ideological Space in East Central Europe." *Communist and Post-Communist Studies* 30 (3): 221–254.

Maroleng, Chris. 2004. "Malawi General Election 2004: Democracy in the Firing Line." *African Security Review* 13 (2): 77–81.

Massetti, Emmanuel. 2009. "Explaining Regionalist Party Positioning in a Multi-dimensional Ideological Space: A Framework for Analysis." *Regional & Federal Studies* 19 (4–5): 501–531.

Maundeni, Zibani. 2005. Succession to High Office: Tswana Culture and Modern Botswana Politics. In *40 Years of Democracy in Botswana: 1965–2005*, ed. Zibani Maudeni, 80–93. Mmegi Publishing House.

Maupeu, Harvé, Musambati Katumanga, and Katumange Mitullah. 2005. *The Moi Succession: The 2002 Elections in Kenya*. Transafrica Press.

Meguid, Bonnie. 2005. "Competition Between Unequals: The Role of Mainstream Party Strategy in Niche Party Success." *American Political Science Review* 99 (3): 347–359.

Melber, Henning. 2003. "From Controlled Change to Changed Control." *Journal of Contemporary African Studies* 21 (2): 267–284.

Merkel, Wolfgang. 2003. *Defekte Demokratien. Band 1: Theorie*. Leskeund Budrich.

Merkl, Peter. 1967. "Political Cleavages and Party Systems." *World Politics* 21 (3): 469–485.

Michels, Robert. 1949. *Political Parties: A Sociological Study of the Oligarchical Tendencies of Modern Democracy*. Free Press.

Miller, Warren. 1996. *The New American Voter*. Harvard University Press.

Mmuya, Maximilian and Amon Chaligha. 1994. *Political Parties and Democracy in Tanzania*. Friedrich Ebert Stiftung.

Mmuya, Maximilian. 1998. *Tanzania: Political Reform in Eclipse. Crises and Cleavages in Political Parties*. Friedrich Ebert Stiftung.

Moegenburg, Ilka. 2002. Die Parteienlandschaft im Senegal. Tragfähige Grundlage der Demokratisierung. LIT Verlag.

Mokopakgosi, Brian, and Mpho Molomo. 2000. "Democracy in the Face of Weak Opposition in Botswana." *Pula: Botswana Journal of African Studies* 14 (1): 3–21.

Momba, Jotham. 2005. *Political Parties and the Quest for Democratic Consolidation in Zambia*. EISA.

Monsch, Grian-Andrea. 2008. *Der Klient und sein Patron – oder warum man nie in Burkina Faso wählen geht*. Center for Comparative and International Studies.

Moore, Barrington. 1967. Social Origins of Dictatorship and Democracy: *Lord and Peasant in the Making of the Modern World*. Beacon Press.

Morgenthau, Ruth Schachter. 1961. *Political Parties in West Africa*. Clarendon Press.

Morgenthau, Ruth Schachter. 1964. *Political Parties in Frenchspeaking West Africa*. Oxford University Press.

Moroff, Anika. 2010. "Party Bans in Africa – An Empirical Overview." *Democratization* 17 (4): 618–641.

Moroff, Anika. 2010. "An Effective Measure of Institutional Engineering? Ethnic Party Bans in Africa." *Democratization* 17 (4): 666–686.

Morrison, Lesa. 2007. "The Nature of Decline: Distinguishing Myth from Reality in the Case of the Luo of Kenya." *Journal of Modern African Studies* 45 (1): 117–142.

Morrison, Minion. 2004. "Political Parties in Ghana through Four Republics. A Path to Democratic Consolidation." *Comparative Politics* 36 (4): 421–442.

Morrison, Minion, and Hong Jaw. 2006. "Ghana's Political Parties. How Ethno-Regional Variations Sustain the National Two-Party System." *Journal of Modern African Studies* 44 (4): 623–647.

Mudde, Cas, and Peter Mair. 1998. "The Party Family and Its Study." *Annual Review of Political Science* 1: 211–229.

Müller, Wolfgang, and Kaare Strom. 1999. *Policy, Office or Votes? How Political Parties in Western Europe Make Hard Decisions*. Cambridge University Press.

Munck, Gerardo. 1998. "Canons of Research Design in Qualitative Analysis." *Studies in Comparative International Development* 33 (3): 18–45.

Munck, Gerardo, and Richard Snyder. 2007. "Debating the Direction of Comparative Politics." *Comparative Political Studies* 40 (1): 5–31.

Mutua, Makau. 2008. *Kenya's Quest for Democracy*. Lynne Rienner.

National Democratic Institute. 2003. *Working to Strengthen and Expand Democracy Worldwide*. National Democratic Institute.

National Development Party. 1997. *Towards a Better Kenya*. National Development Party.

Neumann, Sigmund. 1954. "Towards a Theory of Political Parties." *World Politics* 6 (4): 549–563.
Neumann, Sigmund. 1955. *Modern Political Parties*. University of Chicago Press.
New Patriotic Party. 1998. *Constitution of the New Patriotic Party*. New Patriotic Party.
Newman, Saul. 1996. *Ethnoregional Conflict in Democracies: Mostly Ballots, Rarely Bullets*. Greenwood Press.
Ninsin, Kwame. 1987. "Ghanaian Politics after 1981: Revolution of Evolution?" *Canadian Journal of African Studies* 21 (1): 17–38.
Norris, Pippa, and Robert Mattes. 2003. *Does Ethnicity Determine Support for the Governing Party?* Cape Town: Center for Social Science Research University of Cape Town.
Norris, Pippa. 2005. *Building Political Parties: Reforming Legal Regulations and Internal Rules*. International IDEA.
Nugent, Paul. 1995. *Big Men, Small Boys and Politics in Ghana: Power Ideology and the Burden of History, 1982–1994*. Pinter.
Nugent, Paul. 1999. "Living in the Past: Urban, Rural and Ethnic Themes in the 1992 and 1996 Elections in Ghana." *Journal of Modern African Studies* 37 (2): 287–319.
Nugent, Paul. 2001. "Winners, Losers and Also Rans: Money, Moral Authority and Voting Patterns in the Ghana 2000 Elections." *African Affairs* 100 (400): 405–428.
Nujoma, Sam. 2001. *Where Others Wavered. The Autobiography of Sam Nujoma*. UK: Panaf.
Nyang'oro, Julius. 2004. *Ethnic Structure, Inequality and Governance of the Public Sector in Tanzania*. UNRISD.
Obeng-Odoom, Franklin. 2009. "Transforming Third World Cities Through Good Urban Governance: Fresh Evidence." *Theoretical and Empirical Researchers in Urban Management* 1 (10): 46–62.
Olodo, Kochikpa, and Damaso Sossou. 2008. Militantisme et l'identification Ethnique au Bénin. In *Les Fontionnement des Partis Politiques au Bénin*, ed. Jan Niklas Engels, Alexander Stroh and Léonard Wantchékon, 109–122. Friedrich Ebert Stiftung.
Oloka-Onyango, Joseph and Maria Nassali. 2003. *Constitutionalism and Political Stability in Zanzibar. The Search for a New Vision*. Friedrich Ebert Stiftung.
Omolo, Ken. 2002. "Political Ethnicity in the Democratization Process in Kenya." *African Studies* 61 (2): 209–221.
Oquaye, Mike. 2004. *Politics in Ghana, 1982–1992: Rawlings, Revolution and Populist Democracy*. Tornado Publications.
Osei-Hwedie, Bertha. 1998. "The Role of Ethnicity in Multi-Party Politics in Malawi and Zambia." *Journal of Contemporary African Studies* 16 (2): 227–247.
Osei, Anja. 2010. "Party-Voter Linkage in Ghana and Senegal." PhD thesis. University of Leipzig.
Osei-Hwedie, Bertha. 1998. "The Role of Ethnicity in Multi-Party Politics in Malawi and Zambia." *Journal of Contemporary African Studies* 16 (2): 227–247.
Osei-Hwedie, Bertha. 2001. "The Political Opposition in Botswana: The Politics of Factionalism and Fragmentation." *Transformation* 45: 57–77.

Otayek, René. 1992. "The Democratic 'Rectification' of Burkina Faso." *Journal of Comunist Studies* 8 (2): 83–104.

Ott, Martin, Phiri Kings, and Patel Nandini. 2000. *Malawi's Second Democratic Elections*. Kachere.

Oyugi, Walter. 1997. "Ethnicity in the Electoral Process: The 1992 General Elections in Kenya." *African Journal of Political Science* 2 (1): 41–69.

Palmberg, Mai. 1999. *National Identity and Democracy in Africa*. Human Sciences Research Council.

Peil, Margaret. 1974. "Ghana's Aliens." *International Migration Review* 8 (3): 367–381.

Pelizzo, Ricardo. 2006. *The Cartel Party and the Rise of the New Extreme Right*. Singapore: Research Collection School of Social Sciences.

Peters, Ralph-Michael. 1998. "Die Präsidentschafts- und Parlamentswahlen in Kenia 1997." *Focus Afrika* 10.

Pierson, Paul. 2004. *Politics in Time. History, Institutions and Social Analysis*. Princeton University Press.

Pinto-Duschinsky, Michael. 2002. "Financing Politics: A Global View." *Journal of Democracy* 13 (4): 69–86.

Posner, Daniel. 2003. "The Colonial Origins and Ethnic Cleavages: The Case of Linguistic Division in Zambia." *Comparative Politics* 35 (2): 127–146.

Posner, Daniel. 2004. "The Political Salience of Cultural Difference: Why Chewas and Tumbukas are Allies in Zambia and Adversaries in Malawi." *American Political Science Review* 98 (4): 529–545.

Posner, Daniel. 2005. *Institutions and Ethnic Politics in Africa*. Cambridge University Press.

Puhle, Hans-Jürgen. 2002. Still the Age of Catch-allism? Volksparteien and Parteienstaat in Crisis and Re-equilibration. In *Political Parties. Old Concepts and New Challenges*, ed. Richard Gunther, Jose Ramon-Montero and Juan Linz, 58–83. Oxford University Press, 58–83.

Price, Robert. 1973. "The Pattern of Ethnicity in Ghana." *Journal of Modern African Studies* 11 (3): 470–475.

Protsyk, Olek, and Andrew Wilson. 2003. "Centre Politics in Russia and Ukraine." *Party Politics* 9 (6): 703–727.

Przeworski, Adam, and Henry Teune. 1982. *The Logic of Comparative Social Inquiry*. Kriegler.

Przeworski, Adam. 1991. *Democracy and the Market. Political and Economic Reforms in Eastern Europe and Latin America*. Cambridge University Press.

Pütz, Joachim, Heidi von Egidy, and Oerii Caplan. 1990. *Political Who's Who of Namibia*. Magnus Company.

Qurban, Mitra, and Jan-Niklas Engels. 2007. *Der Sieg der Kauri-Muscheln*. Friedrich Ebert Stiftung.

Rabushka, Alvin, and Kenneth Shepsle. 2009. *Politics in Plural Societies: A Theory of Democratic Instability*. Pearson and Longmen.

Rakner, Lise. 2003. *Political and Economic Liberalization in Zambia 1991–2001*. The Nordic Africa Institute.

Rakner, Lise, and Lars Svasand. 2004. "From Dominant to Competitive Party System. The Zambian Experience 1991–2001." *Party Politics* 10 (1): 49–68.

Randall, Vicky. 2001. Party Systems and Voter Alignments in the New Democracies of the Third World. In *Party Systems and Voter Alignments Revisited*, ed. Lauri Karvonen and Stein Kuhnle, 244–265. Routledge.

Randall, Vicky, and Lars Svasand. 2002. "The Contribution of Parties to Democracy and Democratic Consolidation." *Democratization* 9 (3): 1–10.

Randall, Vicky. 2007. "Political Parties and Democratic Developmental States." *Development Policy Review* 25 (5): 633–652.

Rathbone, Richard. 1973. "Businessmen in Politics: Party Struggles in Ghana 1949–1957." *Journal of Development Studies* 9 (3): 391–401.

Reilly, Ben, and Andrew Reynolds. 1999. *Electoral Systems and Conflict in Divided Societies*. National Academy Press.

Reilly, Ben. 2001. *Democracy in Divided Societies: Electoral Engineering for Conflict Management*. Cambridge University Press.

Reilly, Ben. 2006. *Democracy and Diversity: Political Engineering in the Asia-Pacific*. Oxford University Press.

Reilly, Ben. 2007. "Electoral Systems and Party Systems in East Asia." *Journal of East Asian Studies* 7: 185–201.

Reilly, Ben. 2008. "Electoral Systems and Party Systems in Asia." *Journal of East Asian Studies* 7 (2): 185–202.

Reiter, Howard. 2004, "Factional Persistence Within Parties in the United States." *Party Politics* 10 (3): 251–271.

Reith, Stefan. 2010. *Tanzania After the Parliamentary and Presidential Elections*. Konrad Adenauer Stiftung.

Republic du Benin. 2002. Troisieme Recensement General De La Population et de L'Habilitation. Institut National de la Statistique et de L'Analyse Economique.

Republic of Kenya. 1989. *Kenya Population Census 1989*. Government Publication.

Republic of Kenya. 2008. *Geographic Dimensions of Well-Being in Kenya. Who and Where are the Poor. A Constituency Profile*. Government Publication.

Republic of Namibia. 2008. *A Review of Poverty and Inequality in Namibia*. Central Bureau of Statistics.

Reynolds, Andrew. 2011. *Designing Democracy in a Dangerous World*. Oxford University Press.

Reynolds, Andrew. 1999. *Electoral Systems and Democratization in South Africa*. Oxford University Press.

Reynolds, Andrew. 1995. "Constitutional Engineering in Southern Africa." *Journal of Democracy* 6 (2): 86–99.

Riker, William. 1967. "The Two-Party System and Duverger's Law: An Essay on the History of Political Science." *American Political Science Review* 76 (4): 753–766.

Robinson, James, and Neil Parsons. 2006. "State Formation and Governance in Botswana." *Journal of African Economics* 15 (1): 100–140.

Rokkan, Stein. 1970. *Citizens, Elections, Parties: Approaches to the Comparative Study of the Process of Development*. Universitetsforlaget.

Roper, Steven. 1995. "The Romanian Party System and the Catch-All Party Phenomenon." *East European Quarterly* 28 (4): 519–532.

Rose, Richard, and Derek Urwin. 1974. *Regional Differentiation and Political Unity in Western Nations*. Sage.

Rotberg, Robert. 1966a. "Modern African Studies: Problems and Prospects." *World Politics* 18 (3): 565–578.

Rotberg, Robert. 1966b. "African Nationalism: Concept or Confusion." *Journal of Modern African Studies* 4 (1): 33–46.

Rotberg, Robert. 2002. "The New Nature of Nation-State Failure." *Washington Quarterly* 25 (3): 85–96.

Rudolph, Joseph. 2006. Politics and Ethnicity: *A Comparative Study*. Palgrave Macmillian.

Rutten, Marcel, Ali Mazuri, and Francois Grignon. 2001. *Out for the Count: The 1997 General Elections and Prospects for Democracy in Kenya*. Fountain.

Sachsenröder, Wolfgang, and Ulrike Frings. 1998. *Political Party Systems and Democratic Development in East and Southeast Asia*. Ashgate.

Salih, Mohamed. 2003. *African Political Parties. Evolution, Institutionalization and Governance*. Pluto Press.

Sandbrook, Richard. 1975. The Development of an African Working Class: *Studies in Class Formation and Action*. University of Toronto Press.

Sanger, Clyde, and John Nottingham. 1964. "The Kenya General Election of 1963." *Journal of Modern African Studies* 2 (1): 1–40.

Santiso, Carlos, and Augustin Loada. 2003. "Explaining the unexpected: electoral reform and democratic governance in Burkina Faso." *Journal of Modern African Studies* 41 (3): 395–419.

Sartori, Giovanni. 1970. "Concept Misformation in Comparative Politics." *American Political Science Review* 64 (4): 1033–1053.

Sartori, Giovanni. 1984. *Social Science Concepts. A Systematic Analysis*. Beverly Hills: Sage.

Sartori, Giovanni. 2005a. *Parties and Party Systems. A Framework for Analysis*. ECPR Press.

Sartori, Giovanni. 2005b. "Party Types, Organization and Functions." *West European Politics* 28 (1): 5–32.

Scarritt, James, and Shaheen Mozaffar. 1999. "The Specification of Ethnic Cleavages and Ethnopolitical Groups for the Analysis of Democratic Competition in Contemporary Africa." *Nationalism and Ethnic Politics* 5 (1): 82–117.

Scarritt, James. 2006. "The Strategic Choice of Multiethnic Parties in Zambia's Dominant and Personalist Party System." *Commonwealth & Comparative Politics*, 44 (2): 234–256.

Scarrow, Susan. 2007. "Political Finance in Comparative Perspective." *Annual Review of Political Science* 10: 193–210.

Schattenschneider, Elmer. 1942. *Party Government*. American Government in Action.

Schatzberg, Michael. 1987. *The Political Economy of Kenya*. Praeger.

Schedler, Andreas. 2002. "The Menu of Manipulation." *Journal of Democracy* 13 (2): 36–49.

Schmitter, Philippe, and Terry Karl. 1994. "The Conceptual Travels of Transitologists and Consolidologists: How Far to the East Should They Attempt to Go?" *Slavic Review* 53 (1): 173–185.

Schmitter, Philippe. 2001. Parties Are not What They Once Were. In *Political Parties and Democracy*, ed. Larry Diamond and Richard Gunther, 67–89. The Johns Hopkins University Press.

Schraeder, Peter. 2000. *Teaching African Politics and Society: A Mosaic in Transformation*. St. Martin's Press.

Schröder, Günter. 1998. *The Multi-Party Elections in Kenya, 29 December 1997: A Preliminary Assessment*. National Council of Churches in Kenya.

Schubert, Gunter, and Rainer Tetzlaff. 1995. *Blockierte Demokratie in der dritten Welt*. Germany: Opladen.

Seawright, Jason, and John Gerring. 2008. "Case Selection Techniques in Case Study Research: A Menu of Qualitative and Quantitative Options." *Political Research Quarterly* 61 (2): 294–308.

Seiler, DL. 1980. *Partis et Familles Politiques*. Paris: Press Université de France.

Selolwane, Onalenna Doo. 2002. "Monopoly Politikos: How Botswana's Opposition Parties Helped Sustain One-Party Dominance." *African Sociological Review* 6 (1): 68–90.

Selolwane, Onalenna Doo. 2004. *Ethnic Structure, Inequality and Governance of the Public Sector in Botswana*. United Nations Research Institute for Social Development.

Shayo, Rose. 2005. *Parties and Political Development in Tanzania*. EISA.

Sklar, Richard. 1963. *Nigerian Political Parties: Power in an Emergent African Country*. Princeton University Press.

Simons, Claudia, and Franzisca Zanker. 2012. "Finding the Cases that Fit: Methodological Challenges in Peace Research." German Institute of Global and Area Studies Working Paper 189.

Skocpol, Theda. 1979. *States and Social Revolutions. A Comparative Analysis of France Russia and China*. Cambridge University Press.

Smith, Jennifer. 2009. "Campaigning and the Catch-All Party: The Process of Party Transformation in Britain." *Party Politics* 15 (5): 555–572.

Smith, Gordon. 1989. "A System Perspective on Party System Change." *Journal of Theoretical Politics* 1 (3): 349–363.

Soudriette, Richard, and Andrew Ellis. 2006. "Electoral Systems Today. A Global Snapshot." *Journal of Democracy* 17 (2): 78–88.

Stavenhagen, Rodolfo. 1996. *Ethnic Conflicts and the Nation-State*. St Martin's Press.

Stockton, Hans. 2001. "Political Parties, Party Systems and Democracy in East Asia." *Comparative Political Studies* 34 (1): 94–119.

Stroh, Alexander and Babette Never. 2008a. "Kaurimuschel statt Chamäleon: Dritter demokratischer Präsidentenwechsel in Benin." *Afrika Focus* 8.

Stroh, Alexander. 2008b. Dynamiques et Constantes du Système de Partis Béninois. In *Le Fonctionnement des Partis Politiques au Bénin*, ed. Jan-Niklas Engels, Alexander Stroh and Leonard Wantchekon, 53–79. Friedrich Ebert Stiftung: 53–79.

Stroh, Alexander. 2009. "The Power of Proximity: Strategic Decisions in African Party Politics." German Institute of Global and Area Studies Working Paper.

Stroh, Alexander. 2010. "The Power of Proximity: A Concept of Political Party Startegies Applied to Burkina Faso." *Journal of Contemporary African Studies* 28 (1): 1–29.

Stroh, Alexander. 2011. "Erfolgsbedingungen afrikanischer Parteien. Burkina Faso und Benin im Vergleich." PhD thesis. University of Hamburg.

Stroschein, Sherrill. 2011. "Demography in Ethnic Party Fragmentation: Hungarian Local Voting in Romania." *Party Politics* 17 (2): 189–204.

Subudubudu, David, and Patrick Molutsi. 2009. *Leaders, Elites and Coalitions in the Development of Botswana*. University of Botswana.

Sutton, Francis. 1956. "Political Parties in French-Speaking West Africa." *Journal of Modern African Studies* 3 (2): 299–301.

Swatuk, Larry. 1999. "Botswana: The Opposition Implodes." *Southern Africa Report* 14 (3): 27–30.

Tamarkin, M. 1979. "From Kenyatta to Moi – The Anatomy of a Peaceful Transition of Power." *Africa Today* 26 (3): 21–37.

Temelli, Sinan. 1999. *Demokratisierung im subsaharischen Afrika: Formen und Faktoren einer politischen Landkarte*. LIT.

Tetzlaff, Rainer. 2002. *Die Staaten Afrikas zwischen demokratischer Konsolidierung und Staatenzerfall*. Bundeszentrale für politische Bildung.

Teubert-Seiwert, Bärbel. 1987. *Parteipolitik in Kenia 1960–1969*. Peter Lang.

Thiven, Reddy. 2005. "The Congress Party Model: South Africa's African National Congress (ANC) and India's Indian National Congress (INC) as Dominant Parties." *African and Asian Studies* 4 (3): 271–300.

Throup, David. 1987. *Economic and Social Origins of the Mau Mau*. James Currey.

Throup, David, and Charles Hornsby. 1992. "Multi-Party Elections in Kenya." Paper presented at the African Studies Associational Biennial Conference, September 8–10, 1992.

Throup, David, and Charles Hornsby. 1998. *Multi-Party Politics in Kenya*. Ohio University Press.

Tilly, Charles. 1975. *The Formation of National States in Western Europe*. Princeton University Press.

Tötemeyer, Gerhard, Arnold Wehmhoerner, and Heribert Weiland. 1996. *Elections in Namibia*. Gamsberg Macmillan.

Tötemeyer, Gerhard. 2004. *The Politics of Namibia. From Bantustan to the Positioning of Ethnicity in a Unitary State*. Republic of Namibia.

Toka, Gabor. 1997. "Political Parties and Democratic Consolidation in East Central Europe." University of Strathclyde, Studies in Public Policy Number 279.

Treydte, Klaus-Peter, Nanténe Coulibaly-Seck, and Saliou Kanté. 2005. *Politische Parteien und Parteiensysteme im Senegal*. Friedrich Ebert Stiftung.

United Nations Development Program. 2001. *Kenya National Human Development Report 2001*. Kenya: United Nations.

United Nations Development Program. 2006. *Kenya National Human Development Report 2006*. Kenya: United Nations.

United Nations Development Program. 2007. *Ghana Human Development Report*. Ghana: United Nations.

Van Biezen, Ingrid. 2003. "The Place of Parties in Contemporary Democracies." *West European Politics* 26 (3): 171–184.

Van Biezen, Ingrid. 2004. "How Political Parties Shape Democracy." CSD Working Paper.

Van Biezen, Ingrid. 2005. "On the Theory and Practice of Party Formation and Adaptation in New Democracies." *European Journal of Political Research* 44 (1): 147–174.

Van Cott, Donna. 2005. *From Movements to Parties in Latin America. The Evolution of Ethnic Politics*. Cambridge University Press.

Van de Walle, Nicholas. 2002. "Africa's Range of Regimes." *Journal of Democracy* 13 (2): 66–79.

Van de Walle, Nicholas. 2003. "Presidentialism and Clientelism in Africa's Emergent Party Systems." *Journal of Modern African Studies* 41 (2): 297–321.

Van Donge, Jan Kees. 1995. "Kamuzu's Legacy: The Democratization of Malawi: Or Searching for the Rules of the Game in African Politics." *African Affairs* 94 (375): 227–257.

Van Rooy, Gert, Benjamin Roberts, Christa Schier, Jannie Schwartz, and Sebastian Levine. 2006. "Income Poverty and Inequality." Multi-Disciplinary and Consultant Centre Discussion Paper 1.

Voizey, Guy. 1994. "The Other Parties in Namibia: The Dynamics of SWAPO's Political Rivals." Master thesis. Oxford University.

Wandiba, Simiyu. 1996. *Masinde Muliro: A Biography*. East African Educational Publications.

Ware, Alan. 2005. *Political Parties and Party Systems*. Oxford University Press.

Wattenberg, Martin. 1998. *The Decline of American Political Parties 1952–1996*. Harvard University Press.

Webb, Paul, and Stephen White. 2007. *Party Politics in New Democracies*. Oxford University Press.

Weber, Max. 1978. *Economy and Society: An Outline of Interpretive Society*. University of California Press.

Weissenbach, Kristina. 2010. "Political Party Assistance: The German 'Stiftungen' in sub-Saharan Africa." *Democratization* 17 (6): 1225–1249.

Whitfield, Lindsay. 2008. "'Change for a Better Ghana': Party Competition, Institutionalization and Alternation in Ghana's 2008 Elections." *African Affairs* 108 (433): 621–641.

Wibbels, Erik. 2007. "No Method to the Comparative Politics Method." *Comparative Political Studies* 40 (1): 37–44.

Widner, Jennifer. 1992. *The Rise of a Party-State in Kenya*. USA: University of California Press.

Widner, Jennifer. 1994. *Economic Change and Political Liberalization in Sub-Saharan Africa*. Johns Hopkins University Press.

Wilmsen, Edwin, and Rainer Vossen. 1990. "Labour, Language and Power in the Construction of Ethnicity in Botswana." *Critique of Anthropology* 10 (1): 7–37.

Wisemann, John. 1990. *Democracy in Black Africa: Survival and Revival*. Paragon House Publishers.

Wisemann, John. 1996. *The New Struggle for Democracy in Africa*. Aveburg.

Wollinetz, Steven. 1979. "The Transformation of Western European Party System Revisited." *West European Politics* 2 (1): 4–28.

Wollinetz, Steven. 2002. Beyond the Catch-All Party: Approaches to the Study of Parties and Party Organization in Contemporary Democracies. In *Political Parties. Old Concepts and New Challenges*, ed. Richard Gunther, Jose Montero, and Juan Linz, 136–166. Oxford University Press.

World Bank. 2002. *World Bank Group in Low-Income Countries Under Stress (LICUS): A Task Force Report*. World Bank.

Wrong, Michela. 2009. *It's Our Turn to Eat. The Story of a Kenyan Whistle Blower.* Fourth Estate.

Young, Crawford. 1965. *Politics in the Congo: Decolonization and Independence.* Princeton University Press.

Young, Crawford. 1982. *Ideology and Development in Africa.* Yale University Press.

Young, Daniel. 2009. "Support You Can Count On? Ethnicity, Partisanship, and Retrospective Voting in Africa." Afrobarometer Working Paper.

Zielinski, Jakub. 2002. "Translating Social Cleavages into Party Systems: The Significance of New Democracies." *World Politics* 54 (2): 184–211.

Zollberg, Aristide. 1964. *One-Party Government in the Ivory-Coast.* Princeton University Press.

Databases

Africa Yearbook 2001 to 2011.

Afrobarometer

Economist Intelligence Unit Reports 1999 to 2011.

Index

Made in the USA
Lexington, KY
11 January 2014